I0063975

Data Science for Cyber-Security

Security Science and Technology

ISSN: 2059-1063

Series Editor: Christopher Hankin *(Imperial College London, UK)*

This series will be a collection of monographs presenting science and science policies for mitigating security risks, addressing a range of vulnerabilities including: Individuals in society, their security and wellbeing; National infrastructure and services; and Economic prosperity.

The series will encompass three operational domains: the cyber, physical and social spaces, covering aspects of Prediction (prior to the event), Detection (during the event), and Response (after the event). For example, in cyber space, Prediction includes data mining, data analytics, and threat and vulnerability assessment; Detection includes trustworthy systems, information assurance, and anomaly detection; and Response includes security strategies, decision support, and forensics.

Published

Security Science and Technology – Vol. 3

Data Science for Cyber-Security

Editors

Nick Heard
Imperial College London, UK

Niall Adams
Imperial College London, UK

Patrick Rubin-Delanchy
University of Bristol, UK

Melissa Turcotte
Los Alamos National Laboratory, USA

World Scientific

NEW JERSEY · LONDON · SINGAPORE · BEIJING · SHANGHAI · HONG KONG · TAIPEI · CHENNAI · TOKYO

Published by

World Scientific Publishing Europe Ltd.

57 Shelton Street, Covent Garden, London WC2H 9HE

Head office: 5 Toh Tuck Link, Singapore 596224

USA office: 27 Warren Street, Suite 401-402, Hackensack, NJ 07601

Library of Congress Cataloging-in-Publication Data
Names: Heard, Nicholas, editor. | Rubin-Delanchy, Patrick, editor. | Turcotte, Melissa, editor.
Title: Data science for cyber-security / edited by Nick Heard (Imperial College London, UK),
    Niall Adams (Imperial College London, UK), Patrick Rubin-Delanchy (University of Bristol, UK),
    Melissa Turcotte (Los Alamos National Laboratory, USA).
Description: [Hackensack] New Jersey : World Scientific, [2018] | Series: Security science and
    technology ; volume 3 | Includes bibliographical references and index.
Identifiers: LCCN 2018021228 | ISBN 9781786345639 (hc : alk. paper)
Subjects: LCSH: Internet--Security measures--Data processing--Congresses. |
    Data protection--Statistical methods--Congresses.
Classification: LCC TK5105.59 .D383 2018 | DDC 005.8--dc23
LC record available at https://lccn.loc.gov/2018021228

British Library Cataloguing-in-Publication Data
A catalogue record for this book is available from the British Library.

Copyright © 2019 by World Scientific Publishing Europe Ltd.

All rights reserved. This book, or parts thereof, may not be reproduced in any form or by any means, electronic or mechanical, including photocopying, recording or any information storage and retrieval system now known or to be invented, without written permission from the Publisher.

For photocopying of material in this volume, please pay a copying fee through the Copyright Clearance Center, Inc., 222 Rosewood Drive, Danvers, MA 01923, USA. In this case permission to photocopy is not required from the publisher.

For any available supplementary material, please visit
https://www.worldscientific.com/worldscibooks/10.1142/Q0167#t=suppl

Desk Editors: Anthony Alexander/Jennifer Brough/Shi Ying Koe

Typeset by Stallion Press
Email: enquiries@stallionpress.com

Preface

This volume contains papers submitted by speakers at the workshop *Data Science for Cyber-Security*, held at Imperial College London during September 2017. The primary sponsor for the workshop was the Heilbronn Institute for Mathematical Research,[a] University of Bristol, which is a national centre supporting research across a range of areas of mathematics in the UK. Additionally, generous financial support was also donated by Imperial College London, GlaxoSmithKline and Mentat Innovations.

There is increasing attention being directed from both government and industry towards the use of statistical, machine learning and broader "data science" techniques for improving cyber-security. In 2018, the Head of the UK National Cyber Security Centre, Ciaran Martin, warned that a major cyber-attack on the UK is a matter of when, not if. "Some attacks will get through. What you need to do is cauterise the damage," he added. It is due to this inevitability that data science techniques have such potential to add value: after an attacker has successfully penetrated a network, data-driven analytics which monitor, for example, network traffic, user behaviour or processes running on a host, become the most likely means for detecting the intruder. What follows is a race against time — timely detection of the attacker is paramount if they are to be prevented from achieving a malicious objective — and this drives the need for both broader and deeper data analysis tools, looking at all aspects of statistical cyber-security.

---

[a] https://heilbronn.ac.uk.

The aim of the holding *Data Science for Cyber-Security* workshop and creating this volume was to bring together the diverse research efforts from academia, business and government, both in the UK and overseas, to obtain a global picture of the current state of the art.

Central to the development of good data science techniques for cyber-security is the availability of good data. In Chapter 1, Turcotte *et al.* introduce a new data resource released by Los Alamos National Laboratory (LANL), containing both network traffic records and host logs obtained from their own enterprise network. Previous cyber-data releases made by LANL are central to several chapters of this volume, and so this in-depth exposition of the new resource, including some suggested future research directions, will be keenly welcomed by the community.

Showcasing the diversity of methods that can be applied to the cyber-problem, in Chapter 2, Marchette reviews streaming density estimation, machine learning, graph theory, dimensionality reduction and topological data analysis. These methods are demonstrated on two applications: modelling LANL network flow data, and the classification of malware families. Importantly, Marchette concludes that "One of the take-aways from this work is that very simple ideas can be very powerful".

One fundamental problem in modelling network traffic data is distinguishing human-generated connections from those caused by automated processes. In Chapter 3, Briers *et al.* address this question by modelling the activity levels generating traffic from a computer as a Markov-modulated Poisson process. They demonstrate the method on network flow data obtained from the computer network of Imperial College London.

In Chapter 4, Anderson *et al.* examine data set-level obstacles to successful implementation of machine learning in cyber-security. Their ideas are illustrated with a running example of classifying malicious Transport Layer Security (TLS) encrypted network data.

In Chapter 5, Kalutarage and Shaikh concentrate on the need for timely detection of successful cyber-attacks, focusing on the task of detecting an intruder during the initial "reconnaissance" phase of the cyber-attack life cycle.

In Chapter 6, Spyropoulou *et al.* look at the user-agent string in HTTP traffic from proxy logs, attempting to detect malware disguising its connections as the traffic from an internet browser. Two kernel-based anomaly detectors are proposed, both requiring a novel distance metric tailored to discriminating user-agent strings.

Supporting the conclusion of Marchette that simple techniques can be among the most powerful, in Chapter 7, Zhou *et al.* use simple thresholding and classification rules, combined with behavioural signatures, to identify Twitter botnets with hundreds of thousands of fake users.

Roeling and Nicholls investigate using a more sophisticated technique, fitting the graph-theoretic stochastic block model, to try to identify a botnet in an infected network cluster in Chapter 8. Encouraging results are found with simulated data, demonstrating that the approach has value, but application to real data, overlaid from a number of botnets, proves more challenging.

Conroy also deploys graph-based techniques, motivated by the stochastic block model, to analyse authentication event data from LANL in Chapter 9. Spectral embeddings and random projections are compared as features for a random forest classifier for identifying red team events.

Many of the contributions in this volume rely on well-labelled cybersecurity data sets in order to train new data science-driven analytics. In Chapter 10, Anagnostopoulos considers weakly supervised classification to account for uncertainty or absence of labels. In his proposed framework, primitive labelling functions provided by analysts can be used in place of definitive labels, which may be highly dependent on context and therefore impossible to obtain.

Motivated by devices unable to carry out intrusion detection due to power or processing constraints, such as those to be found within the so-called Internet of Things, Cybenko and Raz address a novel cyber-security side-channel challenge in Chapter 11, analysing the temporal electromagnetic emanations from a microprocessor. A random forest classifier is used to map analogue measurements of these emissions to nodes in a control flow graph, obtaining promising results.

Identification of network intruders in cyber-security has many analogues with fraud detection problems, including managing the costs of false-positive and false-negative detections. In Chapter 12, Bahnsen uses ensembles of cost-sensitive decision trees to address such problems, highlighting the importance of incorporating realistic cost-estimates. In cyber-security, assessing these costs can of course be particularly challenging.

In Chapter 13, Fisk considers the position of the policy decision maker and provides a methodology for quantifying the cost-effectiveness of cyber-security strategies. Factors considered include the impact on an intruder, measured by the delay to access that will be caused by a security measure, and the level of access they will eventually gain.

Contents

Chapter 1

Unified Host and Network Data Set

Melissa J. M. Turcotte[*,‡], **Alexander D. Kent**[*] **and Curtis Hash**[†]

Los Alamos National Laboratory,
Los Alamos, NM 87545, USA
†*Ernst & Young, New Mexico, USA*
‡*mturcotte@lanl.gov*

The lack of data sets derived from operational enterprise networks continues to be a critical deficiency in the cyber-security research community. Unfortunately, releasing viable data sets to the larger community is challenging for a number of reasons, primarily the difficulty of balancing security and privacy concerns against the fidelity and utility of the data. This chapter discusses the importance of cyber-security research data sets and introduces a large data set derived from the operational network environment at Los Alamos National Laboratory (LANL). The hope is that this data set and associated discussion will act as a catalyst for both new research in cyber-security as well as motivation for other organisations to release similar data sets to the community.

1. Introduction

The lack of diverse and useful data sets for cyber-security research continues to play a profound and limiting role within the relevant research communities and their resulting published research. Organisations are reticent to release data for security and privacy reasons. In addition, the data sets that are released are encumbered in a variety of ways, from being stripped of so much information that they no longer provide rich research and analytical opportunities, to being so constrained by access restrictions that key details are lacking and independent validation is difficult. In many cases, organisations do not collect relevant data in sufficient volumes or with high enough fidelity to provide cyber-research value. Unfortunately, there is generally little motivation for organisations to overcome these obstacles.

In an attempt to help stimulate a larger research effort focused on operational cyber-data as well as to motivate other organisations to release useful data sets, Los Alamos National Laboratory (LANL) has released two data sets for public use (Kent, 2014, 2016). A third, entitled the *Unified Host and Network Data Set*, is introduced in this chapter.

The Unified Host and Network Data Set is a subset of network flow and computer events collected from the LANL enterprise network over the course of approximately 90 days.[a] The host (computer) event logs originated from the majority of LANL's computers that run the Microsoft Windows operating system. The network flow data originated from many of the internal core routers within the LANL enterprise network and are derived from router netflow records. The two data sets include many of the same computers but are not fully inclusive; the network data set includes many non-Windows computers and other network devices.

Identifying values within the data sets have been de-identified (anonymised) to protect the security of LANL's operational IT environment and the privacy of individual users. The de-identified values match across both the host and network data allowing the two data elements to be used together for analysis and research. In some cases, the values were not de-identified, including well-known network ports, system-level usernames (not associated to people) and core enterprise hosts. In addition, a small set of hosts, users and processes were combined where they represented well-known, redundant entities. This consolidation was done for both normalisation and security purposes.

In order to transform the data into a format that is useful for researchers who are not domain experts, a significant effort was made to normalise the data while minimising the artefacts that such normalisation might introduce.

1.1. *Related public data sets*

A number of public, cyber-security relevant data sets currently are referenced in the literature (Glasser and Lindauer, 2013; Ma *et al.*, 2009) or

---

[a]The network flow data are only 89 days due to missing data on the first day.

are available online.[b] Some of these represent data collected from operational environments, while others capture specific, pseudo real-world events (for example, cyber-security training exercises). Many data sets are synthetic and created using models intended to represent specific phenomenon of relevance; for example, the Carnegie Melon Software Engineering Institute provides several insider threat data sets that are entirely synthetic (Glasser and Lindauer, 2013). In addition, many of the data sets commonly seen within the research community are egregiously dated. The DARPA cyber-security data sets (Cyber-Systems and Technology Group, 1998) published in the 1990s are still regularly used, even though the systems, networks and attacks they represent have almost no relevance to modern computing environments.

Another issue is that many of the available data sets have restrictive access and constraints on how they may be used. For example, the U.S. Department of Homeland Security provides the Information Marketplace for Policy and Analysis of Cyber-risk and Trust (IMPACT,[c] which is intended to facilitate information sharing. However, the use of any of the data hosted by IMPACT requires registration and vetting prior to access. In addition, data owners may (and often do) place limitations on how and where the data may be used.

Finally, many of the existing data sets are not adequately characterised for potential researchers. It is important that researchers have a thorough understanding of the context, normalisation processes, idiosyncrasies and other aspects of the data. Ideally, researchers should have sufficiently detailed information to avoid making false assumptions and to reproduce similar data. The need for such detailed discussion around published data sets is a primary purpose of this chapter.

The remainder of this chapter is organised as follows: a description of the Network Flow Data is given in Section 2 followed by the Windows Host Log Data in Section 3. Finally, a discussion of potential research directions is given in Section 4.

---

[b]https://www.ll.mit.edu/ideval/data/, http://malware-traffic-analysis.net/, http://www.unb.ca/cic/research/datasets/index.html.
[c]https://www.dhs.gov/csd-impact.

2. Network Flow Data

The network flow data set included in this release is comprised of records describing communication events between devices connected to the LANL enterprise network. Each *flow* is an aggregate summary of a (possibly) bi-directional network communication between two network devices. The data are derived from Cisco NetFlow Version 9 (Claise, 2004) flow records exported by the core routers. As such, the records lack the payload-level data upon which most commercial intrusion detection systems are based. However, research has shown that flow-based techniques have a number of advantages and are successful at detecting a variety of malicious network behaviours (Sperotto *et al.*, 2010). Furthermore, these techniques tend to be more robust against the vagaries of attackers, because they are not searching for specific signatures (for example, byte patterns) and they are encryption-agnostic. Finally, in comparison to full-packet data, collection, analysis and archival storage of flow data at enterprise scales is straightforward and requires minimal infrastructure.

2.1. *Collection and transformation*

As mentioned previously, the raw data consisted of NetFlow V9 records that were exported from the core network routers to a centralised collection server. While V9 records can contain many different fields, only the following are considered: *StartTime, EndTime, SrcIP, DstIP, Protocol, SrcPort, DstPort, Packets* and *Bytes*. The specifics of the hardware and flow export protocol are largely irrelevant, as these fields are common to all network flow formats of which the authors are aware.

This data can be quite challenging to model without a thorough understanding of its various idiosyncrasies. The following paragraphs discuss two of the most relevant issues with respect to modelling. For a comprehensive overview of these issues, among others, readers can refer to Hofstede *et al.* (2014).

Firstly, note that these flow records are uni-directional (*uniflows*): each record describes a stream of packets sent from one network device (*SrcIP*) to another (*DstIP*). Hence, an established TCP connection — bi-directional by definition — between two network devices, *A* and *B*, results in two flow records: one from *A* to *B* and another from *B* to *A*. It follows that there is no relationship between the direction of a flow and the initiator of a bi-directional connection (i.e., it is not known whether *A* or *B* connected first). This is the case for most netflow implementations as bi-directional flow (*biflow*) protocols such as Trammell and Boschi (2008) have yet to gain widespread adoption. Clearly, this presents a challenge for detection of attack behaviours, such as lateral movement, where directionality is of primary concern.

Secondly, significant duplication can occur due to flows encountering multiple netflow sensors in transit to their destination. Routers can be configured to track flows on ingress and egress, and, in more complex network topologies, a single flow can traverse multiple routers. More recently, the introduction of netflow-enabled switches and dedicated netflow appliances has exacerbated the issue. Ultimately, a single flow can result in many distinct flow records. To add further complexity, the flow records are not necessarily *exact* duplicates and their arrival times can vary considerably; these inconsistencies occur for many reasons, the particulars of which are too complex to discuss in this context.

In order to simplify the data for modelling, a transformation process known as *biflowing* or *stitching* was employed. This is a process intended to aggregate duplicates and marry the opposing uniflows of bi-directional connections into a single, *directed* biflow record (Table 1). Many approaches to this problem can be found in the literature (Barbosa, 2014; Berthier *et al.*, 2010; Minarik *et al.*, 2009; Nguyen *et al.*, 2017), all of them imperfect. A straightforward approach was used that relies on simple port heuristics to

Table 1: Bi-directional flow data.

Field Name	Description
Time	The start time of the event in epoch time format.
Duration	The duration of the event in seconds.
SrcDevice	The device that likely initiated the event.
DstDevice	The receiving device.
Protocol	The protocol number.
SrcPort	The port used by the *SrcDevice*.
DstPort	The port used by the *DstDevice*.
SrcPackets	The number of packets the *SrcDevice* sent during the event.
DstPackets	The number of packets the *DstDevice* sent during the event.
SrcBytes	The number of bytes the *SrcDevice* sent during the event.
DstBytes	The number of bytes the *DstDevice* sent during the event.

decide direction. These heuristics are based on the assumption that *SrcPort*s are generally *ephemeral* (i.e., they are selected from a predefined, high range by the operating system), while *DstPort*s tend to have lower numbers that correspond to established, shared network services and will therefore be observed more frequently than ephemeral ports. The heuristics are given below in order of precedence.

- Destination ports are less than 1024 and source ports are not.
- The top 90 most frequently observed ports are destination ports.
- The smaller of the two ports is the destination port.

Each uniflow was transformed into a biflow by renaming the *Packets* and *Bytes* fields to *SrcPackets* and *SrcBytes*, respectively. *DstPackets* and *DstBytes* fields were added with initial values of zero. Next, the port heuristics were considered and, if any were violated or ambiguous, the *Src* and *Dst* attributes were swapped, effectively reversing the direction. Finally, the *5-tuple* was extracted from each record and used as the key in a lookup table.

SrcIP, DstIP, SrcPort, DstPort, Protocol

If a match was found, the flows were aggregated by keeping the minimum *StartTime*, maximum *EndTime* and summing the other attributes. If no match was found, the flow was simply added to the table. This process was performed in a streaming fashion on all of the records in the order in which they were received by the collector. Flows were periodically evicted from the lookup table after 30 minutes of inactivity (i.e., failing to match with any incoming flows). Flows that remained active for long periods of time were reported approximately every 3 hours, but were *not* evicted from the table until inactive.

While biflowing the data mitigates the problems posed by duplicates and ambiguous directionality, it does not address another significant obstacle: the lack of stable identifiers upon which to build models. In some cases, IP addresses are transient (e.g., Dynamic Host Configuration Protocol (DHCP), Virtual Private Network (VPN)). In other cases, devices have multiple IP addresses (e.g., multihoming) or one IP address is shared by multiple devices (e.g., load-balancing, NAT). Whatever the case may be, modelling the behaviour of IP addresses on a typical network is clearly

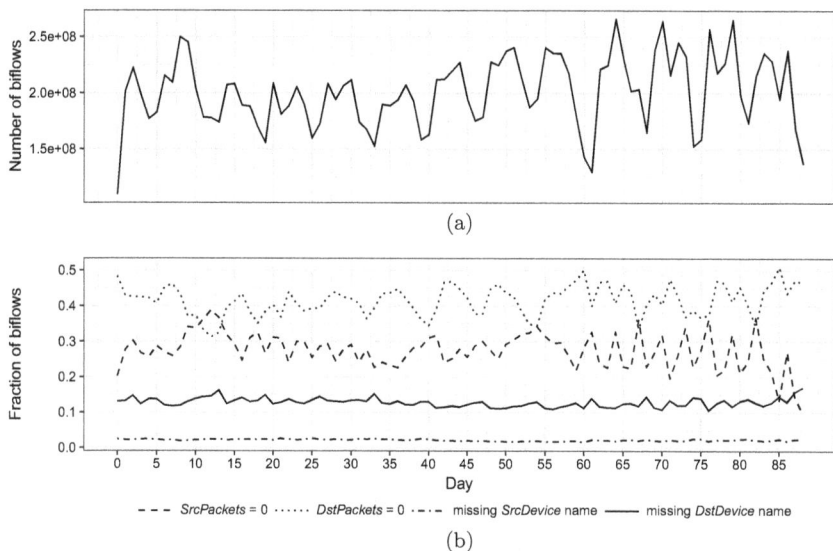

Fig. 1: (a) Daily count of biflows by end time. (b) Fraction of biflows where *SrcPackets* = 0, *DstPackets* = 0, *SrcDevice* FQDN-mapping failed and *DstDevice* FQDN-mapping failed.

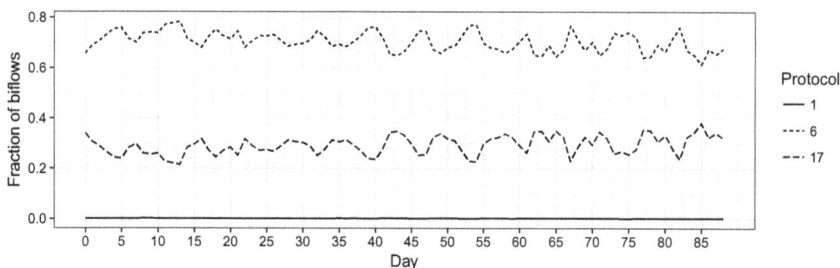

Fig. 2: Daily proportions of each *Protocol*.

error prone. Instead, one should endeavour to map IP addresses to more stable identifiers such as media access control (MAC) addresses or fully-qualified domain names (FQDN), interchangeably referred to as hostnames throughout the rest of the chapter. As with directionality, there is no perfect solution to this problem. The most appropriate identifier will depend greatly on the configuration of the target network, as well as the availability of auxiliary data sources from which a mapping can be constructed. An ideal solution will likely involve some combination of supplementary network data (e.g., Domain Name Service (DNS) logs, DNS zone transfers, DHCP logs, VPN logs, NAC logs), business rules and considerable trial and error.

For this data release, a combination of DNS and DHCP logs was used to construct a mapping of IP addresses to FQDNs over time. The IP addresses in each biflow were then replaced with their corresponding FQDNs at the time of the flow. Where a given IP address and timestamp mapped to multiple FQDNs, business rules were incorporated to give preference to the least-ephemeral name. IP addresses that failed to map to any FQDN were left as is. The resulting mix of names and IP addresses correspond to the *SrcDevice* and *DstDevice* fields in the final data.

Finally, the data were de-identified by mapping *SrcDevice*, *DstDevice*, *SrcPort* and *DstPort* to random identifiers. In the event that the IP-to-FQDN mapping failed, the random identifier was prepended with "IP". Well-known ports were not de-identified. Records with protocol numbers other than 6 (TCP), 17 (UDP) and (1) ICMP were removed entirely. The output from this process is provided in CSV format, one record per line, with fields in the order shown in Table 1.

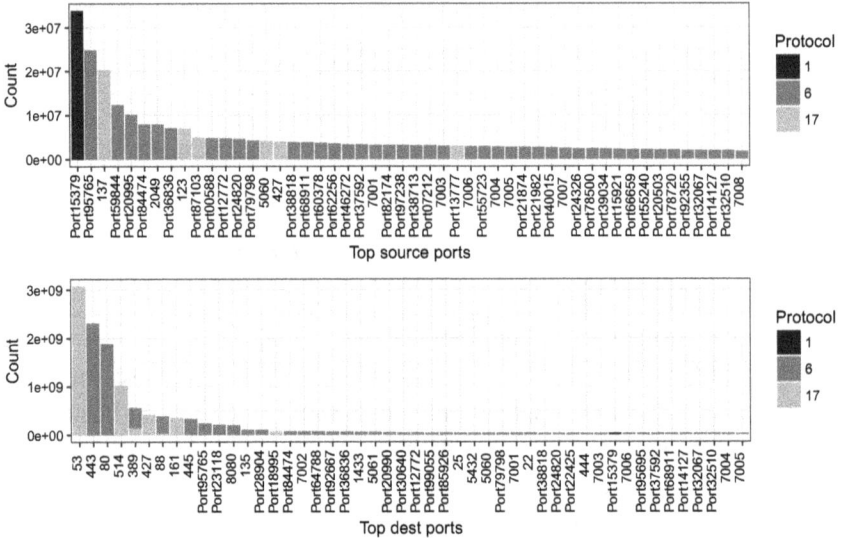

Fig. 3: Histogram of the top 50 *SrcPorts* and *DstPorts*.

2.2. Data quality

Several figures have been provided in order to assess the quality of the network flow data set. The top plot in Figure 1, which shows the number of biflows over time, demonstrates the periodicity that one would expect for data whose volume is driven by the comings and goings of employees during a typical 5-day workweek.

The bottom plot of Figure 1 is intended to measure the success rate of the biflowing and IP-to-FQDN mapping processes. TCP biflows where either *SrcPackets* or *DstPackets* is zero suggests a failure to find matching uniflows for both directions of the exchange. Fifty Seven percent of TCP and approximately 70% of all biflows fall within this category. This can largely be attributed to LANL's netflow sensor infrastructure, which has been specifically configured to export only one direction on many routes. In addition, some devices — namely vulnerability scanners and the like — attempt to connect to all possible IP addresses within a range; this results in a significant number of uniflows for which no response is possible. Likely for the same reason, IP-to-FQDN mapping failed for significantly more *DstDevices* than *SrcDevices*.

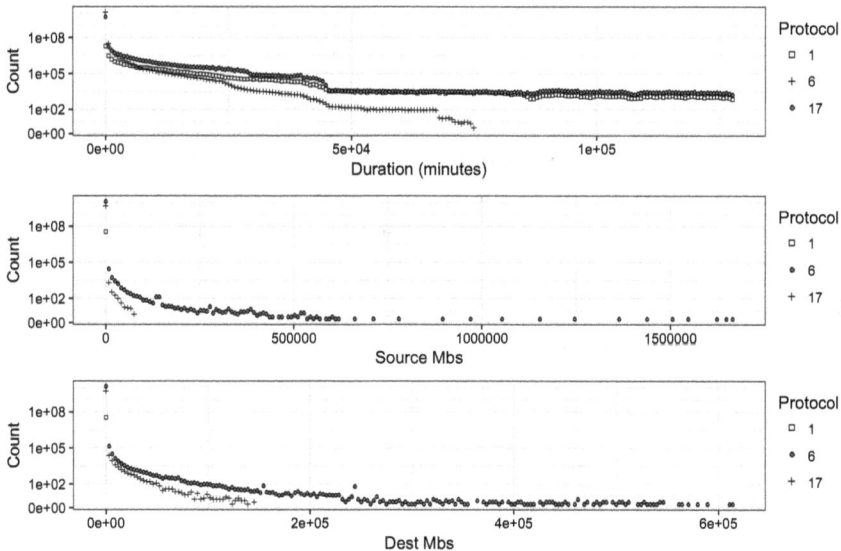

Fig. 4: Distribution of *Duration*, *SrcBytes* and *DstBytes*.

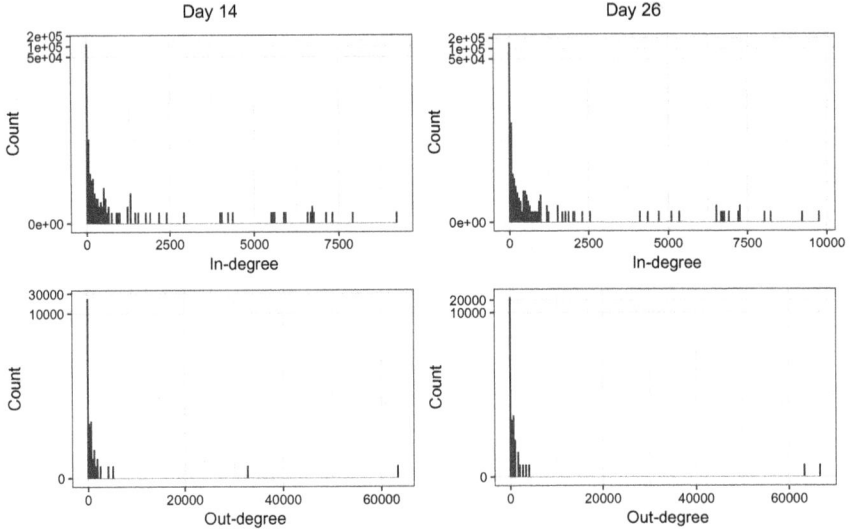

Fig. 5: In-degree and out-degree distribution for two randomly-selected days.

Figure 2 shows the daily proportion of biflows corresponding to each *Protocol*. Figure 3 contains two histograms of the top *SrcPort*s and *DstPort*s respectively. Note the non-uniformity in the *SrcPort* histogram; this illustrates either a consistent failure of the biflowing process to choose the appropriate direction or the presence of protocols that use non-ephemeral source ports. For example, the network time protocol (NTP) uses port 123 for both the source and destination ports per the specification.

Figure 4 shows the distribution of *Duration*, *SrcBytes* and *DstBytes* per *Protocol*. Of particular interest is the presence of many long-lived UDP and ICMP biflows in the data. This indicates frequent, persistent UDP and ICMP traffic sharing the same *5-tuple* and is an unfortunate side effect of not limiting the biflow transformation to TCP uniflows. Finally, Figure 5 shows exemplar in-degree and out-degree distributions for two randomly-selected days.

3. Windows Host Log Data

As remote attackers and malicious insiders increasingly use encryption, network-only detection mechanisms are becoming less effective, particularly those that require the inspection of payload data within the network traffic. As a result, cyber-defenders now rely heavily on endpoint agents and host event logs to detect and investigate incidents. Host event logs capture nuanced details for a wide range of activities; however, given the vast number of logged events and their specificity to an individual host, human analysts struggle to discover the few useful log entries amid the huge number of innocuous entries. Statistical analytics for host event data are in their infancy. Advanced analytical capabilities on this host data, including computer and user profiling, which move beyond signature-based methods, will increase network awareness and detection of advanced cyber-threats.

The host event data set is a subset of host event logs collected from all computers running the Microsoft Windows operating system on LANL's enterprise network. The host logs were collected with windows logging service (WLS), which is a Windows service that forwards event logs, along with administrator-defined contextual data to a set of collection servers.[d] The released data are in JSON format in order to preserve the structure of the original events, unlike the two previously released data sets based on this log source (Kent, 2014, 2016). The events from the host logs included in the data set are all related to authentication and process activity on each machine.

Table 2 contains the subset of *EventID*s included from the event logs in the released data set and a brief description of each; a more detailed description is available online.[e] Figure 6 shows the percentage of *EventID*s contained in the logs, as well as the *LogonType*s for *EventID*s 4624, 4625 and 4634.

Each record in the data set will have some of the event attributes listed in Appendix A and Table B.1 specifies which *EventID*s have each attribute. Note that not all events with a given *EventID* share the same set of attributes. If an expected attribute was missing from the original host log record, then the attribute was not included in the corresponding record in the de-identified data set.

All records will contain the attributes *EventID*, *LogHost* and *Time*. *LogHost* indicates the network host where the record was logged. For

---

[d]http://honeywell.com/sites/aero-kcp/SiteCollectionDocuments/WindowsLoggingServiceSummary. pdf.
[e]https://www.ultimatewindowssecurity.com/securitylog/encyclopedia/default.aspx.

Table 2:   Host log *EventID*s.

EventID	Description
Authentication events	
4768	Kerberos authentication ticket was requested (TGT)
4769	Kerberos service ticket was requested (TGS)
4770	Kerberos service ticket was renewed
4774	An account was mapped for logon
4776	Domain controller attempted to validate credentials
4624	An account successfully logged on, see Logon Types
4625	An account failed to logon, see Logon Types
4634	An account was logged off, see Logon Types
4647	User initiated logoff
4648	A logon was attempted using explicit credentials
4672	Special privileges assigned to a new logon
4800	The workstation was locked
4801	The workstation was unlocked
4802	The screensaver was invoked
4803	The screensaver was dismissed
Process events	
4688	Process start
4689	Process end
System events	
4608	Windows is starting up
4609	Windows is shutting down
1100	Event logging service has shut down (often recorded instead of *EventID* 4609)

*LogonType*s (*EventID*s: 4624, 4625 and 4634)

2 — Interactive	5 — Service	9 — New Credentials
3 — Network	7 — Unlock	10 — Remote Interactive
4 — Batch	8 — Network Clear Text	11 — Cached Interactive
12 — Cached Remote-Interactive	0 — Used only by the system account	

directed authentication events, this attribute will always correspond to the computer to which the user is authenticating, and the source computer will be given by *Source*. For the user associated with the record, if the *UserName* ends in $ then it will correspond to the *computer account* for the specified computer. These computer accounts are host-specific accounts within the

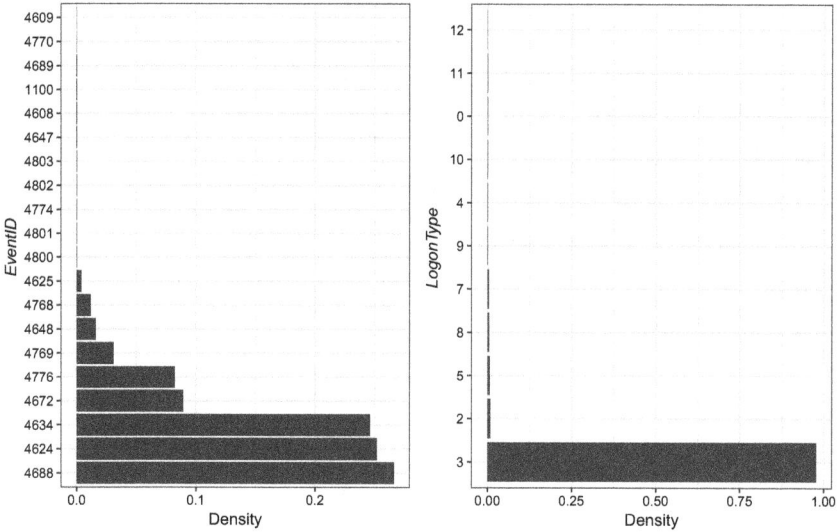

Fig. 6:   Histogram of the *EventID*s and *LogonType*s.

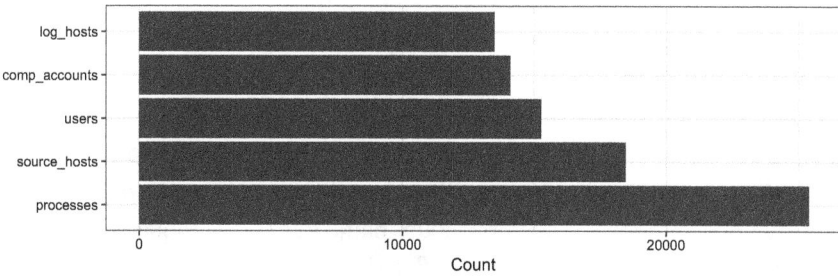

Fig. 7:   Histogram of unique processes, usernames, log hosts (*LogHost*), source hosts (*Source*) and computer accounts for the whole time period.

Microsoft Active Directory domain that allow the computer to authenticate as a unique entity within the network. Figure 7 shows the count of unique processes, log hosts (*LogHost*), source hosts (*Source*), computer accounts (*UserName* ending in $) and users (*UserName* not ending in $) for the 90-day period. Note that the set of source hosts includes devices running non-Windows operating systems, hence there are more source hosts than log hosts. Figure 8 shows the number of wls records on a per-day basis, showing the diurnal patterns that one would expect and good collection

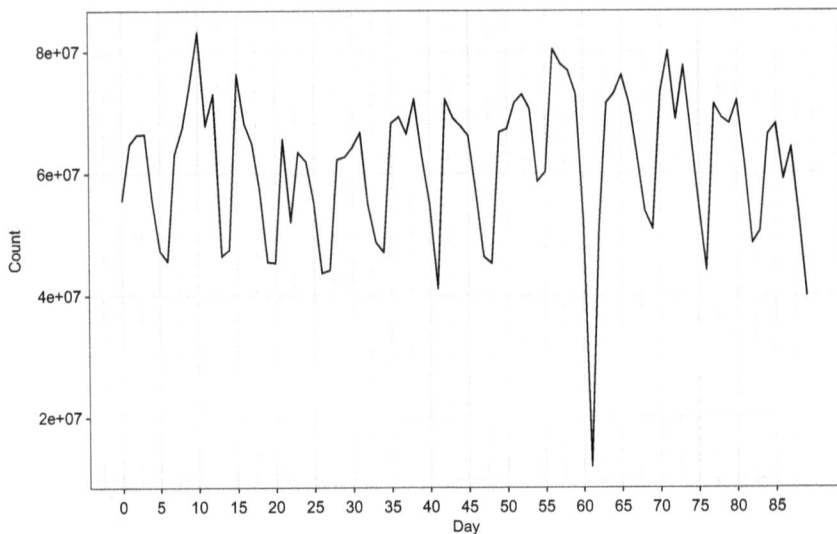

Fig. 8: Daily count of host log records.

throughout the 90 days minus a noticeable drop on day 61 similar to that of the netflow data set, Figure 1.

Requests to the Kerberos ticket granting service (TGS) (*EventID* 4769) correspond to a user requesting Kerberos authentication credentials from the Active Directory domain to a service or account name on a network computer. Hence, the *LogHost* attribute should always be an Active Directory machine and the service or account name the user is requesting access to will be given by *ServiceName*. The *ServiceName* often corresponds to a computer account on the target computer. Because this event only grants a credential, a subsequent network logon event (*EventID* 4624– *LogonType* 3) to the computer indicated by *ServiceName* is common. This differs from the previous data release (Kent, 2016), in which TGS events were assumed to be directed authentication events from the user's machine to the computer indicated by *ServiceName*, ignoring the Kerberos intermediary.

When de-identifying the process events, only the base process name was de-identified and the extension was left as is. Further, the parent process names (*ParentProcessName*) do not have file extensions unlike the child process names (*ProcessName*); this is a direct artefact of how the process information is logged within WLS. The missing extension can be obtained by using the *ParentProcessID* to identify the parent process start event.

Finally, many events include the *DomainName* attribute that indicates what Active Directory domain the event is associated with. The domain, combined with the *UserName*, should be considered a unique account identity. For example, user *u1* with domain *d1* is not necessarily user *u1* in domain *d2*. In addition, the domain may actually be a hostname, indicating the event does not involve a user or account associated with an Active Directory domain, but is instead a local account. Again, these accounts should be considered unique to the host indicated within the *DomainName* attribute. For example, the Administrator account on host *c1* likely does not have a relationship to the Administrator account on *c2* or the Administrator account in domain *d1*. The LANL data sets have a single primary domain, with a number of much smaller, secondary domains, and most computers have a small set of local accounts.

3.1. *Data parsing considerations*

While host logs can be an extremely valuable data resource for cybersecurity research, the formatting and content of the logs can vary drastically between enterprises depending upon the audit policy and technologies used to collect and forward the logs to a centralised server. Hence, parsing the data and extracting the relevant attributes is an important first step in analysing these data; see also Kent (2016).

Even though WLS provides more content and normalisation around the raw Windows logs, some challenges were still faced to provide the de-identified data.

Firstly, the semantics of attribute names are not necessarily the same for different *EventID*s and the attribute names themselves may differ according to what tool is being used to collect and forward the logs. For example, with WLS the *UserName* for *EventID* 4774 is *MappedName*, for *EventID* 4778 and 4779 it is *AccountName* and for most other events it is *TargetUserName*. When parsing the data, these names were all standardised to *UserName*.

As with the network flow data, an extremely important task is mapping IP addresses to FQDNs. Further, unlike netflow, each record may contain both IP addresses and hostnames. The machine where the event is recorded

(*LogHost* for the de-identified data) is provided as a hostname, whereas the *Source* computer for network logons is often given as an IP address.

Finally, both usernames and process names were standardised. In some records, usernames appear with the domain name or additional characters. These discrepancies were removed from the released data in order to ensure all usernames were in canonical form. In addition, some usernames, such as "Anonymous", "Local Service" and "Network Service", do not map to a computer or user account. For some analyses, one may want to remove these events. In the de-identified data these commonly-seen usernames were not anonymised. For the process names, dates, version numbers, operating systems and hexadecimal strings were removed where possible so that processes run on different operating systems or with different versions would map to the same process name. For example, *flashplayerplugin_20_0_0_286.exe* would be mapped to *flashplayer-plugin_VERSION.exe*.

4. Research Directions

Anomaly detection for the defensive cyber-domain is a major yet evolving research area, with much work still to be done in characterising and finding anomalies within complex cyber-data sets. Finding viable attack indicators and per computer, user and computer-to-computer models that enable anomaly detection and fingerprinting are all interesting and important research opportunities.

Although research on anomaly detection for cyber-defence spans more than two decades, operational tools are still almost exclusively rule- or signature-based. Two reasons that statistical methods have not been more widely adopted in practice are a high false-positive rate and un-interpretable alerts. Analysts are inundated with a large number of alerts and triaging them takes significant time and resources; this results in low tolerance for false alarms and alerts that provide no contextual information to guide investigation. Signature-based systems can be finely tuned to reduce false positives as they rely on very specific peculiarities that have been previously identified and documented as indicative of a cyber-attack. Further, they are interpretable as they refer to specific patterns within the data, such as weird domains, network protocols or process names.

However, despite their inherent challenges, anomaly detection methods have the advantage of being able to detect new variants of cyber-attacks and are able to keep pace with the rapidly changing cyber-attack landscape by dynamically learning patterns for normal behaviour and detecting deviations. Further, with the increasing level of encrypted network traffic, the importance of this research and the use of these methods can not be understated. Research into ways to reduce false-positives and providing interpretable anomalies will have significant impact in furthering the use of anomaly detection systems. In fact, providing interpretable anomalies can help overcome the false-positive issue as interpretability leads to quickly identifying alerts that are false positives in the same way it would enable understanding true positives. Research approaches to tackle these problems could include combining different data sets and signals, borrowing strength across entities that are similar by incorporating peer-based behaviour, community detection approaches and ways to provide meaningful context surrounding alerts to human analysts.

When using the host log data set for research, some notable characteristics of these data that need to be considered, especially if looking at the events as a time series, is periodicity and significant correlations between arrivals of different event types. This can be seen clearly in Figure 9, which shows the event times for various *EventID*s for User205265. Periodicity in the data is often an artefact of the computer regularly renewing credentials. This explains why *EventID* 4624–*LogonType* 3 (network logon) constitutes such a significant portion of the events as seen in Figure 6. For a given entity, extrapolating higher-level, interpretable actions from the sequence of low-level events would improve modelling efforts, understanding of these data, and would itself be very useful for security analysts. See Heard *et al.* (2014) and Price-Williams *et al.* (2017) for relevant research in this area.

Another area for research with the host logs is exploring the records related to process starts and stops in detail, in particular looking at process trees. To date, little has been done in this area. Computer systems operate hierarchically; an initial root process starts many other processes, which in turn start and run descendants. A process tree is the dynamic structure that results. In theory, any process can be traced, through its ancestors, to the root process. Unusual or atypical events in process trees could indicate potential cyber-security anomalies.

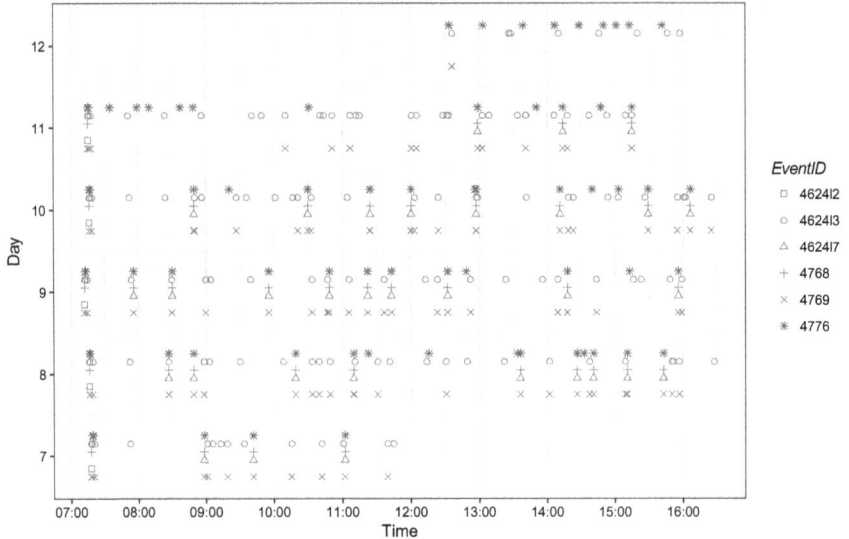

Fig. 9:   Event times for User205265. 462412 corresponds to *EventID* 4624–*LogonType* 2.

Moving beyond anomaly detection, there are other important research directions for which these data could prove useful. For example, preliminary work has been done using similar data to model network segmentation and associated risk (Pope *et al.*, 2017). Using the data to build new, potential network topologies in order to reduce risk and improve security posture are viable directions. Another potential research problem is to quantify and understand data loss within cyber-data sets. The collection and normalisation processes in place for these data can result in information loss and understanding this data loss is an open problem both in general and specific to each element of the data. As most of the data elements represent people and their actions on computers, research on organisational and social behaviour is also viable using these data.

5. Conclusion

Operational cyber-security data sets are paramount to ensuring valuable and productive research continues to improve the state of cyber-defence. The network flow and host log event data discussed in this chapter are intended to enable such research as well as to provide an example for other potential data set providers. In particular, while there is a considerable amount of relevant work on network data, relatively little attention has been given to host log data in the literature. Host log data are becoming increasingly relevant as endpoint security tools gain popularity within the cyber-security ecosystem. It is important that researchers embrace both the opportunity and challenge that they present. Finally, even less consideration has been given to meaningful analyses that combine these and other data sets. This paradigm shift towards a holistic approach to cyber-security defence is critical to advancing the state of the art.

Acknowledgement

This work was supported by the US Department of Energy through the Los Alamos National Laboratory. Los Alamos National Laboratory is operated by Los Alamos National Security, LLC, for the National Nuclear Security Administration of U.S. Department of Energy (Contract DEAC52-06NA25396). The United States Government retains and the publisher, by accepting this work for publication, acknowledges that the United States Government retains a nonexclusive, paid-up, irrevocable, world-wide license to publish or reproduce this work, or allow others to do so for United States Government purposes.

Appendix A. Host Log Fields

- *Time*: The epoch time of the event in seconds.
- *EventID*: Four digit integer corresponding to the event id of the record.
- *LogHost*: The hostname of the computer that the event was recorded on. In the case of directed authentication events, the *LogHost* will correspond to the computer that the authentication event is terminating at (destination computer).
- *LogonType*: Integer corresponding to the type of logon, see Table 2.
- *LogonTypeDescription*: Description of the *LogonType*, see Table 2.
- *UserName*: The user account initiating the event. If the user ends in $, then it corresponds to a computer account for the specified computer.
- *DomainName*: Domain name of *UserName*.
- *LogonID*: A semi-unique (unique between current sessions and *LogHost*) number that identifies the logon session just initiated. Any events logged

subsequently during this logon session should report the same *LogonID* through to the logoff event.

- *SubjectUserName*: For authentication mapping events, the user account specified by this field is mapping to the user account in *UserName*.
- *SubjectDomainName*: Domain name of *SubjectUserName*.
- *SubjectLogonID*: See *LogonID*.
- *Status*: Status of the authentication request. "0×0" means success otherwise failure; failure codes for the appropriate *EventID* are available online.[f]
- *Source*: For authentication events, this will correspond to the the the computer where the authentication originated (source computer), if it is a local logon event then this will be the same as the *LogHost*.
- *ServiceName*: The account name of the computer or service the user is requesting the ticket for.
- *Destination*: This is the server the mapped credential is accessing. This may indicate the local computer when starting another process with new account credentials on a local computer.
- *AuthenticationPackage*: The type of authentication occurring including Negotiate, Kerberos, NTLM plus a few more.
- *FailureReason*: The reason for a failed logon.
- *ProcessName*: The process executable name, for authentication events this is the process that processed the authentication event. *ProcessNames* may include the file type extensions (i.e., exe).
- *ProcessID*: A semi-unique (unique between currently running processes AND *LogHost*) value that identifies the process. *ProcessID* allows you to correlate other events logged in association with the same process through to the process end.
- *ParentProcessName*: The process executable that started the new process. *ParentProcessNames* often do not have file extensions like *ProcessName* but can be compared by removing file extensions from the name.
- *ParentProcessID*: Identifies the exact process that started the new process. Look for a preceding event 4688 with a *ProcessID* that matches this *ParentProcessID*.

---

[f] https://www.ultimatewindowssecurity.com/securitylog/encyclopedia/default.aspx.

Appendix B

Table B.1: Event attributes.

*EventID*s	Attribute
All	*Time*
All	*EventID*
All	*LogHost*
4624, 4625, 4634	*LogonType*
4624, 4625, 4634	*LogonTypeDescription*
All except System Events	*UserName*
All except System Events	*DomainName*
All except 4768, 4769, 4770, 4774, 4776	*LogonID*
4624 (*LogonType* 9), 4648, 4774	*SubjectUserName*
4624 (*LogonType* 9), 4648, 4774	*SubjectDomainName*
4624 (*LogonType* 9), 4648	*SubjectLogonID*
4768, 4769, 4776	*Status*
4624, 4625, 4648, 4768, 4769, 4770, 4776	*Source*
4769, 4770	*ServiceName*
4648	*Destination*
4624, 4625, 4776	*AuthenticationPackage*
4625	*FailureReason*
4624, 4625, 4648, 4688, 4689	*ProcessName*
4624, 4625, 4648, 4688, 4689	*ProcessID*
4688	*ParentProcessName*
4688	*ParentProcessID*

References

Barbosa, R. R. R. (2014). *Anomaly Detection in SCADA Systems — A Network Based Approach*, Ph.D. thesis, Centre for Telematics and Information Technology, University of Twente, Netherlands.

Berthier, R., Cukier, M., Hiltunen, M., Kormann, D., Vesonder, G. and Shelcheda, D. (2010). Nfsight: Netflow-based network awareness tool, in *Proceedings of LISA10: 24th Large Installation System Administration Conference*, p. 119.

Claise, B. (2004). Cisco systems NetFlow services export, Version 9, RFC 3954, Internet Engineering Task Force.

Cyber Systems and Technology Group (1998). DARPA intrusion detection data sets, URL: https://www.ll.mit.edu/ideval/data/.

Glasser, J. and Lindauer, B. (2013). Bridging the gap: A pragmatic approach to generating insider threat data, *2012 IEEE Symposium on Security and Privacy Workshops*, pp. 98–104.

Heard, N., Rubin-Delanchy, P. and Lawson, D. J. (2014). Filtering automated polling traf-
    fic in computer network flow data, in *2014 IEEE Joint Intelligence and Security
    Informatics Conference*, pp. 268–271.

Hofstede, R., Čeleda, P., Trammell, B., Drago, I., Sadre, R., Sperotto, A. and Pras, A. (2014).
    Flow monitoring explained: From packet capture to data analysis with NetFlow and
    IPFIX, *IEEE Communications Surveys & Tutorials* **16**, 4, pp. 2037–2064.

Kent, A. D. (2014). User-computer authentication associations in time, Los Alamos National
    Laboratory, doi:10.11578/1160076.

Kent, A. D. (2016). Cyber security data sources for dynamic network research, in N. Adams
    and N. Heard. eds., *Dynamic Networks and Cyber-Security*, Vol. 1, p. 37, World
    Scientific, UK.

Ma, J., Saul, L. K., Savage, S. and Voelker, G. M. (2009). Identifying suspicious URLs:
    An application of large-scale online learning, in *Proceedings of the 26th Annual
    International Conference on Machine Learning*, pp. 681–688.

Minarik, P., Vykopal, J. and Krmicek, V. (2009). Improving host profiling with bidirectional
    flows, in *International Conference on Computational Science and Engineering, 2009.
    CSE'09.*, Vol. 3, pp. 231–237.

Nguyen, K. V., Tyagi, N. K. and Lau, R. M. (2017). Flow de-duplication for network
    monitoring, US Patent 9,548,908.

Pope, A., Tauritz, D. and Kent, A. (2017). Evolving bipartite authentication graph partitions,
    IEEE Transactions on Dependable and Secure Computing, **99**, pp. 1–1.

Price-Williams, M., Heard, N. and Turcotte, M. (2017). Detecting periodic subsequences in
    cyber security data, in *IEEE European Intelligence and Security Informatics Confer-
    ence (EISIC2017)*, pp. 84–90.

Sperotto, A., Schaffrath, G., Sadre, R., Morariu, C., Pras, A. and Stiller, B. (2010). An
    overview of IP flow-based intrusion detection, *IEEE Communications Surveys and
    Tutorials* **12**, 3, pp. 343–356.

Trammell, B. and Boschi, E. (2008). Bidirectional flow export using IP Flow Information
    Export (IPFIX), RFC 5103, Internet Engineering Task Force.

Chapter 2

Computational Statistics and Mathematics for Cyber-Security

David J. Marchette

Naval Surface Warfare Center,
Dahlgren, VA 22448, USA

david.marchette@navy.mil

Computer and network security relies on many different tools, such as secure programming practices, firewalls, virus scanners and various algorithms to detect attacks and malicious software. The latter require the analysis of complex and varied data such as packet streams, emails, potential malicious binary executable files and user activity on a computer and on the network. Modern data analytics has a number of tools to analyse these data streams and to design detection algorithms. This chapter discusses several such tools that come from the computational statistics literature and from pure mathematics: nonparametric probability density estimation, graph-based manifold learning, topological data analysis. These ideas are illustrated on a problem of malware classification and on network data.

1. Introduction

In an influential paper in statistical science (Breiman, 2001b), Leo Breiman described two cultures of data analysis, which Donoho (2015) refers to as prediction and inference. The idea is that there are those who focus on the bottom line — how well does the algorithm perform on a given task of interest, such as classification or regression — and those who are more concerned with making inference, such as using a model, and the parameters of the model fitted from data, to make statements about the world (or some small piece of it of particular interest to the analyst). Of course, these are not mutually exclusive, and we all (one hopes) have at least some of both of these in our make-up; however, there is a distinct difference in these two cultures. One way of making the distinction, which Donoho discusses at some length, is between those who are primarily interested in elucidating the model that generated the data, and those interested simply in how well the model predicts (some aspect of) future observations.

In cyber-security, one is mostly interested in the latter. While there is considerable interest in things like packet arrival times and other statistics of networks, these are more important for the design and implementations of networks rather than for the security aspects. From a security perspective one mostly cares about whether one can protect the network, computer and data. The focus is more on whether attacks and intrusions can be detected rather than in modelling these attacks. With that said, it is important to note that often one is reduced to modelling what is normal, or at least benign, and looking for deviations from this model, and so one must not completely remove oneself from the inference camp.

In this chapter, I will discuss several statistical methods for analysing, modelling, and predicting in complex data that are of interest for applications in computer security. I will use for illustration a data set provided by Kaggle.[a] The data consist of 10,868 examples of malware, grouped into nine malware families. The task is to construct a classifier that can determine the family of new malware. The data comes in two forms: a byte-dump of the executable programme, and a decompilation of the programme into assembly code. In both cases, some adjustments have been made so that an executable version of the programme cannot be generated by a simple manipulation of the data. I will use the byte-dump data from this data set.

In addition to this data set, I will also utilise the network data available from the Los Alamos National Laboratory (LANL) (Kent, 2016).[b] There are several interesting data sets there, and I will use the network flows data.

The layout of the chapter is as follows. First, I will consider some basic applications of computational statistics in Section 2. In Section 3, I will consider some dimensionality reduction techniques that allow one to go from complex, high-dimensional observations to lower-dimensional data which (one hopes) is easier to model, without losing "too much" of the information in the data. Finally, Section 4 will discuss some new methods

---

[a]https://www.kaggle.com/c/malware-classification.
[b]Data available at http://csr.lanl.gov/data/cyber1/.

derived from algebraic topology that have potential for becoming a new generation of data analysis tools.

2. Computational Statistics

Computational statistics is generally described as the interface between statistics or data analysis and computing.[c] It is the collection of tools and theory developed to model large, high-dimensional and complex data, and the algorithms and computer code that implement these ideas. Generally the tools are nonparametric rather than parametric, and the data of interest are either high dimensional (more than three or four variables), consist of a large number of observations (more than a few hundred), complex (a mix of continuous and categorical variables, or other data types) or a combination of the above. Cyber-security data has all of these properties, and in many cases the data volumes are truly massive. Thus, computationally efficient methods are essential for the analysis of the data. In this section, I will look at a few common methods from computational statistics related to probability density estimation, classification and machine learning.

2.1. *Density estimation*

First, let's focus on univariate data. Everyone is familiar with the histogram, which can be thought of as simply counting the number (proportion) of observations that fall in each of a set of bins.[d] In one extreme case, where the data are discrete, the bins can correspond to the unique values of the data, and the histogram is simply the empirical estimate of the probability mass function. In the continuous case, one generally takes the range of the data and selects equal-sized bins that cover this range. For example, if the data fall in the interval $[0, 1]$ and one wants m bins, the bins can be $\left[0, \frac{1}{m}\right], \left(\frac{1}{m}, \frac{2}{m}\right], \ldots, \left(\frac{m-1}{m}, 1\right]$. It is well known (and often not emphasised enough in school) that the shape of the histogram (the estimate of the probability density function) can vary quite a bit by changing the placement of the bins. For example, instead of placing the center of the first bin at $\frac{1}{2m}$, placing it at the smallest observation will result in a different "picture" and,

---

[c]https://en.wikipedia.org/wiki/Computational_statistics.
[d]For this discussion, the histogram consists of equal-sized adjacent bins.

more importantly, a different estimate of the density.[e] Many solutions have been proposed to solve this problem (David Scott's book (Scott, 1992) is an excellent reference). The one I will consider is kernel density estimation (Silverman, 1986). If one thinks of the histogram as "place the bins, then count the points", the kernel density estimate corresponds to "place the points and count the bins". Formally

$$f_{ke}(x) = \frac{1}{nh} \sum_{i=1}^{n} K \left(\frac{x - x_i}{h} \right).$$

Here, K, the kernel, is a probability density function, such as the normal (Gaussian) distribution.[f] The idea is that one places the "kernel" at every point, and then adds up the contribution from all of the kernels.

Note that the kernel estimator, like the histogram, has a single parameter,[g] h, called the bandwidth.[h] Larger values of h give a smoother estimate of the density, smaller values produce less-smooth estimates, and can detect fine structure in the density. Note that, like the number of bins in a histogram, the bin width should be chosen as a function of n, with larger n corresponding to smaller bandwidths. There are many rules of thumb for bandwidth selection (Silverman, 1986; Wand and Jones, 1994). An important fact about kernel estimators is that they are "consistent", in the sense that (with weak assumptions) the estimate converges to the true density so long as the bandwidth decreases in n, the number of observations, at an appropriate rate. Asymptotic results of this type may not be directly useful in a practical application,[i] but they do provide some confidence that as long as one has "enough" data, one will obtain a "good" estimate, and if this

---

[e]Changing the number of bins will also change the density estimate, and this will be illustrated in discussion of the kernel estimator.

[f]Technically, K needs to be positive, integrate to one, and have finite variance — be square-integrable — but some of these conditions can be weakened.

[g]Technically, as mentioned above, the histogram has a second parameter, the position of the first bin. Since this is almost always set according to the minimum value of the data, or a *priori* by knowledge of the possible data range, it is reasonable to think of the histogram as being parametrised by the bin width.

[h]The bandwidth corresponds to the bin width (or equivalently the number of bins, assuming adjacent bins) of the histogram.

[i]The curse of dimensionality means that for high-dimensional data, asymptotic results are particularly unhelpful.

estimate performs well on the prediction task, there is reason to believe it is likely to perform well on new data.

Although there are good reasons to select the kernel K according to some knowledge of the data, I will use Gaussian (normal density) kernels in this work. The reader is encouraged to look at the discussions about kernels in the references.

The kernel estimator can be seen as an extreme case of a mixture model (McLachlan and Peel, 2000): one fits a mixture of a given density to the data. For example, the Gaussian mixture model (with m terms) is

$$f_{gmm}(x) = \sum_{j=1}^{m} \pi_j \phi(x; \mu_j, \sigma_j).$$

The mixture proportions π_i are positive and sum to one. There are many variations on this theme (Fraley and Raftery, 2002; Marchette *et al.*, 1996; Priebe, 1994). Fitting the parameters of the mixture can be tricky, but there are good methods using variations of the expectation-maximisation (EM) algorithm (McLachlan and Krishnan, 1997) and clever computer science (Moore, 1998). In text data analysis, these show up (using different densities and usually a Bayesian approach to the parameters) as topic models (Blei and Lafferty, 2009; Blei *et al.*, 2003).

Consider the distribution of bytes in malware. That is, for each value from 0 to 255, one computes the proportion of times each byte is found in the file.[j] This seems (and is) a pretty naive set of features to use, but I'll use it to illustrate some of these ideas.

Figure 1 shows the empirical probability distribution (the proportions of times each byte occurs in the file) for one of the pieces of malware. The curve is the kernel estimator. The graph has been scaled — the proportion of 0 bytes for this code is 0.14, which accounts for the vertical offset of the kernel estimator — it is smoothing out this value. It is clear, though, that some of the structure of the data is represented in the kernel estimator. Further, the structure is not simply a random mess — there are what appear to be clusters of similar bytes in the data.

There are multivariate versions of kernel estimators and mixture models. These essentially replace the kernel or mixture component with a

---

[j]In the data provided by Kaggle, there are bytes with value "??", corresponding to obfuscation to prevent the reconstruction of an executable from the data. In these studies, I remove these values.

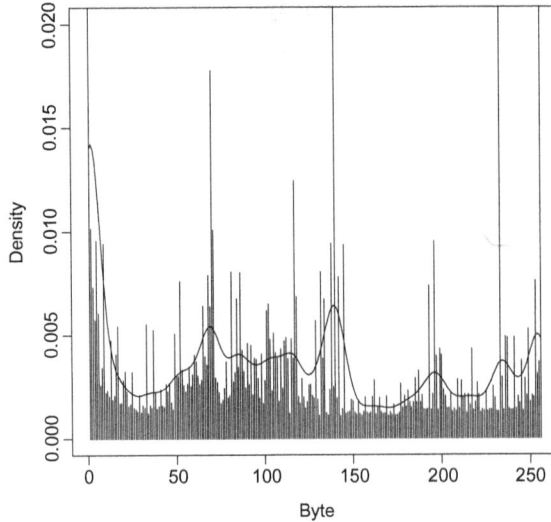

Fig. 1: A one-dimensional kernel estimator of one of the malware programmes. The bars correspond to the empirical estimate of the probability mass function (the histogram with bins centred on the integers). The y-axis has been scaled to show the fine-scale structure.

multivariate kernel or density. Details can be found in the references. See Figure 2 for an example computed on a single malware programme. Here, instead of counting the number of times a byte occurs, we are counting the number of times a pair of adjacent bytes occur.

Now let's investigate the utility of the byte-counts for a simple task: classify the malware according to family. For this, and other tests, I have selected (at random) 100 observations from each class (except for class 5 which only has 42 observations — I select 21 of them) to use as training, and use the rest of the observations for testing. All errors reported in this paper are computed on the testing data.

Using the histogram,[k] a nearest neighbour classifier[l] has an error of 0.162. The kernel estimate of the density function (treating the data as if they were continuous) results in a nearest neighbour error of 0.124. The McNemar test (Agresti, 1990), which is a Chi-square test for symmetry of

---

[k] In this case, the histogram is simply the byte-counts (proportions) for the 256 possible byte values and the bin size is 1. This is the empirical estimate of the probability mass function.

[l] The use of a nearest neighbour classifier is for the purposes of comparison only. As is well known, this classifier is rarely a viable choice for real-world problems, but it can be instructive for getting a feel for the data, and for upper bounds on the error one can expect for the problem.

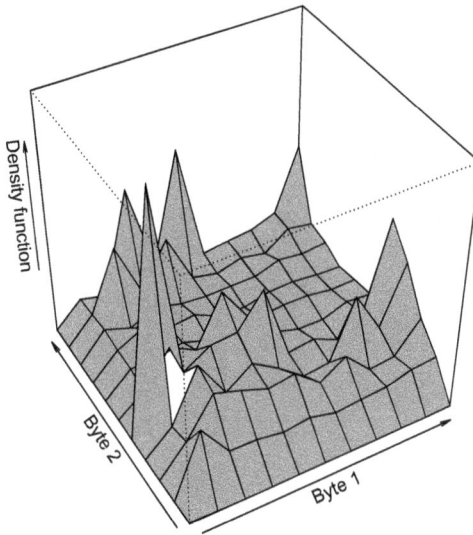

Fig. 2:   A two-dimensional kernel estimator of one of the malware programmes. Adjacent bytes correspond to the two axes. This has been smoothed to a 32×32 grid.

Table 1:   Confusion matrix for the nearest neighbour classifier on byte-counts for the nine class malware data. Blank entries are 0s.

			True Class					
1291	116		6	2	53	12	75	128
5	1525		1		4	1	6	5
0	33	2807	3		1	2	2	0
1	63	29	352		12	2	7	10
27	89			19	13	8	23	21
55	166	2	10		554	2	32	28
30	6	4	3		4	244	45	0
28	243				3	15	920	12
4	137				7	12	18	709

the contingency table (whether the two classifiers miss the same number of observations) has a p-value essentially 0, and so the kernel estimator on these data is a better classifier (see Tables 1 and 2). Note that although the kernel estimator produces better performance overall, it is not better for all classes.

Figure 3 shows how the individual bytes are correlated with class membership, a crude indicator of their importance for classification. Byte value

Table 2: Confusion matrix for the nearest neighbour classifier on a kernel estimator from byte-counts for the nine class malware data.

True Class								
1232	133		1	4	17	9	65	64
16	1816		2		5	6	6	26
0	13	2811	2		1		3	3
4	31	15	363		14		6	7
34	4	1	2	15	9		19	8
52	57	8	4	1	581	2	17	15
7	30	4			1	271	24	1
43	74	3		1	17	7	957	32
53	220		1		6	3	31	757

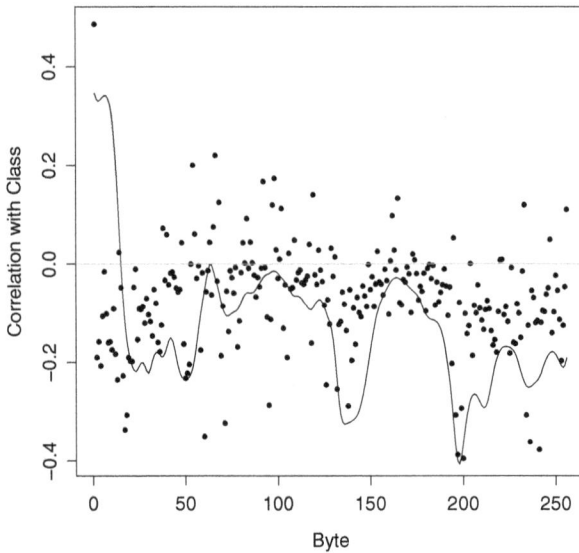

Fig. 3: Correlation with class for the byte proportions (dots) and the kernel estimator (curve).

0 is the most correlated, with values 198, 201, 237 and 242 being the most negatively correlated. The kernel estimator, which smooths the histogram, also smooths this correlation and suggests that the last two may not be as important. Note also that the kernel estimator has a very different profile of correlation.

Criticisms of this little experiment are easy to come by, but I want to make two points. First, simple ideas (byte-counts, nearest neighbour classifiers) can often provide surprising performance and can be used to gain further insight into the problem. Second, statistical ideas such as smoothing (kernel density estimation), variable selection and dimensionality reduction (which we'll see below) and modelling can improve performance dramatically even in the case where domain knowledge does not provide much help.[m]

If one uses only the first 1000 bytes in the file, the results swap: in this case, the histogram obtains an error of 0.130 and the kernel estimator an error of 0.176. Note that the kernel estimate on the entire file is still the superior classifier. Domain knowledge can be used to determine what the optimal approach is: Is it important to process the entire file, or are there particular sections (such as the beginning) that are more informative? Should different sections be weighted differently?

It is important to note that the bytes represent a fairly complicated type of data. On the one hand, they are categorical, representing (one byte of) a machine instruction code. On the other hand, some of them represent memory locations or data, in which case they are integers, and also may correspond to (one byte of) floating point numbers. If the data were purely categorical, the kernel estimator approach above would be nonsensical, and (presumably) this would be reflected in the performance.

Another important consideration when using kernel estimators is to account for a known (or suspected) constraint on the range. Since we know there are no values outside of [0, 255], it makes sense to use a variant of the kernel estimator that constrains the estimate to be within this range. I didn't bother, since the ultimate purpose is not to produce the best estimate of the probability density possible, but to produce the best performance of a classifier.[n]

---

[m]Admittedly, in this case I chose to use no domain knowledge, to illustrate the idea. At a minimum, knowing (and utilising) the word size should be a first step when processing data corresponding to machine instructions.

[n]Note that the Bayes error is given by the classifier that uses the true joint probability distribution of the data, *not* the probability distribution of individual byte-counts. So, it is not the case that a better estimate will necessarily produce a better classifier.

It is important to note that the above is not an estimate of the probability density function of the (256-dimensional) data. Instead, I am using density estimates *as the features* which are then passed to the machine learning algorithm. This is in the spirit of much of the text processing literature (Aggarwal and Zhai, 2012; Gupta and Lehal, 2009), where one often starts with term-frequencies computed on a per-document basis.

2.2. *Streaming data*

The malware problem discussed in the previous section has the property that it comes in discrete chunks (single files) at a relatively slow pace. Internet packet traffic is an example of streaming data: there is an extremely high volume of data that comes at a very rapid pace, making it difficult to store and process all the data in the manner described above. Streaming, or "on-line" methods are needed to allow the processing of the data.

To illustrate, consider the problem of estimating the mean of a univariate random variable X. One observes data in time, $\{x_1, x_2, \ldots\}$ and can only store a small number of bytes. We'd like to know, at any given time, what the sample mean is for all the data seen to date. Fortunately, there is a simple recursive formula for the sample mean that only requires the storage of the current estimate and the number of observations seen to date:

$$\widehat{X}_n = \frac{n-1}{n}\widehat{X}_{n-1} + \frac{1}{n}X_n. \tag{1}$$

Note that (1) is exact: after n observations, $\widehat{X}_n$ is the sample mean of the data $\{x_1, x_2, \ldots, x_n\}$.

One can implement an exponential window on the data, "forgetting" past data, which can be useful in a nonstationary environment, by making a simple change to the equation:

$$\widehat{X}_n = \frac{N-1}{N}\widehat{X}_{n-1} + \frac{1}{N}X_n. \tag{2}$$

Here, N is fixed, with its value controlling the width of the exponential window.

There are many approaches to analysing streaming data in the literature. Various streaming density estimates have been investigated, including kernel estimators (Wegman and Marchette, 2003), wavelet-based density estimators (Caudle *et al.*, 2015) and mixture models (Priebe, 1994). The first two citations were applied to network data, and are thus of particular interest to the computer security community.

The basic idea of most streaming algorithms comes down to a rewriting of (2). For example, a streaming density estimator (Wegman and Marchette, 2003) can be defined as

$$\widehat{f}_n(x) = \theta \widehat{f}_{n-1}(x) + (1 - \theta)\gamma\,(x, X_n). \tag{3}$$

Here, $\gamma\,(\cdot)$ is whatever is appropriate for a single observation (such as the contribution of the observations to a kernel estimator, or an update to the parameters of a mixture model). It is generally straightforward to modify (3) to allow a small number of recent observations to be used, rather than just a single observation, provided the data rates and memory overhead allows for this.

In particular, consider

$$\widehat{f}_n(x) = \theta \widehat{f}_{n-1}(x) + (1 - \theta)\frac{1}{h}K\left(\frac{x - x_n}{h}\right). \tag{4}$$

This presupposes that one knows the values at which one is going to want to apply the estimator: one needs to keep track of (4) at each point at which one wishes to evaluate the kernel estimator. For the malware data of byte-counts, we only have a finite number of possible values. Otherwise one would want to assign a grid to the possible values.

The flows data from Los Alamos consists of number of packets and bytes for a collection of flows between computers over time. Figure 4 depicts the number of packets and bytes for a single day. Note the obvious lines in this plot, indicating flows that have very similar payloads per packet — this is an indication of the type of application that is associated with the flow. The linear structure indicates that a polar coordinates representation is appropriate for these data, and this is depicted in Figure 5. In both cases I have used alpha-blending to reduce the overplotting. Thus, dark regions are regions with many points overplotted within the region.

There is a lot of structure evident in these figures. Diagonal lines in Figure 4 and vertical lines in Figure 5 are indicative of applications with the same ratio of bytes to packets — presumably applications whose flows consist of many same sized packets.

To illustrate the streaming kernel estimator, consider Figure 6. Here, we are estimating the probability density of the log of the number of bytes

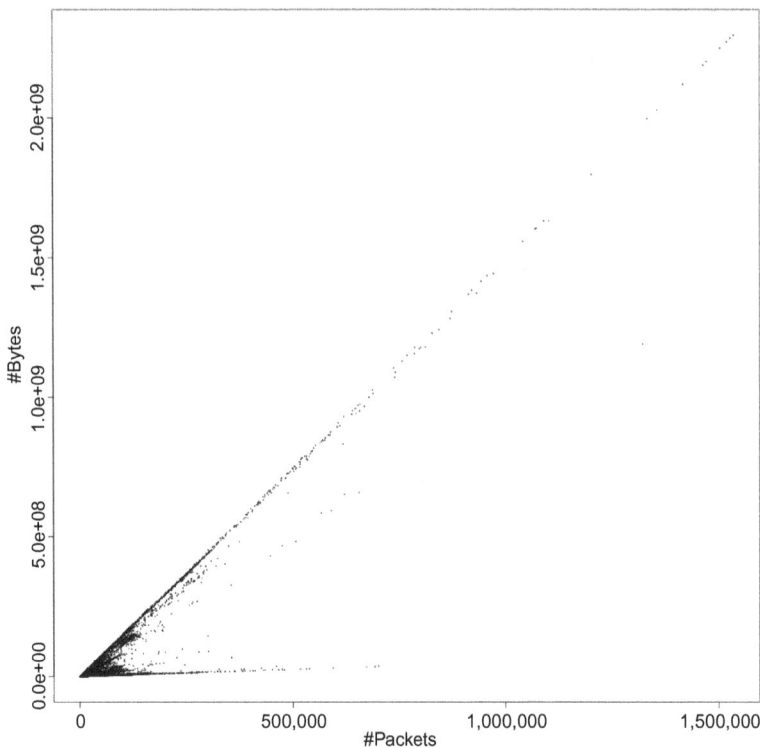

Fig. 4: Number of packets against the number of bytes for one day's worth of data.

in a web session: ports 80, 8080 or 443. We start with an estimate on the first 1000 sessions, and then update the estimate using (4) with each new session. This figure corresponds to 9 hours of data.

There is obvious temporal structure in the data; however, the time period is too short to see if the periodic structures that are apparent in the figure are continued. There is also some structure in the sizes (number of bytes) of the web sessions. Clear peaks are evident, and persist through time. This shows that there is some stability in the application, which is probably due to the way web interactions work; the text of a web page may be transferred via one session while the (substantially larger) images on the page are transferred via other sessions. There is also some standardisation in image size, in the sense that these are often designed to fit in a standard window, and often use the same type of compression (JPEG) throughout.

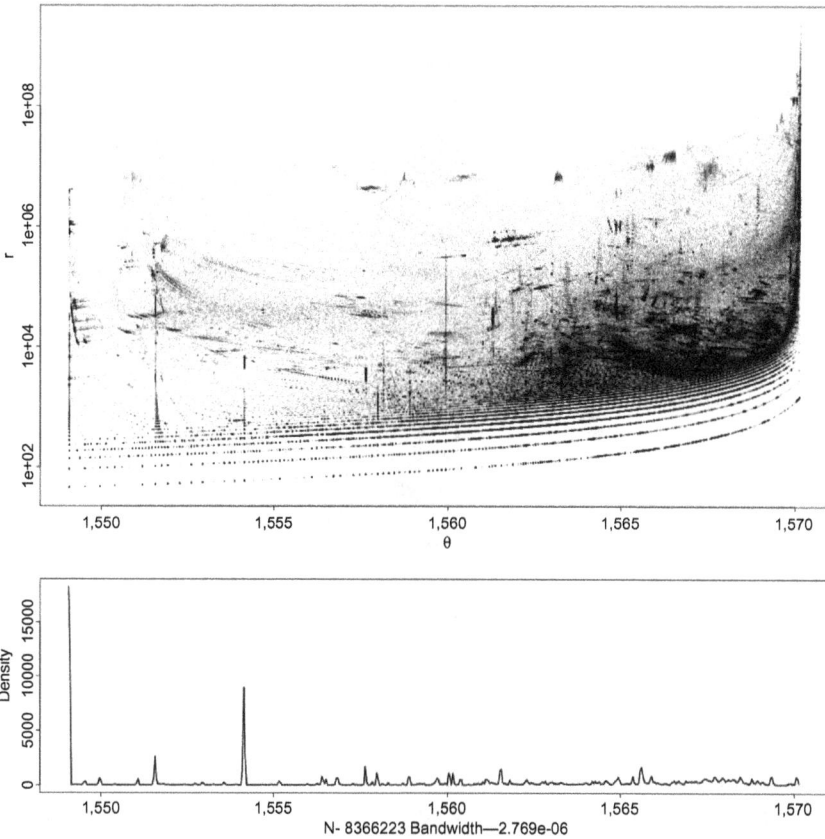

Fig. 5: Polar coordinates of the flows data (top) and a kernel density estimator of the angle θ (bottom). This corresponds to a single day's worth of data.

This may account for the fairly consistent peaks in the higher ranges of the x-axis.

2.3. *Machine learning*

The field of machine learning deals with the problems of developing algorithms to allow the computer to "learn" patterns from data. For the purposes of cyber-data analytics, one wants to perform one of three basic tasks: classification (also called supervised learning), where the computer is given labelled data and the task is to learn how to correctly label new observations; clustering (also called unsupervised learning), where the data are

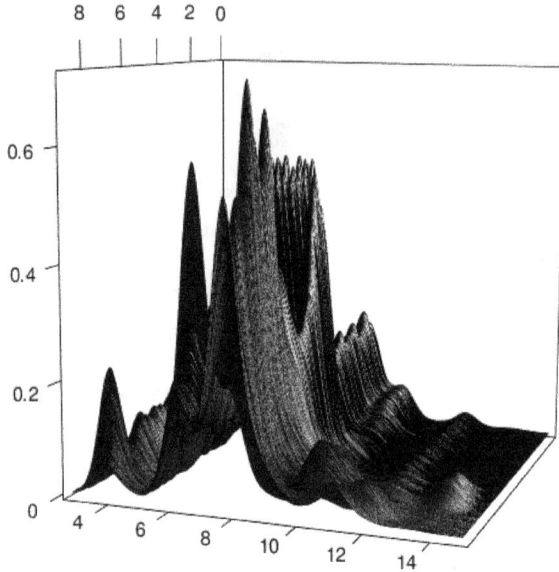

Fig. 6:   Streaming kernel density estimate for web traffic from the flows data. The *x*-axis (front) correspond to the log of the number of bytes in the flow, the *y*-axis (into the page) is time, and the *z*-axis is density.

unlabelled, and the task is to group the data into "appropriate" groups; and outlier or abnormality detection, where the data are "normal", and the computer is tasked to recognise when new data do not fit well with the training data.

There are a myriad of classification algorithms. Recently (Fernández-Delgado *et al.*, 2014), it was observed that from a practical standpoint, there are only a few classifiers that are robust enough to be both easily applicable to a wide range of data sets and at the top of the performance curve. One of the best, if not the best, is random forests (Breiman, 2001a).

The idea of random forests comes from decision trees (Breiman *et al.*, 1984). Think of a physician diagnosing a patient. She may go through a set of rules like: Does the patient exhibit a fever? If not, does the patient complain of abdominal pain? One can imagine building a tree of simple univariate tests of the data, where at each node in the tree, the data are split on the value of the variable, until one reaches a leaf node, where the decision is made based on the class labels of the training data in that node.

This works quite well in practice, and there are a number of software systems that implement variations on this idea. The advantage is that the classifier is easy to understand as a series of if-tests, and a physician can look at the individual decisions to determine whether she believes that the algorithm is computing something that makes sense. The disadvantage is that it is extremely sensitive to the data — changing the training data a little bit, can dramatically change the tree. Also, although the approach works quite well, a single tree is limited in practice and is generally not the best classifier that can be obtained.

The random forest takes advantage of the variability limitation mentioned above. It operates by taking a sample of the data, building a tree on that sample, then repeating many times. The resulting collection of trees (the forest) is then used in a voting scheme to classify new data. In practice, this works amazingly well, as indicated in the reference (Fernández-Delgado *et al.*, 2014). When we apply the random forest to the malware data, we obtain an error of 0.040, far better than the kernel estimator approach. Recall that the data used is simply byte-counts, which we have already noted is a particularly naive set of features, and without a doubt could be improved upon with a bit of domain knowledge, and yet we obtain better than 95% correct classification on the malware task. Note that unlike the nearest neighbour classifier, the random forest does slightly worse on the kernel estimator (an error of 0.064) — it may be that the correlation introduced by the smoothing is harming the performance.

3. Manifold Learning

It is generally believed that most real high-dimensional data fall on or near a lower-dimensional structure. Here, "near" is generally considered in a probabilistic sense; crudely, we think of the data as being drawn from a distribution on this structure, with additive (high-dimensional) noise. This structure is the "manifold" of the section title, but technically it need not be a manifold in the strict topological or geometric sense. Manifold learning, also known as manifold discovery, is a collection of techniques for "discovering" this structure, usually by way of an embedding into a lower-dimensional (Euclidean) space.

This idea that there is a lower-dimensional representation of the data that contains the information relevant for inference is the basis of principal component analysis (Jolliffe, 2002), multi-dimensional scaling (Cox and Cox, 2000), feature selection (Guyon and Elisseeff, 2003), projection pursuit (Friedman and Stuetzle, 1981), etc.

Many manifold learning techniques utilise graphs defined on the data (Belkin and Niyogi, 2003; Cayton, 2005; Huo *et al.*, 2007; Pless and Souvenir, 2009), and so we will start with a discussion of graph theory.

3.1. *Graph theory*

A graph is a set V of vertices (or nodes) and a set of edges $E \subset V \times V$. We assume that there are no self loops (if $(u, v) \in E$ then $u \neq v$). We will also assume the graph is undirected, and so (u, v) and (v, u) correspond to the same edge, so the elements of E are unordered pairs (in spite of the notation). The *order* of a graph $g = (V, E)$ is $|V|$, the number of vertices, and the *size* is $|E|$, the number of edges. The adjacency matrix of a graph is the binary matrix $A = (a_{ij})$ where $a_{ij} = 1$ if and only if there is an edge from vertex i to vertex j. The degree of a vertex is the number of edges incident to it.

One can construct a graph from data by treating the points as vertices and defining edges in terms of proximity. Usually, one defines a distance or dissimilarity measure and uses this to join "close" vertices. The most common such graphs are the k-nearest neighbour graph — in which each vertex is joined to the k points nearest to it — and the ϵ-ball graph — in which each vertex is joined to all points whose distance is within ϵ.

Generally, especially with high-dimensional data, the ϵ-ball graph is disconnected. One way to mitigate this without adding an excessive number of edges, is to add in the edges from a k-nearest neighbour graph, with k chosen to be minimal such that the resulting graph is connected.[o] Performing this operation with the malware training data results in a graph with 13005 edges. Laying the graph out using a spring embedding algorithm (Kamada and Kawai, 1989) is depicted in Figure 7. Here, $k = 9$ connects the graph

---

[o] A (possibly) better approach is to compute the minimal spanning tree first, then add the edges from the ϵ-ball graph.

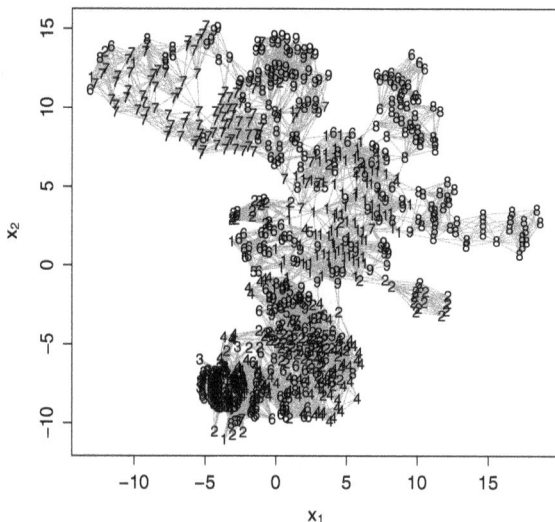

Fig. 7: Two-dimensional layout of the connected $\epsilon = .01$ ball graph on the malware training data. Numbers correspond to the class of the observation.

(the $k = 9$ nearest neighbour graph has two connected components). The 9-nearest neighbour graph is depicted in Figure 8.

3.2. *Dimensionality reduction*

The graph embedding discussed above is one way of reducing the dimension of the data. However, using graph layout algorithms is clearly not what is needed. These algorithms are designed for two- and three-dimensional layouts, and are meant to be visually appealing, or have other measures of quality, that are not necessarily well suited to the inference task at hand.

Instead, we wish to use the graph to provide an embedding into $\mathbb{R}^d$ for any (reasonable) d, and further, we'd like this embedding to be well suited for inference. The Isomap (Tenenbaum *et al.*, 2000) algorithm is one method worth considering.

Given a graph, g, we compute the shortest path distance between each pair of vertices. This produces an inter point distance matrix between each pair of our observations (treated as vertices of the graph). One then applies multi-dimensional scaling (Borg and Groenen, 1997) to this matrix to produce the embedding.

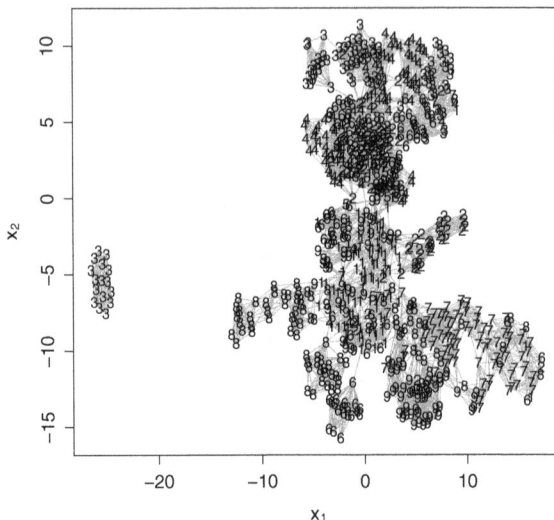

Fig. 8: Two-dimensional layout of the $k = 9$ nearest neighbour graph on the malware training data. Numbers correspond to the class of the observation.

Figure 9 shows the Isomap embedding using the connected ϵ-ball graph. The 9-nearest neighbour graph is problematic, since it is not connected. There are two approaches: embed each component separately, or increase k until the graph is connected. Since the 11-nearest neighbour graph is connected, we use this in Figure 10.

Another popular method of embedding is the Laplacian eigenmap. The Laplacian of a graph is $L = D - A$ where A is the adjacency matrix and D is the diagonal matrix of the degrees of the vertices (the row-sums of A). It is well known that L is positive semi-definite with a 0 eigenvalue for each connected component of the graph. Assuming the graph is connected, the d eigenvectors associated with the d smallest non-zero eigenvalues is often used as an embedding of the graph into $\mathbb{R}^d$. The normalised Laplacian $\mathcal{L} = D^{-\frac{1}{2}} L D^{-\frac{1}{2}}$ is also often used, and empirically seems to provide better embeddings for most classification and clustering tasks.

An interesting model for graphs is the latent position model (Hoff *et al.*, 2002), in which the edges of a graph depend probabilistically on their relationship in a latent (unobserved) "social space". A simple version of this is the random dot product graph (RDPG) (Marchette and Priebe, 2008; Nickel, 2008; Scheinerman and Tucker, 2010). The model is as follows. Assume

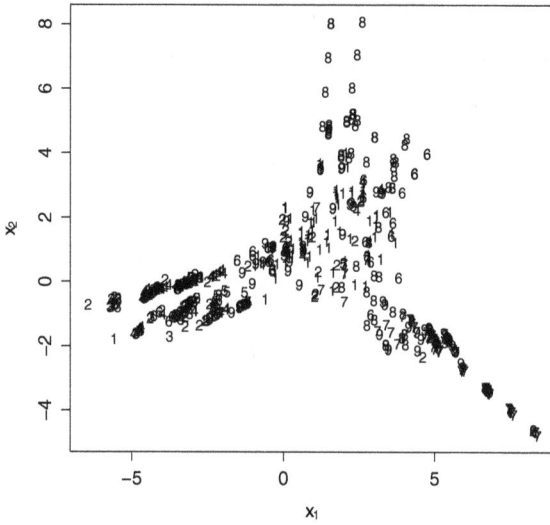

Fig. 9: Two-dimensional Isomap of the connected $\epsilon = .01$ ball graph on the malware training data. Numbers correspond to the class of the observation.

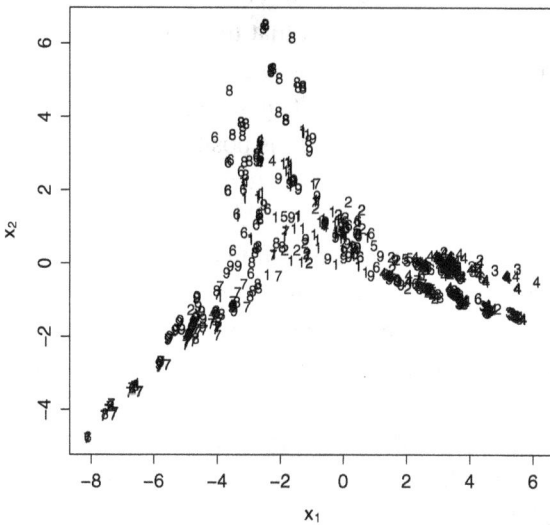

Fig. 10: Two-dimensional Isomap embedding of the $k = 11$ nearest neighbour graph on the malware training data. Numbers correspond to the class of the observation.

there are (unobservable) vectors $(v_1, \ldots, v_n) \in \mathbb{R}^d$, one per vertex, with the property that all pairwise dot products between vectors lie in $[0, 1]$. The graph is generated according to

$$P((i, j) \in E) = v_i^t v_j.$$

The random dot product graph has a couple of nice properties. In particular, it can utilise the spectral theorem to estimate the vectors. Recall that the spectral theorem for symmetric square matrices M can be written as:

$$M = U \Lambda U^t = (U \Lambda^{-\frac{1}{2}})(U \Lambda^{-\frac{1}{2}})^t. \tag{5}$$

The columns of U are the eigenvectors, and Λ is the diagonal matrix of eigenvalues, and U and Λ are real valued. We'll assume the eigenvalues are in decreasing size, so the first column of U corresponds to the largest eigenvalue. Further, the best (in Frobenius norm) representation of M with $(n \times d)$-dimensional matrices is to take the first d eigenvectors in (5).

Given a graph, the obvious thing to do is to use (5) applied to the adjacency matrix, taking the top d eigenvectors/values. There are two problems with this. First is the fact that the adjacency matrix is hollow — the diagonal is structurally zero — and so the statement about the "best d-dimensional representation" isn't quite right. Second is that there's no reason to think the adjacency matrix is positive, and so there is a very real possibility that the square root is going to result in imaginary numbers if d is too large.

The second observation can be eliminated by noticing that the eigenvalues are simply a coordinate-wise scaling, and so one could simply use the eigenvectors, since the purpose is to produce an embedding of the data, not necessarily a good estimate of the latent vectors.[P] The first problem is a bit trickier. If we really want an estimate of the latent vectors, we don't want the diagonal of the resultant dot-product matrix to be 0. What we'd like to do is "fill in" the diagonal matrix with "the right" values — the lengths of the latent vectors. Adding a diagonal matrix to the adjacency matrix changes only the eigenvalues, not the eigenvectors, and so we need an estimate of the lengths of the latent vectors. A reasonable

---

[P]Alternatively, we could simply choose d to be small enough that the first d eigenvalues are positive.

estimate is $D/(n-1)$ where n is the order of the graph. So, we operate on $A + D/(n-1)$.

If the graph is a stochastic block model (Athreya *et al.*, 2016), and one chooses k to be the number of blocks (actually, the rank of the probability matrix), the resultant embedded points are distributed as a mixture of Gaussians.[q] Note that this statement is not changed by whether the vectors are or are not scaled by the eigenvalues — since this is only a scaling of the embedding, the mixture model is still the appropriate model.

Figure 11 depicts the RDPG embedding. As with the other embeddings, this is misleading, since we are depicting a two-dimensional representation, and it is unlikely that this is the intrinsic dimension of the data. However, it illustrates the idea of the RDPG embedding.

3.3. *Fusion*

Often, one has more than one way of looking at an object — more than one sensor or more than one way to construct features. For example, with the

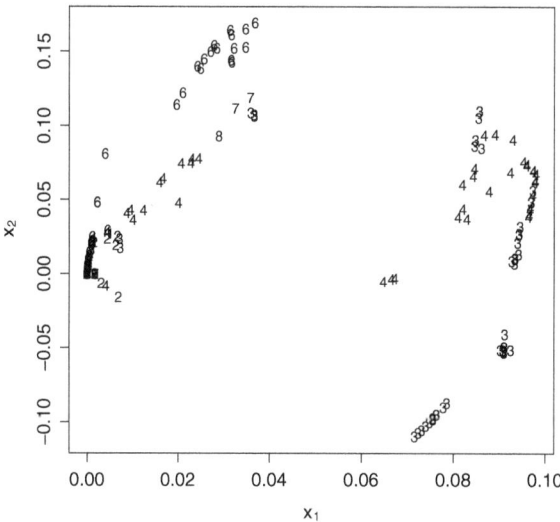

Fig. 11: Random dot product embedding of the connected ϵ-ball graph on the malware training data, with $\epsilon = 0.1$. Numbers correspond to the class of the observation.

---

[q]This is an asymptotic result, and there are a couple of technical details, but from a practical standpoint, a mixture of normals will be a good model for the embedded data.

malware data, one can look at the hex dump of the bytes (as we have done here) or one could look at a decompilation of the programme. Each view of the data can produce features, and we would like to "fuse" these features into a single representation of the data.

The obvious way to do this is to simply stick the features together. That is, if we compute the byte-count histogram from the hex dump and the word-count histogram from the decompilation, we can append these columns and use this (massively large) number of features as our feature set. This is, generally speaking, a bad idea. The curse of dimensionality (Jain *et al.*, 2000; Scott, 1992) says that the noise added by these new features can overcome any extra information inherent in the features. See Trunk (1979) for an excellent illustration of this fact.

One method for "fusing" information can be done at the inter point distance matrix level. Compute the distances from data from the first sensor (the byte-count histogram), producing D_1 and from the second sensor (the word-count histogram), producing D_2. Combine these distances into an *omnibus* inter point distance matrix D and use multi-dimensional scaling to embed these into a manageable space for inference. There are several ways to do this, one of which (Ma *et al.*, 2012; Priebe *et al.*, 2013) is to form the matrix:

$$D = \begin{pmatrix} D_1 & W_\lambda \\ W_\lambda & D_2 \end{pmatrix},$$

where $W_\lambda = \lambda D_1 + (1 - \lambda)D_2$.

Note that the above leads to a similar approach if the distance matrices are replace by the adjacency matrices of graphs defined on the data from the two sensors. This leads to a "joint" manifold discovery approach and is the subject of further research.

4. Topological Data Analysis

The field of algebraic topology seeks to understand topological spaces — such as the support regions of distributions — through the study of invariants computed on the spaces. These measures are invariant to smooth distortions of the space.

Topological data analysis (TDA) utilises the tools of algebraic topology for the analysis of data by first defining a sequence of topological spaces associated with the data and computing certain invariants on these spaces to learn information about the global structure of the data. Information about TDA can be found in Carlsson (2009), and in the book by Ghrist (2014).

Usually one uses TDA to explore a data set of points in some space, and extract features that describe some of the characteristics of the points, or more generally, the distribution from which the points were drawn. I will instead look at applying TDA to the malware data, where each piece of malware is viewed as a set of points, and TDA is used to extract features of the malware.

Much of the topological background we will use can be found in Greenberg and Harper (1981), as well as many other standard algebraic topology books. We will define the basic tools that will be used for TDA, then discuss how these may be used to make inferences about the classification boundary.

4.1. *Simplicial homology*

A (geometric) simplex of dimension d is a set of $d + 1$ points in relative position, see Figure 12. So, a 0-simplex is a point, a 1-simplex a line segment, a 2-simplex a triangle, and so on. We will write a k-simplex as $k+1$ vertices: $[v_0, \ldots, v_k]$, and any subset of k vertices is called a $(k - 1)$-face. We will say that a k-simplex is k-dimensional.

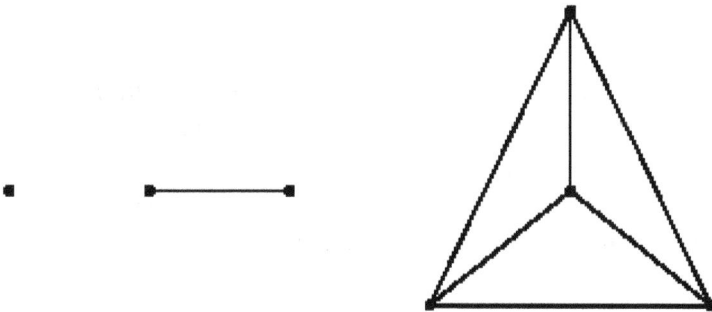

Fig. 12: Examples of a 0-simplex, a 1-simplex, and a 3-simplex (the figure on the right should be considered as a solid three-dimensional tetrahedron).

A simplicial complex is a collection S of simplices that satisfies the following conditions:

(1) If $\sigma \in S$, then so are the faces of σ.
(2) If $\sigma_1, \sigma_2 \in S$ are k simplices, then either they are disjoint or they intersect in a lower-dimensional simplex which is a face of both.

We write the set of k-simplices of S as S_k. We impose an orientation on the simplices by giving a positive orientation to vertices in lexicographic order, and asserting that any odd permutation of a k-simplex $[v_0, \dots, v_k]$ reverses the orientation. Thus, $[v_0, \dots, v_i, \dots, v_j, \dots, v_k] = -[v_0, \dots, v_j, \dots, v_i, \dots, v_k]$.

All of this can be abstracted by defining an abstract simplicial complex as a collection Δ of non-empty finite sets such that $Y \subset X \in \Delta$ implies $Y \in \Delta$. In this case, Y is called a face of X.

Given a simplicial complex, we form the chain complex as follows. For each S_k of k-simplices, we form the vector space (over some field, usually finite) C_k whose basis is the set of k-simplices in S_k. This can be thought of as all formal sums of the form $\sum a_i \sigma_i$ for $a_i \in \mathbb{Z}_p$, $\sigma_i \in S_k$. The boundary of a k simplex is the set of $k - 1$ simplices formed by deleting a vertex. This gives rise to a boundary map $\partial_k : C_k \to C_{k-1}$ for $k \geq 1$ as

$$\partial[v_0, \dots, v_k] = \sum_i (-1)^i [v_0, \dots, v_{i-1}, v_{i+1}, \dots, v_k].$$

The chain complex is the set $\{C_k, \partial_k\}$, often presented as

$$\cdots \xrightarrow{\partial_{k+1}} C_k \xrightarrow{\partial_k} C_{k-1} \cdots \xrightarrow{\partial_2} C_1 \xrightarrow{\partial_1} C_0 \xrightarrow{\partial_0} 0.$$

It is easy to check that $\partial_k \partial_{k+1} = 0$. We call the kernel of ∂_k the k-cycles, written Z_k, and the image of ∂_{k+1} the k-boundaries, written B_k. The homology is the quotient $H_k = Z_k / B_k$.

The rank of the kth homology is referred to as the kth Betti number, and it is these numbers that we will compute. Given a space, one constructs a simplicial complex, for example by triangulating the space, and then computes the homology. This is a topological invariant, meaning that continuous distortions of the space do not change the topology, and in particular do not change the Betti numbers.

In some sense, the homology of a space tells something about the k-dimensional holes, or voids, in the space. For example, Betti_0 is the number of connected components of the space. For an n-sphere, the Betti numbers are 1 for $k = 0, n$ and zero otherwise. The homology of the 2-torus $S^1 \times S^1$ is 2 for $k = 1$ (note that this corresponds to the two circles which generate the torus) and 1 for $k = 0, 2$, zero elsewhere.

Homology has an interesting connection to the Euler characteristic. One defines the Euler characteristic as

$$\chi(X) = \sum_{j=0}^{n} (-1)^j \text{Betti}_j(X). \tag{6}$$

This is equivalent to the standard Euler characteristic one learns in grade school, extended to general topological spaces and higher dimensions.

4.2. *Homology of data*

The above is all in the context of an abstract space — these abstract simplicies and chain complexes. How does one take a data set and apply any of this to learn anything about the data?

Just as with manifold discovery, the idea is to construct a graph on the data, such as a k-nearest neighbour graph, an ϵ-ball graph, or some other graph that encodes the local structure of the data. This graph then defines a simplicial complex through one of a number of mechanisms. The simplest is to treat each clique on $k + 1$ vertices as a k-simplex.

Given a data set, we construct a graph from which we construct a simplicial complex and compute the homology of the complex, which then corresponds to the homology of the data. This procedure is highly dependent on the choices made to define the graph. There are two obvious approaches to consider. The first is to construct a graph that is defined on data without regard to any parameters such as k or ϵ. Relative neighbourhood graphs or Gabriel graphs (Marchette, 2004) are two such graphs. The second is to consider a sequence of graphs (such as several values of k or ϵ) and look at how the homology changes as we change these values. This latter approach leads to the idea of persistent homology: those Betti numbers that "persist" across scales are ones that are indicative of true structure, while those that "come and go" are driven by noise and can be ignored.

4.3. *Euler trajectory*

We define the Euler Trajectory as the Euler characteristic as a function of ϵ in the ϵ-ball graph of the persistent homology. Figure 13 shows the Euler trajectories for the nine families of malware. These trajectories are computed from the persistent homology of the two-dimensional kernel estimators, using the TDA (Fasy *et al.*, 2015) package in R (Ihaka and Gentleman, 1996). There is some difference in the trajectories between the families, but for these data the difference is not large.

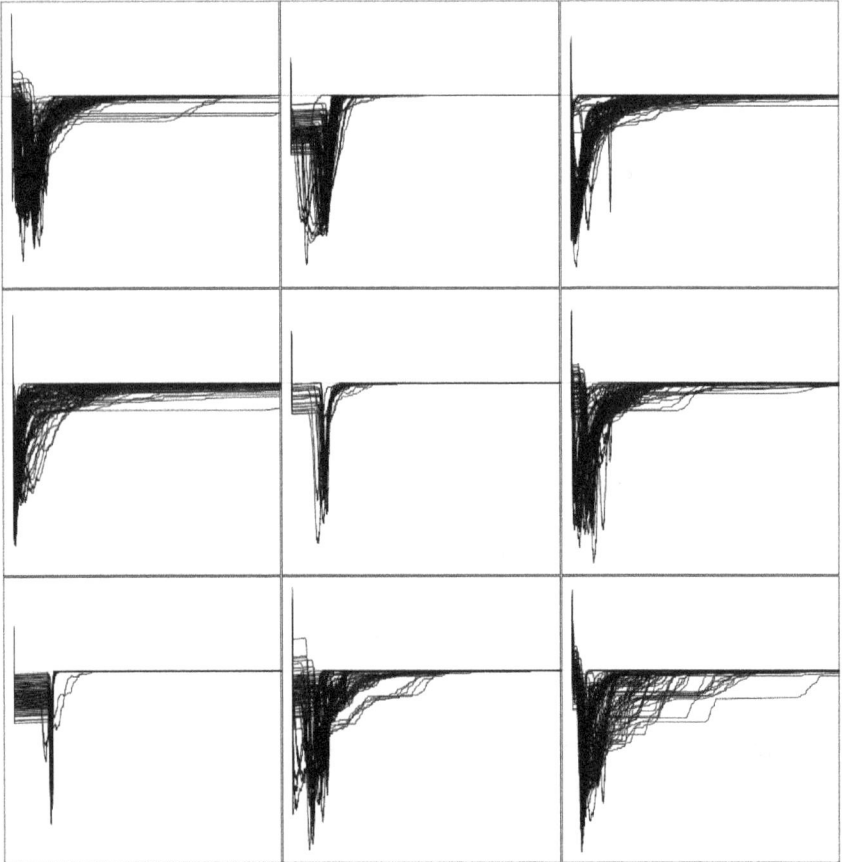

Fig. 13: The Euler trajectories for each of the nine classes of malware. In this figure $\epsilon \in [0, 0.0001]$.

There are several distances between persistent homologies in the literature. The bottleneck distance (Cohen-Steiner *et al.*, 2007; Veltkamp, 2001) looks at all bijections between the pairs of points in the diagram and computes the minimum of the maximum distances between points and their images. Applying multi-dimensional scaling to this distance matrix into $\mathbb{R}^5$ results in Figure 14. This gives another view of the data that may provide insight into its structure, and can provide a set of features to use for subsequent inference.

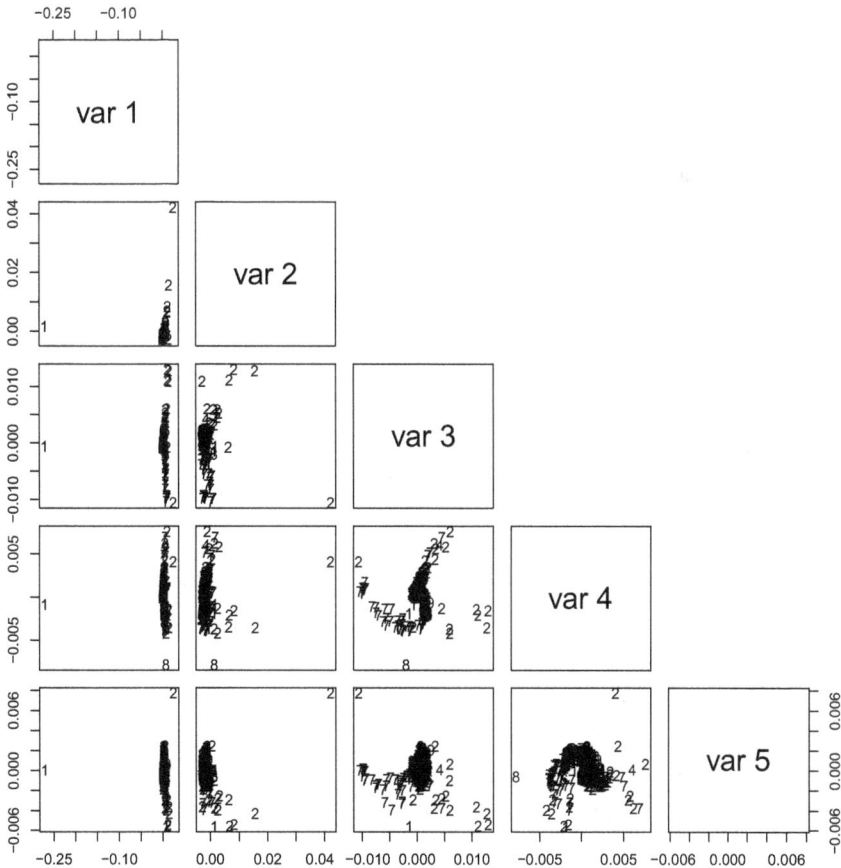

Fig. 14: The multi-dimensional scaling projection of the distances between the persistent homologies for the malware data. Plotting character indicates malware family.

5. Discussion

This has been a very high-level and idiosyncratic look at some techniques from computational statistics and statistical pattern recognition. There is a huge literature in feature selection, manifold discovery, and machine learning that we have only very briefly touched on. It is hoped that this will provide some suggestions for directions to look for future work, and some references for methods that may be of value for the analysis of computer security data.

One of the take-aways from this work is that very simple ideas can be very powerful. The simplistic features extracted from the malware data turn out to go a long way towards providing the information necessary for classification. The very simple idea of averaging — computing the sample mean — is used in the kernel estimator, the streaming data algorithms and the random forest.

Hand (2006) notes the power of simple classifiers and warns against putting too much effort into squeezing out the last bit of performance on a given data set. He points out many problems such as: changes in the underlying distribution of the data; training/testing data that is not representative; model misspecification; uncertainty in the classification labels and issues of interpretability.

With this said, it is important to remember that some things, cybersecurity being one of them, are inherently complicated, and we should be wary of oversimplifying. Careful thought needs to be put into incorporating domain knowledge into the models, and the models need to be adaptable to the changing environment — here streaming methods can be helpful. Interpretation and validation of the model, particularly in the case of random forests, can be quite difficult, and we need more tools to address these issues.

The field of deep learning (neural networks) has been completely missed in this discussion. This is not to denigrate it or to suggest that it is not important. There is reason to believe that the techniques that are currently available for training these deep networks may lead to very useful algorithms and solutions for the problems of cyber-security. These methods do suffer from some of the same issues of interpretability and validation that random forests have, so they should not be viewed as a panacea.

Acknowledgements

This work was funded in part by the Naval Surface Warfare Center (NSWC) In-House Laboratory Independent Research (ILIR) programme.

References

Aggarwal, C. C. and Zhai, C. (2012). *Mining Text Data*, Springer Science & Business Media, LLC, New York, USA.

Agresti, A. (1990). *Categorical Data Analysis*, Wiley, New York.

Athreya, A., Priebe, C. E., Tang, M., Lyzinski, V., Marchette, D. J. and Sussman, D. L. (2016). A limit theorem for scaled eigenvectors of random dot product graphs, *Sankhya A* **78**, 1, pp. 1–18.

Belkin, M. and Niyogi, P. (2003). Laplacian eigenmaps for dimensionality reduction and data representation, *Neural Computation* **15**, 6, pp. 1373–1396.

Blei, D. M. and Lafferty, J. D. (2009). *Topic Models*, Chapman & Hall/CRC.

Blei, D. M., Ng, A. Y. and Jordan, M. I. (2003). Latent Dirichlet allocation, *Journal of Machine Learning Research* **3**, pp. 993–1022.

Borg, I. and Groenen, P. (1997). *Modern Multidimensional Scaling*, Springer, New York.

Breiman, L. (2001a). Random forests, *Machine Learning* **45**, 1, pp. 5–32.

Breiman, L. (2001b). Statistical modeling: The two cultures, *Statistical Science* **16**, 3, pp. 199–231.

Breiman, L., Friedman, J. H., Olshen, R. A. and Stone, C. J. (1984). *Classification and Regression Trees*, Wadsworth & Brooks, Monterey, CA.

Carlsson, G. (2009). Topology and data, *Bulletin of the American Mathematical Society* **46**, 2, pp. 255–308.

Caudle, K. A., Karlsson, C. and Pyeatt, L. D. (2015). Using density estimation to detect computer intrusions, in *Proceedings of the 2015 ACM International Workshop on Security and Privacy Analytics*, pp. 43–48.

Cayton, L. (2005). Algorithms for manifold learning, *University of California at San Diego Technical Report*, pp. 1–17.

Cohen-Steiner, D., Edelsbrunner, H. and Harer, J. (2007). Stability of persistence diagrams, *Discrete & Computational Geometry* **37**, 1, pp. 103–120.

Cox, T. F. and Cox, M. A. (2000). *Multidimensional Scaling*, CRC Press, Boca Raton, FL.

Donoho, D. (2015). 50 years of data science, in *Tukey Centennial Workshop*, Princeton NJ.

Fasy, B. T., Kim, J., Lecci, F., Maria, C., included GUDHI is authored by C. Maria, V. R. T., by D. Morozov, D. and PHAT by U. Bauer, M. K. J. R. (2015). *TDA: Statistical Tools for Topological Data Analysis*, URL: https://CRAN.R-project.org/package=TDA, R package, Version 1.4.1.

Fernández-Delgado, M., Cernadas, E., Barro, S. and Amorim, D. (2014). Do we need hundreds of classifiers to solve real world classification problems? *Journal of Machine Learning Research* **15**, pp. 3133–3181.

Fraley, C. and Raftery, A. E. (2002). Model-based clustering, discriminant analysis and density estimation, *Journal of the American Statistical Association* **97**, pp. 611–631.

Friedman, J. H. and Stuetzle, W. (1981). Projection pursuit regression, *Journal of the American Statistical Association* **76**, 376, pp. 817–823.

Ghrist, R. (2014). *Elementary Applied Topology*, Createspace Independent Publishing Platform.

Greenberg, M. J. and Harper, J. R. (1981). *Algebraic Topology: A First Course*, CRC Press, Boca Raton, FL.

Gupta, V. and Lehal, G. S. (2009). A survey of text mining techniques and applications, *Journal of Emerging Technologies in Web Intelligence* **1**, 1, pp. 60–76.

Guyon, I. and Elisseeff, A. (2003). An introduction to variable and feature selection, *Journal of Machine Learning Research* **3**, pp. 1157–1182.

Hand, D. J. (2006). Classifier technology and the illusion of progress, *Statistical Science* **21**, 1, pp. 1–14.

Hoff, P. D., Raftery, A. E. and Handcock, M. S. (2002). Latent space approaches to social network analysis, *Journal of the American Statistical Association* **97**, pp. 1090–1098.

Huo, X., Ni, X. S. and Smith, A. K. (2007). A survey of manifold-based learning methods, in *Recent Advances In Data Mining Of Enterprise Data*, pp. 691–745, World Scientific, Singapore.

Ihaka, R. and Gentleman, R. (1996). R: A language for data analysis and graphics, *Journal of Computational and Graphical Statistics* **5**, 3, pp. 299–314.

Jain, A. K., Duin, R. P. W. and Mao, J. (2000). Statistical pattern recognition: A review, *IEEE Transactions on Pattern Analysis and Machine Intelligence* **22**, 1, pp. 4–37.

Jolliffe, I. T. ed. (2002). *Principal Component Analysis*, Springer Verlag, New York.

Kamada, T. and Kawai, S. (1989). An algorithm for drawing general undirected graphs, *Information Processing Letters* **31**, 1, pp. 7–15.

Kent, A. D. (2016). Cyber security data sources for dynamic network research, in N. Adams and N. Heard. eds., *Dynamic Networks and Cyber-Security*, Vol. 1, p. 37, World Scientific, Singapore.

Ma, Z., Marchette, D. J. and Priebe, C. E. (2012). Fusion and inference from multiple data sources in a commensurate space, *Statistical Analysis and Data Mining* **5**, 3, pp. 187–193.

Marchette, D. J. (2004). *Random Graphs for Statistical Pattern Recognition*, John Wiley & Sons, New York.

Marchette, D. J. and Priebe, C. E. (2008). Predicting unobserved links in incompletely observed networks, *Computational Statistics and Data Analysis* **52**, pp. 1373–1386.

Marchette, D. J., Priebe, C. E., Rogers, G. W. and Solka, J. L. (1996). Filtered kernel density estimation, *Computational Statistics* **11**, 2, pp. 95–112.

McLachlan, G. J. and Krishnan, T. (1997). *The EM Algorithm and Extensions*, Wiley, New York.

McLachlan, G. J. and Peel, D. (2000). *Finite Mixture Models*, Wiley, New York.

Moore, A. (1998). Very fast EM-based mixture model clustering using multiresolution kd-trees, citeseer.nj.nec.com/moore98very.html.

Nickel, C. L. M. (2008). *Random Dot Product Graphs: A Model For Social Networks*, Ph.D. thesis, Johns Hopkins University, Baltimore, MD.

Pless, R. and Souvenir, R. (2009). A survey of manifold learning for images, *IPSJ Transactions on Computer Vision and Applications* **1**, pp. 83–94.

Priebe, C. E. (1994). Adaptive mixture density estimation, *Journal of the American Statistical Association* **89**, pp. 796–806.

Priebe, C. E., Marchette, D. J., Ma, Z. and Adali, S. (2013). Manifold matching: Joint optimization of fidelity and commensurability, *Brazilian Journal of Probability and Statistics* **27**, pp. 377–400.

Scheinerman, E. R. and Tucker, K. (2010). Modeling graphs using dot product representations, *Computational Statistics* **25**, 1, pp. 1–16.

Scott, D. W. (1992). *Multivariate Density Estimation: Theory, Practice, and Visualization*, Wiley, New York.

Silverman, B. W. (1986). *Density Estimation for Statistics and Data Analysis*, Chapman and Hall, New York.

Tenenbaum, J. B., de Silva, V. and Langford, J. C. (2000). A global geometric framework for nonlinear dimensionality reduction, *Science* **290**, pp. 2319–2323.

Trunk, G. V. (1979). A problem of dimensionality: A simple example, *IEEE Transactions on Pattern Analysis and Machine Intelligence* **1**, 3, pp. 306–307.

Veltkamp, R. C. (2001). Shape matching: Similarity measures and algorithms, in *SMI 2001 International Conference on Shape Modeling and Applications*, pp. 188–197.

Wand, M. P. and Jones, M. C. (1994). *Kernel Smoothing*, Chapman and Hall/CRC, London.

Wegman, E. J. and Marchette, D. J. (2003). On some techniques for streaming data: A case study of internet packet headers, *Journal of Computational and Graphical Statistics* **12**, pp. 893–914.

Chapter 3

Bayesian Activity Modelling for Network Flow Data

Henry Clausen[*,§], Mark Briers[†] and Niall M. Adams[*,‡]

*Department of Mathematics, Imperial College London,
London SW7 2AZ, UK
†Alan Turing Institute, 96 Euston Rd, Kings Cross,
London NW1 2DB, UK
‡Data Science Institute, Imperial College London,
London SW7 2AZ, UK
§henry.clausen@ed.ac.uk

Sophisticated cyber attackers often move through their targeted network by creating a hierarchical chain of controlled computers and thereby create a strong
correlation between the activity on two different computers. To detect such connected activities, an accurate model of network traffic that distinguishes between
automated computer traffic and different user activity states is necessary. In this
chapter, we propose a novel Bayesian model that identifies different states of activity in the arrival times of network flow events on individual computers. Our model
is based on the well-known *Markov-modulated Poisson process*, but overcomes
its drawbacks with the modelling of network data. Our model is embedded in a
fast and scalable Bayesian inference framework. We validate the relation of our
results to actual user activity through a controlled experiment.

1. Introduction

Advanced persistent threats (APTs), which are responsible for many severe
data breaches in enterprise computer networks, are characterised by the
intruder maintaining a presence in the compromised network for long-term
control and data collection, possibly lasting months (Tankard, 2011).

APT attacks often circumvent strong firewalls, which protect high-
value assets, through a technique called *pivoting* (also known as *lateral*

55

movement). This allows the attacker to expand their access from vulnerable computers to ones with higher protection. An attacker often gains a foothold on a system via social engineering and highly targeted phishing emails to selected individuals with no high-level access and the corresponding protection. If the victim system is connected to the network, the attacker will identify available ports and start running services on other systems. This allows the attacker to gain control over new systems without operating a direct connection to the *Command-and-Control* (C&C) server (Neil *et al.*, 2013). Pivoting therefore enables the attacker to explore protected intranets in order to gain control over highly protected operator systems, and search and exfiltrate intellectual property. Figure 1 depicts typical behaviour during a pivoting attack.

Communication between two devices itself is something common in computer networks. A hierarchical chain of controlled devices is not,

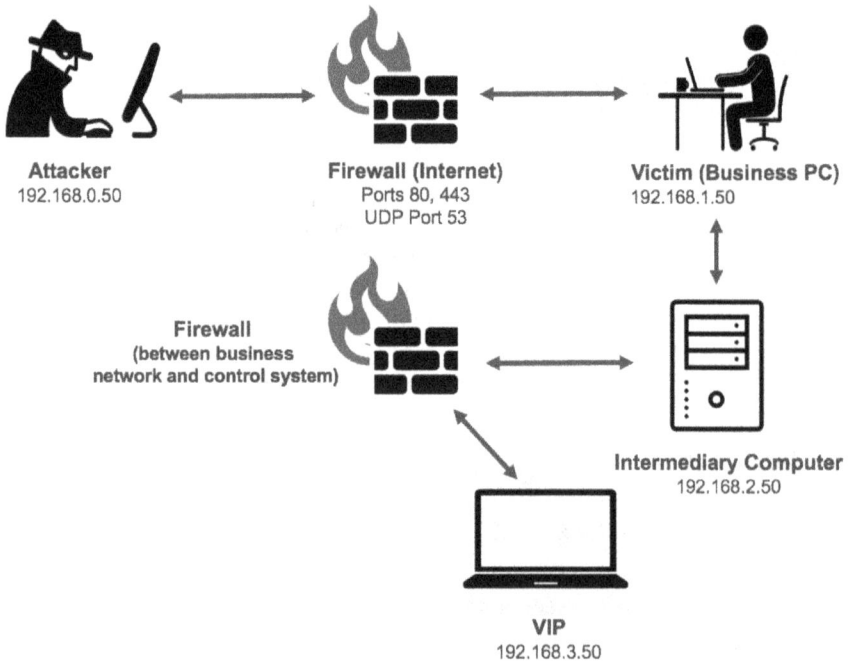

Attacker
192.168.0.50

Firewall (Internet)
Ports 80, 443
UDP Port 53

Victim (Business PC)
192.168.1.50

Firewall
(between business
network and control system)

Intermediary Computer
192.168.2.50

VIP
192.168.3.50

Fig. 1: A typical pivoting attack chain. The attacker penetrates the network at a weak point and moves through the network to find its target.

and the detection of such is a clear indication of an ongoing network intrusion. A key aspect that is necessary to identify such chains is the distinction of human-induced network activity from machine-driven activity, and the classification of different types of the former. This work attempts such a classification on individual machine based on the network traffic leaving and entering them. A future cyber security system might relate identified network activity on pairs of machines with the potential network connections between them in order to identity pivoting behaviour.

1.1. *Network flow arrivals and problems with regular MMPP framework*

A network flow is a summary of a connection between two computers and contains information about the connection such as a timestamp and duration, the transmitted packages and data size, and the involved IP addresses, transmission protocol, and connection ports. Due to their richness of network information, network flow logs are one of the main information sources in network intrusion detection, with both regular network users' as well as attackers' actions leaving trace evidence in it.

The aim of this work is to use the arrival times of network flows on individual computers to identify different states of user activity. Network arrivals are often simulated as Poisson processes for analytic simplicity, and a well-established and tractable model of arrival events with alternating rates is the *Markov-modulated Poisson process* (MMPP), which assumes piece-wise Poisson distributed arrivals with Poisson rates switched via an underlying Markov process. However, a number of traffic studies have shown that packet or flow inter-arrivals are not exponentially distributed, but show among other characteristics a significantly stronger tail behaviour (Leland *et al.*, 1993; Muscariello *et al.*, 2005; Paxson and Floyd, 1995). These tails cannot be accurately modelled by a Poisson distribution. Consequently, in a simple MMPP model tail observations receive a disproportionately low likelihood, which in turn causes state changes in the sampled MMPP for an observed tail event. Therefore, it is crucial to take the shape of the observed event arrival distribution into account.

Recent work argues convincingly that network traffic is much better modelled using self-similar processes (Leland *et al.*, 1993; Park and Willinger, 2000). However, currently none of the mathematical models allow an analytical solution when used for network traffic generation. In this chapter, we will propose a hierarchical extension of the simple MMPP model that is able to capture the tail behaviour of flow arrivals in a more accurate way while still retaining the analytical simplicity of a Markovian arrival process. We will then embed this model in a Gibbs sampling framework and demonstrate how to estimate different states of user activity from network arrival data. We will assume the number of identifiable states to be known. A justified model selection with interpretable activity states will be postponed to future work.

This work has been done in the context of a master's thesis. For more detailed information we refer to Clausen (2017).

2. Methodology

A MMPP is a Poisson process whose intensity depends on the current state of an independently evolving continuous time Markov chain with finite state-space.

An MMPP is parametrised as following:

Definition 1 (Clausen 2017; Rydén 1996). Let $[0, t_{obs}]$ be the time window of observation. Let $\{X_t\}$ for $t \in [0, t_{obs}]$ be a discrete finite-state homogeneous Markov process evolving inside this time window on a state space $\{1, \ldots, M\}$ of cardinality M. Let $\mathbf{Q}$ be the infinitesimal generator of $\{X_t\}$, satisfying $Q_{ii} = -\sum_{j \neq i} Q_{ij}$, $Q_{ii} \leq 0$.

Let $\boldsymbol{\lambda} \triangleq \{\lambda_1, \ldots, \lambda_M\}$ be the Poisson process rates. $N(t)$ is a Poisson process with rate $\lambda(t) = \lambda_{i=X_t}$, i.e., while X stays in state i, events occur with rate λ_i. The two-dimensional set $\{X_t, N(t)\}$ is called the MMPP.

In a typical context, both the state of the Markov process as well as the specific parameters of the MMPP are unknown and have to be estimated while the number of states is assumed to be known. Here, we focus on a completely Bayesian framework that follows Fearnhead and Sherlock

(2006) to sample both the parameters as well as the process states directly using Gibbs sampling.

When dealing with network flow events, two arguments speak against the use of raw arrival times:

(1) The resolution with which flow arrival times are recorded is often in second intervals. Flows recorded within the same second therefore do not have a timely separation, which leads to serious deviation from a Poisson process.
(2) Within an enterprise network, typically between 10^7 and 10^{10} flow events are observed per day. The scalability of any operations acting on the stream of network flows is therefore of particular interest. Consequently, we are interested in an approach that bins multiple flow events together in order to reduce the necessary number of operations.

These two arguments make it particularly attractive to look at network flow arrivals in the format of *accumulation intervals* instead of the raw arrival times. These are a set of intervals $\{I_1 = [t_0 = 0, t_1), \ldots, I_n = [t_{n-1}, t_n = t_{obs})\}$ of equal length $t^* \triangleq t_i - t_{i-1}$. Associated with each interval is a count $z_i = N(t_i) - N(t_{i-1})$ of the number of arrival events during interval I_i.

In order to build a Gibbs sampling framework, we are specifically interested in sampling from the following distribution:

$$P(\{X_t\}|\{z_1, \ldots, z_n\}, \mathbf{Q}, \boldsymbol{\lambda}).$$

We will now outline the steps involved in the sampling procedure.

2.1. Sampling $\{X_t\}$

We will first look at the following probability:

$$P_{jk}^{(z_i)} = P \text{ (there are } z_i \text{ events in } (t_{n-1}, t_n) \text{ and } X_{t^*} = k \,|X_0 = j).$$

We can derive this probability by defining a meta-Markov process V_t: Let $z_{\max} = \max_{i \in \{1, \ldots, n\}}(z_i)$. Define the new $(M \cdot z_{\max} + 1)$-dimensional state-space $S = (1^{(0)}, \ldots, M^{(0)}, 1^{(1)}, \ldots, M^{(1)}, \ldots, 1^{(z_{\max})}, \ldots, M^{(z_{\max})}, 1^*)$. Let $\{t_1', t_2', \ldots\}$ be a (possibly empty) set of event arrival times inside $[t_{n-1}, t_n)$.

$\{V_t\}$ is defined as follows:

$$
V_t = \begin{cases}
X_t^{(0)} & t_{n-1} \leq t \leq t_1' \\
\vdots & \\
X_t^{(i)} & t_i' \leq t < t_{i+1}' \quad t \in (t_{n-1}, t_n). \\
\vdots & \\
1^* & t_{z_{\max}+1}' \leq t.
\end{cases}
\tag{1}
$$

The state of V_t reflects both the state of X_t and the number of occurred events until this number exceeds $z_{\max}$ (which does not occur in the observations).

The infinitesimal generator for $\{V_t\}$ is given by

$$
\mathbf{G_V} = \begin{pmatrix}
\mathbf{Q} - \Lambda & 3 & 0 & \cdots & 0 & 0 \\
0 & \mathbf{Q} - \Lambda & 3 & \cdots & 0 & 0 \\
\vdots & \vdots & \vdots & \vdots & \vdots & \vdots \\
0 & \cdots & \cdots & 0 & \mathbf{Q} - \Lambda & \lambda \\
0 & \cdots & \cdots & 0 & 0 & 0
\end{pmatrix}.
\tag{2}
$$

The transition matrix $P_{jk}^{(z_i)}$ is now given by

$$
P_{jk}^{(z_i)} = P(V_{t_n} = k^{(z_i)} \,|\, V_{t_n-1} = j^{(0)}) = \left[\exp(\mathbf{G_V} t^*) \right]_{j,k+z_i \cdot M}.
$$

For more information on the exact calculation of $P_{jk}^{(z_i)}$, see Clausen (2017); Fearnhead and Sherlock (2006).

2.1.1. *Forward–Backward algorithm*

Due to its Markovian nature, we can formulate the MMPP as a discrete *hidden Markov model* (HMM), with the Markov chain in the model being the state of the Markov process at each time interval. Since the state-space of our Markov model is discrete, we can sample the Markov chain recursively in two steps using the so-called *Forward–Backward algorithm* (Baum, 1972; Devijver, 1985). The backward-part of the Forward–Backward algorithm calculates the posterior distribution of each element of the Markov chain conditional on the number of observations and the previous element recursively while the forward step samples each element sequentially. We will outline the most important steps in the context of the Markov-modulated Poisson process. For a more general description, see Baum (1972); Fearnhead and Sherlock (2006).

Define

$$\mathbf{A}^{(k)} = P(\{z_k, \ldots, z_n\}, X_{t_n} | X_{t_{k-1}}), \quad k \in \{1, \ldots, n\}.$$

For $k = n$, we have

$$\mathbf{A}_{ij}^{(n)} = P_{ij}^{(z_n)} = P(z_n, X_{t_n} = j | X_{t_{n-1}} = i)$$

$$= \left[\exp(\mathbf{G_V} t^*) \right]_{i, j + z_n \cdot M}.$$

We can then calculate $A^{(k)}$ via backward recursion:

$$\mathbf{A}^{(k)} = \mathbf{P}^{(z_k)} \cdot \mathbf{A}^{(k+1)} = \left[\exp(\mathbf{G_V} t^*) \right]_{1:M, 1:M + z_k \cdot M} \mathbf{A}^{(k+1)}.$$

Forward-sampling can then be done as follows: We can sample the initial state of the Markov process using the stationary distribution of the process:

$$P(X_{t_0} = s | \{z_1, \ldots, z_n\}) = \frac{\mu_s \left[\mathbf{A}^{(1)} \mathbf{1} \right]_s}{\mu^T \mathbf{A}^{(1)} \mathbf{1}}.$$

We can then proceed to sample $X_{t_1}, \ldots, X_{t_{n-1}}$:

$$P(X_{t_k} = s | \{z_1, \ldots, z_n\}, X_{t_{k-1}}$$

$$= s_{k-1}) = \frac{\left[\exp(\mathbf{G_V} t^*) \right]_{s_{k-1}, s + z_k \cdot M} \left[\mathbf{A}^{(k+1)} \mathbf{1} \right]_s}{\left[\mathbf{A}^{(k)} \mathbf{1} \right]_{s_{k-1}}}.$$

Finally, we can sample $X_{t_n = t_{\text{obs}}}$

$$P(X_{t_n} = s | \{z_1, \ldots, z_n\}, X_{t_{n-1}} = s_n) = [\exp(\mathbf{G_V} t^*)]_{i, j + z_n \cdot M}.$$

2.1.2. *Simulate full underlying Markov process*

We are now able to sample the state of the Markov process $\{X_t\}$ at the times $\{t_0, \ldots, t_n\}$. Finally, we want to sample the whole trajectory of the Markov process conditionally, i.e., we want to sample from all

$$P(\{X_t\}, \text{ there are } z_k \text{ Y-events in } (t_{k-1}, t_k) | X_{t_{k-1}} = i, \ X_{t_k} = j)$$

$$= P(\{V_t, t \in (t_{k-1}, t_k)\} | V_{t_{k-1}} = i^{(0)}, \ V_{t_k} = j^{(z_k)}),$$

where we used the definition of $\{V_t\}$ and its generator from (1) and (2). We are therefore simply looking at the evolution of the Markov process $\{V_t\}$ with specified endpoints. Sampling the trajectory of $\{V_t\}$ gives us both a sampled trajectory of $\{X_t\}$ as well as a sample of the exact arrival times $\{t'_1, \ldots, t'_l\}$ where l is the number of all observed flows.

Drawing sample paths for endpoint-conditioned continuous time Markov processes is not trivial. Two common techniques to solve this problem are *Modified Rejection Sampling* and *Uniformization Sampling*. We use both techniques where appropriate during the sampling of $\{V_t\}$, depending on the particular endpoint states V_{t_k}, $V_{t_{k+1}}$ to benefit from the advantages of both methods. A detailed description of both algorithms and their particular advantages and disadvantages is given in Clausen (2017); Hobolth and Stone (2009).

2.2. *Hierarchical MMPP extension*

It is known that flow arrivals are not piecewise exponentially distributed, but have a strong tail behaviour which has severe consequences when trying to fit a simple MMPP. Muscariello *et al.* (2005) suggests the use of a hierarchical Markovian Poisson model in order generate characteristics that match those measured on network traffic while still maintaining analytical tractability. However, in their work they neither provide a general approach to fit the involved parameters nor a way to calculate or sample from $P(\{X_t\}|\{z_1, \ldots, z_n\})$, which eventually is our ultimate interest in this work. We now propose a model that adopts the idea of MMPP arrivals acting as a latent generator of observed events while remaining analytically tractable. We will then embed our model in a Gibbs sampling framework that samples the Markov process trajectory and the model parameters jointly. A graphical model representation of the proposed model is given in Figure 2.

As before, let $\{X_t\}$ for $t \in [0, t_{\text{obs}}]$ be the unobserved discrete Markov process with infinitesimal generator $\mathbf{Q}$, and let $N(t)$ be a Poisson process with rate $\lambda(t) = \lambda_{i=X_t}$. However, $N(t)$ does not generate flow events anymore, but unobserved events called *sessions*.[a] Let

---

[a] In reference to Muscariello *et al.* (2005).

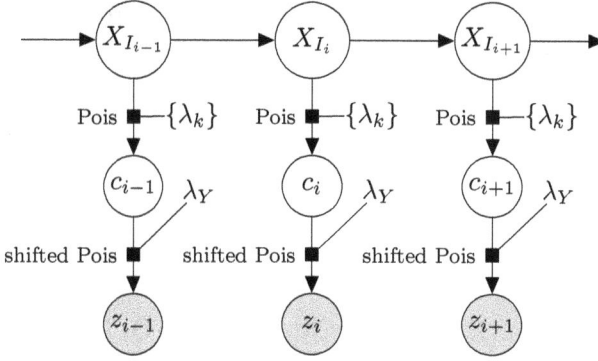

Fig. 2: Graphical model for our proposed hierarchical MMPP.

$\{I_1 = [t_0 = 0, t_1), \ldots, I_n = [t_{n-1}, t_n = t_{obs})\}$ be our accumulation intervals, and let $c_k \triangleq N(t_k) - N(t_{k-1})$ be the number of sessions in I_k.

Upon generation, a session s_i instantaneously generates y_i events that are observed. $y_i \in \mathbb{N}_{>0}$ is a discrete random variable following a shifted Poisson distribution:

$$y_i - 1|\mathbf{2} \sim \text{Pois}(\lambda_Y).$$

The shift introduced is beneficial since it ensures that every session generates at least one flow event. The flow events z_k observed during interval I_k are now defined as

$$z_k \triangleq \sum_{i=1}^{l} y_i \mathbb{1}_{t_{k-1} < t'_i \le t_k}.$$

Since the sum of Poisson-distributed variables is also Poisson-distributed, we can easily derive $P(z_k|c_k, \lambda_Y)$ to be

$$P(z_k|c_k, \lambda_Y) = \frac{(c_k \lambda_Y)^{z_k - c_k} \exp(-c_k \lambda_Y)}{(z_k - c_k)!}.$$

2.3. *Gibbs sampler*

Fearnhead and Sherlock (2006) proposed a Gibbs sampling framework for MMPP models that estimates $\{X_t\}$ and the model parameters jointly. We now extend this Gibbs sampler to sample from the following distribution:

$$P(\{X_t\}, \{c_1, \ldots, c_n\}, \mathbf{Q}, \lambda | \{z_1, \ldots, z_n\}, I),$$

where I represents the available prior information. To implement such a Gibbs sampler, we use the following conditional distributions:

1. $P(\{X_t\}, \{t_1', \ldots, t_l'\}|\{z_1, \ldots, z_n\}, \{c_1, \ldots, c_n\}, \mathbf{Q}, \boldsymbol{\lambda}, \lambda_Y)$
2. $P(\{c_1, \ldots, c_n\}|\{z_1, \ldots, z_n\}, \{X_t\}, \mathbf{Q}, \boldsymbol{\lambda}, \lambda_Y)$
3. $P(\mathbf{Q}, \boldsymbol{\lambda}, \lambda_Y|\{z_1, \ldots, z_n\}, \{c_1, \ldots, c_n\}, \{X_t\}, I)$

1. In Section 2.1.2, we have seen how to sample the trajectory of an MMPP,[b] i.e., how to sample from

$$P(\{X_t\}, \{t_1', \ldots, t_l'\}|\{c_1, \ldots, c_n\}, \mathbf{Q}, \boldsymbol{\lambda}).$$

Since $\{z_1, \ldots, z_n\}$ and $\{X_t\}$ are independent conditional on $\{c_1, \ldots, c_n\}$, we can rewrite

1. $P(\{X_t\}|\{z_1, \ldots, z_n\}, \{c_1, \ldots, c_n\}, \mathbf{Q}, \boldsymbol{\lambda}, \lambda_Y)$

$$= P(\{X_t\}|\{c_1, \ldots, c_n\}, \mathbf{Q}, \boldsymbol{\lambda})$$

to be equal to the expression we already know how to sample from.

2. We define

$$\lambda_{I_k} \triangleq \left(\sum_{i=1}^{M} \int_{t_{k-1}}^{t_k} \mathbb{1}_{X_t=i} \cdot \lambda_i \, dt \right).$$

Since the increments of a Poisson process are independently Poisson-distributed, the number of sessions in I_k conditional on $\{X_t\}$ is Poisson-distributed with rate λ_{I_k}:

$$P(c_k|\{X_t, \ t \in I_k\}, \boldsymbol{\lambda}) = \frac{\lambda_{I_k}^{c_k} \exp(-\lambda_{I_k})}{(c_k)!}.$$

This allows us to calculate the posterior distribution of c_k:

2. $P(c_k|z_k, \{X_t, \ t \in I_k\}, \boldsymbol{\lambda}, \lambda_Y)$

$$\propto P(c_k|\{X_t, \ t \in I_k\}, \boldsymbol{\lambda}) P(z_k|c_k, \lambda_Y)$$

$$= \frac{\lambda_{I_k}^{c_k} \exp(-\lambda_{I_k})}{(c_k)!} \frac{(c_k \lambda_Y)^{z_k - c_k} \exp(-c_k \lambda_Y)}{(z_k - c_k)!}$$

---

[b]Please note that c_i replaced z_i as the arrivals of the MMPP which are now latent while z_i now represents the observed events in the extended model.

Since $P(z_k < c_k | c_k) = 0$, this expression is easily normalisable. We can therefore also sample the sessions counts $\{c_1, \ldots, c_n\}$ conditional on $\{Z_1, \ldots, Z_n\}, \{X_t\}, \lambda$ and λ_Y.

3. The likelihood of $\{X_t\}$ and $\{t'_1, \ldots, t'_l\}$ is given by

$$L\left(\{X_t\}, \{t'_1, \ldots, t'_l\} | \mathbf{Q}, \lambda\right)$$

$$\propto v_{X_{t'_0}} \prod_{i=1}^{M} \left(\lambda_i^{n_i} \exp(-\lambda_i \tilde{t}_i) \prod_{j \neq i} q_{ij}^{r_{ij}} \exp(-q_{ij} \tilde{t}_i) \right),$$

where

$$\tilde{t}_i \triangleq \int_0^{t_{obs}} \mathbb{1}_{X_t = i} \, dt,$$

is the time spent in state i,

$$n_i \triangleq \sum_{k=1}^{l} \mathbb{1}_{X_{t'_k} = i},$$

is the number of arrival events taking place while $X_t = i$, and

$$r_{ij} \triangleq |\{t_k, X_{t_k} = i \text{ and } X_{t_k+} = j\}|,$$

is the number of transitions from state i into state j (Fearnhead and Sherlock, 2006). It is clear that the densities of λ_i and q_{ii} are Gamma while the joint densities of q_{ij}/q_{ii}, $j \in \{1, \ldots, M\}/i$ are Dirichlet distributed. Moreover, we know that the likelihood of $\{z_1, \ldots, z_k\}$ conditional on $\{c_1, \ldots, c_n\}$ is the product of shifted Poisson distributions with rates $c_k \lambda_Y$. If we employ a Bayesian framework with conjugate priors, it is possible to calculate the posterior distributions of $\mathbf{Q}, \lambda, \lambda_Y$ conditional on $\{X_t\}, \{t'_1, \ldots, t'_l\}$, and $\{z_1, \ldots, z_n\}$.

We impose Gamma-priors on λ_i, q_{ii}, and λ_Y with hyper-parameters $\alpha_{\lambda,i}$, $\alpha_{q,i}$, $\alpha_{Y,i}$ and $\beta_{\lambda,i}$, $\beta_{q,i}$, $\beta_{Y,i}$:

$$\lambda_i \sim \Gamma(\alpha_{\lambda,i}, \beta_{\lambda,i}),$$

$$q_{ii} \sim \Gamma(\alpha_{q,i}, \beta_{q,i}),$$

$$\lambda_Y \sim \Gamma(\alpha_{Y,i}, \beta_{Y,i}).$$

For $q_{i \neq j}/q_{ii}$, we impose a Dirichlet prior with hyper-parameter $\alpha_{D,i}$:

$$\frac{(q_{1,i}, \ldots, q_{i-1,i}, q_{i+1,i}, \ldots q_{M,i})^T}{q_{ii}} \sim \text{Dir}(\alpha_{D,i}).$$

The posterior distributions are then given by

$$\lambda_i | \{X_t\}, \{t'_1, \ldots, t'_l\} \sim \Gamma(\alpha_{\lambda,i} + n_i, \beta_{\lambda,i} + \tilde{t}_i)$$

$$q_{ii} | \{X_t\}, \{t'_1, \ldots, t'_l\} \sim \Gamma\left(\alpha_{q,i} + \sum_{j \neq i} r_{ij}, \beta_{q,i} + \tilde{t}_i\right)$$

$$\lambda_Y | \{z_k\}, \{c_k\} \sim \Gamma(\alpha_{\lambda_Y} + z_k - c_k, \beta_{\lambda_Y} + z_k)$$

$$\frac{(q_{1,i}, \ldots, q_{i-1,i}, q_{i+1,i}, \ldots q_{M,i})}{q_{ii}} | \{X_t\}, \{t'_1, \ldots, t'_l\} \sim \text{Dir}(\alpha_{D,i} + \mathbf{r}_i),$$

where $\mathbf{r}_i = (r_{1,i}, \ldots, r_{i-1,i}, r_{i+1,i}, \ldots r_{M,i})^T$.

3. Data

3.1. *LANL data*

This work was motivated by a data set containing 16 consecutive days of network flow data from the LANL's corporate, internal computer network (Kent, 2015). The network consists of 17,684 computers which can be identified through their individual label through the data. We applied our developed Gibbs sampler to several selected computers that were identified to be subject to human control. Our framework was able to identify different types of computer activity, which appear to resemble a very reasonable trace of human activity on the individual computers. However, we do not have any information about the actual activity conducted on each computer to verify our sampled results. Therefore, we conducted a controlled experiment on a specific computer which is described in the next section in order to validate the results of our model. We will focus on the data obtained from that experiment in this work. Results and further details on the LANL data can be found in Clausen (2017).

3.2. *Imperial College data*

Network flows do not give direct insight in specific user activities. To acquire some ground truth about the traces of human activity in network flow logs, we conducted a controlled experiment during which a user conducts different selected activities on a single computer inside the Imperial College network.

The data set contains network flow data originating from a single source IP address inside the Imperial College network over a 3-hour time span. The computer corresponding to this IP address is a college computer running Microsoft Windows, and is accessible via user log-in. The purpose of the experiment was to see how different activities on a computer influence the flow arrival distribution. We therefore chose a diverse selection of activities that resemble all possible user states in an accurate way. For this, we included phases with video and social media consumption, with surfing and information gathering, but also without any user activity. Log-in and log-off processes are suspected to cause spikes in the activity, so we logged the user in and out frequently. The activity schedule looks as following:

14:00   User log-in
        Open Mozilla Firefox
        Scrolling on www.facebook.com, opening occasional videos on this site
14:08   Open Google Chrome, close Mozilla Firefox
        Scrolling on www.9gag.com
14:20   User log-out
        User log-in
        No further activity (no browser or other programme open)
14:40   User log-out
        User log-in
14:42   Open Mozilla Firefox, open several sites[c]
        No further activity
15:00   Visiting www.soundcloud.com, downloading three files with a total size of 2 GB

15:04   Watching several videos on www.youtube.com, all of which are several minutes long

---

[c]www.facebook.com, www.gmail.com, www.9gag.com, www.faz.de, www.outlook.com.

15:20 Intense surfing, clicking from site to site
Listening to music on `soundcloud.com`
15:40 User log-off
16:00 User log-in
16:02 Open Mozilla Firefox
Playing multiplayer online game on `www.splix.io`
16:20 Establishing SSH-connection to `bazooka.ma.ic.ac.uk`
Sending Unix-commands via ssh
Occasional look-up of information using Mozilla Firefox
16:40 End of experiment

A significant amount of a computer's flow traffic is caused by strictly periodic communication. This sort of communication might manifest itself in periodic update requests or flows restarting due to exceeding specific time limits. Any form of periodic communication is highly deterministic and will alter the observed flow arrival distribution without giving us any information about the state of the user. We therefore remove this communication from our data. More information about this process can be found in Clausen (2017).

Figure 3 depicts the number of cleaned flow events binned into 5-second intervals during the experiment. The colours represent the activity schedule.

3.2.1. *Spikes*

In the Imperial College data, we observe several large spikes, standing out from the rest of the data. These spikes primarily stem from new web

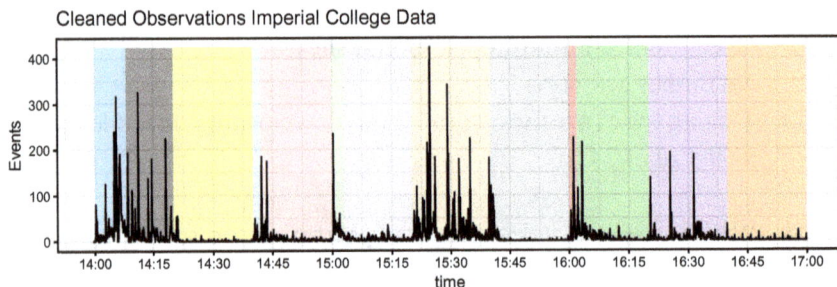

Fig. 3: Number of Imperial College flow events, binned into 5-seconds intervals. The coloured intervals correspond to the different stages during the experiment.

processes being started on the computer which trigger many DNS requests to a single IP-address. For instance, the largest spike in the Imperial Data at 15:24:34 contains 656 flow events, of which 297 are directed to the IP-address `155.198.142.8`, all via UDP-port 53 (which is responsible for DNS requests). We will identify these DNS-spikes as an additional new device state in our framework since their detection might be of interest for a broader intrusion detection framework.

3.3. *Distribution comparison*

Figure 4(a) depicts an excerpt of the Imperial College data during which the flow arrival rate supposedly stays constant, while Figure 4(b) shows the

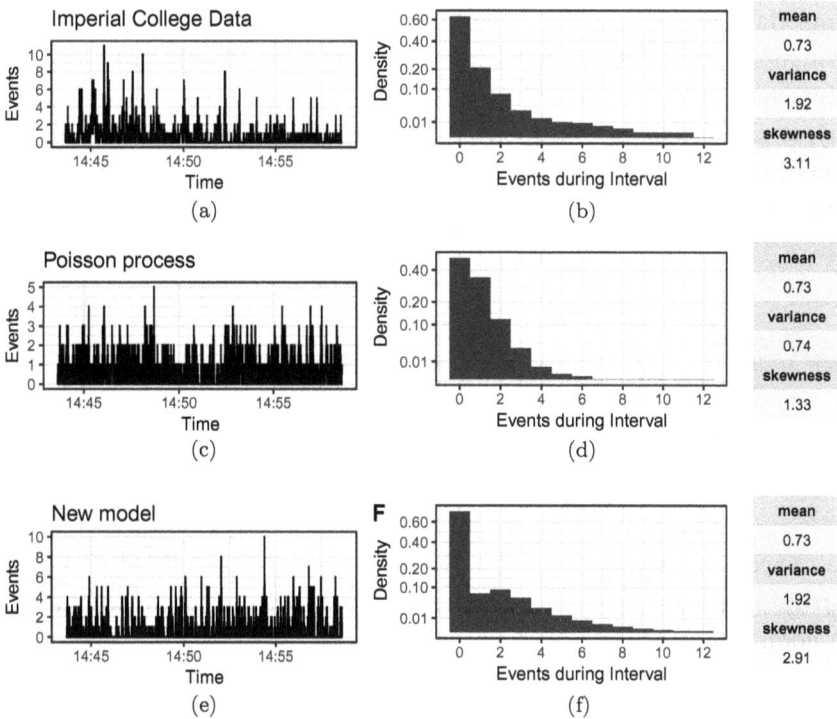

Fig. 4: Plot (a) shows an interval of the Imperial College flow data during which the flow arrival rate was supposedly constant (bin size 2 seconds). Plot (b) shows the corresponding empirical flow count distribution. Plots (c) and (d) show simulated arrivals from Poisson processes with the same mean as the data in (a). Plots (e) and (f) show simulated arrivals from our proposed model.

distribution of the observed counts during each interval. Plots (c)/(d) and
(e)/(f) show a comparison with events generated from a Poisson process and
from our proposed hierarchical Poisson model. λ for the Poisson process
was chosen such that the data generated has the same mean as the Imperial
College interval, while λ and λ_Y for the hierarchical model were chosen to
adjust both the mean and the variance.

A comparison of the first three moments of the depicted data shows that
our proposed hierarchical Poisson model is better suited to imitate the tail
behaviour of the observed data distribution.

3.4. *Results*

Using our proposed Gibbs sampler, we fit a 4-state MMPP model to the
Imperial College data. We have to make sure that we choose the model
parameter priors wide enough to allow for proper convergence of the posterior, but narrow enough to initialise the parameters correctly. Our choice of
hyper parameters for λ_i is motivated by the range of observed flow events
per bin while hyper parameters for q_{ii} are chosen to exclude unreasonable
state decay times:

$$\alpha_{\lambda,i} = 1.2\frac{1}{\text{sec}}, \quad \beta_{\lambda,i} = 1,$$

$$\alpha_{q,1} = \alpha_{q,2} = \alpha_{q,3} = 5\frac{1}{\text{sec}},$$

$$\beta_{q,1} = \beta_{q,2} = \beta_{q,3} = 1000,$$

$$\alpha_{q,4} = 5\frac{1}{\text{sec}}, \quad \beta_{q,4} = 100.$$

Experience shows that $\lambda_Y > 10$ does not match the shape of a flow
arrival distribution anymore, the hyper parameters are therefore chosen
accordingly:

$$\alpha_{\lambda_Y} = 2, \quad \beta_{\lambda_Y} = 1.$$

Lastly, we employ an uninformative Dirichlet prior with $\alpha_{D,i} = (1, 1, 1)^T$. We then proceed to generate 500 samples of $\{X_t\}, \mathbf{Q}, \boldsymbol{\lambda}$,
$\lambda_Y | \{z_1, \ldots, z_n\}$ using our described Gibbs sampler. Figure 5 depicts an
excerpt of the sampled $\{X_t\}$ for the Imperial College data.

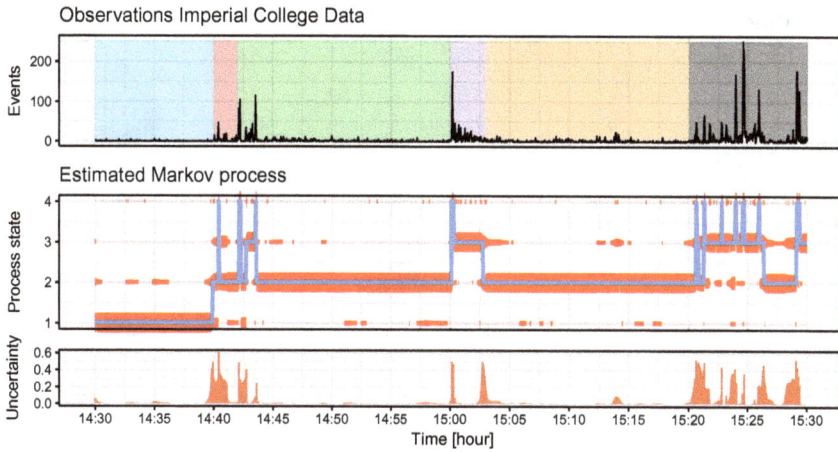

Fig. 5: Excerpt of sampled $\{X_t\}$ for the Imperial College data. Binned flow data (top), 500 samples of $\{X_t\}$ (using the Gibbs sampler described in Section 2.3) (middle), and uncertainty of the inferred state (bottom). The blue line indicates the sample mode at each point in time, while the thickness of the red lines indicates the amount of samples in each state. The uncertainty is calculated by $1 - \alpha_{t_i}$ where α_{t_i} is the fraction of the sample mode at time t_i.

Especially in comparison to the results (Figure 6) from a conventional MMPP model using the Gibbs sampler from Fearnhead and Sherlock (2006), the improvements of our model are apparent: While we are not able to identify any activity state coherently with the simple MMPP framework, our new model is able to distinguish several states of user activity throughout the whole data. The identified states are in good correspondence to the actual activity on the computer, i.e., similar experiment phases are identified by the same state. The state estimates are consistent and stable during each activity phase. As expected, the described DNS-spikes are identified as a separate state. Furthermore, the overall uncertainty of the $\{X_t\}$ samples is small. An exception are points where the user activity changes since the exact time of the state change has a high uncertainty.

The interpretation of the 4-state model in terms of human activity results are straightforward:

- State 1 corresponds to pure standby activity, no human actions are taken nor are any programmes open.
- State 2 corresponds to the presence of an inactive user, i.e., the internet browser or a similar programme is open, but no actions are taken. It is

Observations Imperial College Data

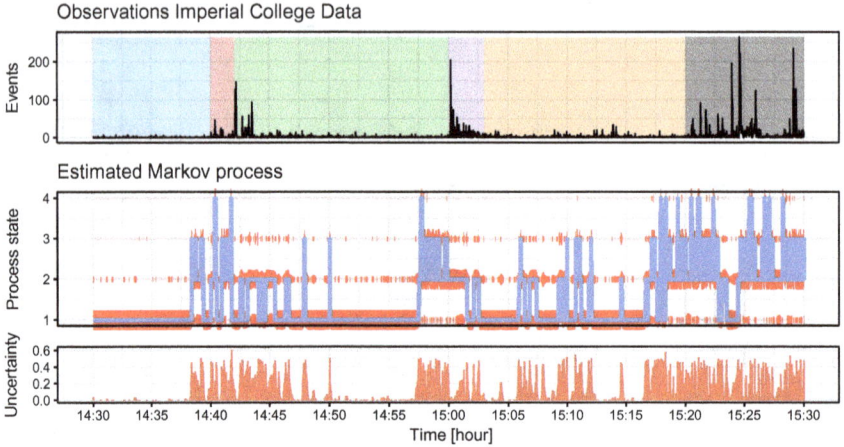

Fig. 6:   Results from a conventional MMPP model. 500 samples were generated using the Gibbs sampler described in Fearnhead and Sherlock (2006).

remarkable that the watching of internet videos or ssh-communication create flow events at a similar rate and is therefore identified as state 2. Differences between these two activities are however visible when looking at the length and the size of the transmitted flows.

- State 3 identifies surfing activity of the user.
- State 4 captures the above described DNS spikes. Since these spikes are very short, they do not correspond to a change in user activity, but are more or less a nuisance. State 4 should therefore also be seen as a nuisance state that ensures the model stability without indicating a user state. In a cyber security framework, the identification of the spikes through state 4 might also be of other interest.

Obviously, our framework models the state of the user only as perceived through the machine. For instance, we observe multiple short drops of the perceived activity from state 3 to state 2, indicating user inactivity, while it is most likely that the user just stopped his actions shortly to read something of interest or similar. To make inference from activity on the computer to a general state of the person sitting behind the computer, we need additional assumptions and post-process modelling. All in all, there is a great correspondence of these four activity states that are sampled with our model, and the actual user activity.

3.4.1. *Convergence*

Figure 7 shows the sampled marginal posterior distributions of $\mathbf{Q}$, λ and λ_Y. All λ_i are sampled well within our previously estimated range, as is λ_Y. Furthermore, the decay rates Q_i for states 1 to 3 are sampled in a reasonable range, corresponding to state half-lives of 2–15 minutes, which is a good reflection of the activity phases in the experiment. Since state 4 is capturing the above described DNS-spikes, the values for Q_4 are much higher, corresponding to a half-life of around 9 seconds.

The posterior distributions of the generated sample chain of $\mathbf{Q}$, λ and λ_Y, depicted in Figure 7, all appear to be well explored with a single pronounced mode. Figure 8 depicts trace plots and auto-correlation plots of our sampled chain for selected parameters. All parameters show a fast convergence towards a stationary distribution, and a low auto-correlation, indicating a great efficiency of our sampler. The first 50 samples were discarded as burn-in.

Since the individual Markov process states are interchangeable, an important aspect to be considered is the *label switching* problem (Jasra

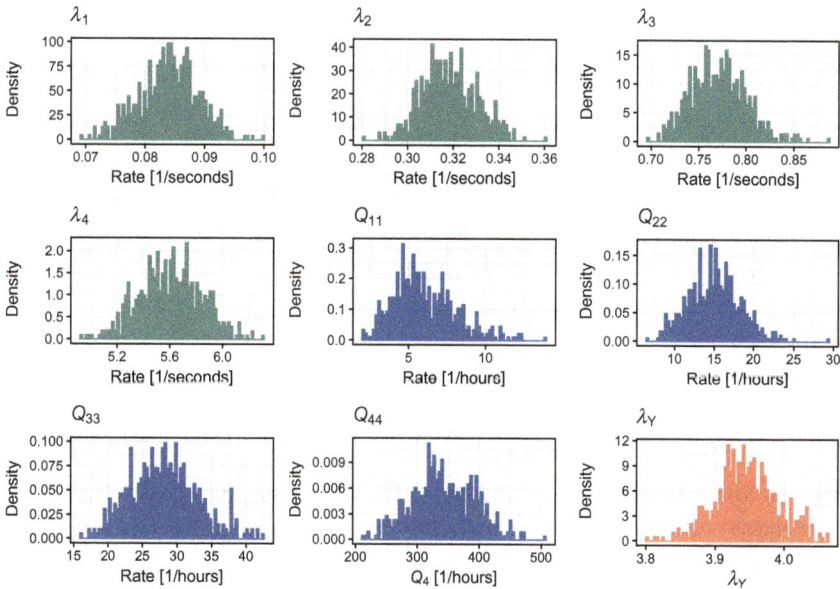

Fig. 7: Sampled posterior distributions of Q_{ii} (blue), λ_i (green) and λ_Y (red).

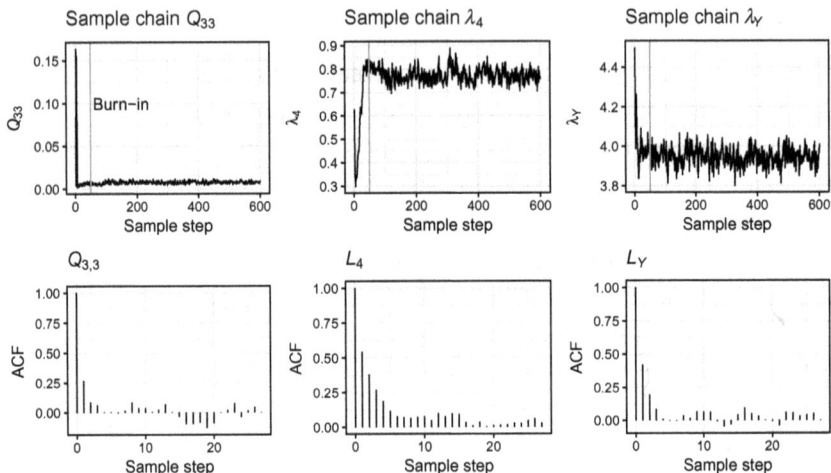

Fig. 8: Trace and auto-correlation plots for selected parameters. The blue line indicates the discarded burn-in.

et al., 2005). Since the marginal posterior distributions are well separated, we avoid this problem by ordering the initial samples of the model parameters. A more detailed discussion of this problem can be found in Clausen (2017).

4. Conclusion

In this chapter, we have established a novel Bayesian framework that is able to identify temporal patterns in the network flow generation of individual personal computers. We proposed a new hierarchical model that addresses the deviations of network flow arrivals from a Poisson process problem sufficiently while retaining the computational simplicity and scalability of a conventional MMPP-based model. Our model extends the MMPP model adding a latent layer that separates the observations from the observations. We then adopted the concept of the exact Gibbs sampler of Fearnhead and Sherlock (2006) and extended it to incorporate our proposed model. Our model is fully Bayesian, and samples the posterior distribution of the Markov process that represents the user's activity state. Our implementation samples 500 process trajectories in less than a minute for approximately 30,000 observed flow events.

Our model has identified different activity states with converging model parameters on multiple computers in the LANL data set. A controlled experiment which was the focus in this work verified that the identified patterns can be linked quite closely to states of human activity. In order to achieve a finer distinction of different activities with similar arrival rates, the incorporation of other flow quantities in a broader model based on MMPPs is possible. A discussion of a possible model extension including the flow durations is discussed in Clausen (2017).

The estimation of human activity states has direct applications in modelling human behaviour in order to identify intruders operating inside enterprise computer networks, and is intended as a building block in a larger Bayesian cyber security model. Several other potential applications such as Internet traffic modelling for engineering and performance evaluations, or user monitoring in online marketing, might benefit from both its advantages over conventional MMPP models and its computational scalability. Furthermore, our model can be used for multiple applications outside of network modelling in which events arrivals are not exactly Poisson-distributed. The release of heavily optimised computational routines is planned in the form of an R-C++-package.

References

Baum, L. E. (1972). An inequality and associated maximization technique in statistical estimation for probabilistic functions of Markov process, *Inequalities* **3**, pp. 1–8.

Clausen, H. (2017). *A Bayesian Approach to Human Behaviour Modelling in Computer Networks*, Master's thesis, Imperial College London.

Devijver, P. A. (1985). Baum's Forward-Backward algorithm revisited, *Pattern Recognition Letters* **3**, 6, pp. 369–373.

Fearnhead, P. and Sherlock, C. (2006). An exact Gibbs sampler for the Markov-modulated Poisson process, *Journal of the Royal Statistical Society: Series B (Statistical Methodology)* **68**, 5, pp. 767–784.

Hobolth, A. and Stone, E. A. (2009). Simulation from endpoint-conditioned, continuous-time Markov chains on a finite state space, with applications to molecular evolution, *The Annals of Applied Statistics* **3**, 3, pp. 1204–1233.

Jasra, A., Holmes, C. C. and Stephens, D. A. (2005). Markov chain Monte Carlo methods and the label switching problem in Bayesian mixture modeling, *Statistical Science* **20**, 1, pp. 50–67.

Kent, A. D. (2015). Comprehensive, multi-source cyber-security events data set, Tech. rep., Los Alamos National Lab. (LANL), Los Alamos, NM, United States.

Leland, W. E., Taqqu, M. S., Willinger, W. and Wilson, D. V. (1993). On the self-similar nature of Ethernet traffic, in *ACM SIGCOMM Computer Communication Review*, Vol. 23, pp. 183–193.

Muscariello, L., Mellia, M., Meo, M., Marsan, M. A. and Cigno, R. L. (2005). Markov models of internet traffic and a new hierarchical MMPP model, *Computer Communications* **28**, 16, pp. 1835–1851.

Neil, J., Hash, C., Brugh, A., Fisk, M. and Storlie, C. B. (2013). Scan statistics for the online detection of locally anomalous subgraphs, *Technometrics* **55**, 4, pp. 403–414.

Park, K. and Willinger, W. (2000). *Self-similar Network Traffic and Performance Evaluation*, Wiley Online Library.

Paxson, V. and Floyd, S. (1995). Wide area traffic: The failure of Poisson modeling, *IEEE/ACM Transactions on Networking (ToN)* **3**, 3, pp. 226–244.

Rydén, T. (1996). An EM algorithm for estimation in Markov-modulated Poisson processes, *Computational Statistics & Data Analysis* **21**, 4, pp. 431–447.

Tankard, C. (2011). Advanced persistent threats and how to monitor and deter them, *Network Security* **2011**, 8, pp. 16–19.

Chapter 4

Towards Generalisable Network Threat Detection

Blake Anderson*, Martin Vejman†, David McGrew‡
and Subharthi Paul§

Cisco Systems, Inc., North Carolina, USA
*blake.anderson@cisco.com
†mvejman@cisco.com
‡mcgrew@cisco.com
§subharpa@cisco.com

Network traffic analysis presents a number of key challenges including concept drift, noisy ground truth and noisy features introduced by endpoint and network-level artefacts. In this chapter, we demonstrate current applications of machine learning to this domain, and then provide an overview of common problems and how they manifest themselves in our data sets. Specifically, we demonstrate the changing popularity of different protocols and services, pitfalls in assuming ground truth for sandbox data and how different operating systems and collection points affect commonly used data features. Given this enhanced understanding of the network domain, we show how to develop machine learning solutions that can address each of these challenges to provide generalisable threat detection. While the themes of this chapter are applicable to many application layer protocols, our focus will be on identifying malware in TLS-encrypted traffic.

1. Introduction

Using the network to perform threat detection and prevention is a fundamental component of an enterprise network's security posture. The most common tools are intrusion detection systems (IDS) and intrusion prevention systems (IPS) (Paxson, 1999; Roesch, 1999), which are extremely effective for known threats over unencrypted traffic. The widespread adoption of protocols such as transport layer security (TLS) have severely reduced the amount of unencrypted Internet traffic, and we have observed malware authors also using these techniques to evade detection (Anderson *et al.*, 2017). Due to this transition and other evasion techniques, traditional rule-based systems have become less effective, which has prompted researchers to investigate machine learning solutions to fill the gaps (Anderson and McGrew, 2016; Bilge *et al.*, 2012; Gu *et al.*, 2008; Moore and Zuev, 2005).

Network threat detection has proven to be a complex domain where many of the proposed solutions have seen little adoption, causing some critics to question the applicability of machine learning for this problem domain (Harrigan, 2016; Sommer and Paxson, 2010). In this chapter, we highlight concrete reasons why many of the previous approaches have failed to generalise. Two broad categories are introduced: feature-level and data set-level obstacles. Feature-level obstacles refer to the artefacts that are introduced for a specific environment. For example, the behaviour of requesting a javascript file from a server can result in very different feature vectors depending on the endpoint, the current network conditions, and the system used to collect the data. By ignoring these factors, both supervised and unsupervised machine learning algorithms will overfit their known environments resulting in unexpected responses to network traffic that would otherwise be handled properly.

The data set-level obstacles highlight the difficulties that we must overcome in order to train and maintain a network threat detection model. Assuming a perfectly robust feature representation, there are still two major issues: the non-stationarity inherent in network data and the ability to accurately determine ground truth. Most browsers release a major version upgrade at least every two months, which can lead to significant change-points that can affect both supervised and unsupervised methods. Determining ground truth labels is difficult and often requires skilled incident responders, which obviously does not scale. In the supervised domain, shortcuts are often taken where most traffic generated by a known malware sample in a sandbox environment is taken as malicious, but this approach can fail to differentiate the benign traffic that occurs during the run. Unsupervised methods have these same pitfalls in their baselining stages.

We begin this chapter with a brief introduction to the TLS protocol, and then walk through our problem space by presenting the design and results of a malware vs benign TLS classification problem. We then describe and give real-world examples of each potential pitfall. Finally, we provide suggestions to overcome these challenges and conclude.

2. Preliminary Analysis

2.1. *TLS background*

TLS 1.2 (Dierks and Rescorla, 2008) is the most prevalent protocol used to encrypt application layer protocol plain-text data, e.g., HTTPS is the plain-text HTTP protocol over TLS. Figure 1 provides a graphical representation of a simple TLS connection. The client initially sends a `ClientHello`

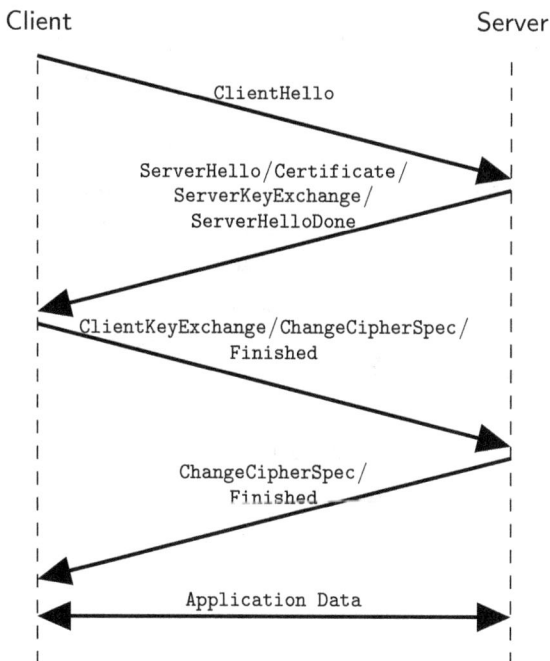

Fig. 1: The initial TLS handshake is used to verify identities and derive shared secrets. With the shared secrets in place, the client and server can exchange encrypted application data.

message that provides the server with, among other fields, a list of cipher suites and a set of TLS extensions that the client supports. The cipher suite list is ordered by the client's preference, where each cipher suite defines a set of cryptographic algorithms needed for TLS to operate. The set of extensions provides additional information to the server that facilitates extended functionality, e.g., the server name extension indicates the server's hostname that the client is trying to connect to, which is important for virtual hosting environments. As explained in Section 2.2, all of the TLS data features are taken from the unencrypted `ClientHello` message.

After the `ClientHello`, the server sends a `ServerHello` message that contains the selected cipher suite, selected from the client's offer list, which defines the set of cryptographic algorithms that will be used to derive the master secret and secure the exchanged application data. The `ServerHello` message also contains a list of extensions that the server supports, where this list is a subset of what the client supports. At this time, the server also sends a `Certificate` message containing the server's certificate chain, which can be used to authenticate the server, and the `ServerKeyExchange` message containing the server's public key material.

The client then sends a `ClientKeyExchange` message that establishes the premaster secret of the TLS session. Then the client and server send `ChangeCipherSpec` messages indicating that future messages will be encrypted with the negotiated cryptographic parameters. Finally, the client and server begin to exchange application data. The current TLS 1.2 handshake protocol provides many interesting, unencrypted data features. To enhance privacy, TLS 1.3 (Rescorla, 2017) will be encrypting more of the handshake, e.g., the `Certificate` message will be encrypted, but the data features used in this chapter will still be available. Many important protocol details were omitted in this explanation, but the associated RFC's provide the full specification (Dierks and Rescorla, 2008; Rescorla, 2017).

2.2. *Feature representation*

For this experiment, we have focused on straightforward feature representations of three data types: traditional NetFlow, packet lengths and information taken from the TLS `ClientHello`. These data types are all extracted from a single TLS session, but models that incorporate features from multiple flows have also been investigated (Anderson and McGrew, 2016). All features were normalised to have zero mean and unit variance before training.

Legacy. We utilised five features that are present in traditional NetFlow: the duration of the flow, the number of packets in each direction and the number of bytes in each direction. Information about ports and IP addresses were omitted, but could be included if the appropriate auxiliary data feeds were available, e.g., IP blacklist.

Sequence of Packet Lengths (SPL). We create a length-20 feature vector, where each entry is the corresponding packet size in the bidirectional flow. Packet sizes from the client to the server are positive, and packet sizes from the server to the client are negative.

TLS Metadata (TLS). We analyse both the offered cipher suite list and the list of advertised extensions contained in the `ClientHello` message. In our data sets, we observed 176 unique cipher suites and 21 unique extensions, which resulted in a length-197 binary feature vector. The appropriate feature is set to 1 if that cipher suite or extension appeared in the `ClientHello` message. This feature set provides information about the client application's identity, and it would be straightforward to include features that provide information about the server's identity, e.g., features derived from the `Certificate` or DNS responses.

2.3. *Learning*

The presented results use the `scikit-learn` random forest implementation (Pedregosa *et al.*, 2011). Based on previous longitudinal studies that we conducted (Anderson and McGrew, 2017a), the number of trees in the ensemble was set to 125 and the number of features considered at each split of the tree was set to the square root of the total number of features. The feature set used by the random forest model was composed of some subset of the Legacy, SPL, and/or TLS features.

2.4. *Results*

We sampled 1,621,910 TLS flows from one enterprise network, Site1, and 324,771 flows from a malware analysis sandbox (collected between August

Table 1: The validation results are demonstrated for several different threshold values.

Data Features	Data Source	0.5 (%)	0.95 (%)	0.99 (%)
All	Benign	98.38	99.99	100.00
	Malware	99.35	85.80	68.83
Legacy + TLS	Benign	99.78	99.96	99.99
	Malware	97.67	78.42	72.75
Legacy + SPL	Benign	98.32	98.53	98.95
	Malware	97.45	78.05	69.81
Legacy	Benign	98.76	99.96	99.99
	Malware	66.79	23.04	10.05

Note: The malware/benign accuracies are kept separate to demonstrate feature subsets that overfit the benign class.

2015 and December 2016) to train our random forest model. We then simulated deploying the model on unseen data from a separate enterprise network, Site 2, and malware data collected during the 2 months following the previous data set. There were 2,638,559 sampled TLS flows from Site 2 and 57,822 TLS flows from the malware sandbox during January and February of 2017. Table 1 presents the results of this experiment at different thresholds. 0.5 is the default threshold of the classifier, and the higher the threshold, the more certain the trained model has to be to determine that the TLS flow was generated by malware. The malware/benign accuracies are kept separate to demonstrate feature subsets that overfit to a particular class. For example, Legacy can achieve near perfect accuracy on the benign set, but these features fail to generalise to the malware data set.

At a threshold of 0.99, the classifier using the Legacy/SPL features correctly classified 98.95% of the benign samples, and 69.81% of the malicious samples. These results are significantly improved upon if we combine information about the application (TLS) with the behavioural characteristic of the network traffic (SPL). The combination of Legacy/SPL/TLS was the best performing model on the benign and malware samples. At a threshold of 0.95, this model achieved accuracies of 99.99% and 85.80% for the benign and malicious hold out data sets, respectively.

2.5. *Assumptions and limitations*

The previous results assume that the data sets are representative of diverse operating conditions, and generalisability assumes that future data sets will come from the same data-generating process, i.e., be collected from environments that have the same biases and artefacts. These are unreasonable assumptions. We did go through many steps to ensure that the data had as few artefacts as possible, and we will spend the remainder of this chapter highlighting our observations.

3. Feature-level Obstacles

If we assume that network data is stationary and we have an oracle labelling all samples, there will still be deficiencies due to the inability of obtaining a representative data set. Most importantly, environment-dependent artefacts in the feature representation can result in network connections that should be identical having very dissimilar feature vectors. Due to the higher-order interactions between the endpoint and the network, it is difficult to curate a data set that has acceptable coverage. There are three main sources for these artefacts: endpoint, network and collection point.

3.1. *Endpoint*

Among other functions, the TCP stack of an operating system ensures reliable transmission of data, flow control and congestion control. Many operating systems will use different algorithms or parameters to achieve these goals, which makes operating system fingerprinting possible.[a] These differences can also affect the inter-arrival times and the sizes of the packets. For example, the window scale TCP option indicates the amount of unacknowledged data to send. The size of the TCP options will also limit the space available within a single MTU to store application data, increasing the number of transmitted bytes and increasing the number of packets in some cases. Operating systems also vary in how they handle allocating source ports. Figure 2 shows the IANA recommended port ranges for system, registered

---

[a] http://seclists.org/bugtraq/2000/Jun/141.

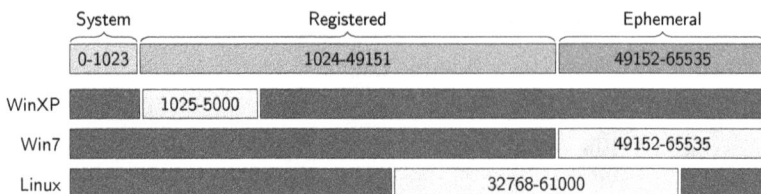

Fig. 2:   IANA port ranges.

and ephemeral ports. This figure also shows how Windows XP, Windows 7, and Linux allocates their ephemeral ports. Further confusion is caused by the different port allocation strategies, e.g., uniform random or sequential within the ephemeral range. As an example, both Windows 7 and OS X use the IANA defined range for ephemeral ports, but Windows uses a random allocation strategy and OS X uses a sequential allocation strategy.

The applications and libraries installed on the endpoint obviously play an important role shaping the observed data features. This can be one of the biggest pitfalls when utilising malware sandbox data. Operational malware sandboxes typically support the most popular and vulnerable operating systems, with little diversity due to resource constraints. Windows 7 and XP are often supported, but all of the vulnerable operating systems on an enterprise network clearly do not belong to this subset. This can bias the learned classifiers if the data features are dependent on libraries native to those systems. In the case of TLS, Schannel is the default Microsoft library, and the TLS ClientHello features would be the default settings unless manually changed. These features would be completely different if the malware was executed on a Windows 10 machine. HTTP has similar behaviour, with the User-Agent header being the closest analogy. To see how often malware relied on the default libraries provided by Windows and to better understand which features were robust across environments, we analysed samples that successfully ran in both environments.

From November 2016 until June 2017, we collected 1,236 unique malware samples that had successful TLS connections in both environments. 971 (~78.6%) samples used the TLS libraries provided by the operating system, and 265 (~21.4%) samples used the same TLS library in both environments. The majority of these samples either downloaded or contained Chrome or Tor. For HTTP, we collected 2,045 unique malware samples over the same time frame that successfully connected in both environments. 1,353 (~66.2%) samples had the same `User-Agent` string in both environments, and 692 (~33.8%) samples used the same `User-Agent` string. The higher percentage of stable `User-Agent` strings most likely is a side-effect of malware modifying the default value, which is less error-prone than modifying the default TLS cryptographic parameters.

3.2. Network

The network topology and geography can dramatically affect the packet lengths and inter-arrival times of observed network connections. There has been previous research into methods that account for some of these effects, e.g., normalising a connection's RTT (Celik *et al.*, 2011) or properly handling retransmissions (Vutukuru *et al.*, 2008). The higher order interactions between the network, client and server further complicates matters, and previous approaches can sometimes fail to capture these complexities.

Figure 3 graphically represents an application downloading a static resource from the same server, but the traffic is proxied through two different, remote VPN servers in Amsterdam, Netherlands and Bangalore, India.

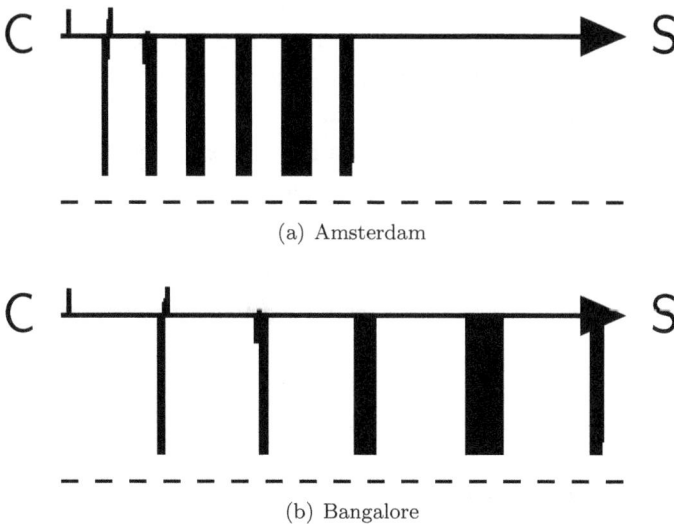

(a) Amsterdam

(b) Bangalore

Fig. 3: Varying flow durations based on location.

The x-axis represents elapsed time, the upward lines represent the size of packets that are sent from the client to the server and the downward lines represent the size of packets that are sent from the server to the client. After the TLS handshake and HTTP GET, the connection proxied through Amsterdam has five distinct server bursts, and transmits the resource in ~0.82 seconds. The connection proxied through Bangalore has four distinct server bursts, and transmits the resource in ~1.75 seconds. Even for the simple case of a single network connection requesting a static resource, the geography of the proxy significantly affected the duration and number of bursts within the connection. This becomes more complicated with real traffic and protocols such as HTTP/2 (Belshe *et al.*, 2015) that support multiplexing.

Network topology also affects the protocol-specific features used to analyse network data. Web proxies often inject HTTP headers into a connection, e.g., the Via header. When Man-in-the-Middle boxes are present, managed endpoints are configured to accept the certificates of the Man-in-the-Middle device instead of the server's certificate. Man-in-the-Middle devices can also rewrite the information in the ClientHello message, e.g., the cipher suites and extensions. Depending on the protocol-specific features the model uses, the absence or presence of these devices in the training or testing environments can lead to suboptimal results. Network devices can also add a considerable amount of noise to the packet length and inter-arrival time measurements. Man-in-the-Middle will normalise the lengths of certificates and can normalise the lengths of ClientHello messages. Man-in-the-Middle requires non-negligible computational resources, adding possibly non-uniform delays between packets.

3.3. *Collection point*

To further confuse matters, *where* network data is collected on the network also has an impact on the observed features. Obviously, we cannot assume that all network administrators will deploy identical monitoring devices at identical locations in the network. In the previous Man-in-the-Middle examples, we saw that both the ClientHello and Certificate messages could be altered, but in most network monitoring deployments, you would only see one or the other. For instance, if the monitoring device is located between the endpoint and the Man-in-the-Middle device, the

ClientHello message would be unaltered, but all Certificate messages would be generated by the Man-in-the-Middle device. This situation is reversed if the monitoring device is located between the Man-in-the-Middle device and the Internet.

Generic Receive Offload (GRO) is a feature of some network interface controllers (NIC) that will merge the TCP payload of several TCP packets. This reduces the computational overhead needed by the CPU to process individual packets. This feature is turned on by default for many Linux distributions if the installed NIC or virtual NIC supports the option. Figure 4 illustrates the effect that this feature has on the collected data. In this figure, both Figures 4(a) and 4(b) represent the same network data being simultaneously collected on a Windows 7 host machine and in an Ubuntu virtual machine. The connection was initiated by the Ubuntu virtual machine. Despite the fact Figures 4(a) and 4(b) represent the same connection, selected features, such as the number of packets, the individual packet lengths, or various statistics derived from the packet lengths, can result in very different looking responses!

In any of the above cases, inconsistency in this collection infrastructure could result in a trained model not being able to generalise to the collected data. It could also be the case that a network reconfiguration could

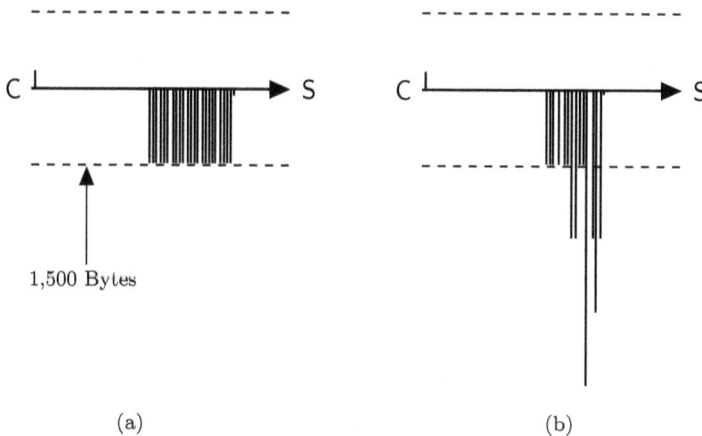

(a)   (b)

Fig. 4: Two different views of the same, Ubuntu VM-initiated connection. (a) The traffic is collected on a Windows 7 host machine. (b) The same traffic is collected in the Ubuntu 16.04 VM with generic receive offload turned on.

introduce an abrupt change-point in the collected data, which again could cause problems for the machine learning solution. Clearly, it is not reasonable to assume the incoming data will always be uniformly generated and collected, and this responsibility needs to be explicitly handled by those who are analysing the data.

4. Data Set-level Obstacles

If we assume we have perfectly robust feature representations, despite the endpoint, network and collection point configurations, we still have to contend with the inherent traits of the network security domain: data non-stationarity and noisy class labels. Operating on robust data features, curating representative data sets and timely re-training of robust machine learning models helps to limit the impact of these obstacles. In this section, we will provide some intuition about these problems, and refer the reader to Anderson and McGrew (2017a) for a more detailed analysis.

4.1. *Non-stationarity*

The non-stationary nature of network data for a fixed network topology can be attributed to changes in user behaviour and protocol standards. On a user level, the popularity of websites and services frequently change. For instance, transitioning your cloud-hosted storage from box.com to google.com/drive/ will have an impact on the encrypted traffic patterns observed. The user's browser preference and the release schedules for modern browsers also play a prominent role in ensuring that network data constantly changes. From July 2016 until June 2017, Firefox and Safari released seven major version upgrades, and Chrome released 8 major version upgrades. Although some of these upgrades had little effect on the data features observable through network monitoring, upgrades to the TLS libraries or performance optimisations often result noticeable differences.

On the protocol level, dramatic change-points can be introduced when new protocols such as TLS 1.3 (Rescorla, 2017) or HTTP/2 (Belshe *et al.*, 2015) are released. TLS 1.3 introduces a Zero-RTT mode and begins to encrypt all messages starting with the Certificate. HTTP/2 allows multiple streams to be multiplexed over the same connection. These revisions are less frequent than typical browser upgrades, but they do significantly affect the structure and available data within a network connection, impacting the features available for classification or anomaly detection.

4.2. *Inaccurate ground truth*

The most straightforward method to acquire malicious network data for training is to use a sandbox environment to run malware, and collect the submitted sample's associated packet capture files for positively labelled, malicious data. Malware samples often perform connectivity checks to sites like `google.com` that are indistinguishable from benign traffic on a per-flow basis. It is also not uncommon for all of the network activity from these sandboxes to be composed of "benign" activities, possibly as a means of execution stalling. Many malware samples will use reputable sites to perform command and control, e.g., `twitter.com`. While malware connections to these sites should be considered malicious, the contextual connections to content delivery networks that download static resources are not necessarily malicious.

To collect benign or baseline data, researching typically monitor a set of networks and collect all connections. In this case, even after filtering the data set using some set of IP blacklists (Cisco Talos, 2017), there will typically be a non-negligible percentage of network traffic that would be at least considered suspicious. It is nearly impossible to identify all of the cases where your assigned labels are incorrect. Filtering strategies to remove samples with low-confident labels will result in sparse, homogeneous data sets that do not reflect the problem domain. For example, we recently used a set of strong filtering rules that reduced our malicious data set from ~450,000 TLS connections to ~4,000 TLS connections; the resulting performance was worse on all metrics, including false positives.

5. Moving Forward

Given the obstacles presented by network data, we now sketch out several best practices that we employ. This section is not meant to be exhaustive nor the analysis complete, but to only serve as a jumping-off point.

5.1. *Utilising robust data features*

A deep understanding of the data features should be the foundation of any machine learning solution, specifically an understanding of how the chosen data features can vary with an environment. This necessitates the need to identify the current environment for a given network connection. Identifying common applications on the endpoint and enterprise, inferring popular web services per user (Gonzalez *et al.*, 2016) and fingerprinting operating systems (Anderson and McGrew, 2017b) should be done to help normalise the data features. For example, client ports can be mapped to the appropriate IANA categories, retransmissions removed, packet lengths and times can be normalised based on TCP stacks, operating system-dependent libraries can be taken into account and HTTP headers inserted by web proxies can be removed.

5.2. *Synthetic samples*

Training on malicious network traffic from a Windows 7 sandbox, with updates turned off, will not necessarily generate traffic similar to what would be seen from the same malicious executable on real enterprise endpoints. We explored a simple solution: create synthetic malware traffic by replacing the TLS client features of the sandbox data with TLS client features that would be observed on a real network. For the malware samples that take advantage of the built-in Windows library, Schannel, this meant changing the offered cipher suite vectors and extension lists so that the malware training data set's use of Schannel roughly matched that of the enterprise network's use of Schannel. The relevant packet lengths also need to be changed, e.g., the ClientHello message's size depends on the number of cipher suites and extensions offered.

To test this approach, we had three data sets: two sets of 150,000 TLS flows were taken from two geographically distinct networks, and 50,000 TLS flows were taken from the malware sandbox. In the first experiment, we left the data unchanged, trained on one enterprise network and the sandbox data, and applied this model to the traffic from the second enterprise network. There were 1,075 alarms for this experiment, with 118 being deemed suspicious by a network analyst. We repeated this experiment, but instead used synthetic malware samples that matched the TLS client distribution found in the enterprise data we trained on. There were 813 total alarms for this experiment, with 685 being deemed suspicious by a network analyst. The synthetic sampling approach resulted in a much improved precision on the validation network data set.

5.3. *Longitudinal studies*

The next two experiments highlight the importance of an informative feature set. We analysed the use of a standard set of data features that can be derived from NetFlow (Claise, 2004), and an enhanced set that provides more detail on the behaviour of the connection. For the standard representation, we used common features found in the literature (Williams *et al.*, 2006). These 22 features included the minimum, mean, maximum and standard deviation of:

- client → server packet lengths
- server → client packet lengths
- client → server packet inter-arrival times
- server → client packet inter-arrival times.

The protocol, duration of the network connection, number of client → server packets and bytes and number of server → client packets and bytes were also used. Williams *et al.* (2006) provides a complete list of these features in their Appendix C: Table of Features. The enhanced feature set adds the packet lengths and TLS specific information described in Section 2.2. We also tested several machine learning models, including linear regression, logistic regression with different regularisation penalties, a multi-layer perceptron, support vector machine and a random forest model (Anderson and McGrew, 2017a). In this experiment, the model is fixed at time t, and then its performance is evaluated on data collected over the next 5 months.

Using the standard representation, a random forest ensemble was clearly the best performing algorithm over time, maintaining ∼99.9% accuracy on the enterprise data set over a 5-month period. The random forest model outperformed other models over a 5-month period on the malware data set, but its performance still fell significantly over time with ∼35% recall on the fifth month.

With respect to the enterprise data, the random forest using the enhanced representation almost exactly maintained its ~99.99% cross-validation accuracy across all 5 months. The random forest model was again one of the most competitive algorithms when detecting malicious TLS sessions across all 5 months, with ~77% recall on the fifth month. It is interesting to note the robustness of linear regression when using the enhanced representation: this simple model easily outperformed all other methods based on the standard representation.

5.4. *Noisy labels*

In this experiment, we randomly changed the class of a fixed percentage of samples in the training data set, trained the classifiers and then tested the classifiers on the data collected 5 months later from the original enterprise network and the malware sandbox. The label noise was varied from 0.5% to 5.0% in increments of 0.5%. For the enhanced data representation, the support vector machine was by far the least robust with respect to label noise. This has been independently observed, and although not addressed in this chapter, solutions have been proposed (Biggio *et al.*, 2011).

Interestingly, logistic regression with both an l_1 and l_2 penalty was helped by the label noise. These methods were biased towards the malware samples, and introducing the label noise at a rate of 1.5–5.0% significantly increased the classification accuracy on the enterprise data set, and had no further degradation past 1.5% on the malware data. The multi-layer perceptron model and linear regression were both stable across all levels of label noise when using the enhanced data. The random forest ensemble maintained its accuracy on the enterprise data despite the noisy labels. It was also significantly better on the malware data than all other classifiers with reasonable enterprise performance: maintaining ~89% recall vs ~72–74% recall on the malicious data set. Again, the enhanced feature representation significantly helped the classifiers account for the noisy labels.

6. Conclusion

The network security domain presents a number of interesting data science challenges. We believe that these challenges cannot be overcome with an algorithm-first, domain-agnostic view. Many of the observations in this chapter are the direct result of deeply studying the data and working closely with networking, software and security experts. Many of the unintuitive outcomes of our experiments were easily explained with a deeper knowledge of the data, and these missteps have allowed this line of research to steadily progress.

References

Anderson, B. and McGrew, D. (2016). Identifying encrypted Malware traffic with contextual flow data, in *ACM Workshop on Artificial Intelligence and Security (AISec)*, pp. 35–46.

Anderson, B. and McGrew, D. (2017a). Machine learning for encrypted Malware traffic classification: Accounting for noisy labels and non-stationarity, in *ACM SIGKDD International Conference on Knowledge Discovery in Data Mining (KDD)*, pp. 1723–1732.

Anderson, B. and McGrew, D. (2017b). OS fingerprinting: New techniques and a study of information gain and obfuscation, in *IEEE Conference on Communications and Network Security (CNS)*, pp. 1–9.

Anderson, B., Paul, S. and McGrew, D. (2017). Deciphering malware's use of TLS (without decryption), *Journal of Computer Virology and Hacking Techniques*. doi:10.1007/s11416-017-0306-6.

Belshe, M., Peon, R. and Thomson, M. (2015). Hypertext transfer protocol, Version 2 (HTTP/2), RFC 7540 (Proposed Standard), URL: http://www.ietf.org/rfc/rfc7540.txt.

Biggio, B., Nelson, B. and Laskov, P. (2011). Support vector machines under adversarial label noise, in *Asian Conference on Machine Learning*, pp. 97–112.

Bilge, L., Balzarotti, D., Robertson, W., Kirda, E. and Kruegel, C. (2012). Disclosure: Detecting botnet command and control servers through large-scale NetFlow analysis, in *ACM Annual Computer Security Applications Conference (ACSAC)*, pp. 129–138.

Celik, Z. B., Raghuram, J., Kesidis, G. and Miller, D. J. (2011). Salting public traces with attack traffic to test flow classifiers, in *USENIX Conference on Cyber Security Experimentation and Test (CSET)*, pp. 17–24.

Cisco Talos (2017). IP Blacklist Feed, URL: http://www.talosintel.com/feeds/ip-filter.blf, accessed: 2017-04-19.

Claise, B. (2004). Cisco Systems NetFlow services export, Version 9, RFC 3954 (Informational), URL: http://www.ietf.org/rfc/rfc3954.txt.

Dierks, T. and Rescorla, E. (2008). The transport layer security (TLS) protocol, Version 1.2, RFC 5246 (Proposed Standard), URL: http://www.ietf.org/rfc/rfc5246.txt.

Gonzalez, R., Soriente, C. and Laoutaris, N. (2016). User profiling in the time of HTTPS, in *ACM SIGCOMM Internet Measurement Conference (IMC)*, pp. 373–379.

Gu, G., Perdisci, R., Zhang, J. and Lee, W. (2008). BotMiner: Clustering analysis of network traffic for protocol-and structure-independent botnet detection, in *USENIX Security Symposium*, pp. 139–154.

Harrigan, M. (2016). Machine learning is not the answer to better network security, URL: https://techcrunch.com/2016/02/29/machine-learning-is-not-the-answer-to-better-network-security/, accessed: 2017-07-30.

Moore, A. W. and Zuev, D. (2005). Internet traffic classification using Bayesian analysis techniques, *SIGMETRICS Performance Evaluation Review* **33**, pp. 50–60.

Paxson, V. (1999). Bro: A system for detecting network intruders in real-time, *Computer Networks* **31**, 23–24, pp. 2435–2463.

Pedregosa, F., Varoquaux, G., Gramfort, A., Michel, V., Thirion, B., Grisel, O., Blondel, M., Prettenhofer, P., Weiss, R., Dubourg, V., Vanderplas, J., Passos, A., Cournapeau, D., Brucher, M., Perrot, M. and Duchesnay, E. (2011). Scikit-learn: Machine learning in Python, *Journal of Machine Learning Research* **12**, pp. 2825–2830.

Rescorla, E. (2017). The transport layer security (TLS) protocol, Version 1.3 (draft 20), Intended status: Standards track, URL: https://tools.ietf.org/html/draft-ietf-tls-tls13-20.

Roesch, M. (1999). Snort — lightweight intrusion detection for networks, in *USENIX Large Installation System Administration Conference (LISA)*, pp. 229–238.

Sommer, R. and Paxson, V. (2010). Outside the closed world: On using machine learning for network intrusion detection, in *IEEE Symposium on Security and Privacy (S&P)*, pp. 305–316.

Vutukuru, M., Balakrishnan, H. and Paxson, V. (2008). Efficient and robust TCP stream normalization, in *IEEE Symposium on Security and Privacy (S&P)*, pp. 96–110.

Williams, N., Zander, S. and Armitage, G. (2006). A preliminary performance comparison of five machine learning algorithms for practical IP traffic flow classification, *SIGCOMM Computer Communication Review* **36**, 5, pp. 5–16.

Chapter 5

Feature Trade-Off Analysis for Reconnaissance Detection

Harsha Kumara Kalutarage*,‡ and Siraj Ahmed Shaikh†,§

*School of Computing Science & Digital Media,
Robert Gordon University, Aberdeen, UK
†Research Institute for Future Transport and Cities, Coventry University,
CV1 5FB Coventry, UK

‡h.kalutarage@rgu.ac.uk
§s.shaikh@coventry.ac.uk

An effective cyber early warning system (CEWS) should pick up threat activity at an early stage, with an emphasis on establishing hypotheses and predictions as well as generating alerts on (unclassified) situations based on preliminary indications. The design and implementation of such early warning systems involve numerous challenges such as generic set of indicators, intelligence gathering, uncertainty reasoning and information fusion. This chapter begins with an understanding of the behaviours of intruders and then related literature is followed by the proposed methodology using a Bayesian inference-based system. It also includes a carefully deployed empirical analysis on a data set labelled for reconnaissance activity. Finally, the chapter concludes with a discussion on results, research challenges and necessary suggestions to move forward in this research line.

1. Introduction

Our national critical infrastructures depend heavily on the Internet. More devices rapidly get connected to the "Internet of Things" including cars and homes. This is due to increasing shift of service and production systems to IP-based infrastructures. Though convenient and cost-effective, IP-based infrastructures can be easily compromised by an attacker to create a disaster against either an individual or a whole nation state. Recent cyber attacks such as 2017 cyber attacks on Ukraine, WannaCry, Heartbleed bug (which kills security on millions of websites worldwide) and Stuxnet (frequently described as a jointly built Cyberweapon by two countries to attack a third country) are examples for this movement. Proactive measures such as early warnings on computer networks are required to reduce such a risk.

Traditional security solutions such as firewalls cannot assure that data, objects and resources are restricted from unauthorised subjects. Such defensive approaches are increasingly insufficient for modern-day attacks as threat actors circumvent perimeter-based defences in a creative, stealthy, targeted and persistent manner that often goes undetected for significant periods of time. These attacks are multistage in nature. If we can detect them *early* and respond quickly, then high-impact cyber incidents can be avoided. So, an active approach to cyber defence is needed, which in turn needs to effectively detect early stages of threat activity to deploy effective potential responses. A cyber early warning system (CEWS) hence should serve such a goal.

One definition for a CEWS is that it "aims at alerting *unclassified* but potentially harmful system behaviour based on *preliminary indications* before possible damage occurs, and *contribute* to an integrated and aggregated situation report" (Biskup *et al.*, 2008).

Although there can be many overlaps between a typical intrusion detection system (IDS) and a CEWS, a particular emphasis for a CEWS is to establish hypotheses and predictions as well as to generate advice on unclassified activity based on preliminary indications (Biskup *et al.*, 2008).

This chapter sets off by attempting to present a generic attack model in Section 2. Section 3 presents an analytical approach building over prior work to threat monitoring (Kalutarage *et al.*, 2012, 2013, 2015; Shaikh and Kalutarage, 2016). Section 4 delves into the data set and experimental set up used for this effort, and Section 5 describes the results of the proposed method. Section 6 provides an overview for related work, and Section 7 concludes the chapter with some thoughts on open challenges in this area.

2. Cyber-Attack Life Cycle

The notion of *early* can be explained using the cyber attack life cycle. As mentioned above, modern attacks are multistage and producing evidence at each stage of the attack life cycle. In principal, these evidence can be collected and analysed to alarm the attack, but it is difficult in practice due to a number of constraints. The typical stages of a modern-day cyber-attack life cycle can be summarised as follows:

Stage 1 Reconnaissance — The attacker conducts initial surveys on potential targets which can be either systems or people. Once a target is identified, she starts to search more specific information such as internet facing services and individuals in order to decide which weapon to use. It could be a zero-day exploit, social engineering, spear phishing or even bribing an insider.

Stage 2 Initial compromise — The attacker successfully executes malicious code on one or more systems on the target. She bypasses the perimeter defences and gains access to the internal network. This can be through a compromised system or user account; often attackers use phishing for initial compromise, as exploiting user vulnerability is relatively easier than software/hardware vulnerabilities.

Stage 3 Command & control — The attacker maintains continued control over the compromised system by installing a persistent backdoor. This can be done via downloading additional utilities such as remote access Trojan (RAT) on to the victim system.

Stage 4 Escalate privileges — The attacker attempts to escalate her privileges in order to gain wider access to systems and data. This could be done via a pass the hash technique, keylogging, obtaining public key infrastructure (PKI) certificates, leveraging privileges held by an application, exploiting a vulnerable piece of software on the victim node or using any other method.

Stage 5 Internal reconnaissance — The attacker gains a better understanding of the environment, security in place, assets, and the roles and responsibilities of key subjects.

Stage 6 Lateral movement — The attacker compromises additional systems and user accounts moving from system to system using the access she gained from previous stages. This can be accessing network shares, using task schedulers, remote desktop clients or virtual network computing. Since the attacker is often impersonating a legitimate user, evidence of their existence can be hard to find at this stage.

Stage 7 Maintain presence — The attacker installs multiple remote access entry points (e.g., variants of malware back doors) and may have compromised a number of internal systems and user accounts to ensure that continued access to the environment. At this stage, she deeply understands the environment and is within reach of her target at anytime.

Stage 8 Complete mission — The attacker executes the final aspects of her mission. This could be stealing sensitive information (e.g., intellectual property, financial data), corrupting mission critical systems or making computer resource unavailable for functioning the business via a denial of service attack. Once the mission has completed, she might either leave the environment (without leaving evidence) or maintain access in case a new mission is directed.

Readers are invited to notice the final stage of the above life cycle where exfiltration, corruption and disruption happen. Damage of the attack rises exponentially at this stage if the attack is not defeated. Therefore, any system that can alert the ongoing malicious attempt using preliminary indicators before it reaches the "mission completion" stage can be considered as a CEWS.

2.1. *Automated threat detection*

As mentioned above, a modern cyber attack doesn't just happen. It evolves in a multistage process which includes early stages of reconnaissance and planning. Humans take too long to notice these activities, which would be in favour of the attackers. Automated CEWSs are necessary. Automation dramatically increases scalability and effectiveness of security monitoring. However, due to the targeted nature, attack vector varies from one entity to another. Thus, signature-based pattern matching techniques are not useful and more sophisticated techniques are required. As shown in Figure 1, our ultimate goal in this work is to employ cognitive technologies to "early detect". However at this stage of the work, we propose a simple but systematic behaviour analytic model aiming at two essential features of future

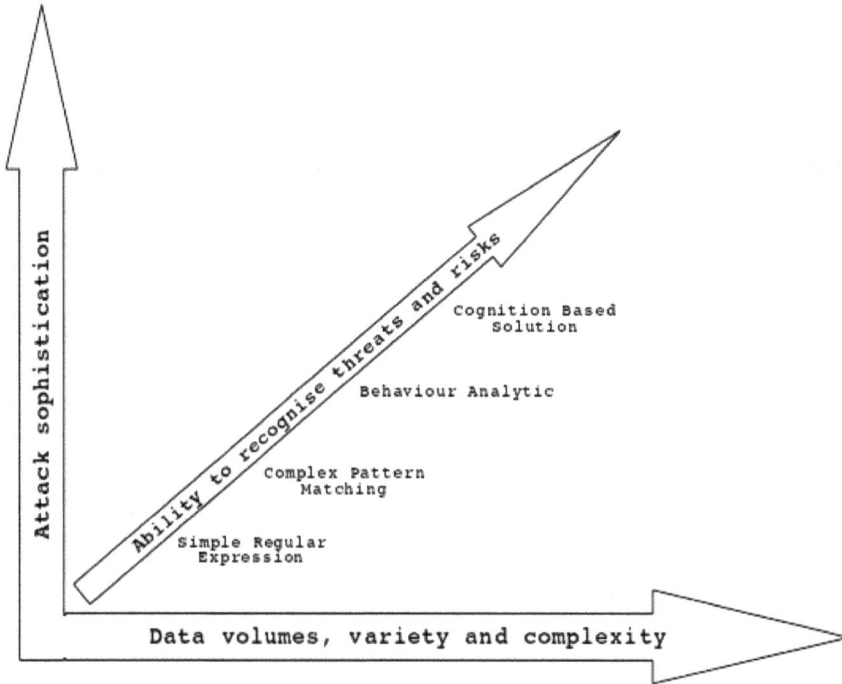

Fig. 1:   Automated threat detection: Attack sophistication vs detection technique to employ.

CEWS (Golling and Stelte, 2011), which can be summarised based on its ability to answer the following:

- Has the attack begun/about to begin?
- What is the target?

3. Methodology

An incident occurs when an attack is carried out. Each incident area (e.g., scanning, compromising, malicious code) produces different event data which spread out over the time and space. Event data can be classified into four types: suspicious, malicious, legitimate and not reported. Suspicious events belong to the "grey area" in security decisions. They can occur due to either a malicious attempt or a legitimate activity — for example, an execution of *cmd.exe*, multiple logging attempts or an overwhelming number of ICMP unreachable messages; a major router failure could generate many ICMP unreachable messages, while some viruses and worms (for example, CodeRed and Nimda) generate the same in the probing process. Writing black/white list rules to distinguish these types of activities is difficult.

Given that the mean time to detect (MTTD) of a modern-day attack is 146 days,[a] it is necessary to maintain a long history of what is happening in the environment. Most systems cannot keep enough event data to track across extended time intervals due to the storage overheads. As a result, the scarcity of attack data within a short period of time allows the attacker to go undetected. On the other hand, as contemporary enterprise networks scale up in size and speed, huge volume of traffic has a cost ramification for collection and processing. Resources of network devices are comparatively expensive and scarce. Such resources need to be utilised for their regular activities rather than utilised on monitoring activities. Therefore, in order to be a practical automated solution, proposed system should be computationally inexpensive. We propose continuous monitoring via node profiling. It uses information fusion and evidence accumulation as in our previous works (Kalutarage *et al.*, 2012, 2013, 2015; Shaikh and Kalutarage, 2016).

3.1. *Computing node profiles*

Node profiling is the method of evidence fusion across space and time by updating node score dynamically based on changes in evidence. Profiling computes a suspicion score s_w for each node in the system during a smaller time window w. That score is updated as time progresses to compute a node score N_W such that

$$N_W = \sum s_w,$$

for a larger observation window $W = \sum w$. Various machine learning algorithms, either supervised or unsupervised, can be employed to estimate s_w depending on the context and data availability.

---

[a]https://www.fireeye.com/company/press-releases/2016/fireeye-releases-first-mandiant-mtrends-eme a-report.html.

3.1.1. *Computing s_w using supervised learning*

Evidence to compute s_w can be collected from any source of information to generate predictors; these sources can be packet/flow information from L3 switches or outputs of signature-based IDSs, anomaly detection components, antivirals, file integrity checkers, SNMP-based network monitoring systems or any other relevant information. The choice of predictors, say $D = \{d_1, d_2, d_3, \ldots, d_n\}$, is subject to the condition that they have some sort of predictive power of the target variable defined as H — the hypothesis that given node is under attack. If H is true, it means that an attacker has initiated at least the first step of the attack life cycle (see Section 2) against the victim node. Then s_w is defined as

$$s_w = \begin{cases} 1 & \text{if } \Lambda = \ln \dfrac{L(H \mid D)}{L(\neg H \mid D)} > 0, \\ 0 & \text{otherwise,} \end{cases}$$

where $L(.)$ denotes the likelihood. Λ expresses how many times more likely the observed evidence in D is under one model (H) than the other ($\neg H$).

3.1.2. *Computing Λ using naive Bayes model*

One of the key applications of predictive analytics is to classify entities or events based on a knowledge of their attributes. In this chapter, for the purpose of demonstration, we will employ a naive Bayes classifier and knowledge of communication flow attributes to compute Λ as follows.

Let $D = [d_1, \ldots, d_n]$ be an n-dimensional space, where n is the total number of attributes (predictors) chosen to describe a communication flow in a computer network. Note that we assume remote attacks here and hence victim nodes receiving malicious communication flows during the attack life cycle. Using the notation of conditional probability and well-known Bayes theorem,

$$P(H|D) = \frac{\prod_{k=1}^{n} P(d_k|H) \cdot P(H)}{P(D)}, \tag{1}$$

$$P(\neg H|D) = \frac{\prod_{k=1}^{n} P(d_k|\neg H) \cdot P(\neg H)}{P(D)}. \tag{2}$$

Dividing Equation (1) by (2) and taking logarithm,

$$\ln \frac{P(H|D)}{P(\neg H|D)} = \ln \frac{P(H)}{P(\neg H)} + \sum_{k=1}^{n} \ln \frac{P(d_k|H)}{P(d_k|\neg H)}. \qquad (3)$$

Equation (3) is the well-known "Log likelihood ratio". $P(H)$, $P(d_k|H)$ are prior and likelihoods terms while $P(H|D)$ is the posterior probability. Taking $\ln \frac{L(H|D)}{L(\neg H|D)} \cong \ln \frac{P(H|D)}{P(\neg H|D)}$,

$$\Lambda = \ln \frac{P(H|D)}{P(\neg H|D)}.$$

The key assumption in Equations (1) and (2) is that the conditional probability of each feature given the class is independent of all other features. It means that the features are completely independent of each other. This is clearly not the case in many practical problems including ours. For example, the conditional probability of network service (e.g., http, ftp, smtp, ssh, dns) and the port number in a communication flow are definitely not independent of each other. But in practice, even when the independence assumption is violated and there are clear known relationships between attributes, it works anyway. A good example for this is spam filtering in which features are individual words in an email. In this case certain word combinations tend to show up consistently in spam — for example, "pharmacy", "online", "meds" and "viagra". So, their occurrences are not independent of each other. Nevertheless, in filtering spam from ham, naive Bayes-based spam filters work very well. This can happen for two reasons. First, prediction in Equation (3) depends only on the maximum, not the value of the maximum. Hence the naive Bayes classifier gets it right even if there are dependencies between features given that such dependencies do not change which class has the maximum probability value. The second reason might be that such dependencies often cancel out across a large set of features. However, the performance of naive Bayes can be degraded if the data contains highly correlated features. Such features over-inflate their importance by voting twice in the model. Therefore it is better to treat highly correlated attributes and test the performance before and after such treatments and stick with better performance.

3.1.3. *Pros and cons of using naive Bayes*

There are some *pros* and *cons* of using naive Bayes in this problem. As mentioned above, due to the nature of the problem, proposed system should be computationally inexpensive and lightweight. Using naive Bayes, calculating the probabilities for each attribute is very fast which means that the system can recalculate the probabilities as the data changes since temporal drift is a major issue in cyber security. Another advantage of naive Bayes is its naive (independent) assumption can be exploited to speed up the execution of the algorithm. Attribute probabilities can be calculated in parallel using different CPUs, machines or clusters in real-world applications. This is useful as global networks scale up in traffic, volume and speed. Naive Bayes does not need a lot of training data to perform well. Given that interactions between attributes are ignored in the model, it does not need examples of these interactions and therefore generally requires less training data than other algorithms (e.g., logistic regression). However, naive Bayes will not be reliable if there are significant differences in the attribute distributions between training and test cases. Zero observations problem is a special case of this. After such cases have been identified, the model should be updated.

3.1.4. *Computing s_w using unsupervised learning*

This section discusses how to employ unsupervised learning, in particular an autoencoder neural network model, in estimating s_w. An autoencoder neural network is an unsupervised learning algorithm. It applies backpropagation, setting the output values to be equal to inputs (i.e., $\hat{D} \approx D$), by learning an approximation to the identity function in the model. Figure 2 depicts an autoencoder model.

To compute suspicion score, s_w is defined as

$$s_w = \sqrt{\frac{1}{n}\sum_{i=1}^{n}(d_i - \hat{d}_i)^2}.$$

In other words, s_w is the reconstructed mean squared error (MSE) of autoencoder model during a smaller time window w. As far as anyone

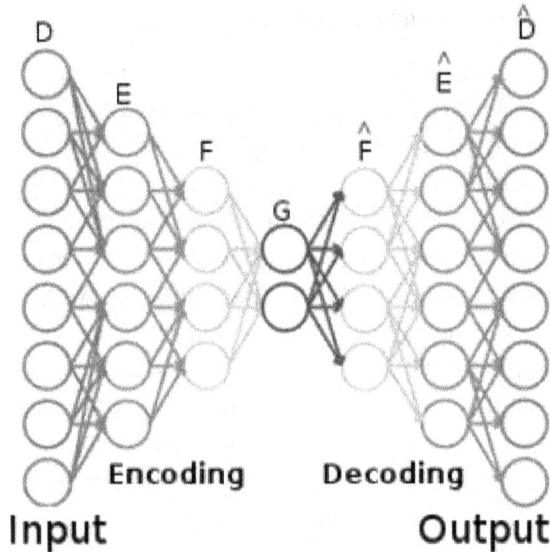

Fig. 2: An auto-encoder model.

knows, total number of malicious class data is far less than the total number of benign class data in many real-world network security problems. Hence, we can expect that the model learns patterns in the benign data that it can't see as easily in the malicious data. As a result, high reconstructed MSE (s_w) values can be expected for malicious observations, which could be useful to stand out victim nodes from normal nodes.

Nevertheless, from the machine learning perspective, it is still important to evaluate different algorithms to see which algorithm performs best in terms of false alarms and computational cost in estimating s_w. However, it is out of the scope of this work.

3.2. *Analysis*

We compute a node score for each node in the system as described above. Aggregating suspicious scores over the time helps to accumulate relatively weak evidence for long periods. These accumulated terms can be used as a measurement of the level of suspicion of a given node at any given time with respect to the peers. Hence, our task is detecting anomalous profiles, in a given set of node profiles. If attacker activity pattern is sufficiently reflected by profiles, then detecting anomalous profiles would be sufficient to identify attackers. We use a statistical method to detect anomalies subject to the assumption that normal node profiles in a given set follow an unknown Gaussian distribution. Testing of our hypothesis for any given time is a Bernoulli trial. Accumulated Bernoulli trials makes a binomial distribution which can be approximated by a normal distribution. In practice, the setup where we have the distribution would be very well modelled with a mixture of Gaussians.

For each profile score N_W, its Z score is computed as

$$z = \frac{N_W - \mu_W}{\sigma_W},$$

where μ_W and σ_W are the mean and standard deviation of the data set at time window W. A test instance is declared to be anomalous if $z \geq T = k$. Note that the threshold T adjusts itself according to the current state of a network as μ_W and σ_W change. k can be setup to 1, 2 or 3 using the 68%–95%–99.7% rule of detecting outliers with Z-scores. For example, by setting $k = 2$, Z-scores in 2–3 range can be considered as borderline outliers. If the data (N_W values) is skewed, it is recommended to apply a transformation technique (e.g., power transformation or logarithms) first to move the data set back to the normal bell shape and then apply the outlier detection technique.

The simple outlier detection method above is subject to the masking and swamping effects. Multiple outliers may influence the value of the test statistic enough so that no points are declared as outliers. On the other hand, swamping can occur when there is no outlier (or an outlier with very slight deviation). Therefore we complement the outcome of the above outlier detection method with graphical methods. Graphics can often help identify cases where masking or swamping may be an issue.

Our analysis compares each node's activity changes to activity changes of her peer group. Looking at one's aberrant behaviour within similar peer groups (e.g., same user types, subnet, departments, job roles) would give better results in terms of false alarms than setting a universal baseline. Hence, first classifying similar nodes into peer groups (e.g., web servers, file servers, clients), based on behaviour related attributes/features, and then applying the monitoring algorithm is recommended. Investigations of suitable classification algorithms for this task is left as a future work.

4. Experimental Setup

4.1. *Data set description*

A third-party data set consisting of malicious and normal traffic captures is used in this work. According to the authors of the data set, Moustafa and Slay (2016), IXIA PerfectStormOne Tool[b] has been used to generate synthetic contemporary attacks within realistic modern normal activities. 100GB of raw network traffic has been captured.

4.1.1. *Initial features*

Forty nine features are extracted and categorised into five groups (Moustafa and Slay, 2016):

- Flow related features — these features includes the flow related attributes between two nodes in a computer network such as source and destination IP addresses, port numbers and the protocol type (e.g., TCP, UDP).
- Basic features — attributes that represent protocol connections (e.g., duration, source to destination bytes, time to live, packets loss, service, bits per second, packet count).
- Content-related features — encapsulates the TCP/IP layer-related attributes (e.g., TCP window advertisement value, TCP base sequence number, packet size).
- Time related features — contains the time-related attributes (e.g., jitter, start time, inter packet arrival time, round-trip time, time between SYN and SYN_ACK, time between SYN_ACK and the ACK).
- Additional generated features: divided into two groups: general-purpose features (each feature has its own purpose) and connection features (built from the flow of 100 record connections based on the sequential order of the last time feature).

It should be noted that none of the features above are attack dependent and can be extracted from any given traffic flow, and hence can be considered as a general-purpose feature set for monitoring. Readers are invited to refer

---

[b]https://www.ixiacom.com/products/ixnetwork.

to Moustafa and Slay (2016) for more details of data generation, feature extraction and attack types.

4.1.2. *Attack types*

The following activity (attack) types have been produced in the data set in addition to the day to day normal activities. Note that one or more activity types described below can be presented at different stages of the attack life cycle. For example, Fuzzers and Exploit can be presented at either stage 1, 2 or 5 of the attack life cycle. Hence, ability to detect any of them will stop the attacker reaching the final stage where exfiltration, corruption and disruption happen and can be considered as an early detection. However, we will mostly focus on reconnaissance activities in this work as it would be naturally the first step of many network-based computer attacks.

- **Reconnaissance:** Can be defined as a probe in which attacker gathers information about a computer network to evade its security controls.
- **Fuzzers:** Attacker attempts to discover security loopholes in a programme, operating system or network by feeding it with the massive inputting of random data to make it crash.
- **Analysis:** A type of variety intrusions that penetrate the web applications via ports (e.g., port scans), emails (e.g., spam) and web scripts (e.g., HTML files).
- **Backdoor:** A technique of bypassing a stealthy normal authentication, securing unauthorised remote access to a device and locating the entrance to plain text as it is struggling to continue unobserved.
- **Exploit:** A sequence of instructions that takes advantage of a glitch, bug, or vulnerability to be caused by an unintentional or unsuspected behaviour on a host or network.
- **Generic:** A technique that establishes against every block cipher using a hash function to collision without respect to the configuration of the block-cipher.
- **Shellcode:** Attacker penetrates a slight piece of code starting from a shell to control the compromised machine.
- **Worm:** Attack replicates itself in order to spread on other computers. Often, it uses a computer network to spread itself, depending on the security failures of the target computer to access it.

- **DoS:** An intrusion which disrupts the computer resources via memory, to be extremely busy in order to prevent the authorised requests from accessing a device.

4.1.3. *Exploring the data set*

In order to investigate distributions of each feature in two different classes (i.e., malicious and benign), first we encoded categorical variables into numerical variables and then plot box-plots as shown in Figure 3. Due to the space constraints, only twenty box-plots are presented. There is a certain group of features which have different distributions in malicious class than benign class (see Figure 3). These features have the discriminating power and hence inform more in classification/anomaly detection model. In order to reduce computational cost, features having same distributions in both classes can be removed from D, unless they are not important collectively with other features or have any other form of information such as semantic information which is not encoded in the data. Therefore, feature selection and reduction is necessary to remove unnecessary features, such as features not informed in the model and highly correlated features.

4.2. *Feature selection using empirical analysis*

As mentioned above, due to the scarcity of resources on monitoring devices, reduction of the computational cost is vital in our problem. Hence, feature selection and reduction play an important role. Features described in Section 4.1.1 were chosen as the initial feature set, and then a random forest model (Breiman, 2001) was built and tuned using R's random forest package (version 4.6-12) (Liaw and Wiener, 2002). Then, for the feature trade-off analysis in Section 5.2, top importance features are selected using the mean decrease Gini (see Figure 4).

For example, as shown in Figure 3, variable "dwin" has similar distributions in both classes, and has not been selected as an importance feature in Figure 4. Should "dwin" be excluded from our feature set? Variable "dwin" denotes the destination TCP window advertisement value in a TCP packet. If it set to zero, then connection will be halted. If the attacker is smart enough, "dwin" can be exploited to create a service disruption. Hence domain experts think "dwin" as an important feature to look at. Therefore,

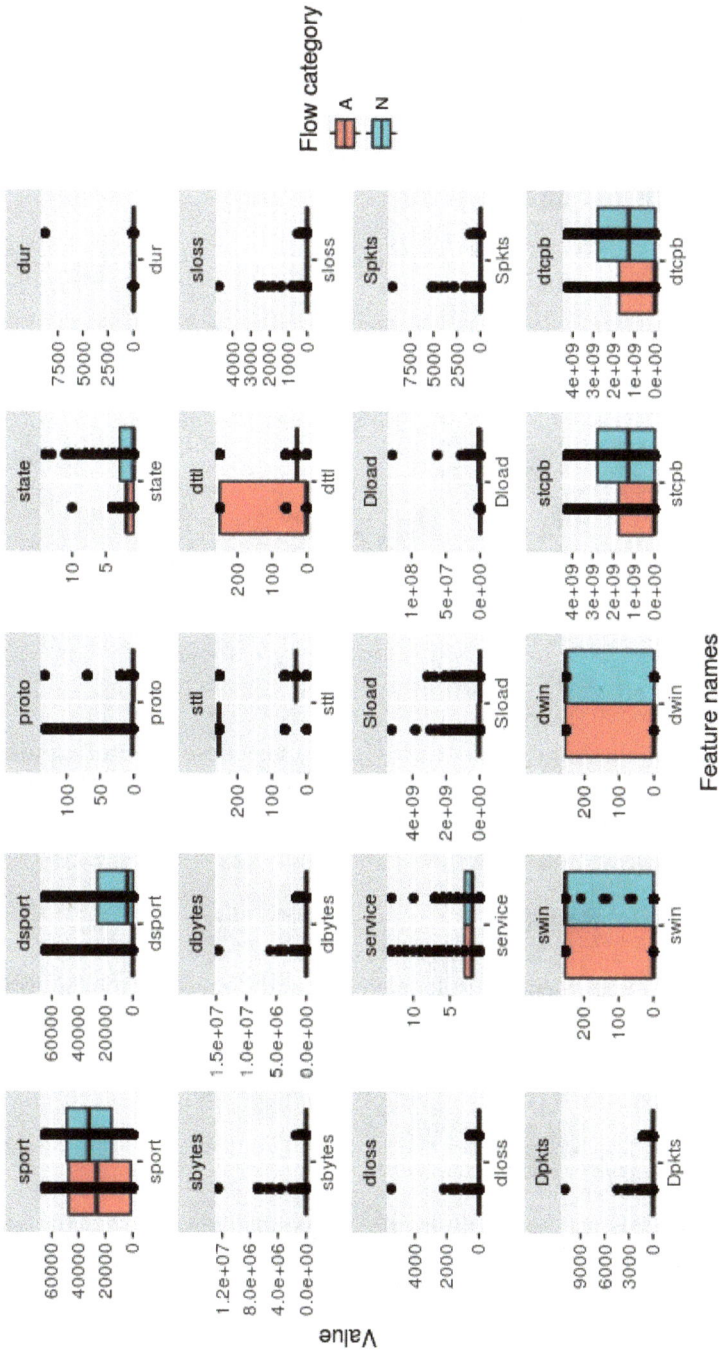

Fig. 3: Distributions of each feature in two classes (A — attack, N — normal).

Feature Importance

Feature Importance

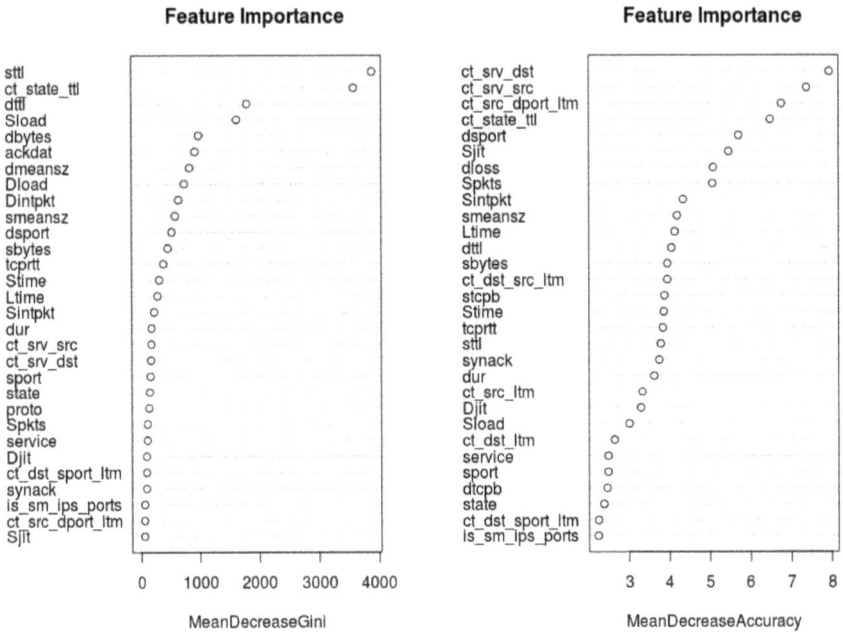

Fig. 4:   Feature selection: Using empirical analysis.

instead of depending entirely on data for feature selection, a hybrid approach which combines expert judgements with the knowledge gained from training data is recommended.

5.   Experimental Results

In this section, experimental results are presented. We use graphical forms (e.g., Z-Score graphs) to present information. Visualisation helps to quickly recognise patterns in data as well as spotting masking and swamping effects mentioned above.

5.1.   *Monitoring for reconnaissance*

Reconnaissance is a type of intrusion activity that can occur at the very early stages of the attack life cycle. In an active reconnaissance, an intruder engages with the targeted system to gather information about vulnerabilities.

Victim IP: all nodes

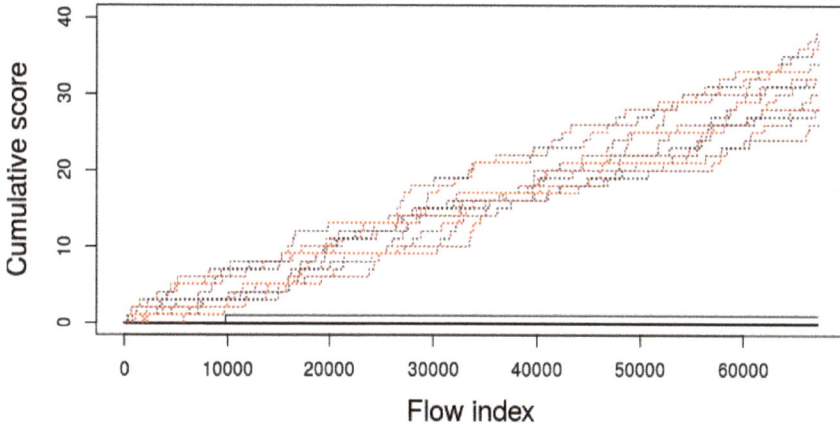

Fig. 5: Monitoring for all nodes (forty nodes in the subnet). Victims of reconnaissance attempts are denoted by red dotted lines. All other nodes denoted by black lines in the above graph keep suspicious score near zero.

Our proposed technique was investigated against reconnaissance activities in the data set. As shown in Figure 5, the proposed approach can detect all victims of reconnaissance activities in the data set. It includes ten IP addresses, namely, 149.171.126.18, 149.171.126.17, 149.171.126.11, 149.171.126.12, 149.171.126.13, 149.171.126.15, 149.171.126.16, 149. 171.126.19, 149.171.126.14 and 149.171.126.10. These IP addresses are denoted by red dotted lines in Figure 5. All other nodes (30 IP addresses) are normal and denoted by black lines. As expected, they keep suspicious score near zero as they are not targeted by any reconnaissance attempt during the monitoring period for our experiments.

In order to closely investigate how our algorithm increment profile scores over the time, Figure 6 visualises the profile scores of node 149.171.126.18 against time and event arrivals. In Figure 6, data points with + sign denote a reconnaissance attempt as it happens over the time from multiple source IPs while all other points denote a normal activity. As is obvious, reconnaissance always increments the suspicious score of a node in the graph.

It should be noted that computing cumulative scores N_W itself and then presenting them as in Figure 5 is not enough for detecting ongoing malicious

Victim IP: 149.171.126.18

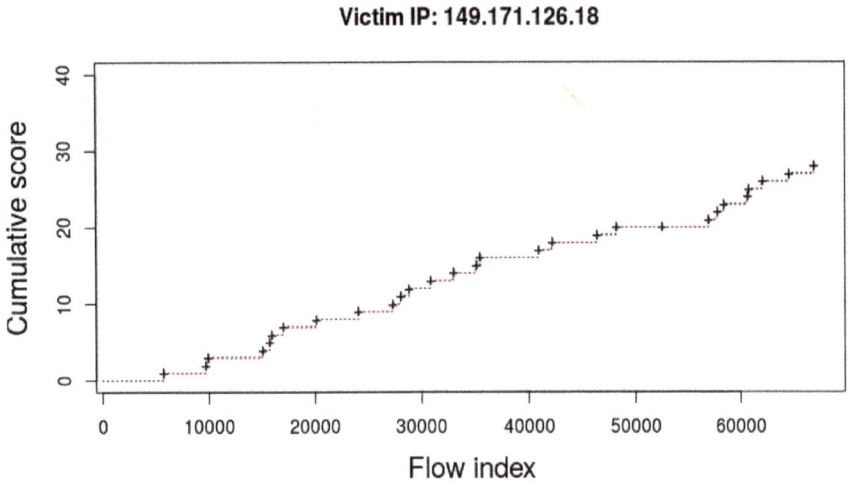

Fig. 6: Increasing the suspicious score: + sign denotes a reconnaissance attempt as it happens over the time from multiple source IPs.

Z-scores: all nodes

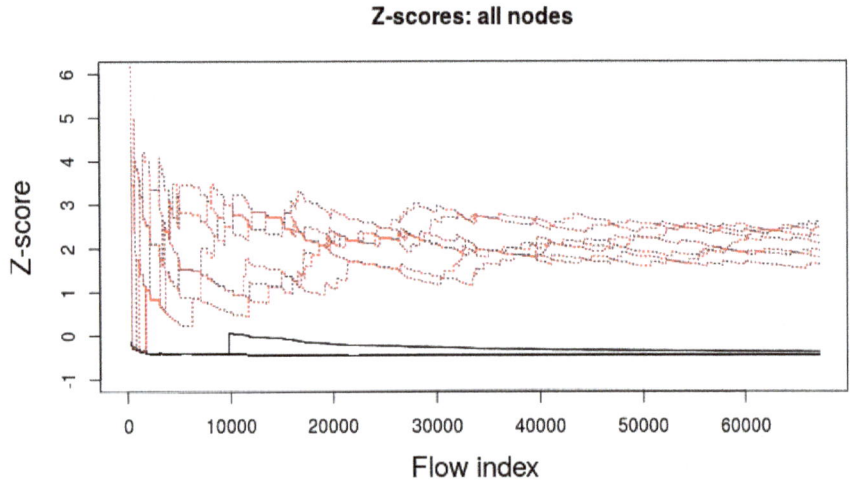

Fig. 7: Z-scores: Compassion within the peer group. Red dotted lines denote victim nodes.

activities, because there is no sense of a threshold in that representation. Converting to Z-scores is required. In Z-score graphs in Figure 7, nodes corresponding to red dotted lines denote victims. We set the threshold as $T = 2$ in this work and then victim nodes are near the T, and importantly there is a clear visual separation between the set of normal nodes and anomalous nodes. Hence, it is possible to recognise victims using the proposed method.

5.2. *Feature trade-off analysis*

As contemporary enterprise networks scale up in size and speed, huge volume of traffic has a cost ramification for security monitoring. You may not see a few milliseconds delay as much time. But if we suffer this delay millions of times, then the accumulated delay can be significant and our solution may not be viable in practice. Therefore, as mentioned in Section 3, in order to be a practical automated CEWS solution, a proposed system should be computationally inexpensive. Feature reduction plays an important role in developing lightweight solutions, which could be motivated as long as it preserves the required level of precision. We will investigate how the number of features affects the performance as follows.

First, the five most important features (top 5) were selected as input features (see Section 4.2) to the proposed algorithm, and then training time, testing time (per test case) and false alarm rates were recorded. With regards to the false alarms, misclassification of flows were counted. The same experiment was repeated nine times by keeping all parameters unchanged, except number of features which were varied as top 5, top 10, top 15 and so on until top 45 as described above. Training and testing time were calculated on a laptop with an Intel(R) Core(TM) i7-6820HQ CPU @ 2.70 GHz and 8 GB of RAM. Ubuntu 16.04 operating system was running on the laptop.

Figure 8 presents the number of features vs training time. As shown in Figure 8, number of features is proportional to the model training time. Lower numbers of features selected is better for training time. Figure 9 presents the number of features vs testing time. Though there are slight drops at points 15 and 40, the graph has a increasing trend in general for test time. Figures 10 and 11 present false alarm rates against number of features used in the model. As is obvious from the figures, increasing the number of features does not always reduce the false alarms. In fact, in this particular case, it will start to increase false-negative rates if we increased the number of features beyond 20. From the security point of view, false

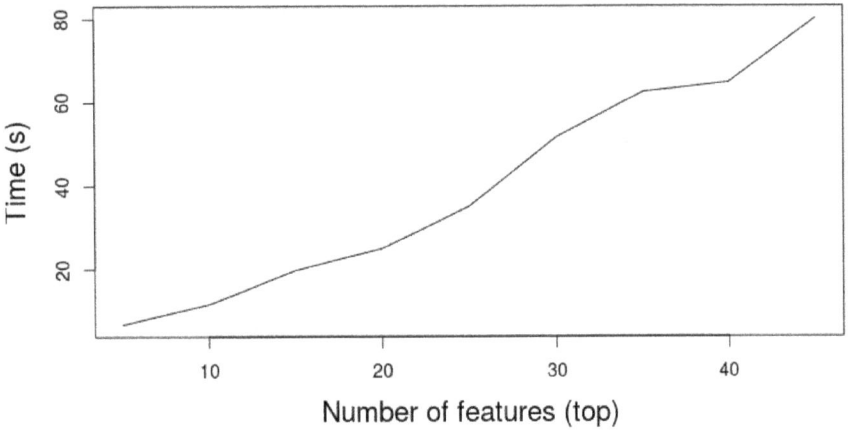

Fig. 8: Number of features vs training time.

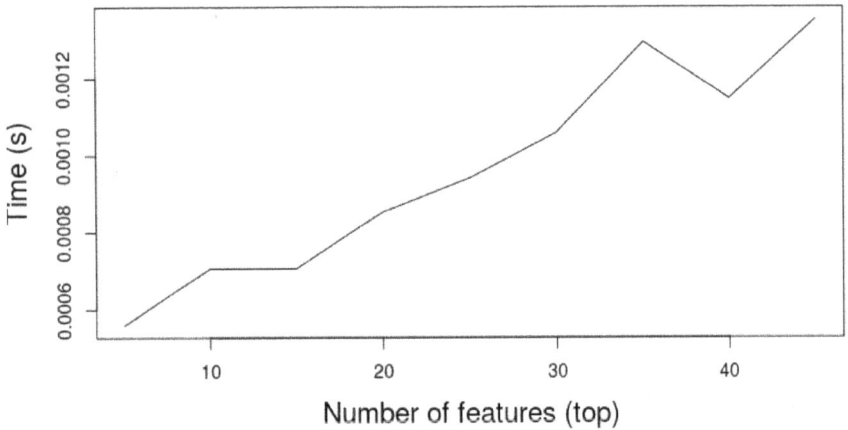

Fig. 9: Number of features vs testing time (per test case).

negatives are more critical than false positives though the latter would affect user convenience. As per this analysis, using top 10 importance features would be the best combination in terms of computational cost and false alarm rates.

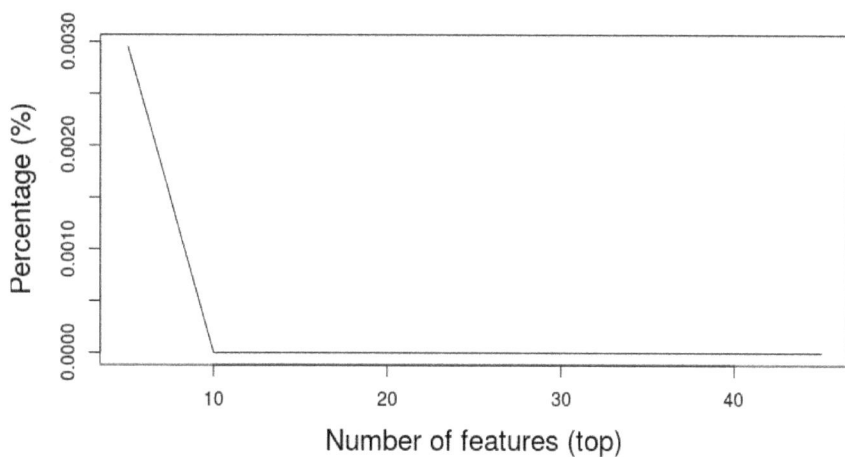

Fig. 10: Number of features vs false positive rates.

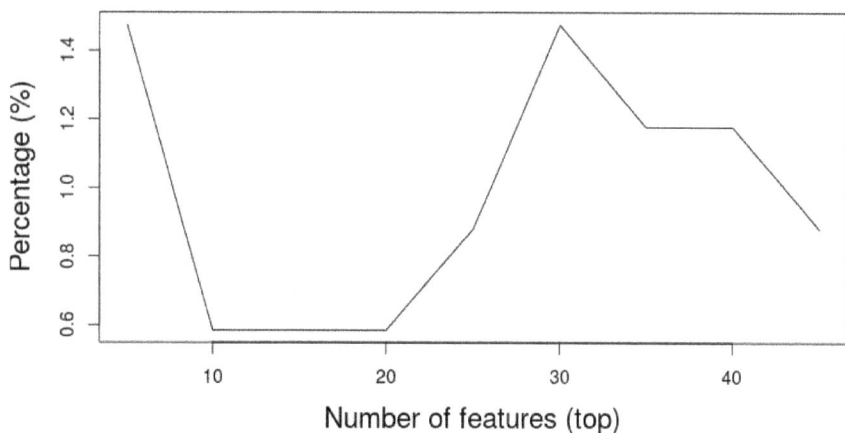

Fig. 11: Number of features vs false negative rates.

5.3. *Monitoring for other activities*

As explained in Section 4.1.2, ability to detect any intruder activities simulated in the data set will stop the attacker reaching final stage of the attack where exfiltration, corruption and disruption happen, and hence can be

Data Science for Cyber-Security

Victim IP: all nodes

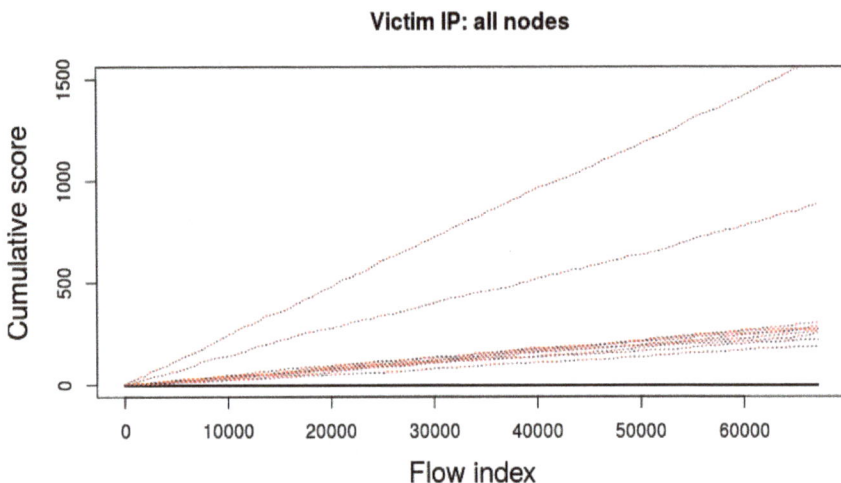

Fig. 12: Profile scores: Cumulative scores of all nodes in the network while being a target of all possible malicious activities including reconnaissance. Victims of malicious activities are denoted by red dotted lines.

considered as an early detection. Therefore, this section briefly investigates ability to employ the proposed method to detect other intruder activities included in the data set.

We use the entire data set, without excluding any specific type of malicious activities, to produce the cumulative and Z-sore graphs as mentioned above. Figures 12 and 13 presents the cumulative and Z-score graphs respectively. Red dotted lines denote the victim nodes of different attack activities simulated in the data set. Note that it includes the same victim IPs mentioned in Section 5.1. Readers should notice the changes to the limits of cumulative scores in Figure 12. Its value increases from 40 (in Figure 5) to 1,500 for one node. This has happened due to the contribution of other activities to increment node score in addition to the reconnaissance. While this helps to spot that node quickly, at the same time it influences the values of the test statistic of other nodes to suppress (see Figure 13). However, in practice, this won't be a problem since as soon as a highly deviated victim is spotted and stopped, the rest of the nodes start to stand out as μ_W, σ_W and T adjust according to the current state of the network. Therefore, higher numbers of suspicious activities are better for early detection using the proposed method.

Z-scores: all nodes

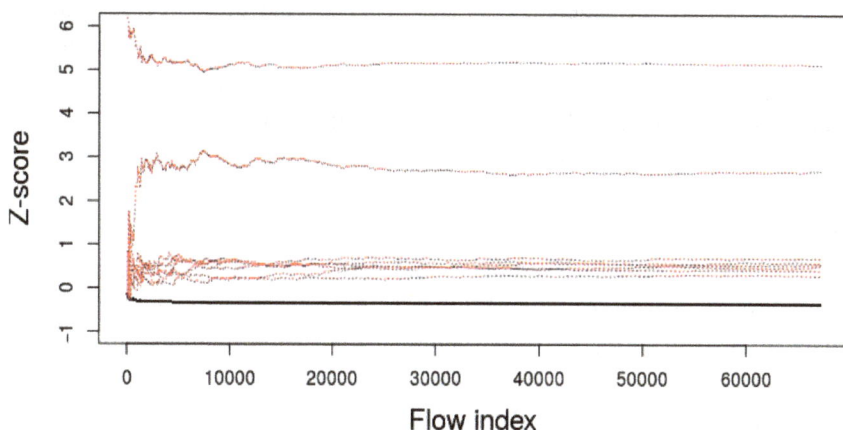

Fig. 13: Profile scores: Z-scores of all nodes in the network while being a target of all possible malicious activities including reconnaissance. Victims of malicious activities are denoted by red dotted lines.

6. Related Literature

An extensive survey of collaborative intrusion detection proposals can be found in Zhou *et al.* (2010). Collaborative intrusion detection works aim at sharing, correlating and cooperatively analysing sensor data collected from a number of organisations located in different geographical locations and hence producing early warnings on ongoing malicious activities. An infrastructure and organisational framework for situational awareness and early warning system is presented in Grobauer *et al.* (2006). eDare (Early Detection, Alert and Response system) (Elovici *et al.*, 2007) and the Agent-based CEWS (Bsufka *et al.*, 2006) are similar efforts. However, information exchange can be seen as a major barrier for CEWS' advances. The Internet motion sensor, a globally scoped Internet monitoring system, statistically analyses dark net traffic that needs to be interpreted by humans (Bailey *et al.*, 2005). DShield internet storm centre collects firewall and IDS logs world-wide and incorporates human interpretation and action in order to generate predictions and advice (Zhou *et al.*, 2010), while eCSIRT.net[c] comprises

---

[c]http://www.ecsirt.net/.

a sensor network which collects and correlates alerts for human inspection. DeepSight intelligence collects, analyses and delivers cyber threat
information through an editable portal and datafeeds, enabling proactive
defensive actions and improved incident response.[d] Human analysis and
data mining is incorporated in order to provide statistics. In the context of
security, data and information sharing is difficult between different organisations and nations due to various reasons (Brunner *et al.*, 2011; Koch *et al.*,
2013).

Situational awareness is an essential part of a CEWS, which includes
awareness of suspicious network-related activities that can take place at all
levels in the TCP/IP stack (Franke and Brynielsson, 2014). Such activity can
range from low-level network sniffing to suspicious linguistic contents on
social media. Various network measurements and techniques (e.g., packet
inter arrival times (Harmer *et al.*, 2011), deep packet inspection (King *et al.*,
2012), game theory (He *et al.*, 2009)) have been employed. The idea for a
common operational picture (big picture) is presented (Cheng *et al.*, 2012;
Preden *et al.*, 2011). A systematic review of cyber situational awareness can
be found in Franke and Brynielsson (2014). However instead of addressing
the full complexity, the above solutions concentrate on a particular issue of
the problem, and some solutions (e.g., deep packet inspection) are neither
feasible in practice nor suitable for real-time analysis yet.

Sensing in-progress attacks requires strategically placed sensors
throughout the cyberspace. Current sensor networks for CEWS have a simple monolithic structure (Theilmann, 2010), where data is acquired at the
network edges and then transmitted over a dumb infrastructure to a central
location for analysis. This can cause various issues to the analysis due to
many reasons such as nonidentical measurements, nonidentical local detectors and noisy channels (Aldosari *et al.*, 2007). High computational cost is
another significant issue. Hence, computationally fast and accurate methodology to evaluate the error, detection and false alarm probabilities in such
networks is essential. Optimal sensor placement strategies for CEWS are
discussed in Göbel and Trinius (2010). Authors study correlation between
attack patterns of different locations (national and international) and explore
how sensors should be located accordingly. The design and analysis of

---

[d]http://www.symantec.com/deepsight-products.

sensor networks for detection applications has received considerable attention during past decades (Varshney, 1997).

In order to early warn, fusion of different network measurements from different sources is essential. Fusion of cyber-related information from a variety of resources including commercial news, blogs, wikis and social media sources is proposed in Morris *et al.* (2011). Bayesian fusion for slow activity monitoring (Chivers *et al.*, 2013; Kalutarage *et al.*, 2015), high-speed information fusion for real-time situational awareness (Sudit *et al.*, 2005), JDL data fusion model for computer networks (Schreiber-Ehle and Koch, 2012), detecting network data patterns (Paffenroth *et al.*, 2013), combining data from sensors using ontology methods (Mathews *et al.*, 2012) and fusing security audit data with data from a psychological model (Greitzer and Frincke, 2010) to mention a few. Using web-based text as a source for identifying emerging and ongoing attacks can be found in Grothoff *et al.* (2011).

An open, adaptable and extensible visual analytic framework is provided in Jonker *et al.* (2012). All data is treated as streaming and visualised using machine learning techniques (Harrison *et al.*, 2012). A live network situational awareness system that relies upon streaming algorithms (Streilein *et al.*, 2011), fast calculations of important statistical properties of high-speed and high-volume data (Streilein *et al.*, 2011), sophisticated visualisation of attack paths and automatic recommendations for mitigation (Jajodia *et al.*, 2011) are some interesting works.

Threat scenario provides an important aspect to the early warning discussion. For example, early warning on malware propagation can be easier than warning on a DOS attack. Focus on early warning of a particular threat type is common (for example Apel *et al.*, 2010; Engelberth *et al.*, 2010; Kollias *et al.*, 2014; Magkos *et al.*, 2013; Zou *et al.*, 2003). A malware warning centre is proposed in Zou *et al.* (2003), while Engelberth *et al.* (2010) aims for distributed and large-scale malware on the Internet. A worm propagation stochastic model is built (Magkos *et al.*, 2013). Authors propose a logical framework for a distributed early warning system against unknown and fast-spreading worms. An open-source early warning system to estimate the threat level and the malicious activities across the Internet is provided (Kollias *et al.*, 2014). Limiting to a certain threat type is a major drawback of these proposals. They cannot simply extend for newly emerging threats.

7. Research Challenges

Traditional defences are simply not a match for today's adversaries as less than 1 percent of successful advanced threat attacks are spotted by SIEM systems, according to the Verizon 2014 Data Breach Investigations Report.[e] Once passed through the perimeter defences, the attackers persist for long periods of time and manage to maintain seemingly legitimate actions. Hence, continuous monitoring of behaviour of systems/users is required. Unlike most traditional solutions which focus on one or two steps in the attack life cycle, as shown in this work, our proposed method can counter an adversary's activities at early stages of the attack life cycle. As a result, by analysing the data and following the digital footprints of the attacker, security professional can focus on disrupting the adversary's attack before he or she can achieve their goal. However, ability to early warn depends upon three factors: the progression rate of attack life cycle (e.g., a malware propagation vs DOS attack), amount of evidence accessible at each stage and the ability to acquire such evidence by sensors. The rest of the section highlights a few challenges associated with these factors.

7.1. *Generic set of indicators*

In other domains such as natural disasters (e.g., tsunami), early warnings are well established and arguably simple when compared to early warnings on the cyberspace. For example, in kinetic warfare, intelligence officers study different sources of intelligence (e.g., listen to communications, satellite imagery) to look for known preliminary indicators of military mobilisation. In medical diagnosis, preliminary indicators such as feeling thirsty, tired, losing weight and blurred vision act as an early warning system in an individual for diabetes. But on the cyberspace, it is not clear what these indicators are or how they can be observed (Robinson *et al.*, 2015). This presents a huge problem when trying to develop CEWS. As some scholars argue (Robinson *et al.*, 2015; Sharma *et al.*, 2010), CEWS cannot be developed from a purely technical perspective. They must consider more than just technical indicators and require significant input from other disciplines such as international relations and sociology since the focus of CEWS should be

---

[e]http://www.verizonenterprise.com/resources/reports/rp_Verizon-DBIR-2014_en_xg.pdf.

to warn of an impending attack rather than detecting when it in progress. However the biggest challenge, a generic set of indicators (signs) of preparation for an attack on the cyberspace is not well established (understood) yet (Kalutarage *et al.*, 2016). One might propose to apply deep learning for automatic feature extraction as it works very well in some other domains (e.g., object recognition). But cyber data is infinite, rapidly changing, varying and with a high concept drift. Hence, it is very difficult to set up norm shapes for malicious (e.g., zero-day attacks) and even for the benign class since the normality is changing rapidly over time.

7.2. *Gathering evidence, integrity and retention*

The cyberspace has a huge diversity. It consists of different topological structures (e.g., PAN, LAN, MAN, WAN), different kind of networks (e.g., open Internet, darknet, honeynet, demilitarised zones) and different types of users (e.g., universities, health care systems, traffic systems, SCADA systems, trade, military networks). These entities produce events at different types and rates and have different analysis objectives and privacy requirements. In order to provide a representative image of the cyberspace at any given time, CEWS have to collect and process data from a range of these different entities. Employing a large monolithic sensor network for intelligence gathering on the cyberspace would not be possible due to these variations. Data integrity and retention would be another concern. No matter how persuasive evidence may be, it could be thrown out of the court if altered during the collection process. Hence, integrity should be maintained throughout the monitoring process and proved.

7.3. *Information fusion*

As mentioned earlier, CEWS has to gather information from various heterogeneous sources. Given the huge number of possible data sources and overwhelming amount of data they generate, a data reduction method is essential to enable continuous security monitoring (Dempsey, 2011). Future CEWS require fusing as many data sources as possible. Though it is not an exhaustive list, some possible data sources for this task would be network data traffic, log files, social media, mobile location traces, mobile call traffic, web browsing traces, content popularity, user preferences, spatial/geographic distribution of network elements, network topology (router and AS level), network paths, protocol traces, social network structure and other security intelligence, either at a system or social level.

7.4. *Training, verifying and testing data*

Getting validity for a novel method is only possible through a proper evaluation. In this research area, it is necessary to have good representative data samples as network data is infinite, changing, varying and with a high concept drift. Before deployment on live systems, machine learning algorithms need to verify precisely to find their performance against real data. But real network traffic traces with ground truth data on attack activities are difficult to obtain. Any such effort faces uncertainty of success in investigating relevant patterns of activity. Evaluation of novel algorithms against production network is also difficult. Currently, three alternative methods are available: using benchmark data sets, network simulators/emulators and network test beds. Each method has pros and cons. In particular, benchmark data sets have several limitations. They are not representative to every possible situations of a live network (biased). Hence, working against one data set does not guarantee a proposed method works in all situations. Developing monitoring algorithms based on benign class (e.g., unary classification) would be another option, because finding benign samples is relatively easier than malicious samples.

7.5. *Uncertainty reasoning*

The cyberspace is an uncertain place. Hence, cyber defenders have to deal with a great deal of uncertainty (Kalutarage, 2013; Kalutarage *et al.*, 2015) which is compounded by the nature of computing. Any future CEWS that seeks to model and reason on the cyberspace has to accept this ground truth and must deal with incompleteness (compensate for lack of knowledge), inconsistencies (resolve ambiguities and contradictions) and change (update the knowledge base over time). For example, entering a misspelled password can be a simple mistake by an innocent user or a password guessing attempt by an attacker. Cyber defenders do not know who the attackers are nor their location. Some suspicious events can appear as part of an attack or can originate from normal network activities. For example, a major router failure could generate many ICMP unreachable messages, while some computer worms (e.g., CodeRed and Nimda) generate the same in active probing process. The subtlest change in activity and context would be the key to narrow down the meaning of such data (Kalutarage *et al.*, 2015). Adversaries often operate in the grey area of security decisions, as a result existing security solutions produce significant amount of false alarms. In production environments, security analysts have to analyse these alarms and decide what to act on and what to ignore by utilising their cognitive abilities. Therefore, incorporating cognitive abilities with CEWS would be one way to move forward. Such systems should utilise data mining, machine learning and natural language processing to mimic the way analysts build their body of knowledge through self-learning.

References

Aldosari, S., Moura, J. M. *et al.* (2007). Detection in sensor networks: The saddlepoint approximation, *Signal Processing, IEEE Transactions on* **55**, 1, pp. 327–340.

Apel, M., Biskup, J., Flegel, U. and Meier, M. (2010). Towards early warning systems– challenges, technologies and architecture, in *Critical Information Infrastructures Security*, pp. 151–164, Springer, Berlin, Heidelberg.

Bailey, M., Cooke, E., Jahanian, F., Nazario, J., Watson, D. *et al.* (2005). The internet motion sensor-a distributed blackhole monitoring system, in *The 12th Annual Symposium on Network and Distributed Security Security (NDSS), 2005*.

Biskup, J., Hämmerli, B., Meier, M., Schmerl, S., Tölle, J. and Vogel, M. (2008). 2. 08102 working group — Early warning systems, in G. Carle, F. Dressler, R. A. Kemmerer, H. König and C. Kruegel. eds., *Perspectives Workshop: Network Attack Detection and Defense*, no. 08102 in Dagstuhl Seminar Proceedings, Schloss Dagstuhl — Leibniz-Zentrum fuer Informatik, Germany, Dagstuhl, Germany.

Breiman, L. (2001). Random forests, *Machine Learning* **45**, 1, pp. 5–32.

Brunner, M., Hofinger, H., Roblee, C., Schoo, P. and Todt, S. (2011). Anonymity and privacy in distributed early warning systems, in *Critical Information Infrastructures Security*, pp. 81–92, Springer, Berlin, Heidelberg.

Bsufka, K., Kroll-Peters, O. and Albayrak, S. (2006). Intelligent network-based early warning systems, in *Critical Information Infrastructures Security*, pp. 103–111, Springer, Berlin, Heidelberg.

Cheng, Y., Sagduyu, Y., Deng, J., Li, J. and Liu, P. (2012). Integrated situational awareness for cyber attack detection, analysis, and mitigation, in *SPIE Defense, Security, and Sensing*, pp. 83850N–83850N.

Chivers, H., Clark, J. A., Nobles, P., Shaikh, S. A. and Chen, H. (2013). Knowing who to watch: Identifying attackers whose actions are hidden within false alarms and background noise, *Information Systems Frontiers* **15**, 1, pp. 17–34.

Dempsey, K. (2011). *Information Security Continuous Monitoring (ISCM) for Federal Information Systems and Organizations*, US Department of Commerce, National Institute of Standards and Technology.

Elovici, Y., Shabtai, A., Moskovitch, R., Tahan, G. and Glezer, C. (2007). Applying machine learning techniques for detection of malicious code in network traffic, in *KI 2007: Advances in Artificial Intelligence*, pp. 44–50, Springer, Berlin, Heidelberg.

Engelberth, M., C. Freiling, F., Gbel, J., Gorecki, C., Holz, T., Hund, R., Trinius, P. and Willems, C. (2010). The InMAS approach, in *1st European Workshop on Internet Early Warning and Network Intelligence (EWNI), 2010*, pp. 1–14.

Franke, U. and Brynielsson, J. (2014). Cyber situational awareness — a systematic review of the literature, *Computers & Security* **46**, pp. 18–31.

Göbel, J. and Trinius, P. (2010). Towards optimal sensor placement strategies for early warning systems. in *Sicherheit*, pp. 191–204.

Golling, M. and Stelte, B. (2011). Requirements for a future ews-cyber defence in the internet of the future, in *Cyber conflict (ICCC), 2011 3rd international conference on*, pp. 1–16.

Greitzer, F. L. and Frincke, D. A. (2010). Combining traditional cyber security audit data with psychosocial data: Towards predictive modeling for insider threat mitigation, in *Insider Threats in Cyber Security*, pp. 85–113, Springer, Boston, MA.

Grobauer, B., Mehlau, J. I. and Sander, J. (2006). Carmentis: A co-operative approach towards situation awareness and early warning for the internet, in *International Conference on IT-Incident Management & ITForensics (IMF), 2006*, pp. 55–66.

Grothoff, K., Brunner, M., Hofinger, H., Roblee, C. and Eckert, C. (2011). Problems in web-based open source information processing for it early warning, URL: https://e-reports-ext.llnl.gov/pdf/486769.pdf.

Harmer, P., Thomas, R., Christel, B., Martin, R. and Watson, C. (2011). Wireless security situation awareness with attack identification decision support, in *2011 IEEE Symposium on Computational Intelligence in Cyber Security (CICS)*, pp. 144–151.

Harrison, L., Laska, J., Spahn, R., Iannacone, M., Downing, E., Ferragut, E. M. and Goodall, J. R. (2012). situ: Situational understanding and discovery for cyber attacks, in *2012 IEEE Conference on Visual Analytics Science and Technology (VAST)*, pp. 307–308.

He, H., Xiaojing, W. and Xin, Y. (2009). A decision-support model for information systems based on situational awareness, in *International Conference on Multimedia Information Networking and Security, 2009, MINES '09*, Vol. 2, pp. 405–408.

Jajodia, S., Noel, S., Kalapa, P., Albanese, M. and Williams, J. (2011). Cauldron mission-centric cyber situational awareness with defense in depth, in *Military Communications Conference, 2011 — MILCOM 2011*, pp. 1339–1344.

Jonker, D., Langevin, S., Schretlen, P. and Canfield, C. (2012). Agile visual analytics for banking cyber "big data", in *IEEE Conference on Visual Analytics Science and Technology (VAST), 2012*, pp. 299–300.

Kalutarage, H. (2013). *Effective Monitoring of Slow Suspicious Activities on Computer Networks*, Ph.D. thesis, Coventry University.

Kalutarage, H., Shaikh, S., Lee, B.-S., Lee, C. and Kiat, Y. C. (2016). *Early Warning Systems for Cyber Defence*, pp. 29–42, Springer International Publishing, Cham.

Kalutarage, H. K., Shaikh, S. A., Wickramasinghe, I. P., Zhou, Q. and James, A. E. (2015). Detecting stealthy attacks: Efficient monitoring of suspicious activities on computer networks, *Computers & Electrical Engineering* **47**, pp. 327–344.

Kalutarage, H. K., Shaikh, S. A., Zhou, Q. and James, A. E. (2012). Sensing for suspicion at scale: A Bayesian approach for cyber conflict attribution and reasoning, in *2012 4th International Conference on Cyber Conflict (CYCON)*, pp. 1–19.

Kalutarage, H. K., Shaikh, S. A., Zhou, Q. and James, A. E. (2013). Monitoring for slow suspicious activities using a target centric approach, in *Information Systems Security*, pp. 163–168, Springer.

King, D., Orlando, G. and Kohler, J. (2012). A case for trusted sensors: encryptors with deep packet inspection capabilities, in *Military Communication Conference, MILCOM 2012*, pp. 1–6.

Koch, R., Golling, M. and Dreo, G. (2013). Evaluation of State of the Art IDS Message Exchange Protocols, *International Journal of Electrical, Computer, Energetic, Electronic and Communication Engineering* **7**, 8, pp. 1017–1026.

Kollias, S., Vlachos, V., Papanikolaou, A., Chatzimisios, P., Ilioudis, C. and Metaxiotis, K. (2014). Measuring the internet's threat level: A global-local approach, in *2014 IEEE Symposium on Computers and Communication (ISCC)*, pp. 1–6.

Liaw, A. and Wiener, M. (2002). Classification and regression by randomForest, *R news* **2**, 3, pp. 18–22.

Magkos, E., Avlonitis, M., Kotzanikolaou, P. and Stefanidakis, M. (2013). Toward early warning against internet worms based on critical-sized networks, *Security and Communication Networks* **6**, 1, pp. 78–88.

Mathews, M. L., Halvorsen, P., Joshi, A. and Finin, T. (2012). A collaborative approach to situational awareness for cybersecurity, in *2012 8th International Conference on Collaborative Computing: Networking, Applications and Worksharing (Collaborate-Com)*, pp. 216–222.

Morris, T., Mayron, L., Smith, W., Knepper, M., Ita, R. and Fox, K. (2011). A perceptually-relevant model-based cyber threat prediction method for enterprise mission assurance, in *2011 IEEE First International Multi-Disciplinary Conference on Cognitive Methods in Situation Awareness and Decision Support (CogSIMA)*, pp. 60–65, doi: 10.1109/COGSIMA.2011.5753755.

Moustafa, N. and Slay, J. (2016). The evaluation of network anomaly detection systems: Statistical analysis of the unsw-nb15 data set and the comparison with the kdd99 data set, *Information Security Journal: A Global Perspective* **25**, 1–3, pp. 18–31.

Paffenroth, R., Du Toit, P., Nong, R., Scharf, L., Jayasumana, A. P. and Bandara, V. (2013). Space-time signal processing for distributed pattern detection in sensor networks, *IEEE Journal of Selected Topics in Signal Processing* **7**, 1, pp. 38–49.

Preden, J., Motus, L., Meriste, M. and Riid, A. (2011). Situation awareness for networked systems, in *2011 IEEE First International Multi-Disciplinary Conference on Cognitive Methods in Situation Awareness and Decision Support (CogSIMA)*, pp. 123–130, doi:10.1109/COGSIMA.2011.5753430.

Robinson, M., Jones, K. and Janicke, H. (2015). Cyber warfare: Issues and challenges, *Computers & Security* **49**, pp. 70–94.

Schreiber-Ehle, S. and Koch, W. (2012). The JDL model of data fusion applied to cyber-defence: a review paper, in *2012 Workshop on Sensor Data Fusion (SDF): Trends, Solutions, Applications*, pp. 116–119.

Shaikh, S. A. and Kalutarage, H. K. (2016). Effective network security monitoring: from attribution to target-centric monitoring, *Telecommunication Systems* **62**, 1, pp. 167–178.

Sharma, A., Gandhi, R., Mahoney, W., Sousan, W., Zhu, Q. *et al.* (2010). Building a social dimensional threat model from current and historic events of cyber attacks, in *2010 IEEE Second International Conference on Social Computing (SocialCom)*, pp. 981–986.

Streilein, W. W., Truelove, J., Meiners, C. R. and Eakman, G. (2011). Cyber situational awareness through operational streaming analysis, in *Military Communication Conference, MILCOM 2011*, pp. 1152–1157.

Sudit, M., Stotz, A. and Holender, M. (2005). Situational awareness of a coordinated cyber attack, in *Data Mining, Intrusion Detection, Information Assurance, and Data Networks Security*, pp. 114–129, International Society for Optics and Photonics, Orlando, Florida.

Theilmann, A. (2010). Beyond centralism: The herold approach to sensor networks and early warning systems, in *Proceedings of First European Workshop of Internet Early Warning and Network Intelligence (EWNI 2010)*.

Varshney, P. K. (1997). *Distributed Detection and Data Fusion*, Springer Science & Business Media, New York.

Zhou, C. V., Leckie, C. and Karunasekera, S. (2010). A survey of coordinated attacks and collaborative intrusion detection, *Computers & Security* **29**, 1, pp. 124–140.

Zou, C. C., Gao, L., Gong, W. and Towsley, D. (2003). Monitoring and early warning for internet worms, in *Proceedings of the 10th ACM Conference on Computer and Communications Security*, pp. 190–199.

Chapter 6

Anomaly Detection on User-Agent Strings

Eirini Spyropoulou*, Jordan Noble[†]
and Christoforos Anagnostopoulos[‡,§]

*Barclays, UK
[†]Imperial College London, UK
[‡]Mentat, UK

[§]*canagnos@ment.at*

Malicious software often uses HTTP traffic to penetrate an organisation or communicate with its command and control centre. This type of traffic is hidden in vast amounts of legitimate HTTP traffic, often remaining undetected. Signature-based techniques for detecting such traffic are only useful for known malware types. Anomaly detection techniques attempt instead to understand how HTTP traffic typically looks like, and flag any abnormal behaviour for further scrutiny. One aspect of HTTP traffic is captured by the user-agent string (UAS), a field of the HTTP header containing information about the application and operating system used by the client. Typically corresponding to a browser, it allows servers to determine which type of content to deliver to the client so that it is properly rendered. Malware will sometimes masquerade as a browser, which requires them to fake the UAS, making it an interesting feature to consider when looking for suspicious activity in HTTP traffic. In this chapter, we present an anomaly detection method for UASs that relies on a novel and efficient approach for computing distances between UASs on large amounts of data.

1. Introduction

Cybersecurity is in many ways the ultimate needle-in-a-haystack problem. Users generate vast amounts of normal traffic via their use of legitimate applications, and cyber attacks explicitly attempt to masquerade as normal traffic to evade detection. For a large enterprise, the task of detecting attacks

127

represents an attempt to spot a handful of abnormal events in terabytes of legitimate traffic. Traditionally, the approach involved the use of fixed signatures, which meant that the task at hand was one of *search*, rather than *learning*: vast amounts of logs had to be searched for occurrences of these known signatures. This approach is still valid today, and has been augmented by the use of *indicators of compromise*: attributes of traffic that are not unique signatures of malware *per se*, but are rather known to be associated with some degree of probability to malicious actors. Both approaches benefit from their simplicity, and scalability, as they fundamentally rely on search. However, they suffer from a major drawback: they can only identify malware or malicious activity that is identical to past, known examples of such behaviour. This is a problem for several reasons. First, as cyber criminals evolve in an attempt to evade detection, they use a number of techniques to obfuscate and randomise their code which result in absence or near-absence of fixed signatures (Scott, 2017; Shackleford, 2016). Second, for a fixed signature to become known, it has to be detected or reported to a security vendor. Given the general acknowledgement that only a small number of actual threats are ever detected or reported, this is bound to compromise the degree of protection offered by this approach.

Machine learning seeks to fill this void, by using predictive methodology to detect previously unseen threats. There are two main approaches. Supervised techniques attempt to generalise from previously seen threats in order to detect novel ones (Pfahringer, 2000). In practice, these methods tend to succeed in detecting variations of existing threats, rather than altogether novel approaches (e.g., zero-day threats). Moreover, they require a large number of labelled examples, which is sorely lacking in cybersecurity. Attention has therefore recently shifted away from classification approaches towards unsupervised approaches based on anomaly detection. These focus instead on normal, legitimate traffic, and attempt to profile it sufficiently well so that any activity by an external actor will immediately seem out-of-place and can be flagged for scrutiny.

Large enterprise security in principle holds an advantageous position with respect to anomaly detection techniques: due to software controls and centralised IT, as well as a relatively disciplined work environment, variability within the network is likely to be far smaller than variability outside it. For example, it is very likely that at any given point, all Windows computers in a given enterprise will be using the same version of Internet Explorer. Despite this relative homogeneity, the variation within the network remains vast, with thousands of applications generating terabytes of daily traffic, and cannot possibly be captured by human visual inspection. Moreover, homogeneity itself is slowly eroding, with the advent of bring-your-own-device and flexible working policies. Scalable technologies to assist cyber defenders in "knowing-their-network" are therefore more pertinent than ever.

In this work, we focus on one slice of cyber activity, namely, HTTP traffic. Malware uses the HTTP protocol for two phases of a cyber attack: delivery, i.e., when a malware manages to download itself to a machine by someone clicking on a malicious link or visiting a website that has been compromised; and command and control, i.e., when previously installed malware communicates to its command and control centre to accomplish its goal. HTTP headers can be logged by proxy servers that are situated at the edge of the network, between clients and the Internet. These logs can then be analysed to detect malicious traffic.

One of the fields of the HTTP header is the user-agent string (UAS), a string which is automatically populated by the browser or application making the request and includes information about the name, version and type of the application or browser as well as the name, version and type of the operating system. Malware might try to blend in with the normal traffic by mimicking one of the well-known UASs, or try to take advantage of the fact that the UAS need not follow a pre-specified format, in order to use it to communicate to its command and control centre. This masking attempt can often go wrong, which motivates the detection of anomalous UAS. There have even been cases of attacks that used the UAS as part of the payload, with a notable example being Shellshock (Graham-Cumming, 2014).

In this chapter, we study the UAS in depth and propose an anomaly detector that relies on a bespoke distance metric. Our framework is generalisable to other semi-structured logs, such as URIs, or even system logs. We present the results of an empirical study showing great promise.

2. Problem Definition and Methodological Approach

The purpose of this paper is to develop a methodology for the detection of suspicious-looking UASs, given a large number of unlabelled UASs.

The main challenge in applying anomaly detection on UAS data, besides the fact that it is not numerical, is that the UASs do not adhere to specific rules about their format. Indeed, in principle, any string can be a UAS. In the case of browsers, a number of conventions have evolved that need to be respected in order for the server to understand how to render the content. Nevertheless, a lot of variability is still present. It is notable that in one of the real-world proxy logs data sets we analysed, 23% of unique UASs were Internet Explorer, amounting to many thousands of possible variations.

As with any unstructured format, we have at our disposal two different methodological approaches. We could either *featurise* the strings, by converting each UAS into a numeric vector whose components quantify different aspects of the string (e.g., the presence/absence of a specific token, or its length) and then proceed with standard tools, or we could define a distance metric that quantifies the distance (respectively, the similarity) between any two strings, and then use it as the kernel of our chosen machine learning method. The latter approach is particularly powerful in the case of strings, because, unlike in featurisation, it does not assume a fixed dictionary of tokens and can be robust to typos/variations. In the case of UASs any dictionary of tokens will quickly become obsolete as version numbers and new applications arise. Moreover, tokenisation itself is challenging, given the lack of standardised formats and the inconsistent use of separators and space.

As is generally the case in cyber-security research, there is a lack of explicit labelled data. This is due to a perfect storm of massive data, highly imbalanced classes with genuine attacks being very rare and a fast-paced environment that quickly renders past examples of attacks obsolete. Therefore, we opt for an unsupervised approach, which relies on the key insight that the vast majority of enterprise traffic is benign in order to flag any events that fail to follow the norm as possibly malicious.

In unsupervised techniques, expert knowledge can be used in making an appropriate choice of distance metric. For example, users can be asked to group objects according to their similarity, and this can be used as a test case for the distance metric. We performed such an exercise with the cyber security team of a large organisation, and we modified standard string distance metrics to agree with these expert insights.

To set the scene, we start by introducing the idiosyncrasies of the UAS in Section 2.1. In Section 2.2, we proceed to review standard methods for measuring distance between strings, their shortcomings in the case at hand and how these can be overcome. Finally, in Section 2.3 we discuss how one-class classifiers and outlier detection techniques can be combined with our choice of distance metric to yield an unsupervised anomaly detector. Results are presented in Section 3, where we aim to distinguish between two different data sets, one of which represents data observed in a high-risk, honeypot environment.

2.1. *UAS data format*

In its raw form, a UAS is a string comprising both alphanumeric and special characters. For most applications, the string is not entirely unstructured, but that structure varies across different applications as well as, sometimes, within applications. The vast majority of UASs found in the wild are generated by web browsers, in which case they are fairly structured as seen in Table 1. For example, the last entry represents an Internet Explorer browser (`Mozilla/4.0 compatible`) of version 6 (`MSIE 6.0`) running on a Windows NT operating system (`Windows NT 5.1`) with an Opera rendering engine (`Opera 7.54`). Attempts to parse and tokenise the UAS can be quite successful in the case of browsers and other applications that employ a standard format. Because of a non-standard use of separators, a

Table 1: A list of browser UASs.

```
Mozilla/4.0 (compatible; MSIE 5.0; Windows NT 5.1;
  PlaceWare Quicksilver 5.1.2.213)
```

```
Mozilla/4.0 (compatible; MSIE 6 0; Windows NT 5.1)
```

```
Mozilla/4.0 (compatible; MSIE 6.0; AOL 8.0;
  Windows NT 5.1; SV1; .NET CLR 1.1.4322)
```

```
Mozilla/4.0 (compatible; MSIE 6.0; AOL 9.0;
  Windows NT 5.1; .NET CLR 1.1.4322)
```

```
Mozilla/4.0 (compatible; MSIE 6.0; AOL 9.0;
  Windows NT 5.1; FunWebProducts; .NET CLR 1.0.3705)
```

```
Mozilla/4.0 (compatible; MSIE 6.0; America Online Browser 1.0;
  Windows NT 5.1)
```

```
Mozilla/4.0 (compatible; MSIE 6.0; MSIE 5.5; Windows NT 5.1)
  Opera 7.01 [en]
```

```
Mozilla/4.0 (compatible; MSIE 6.0; Windows NT 5.1)
```

```
Mozilla/4.0 (compatible; MSIE 6.0; Windows NT 5.1) Java/1.4.2_06
```

```
Mozilla/4.0 (compatible; MSIE 6.0; Windows NT 5.1) Opera 7.54 [en]
```

Table 2: A list of non-standard UASs.

```
Datek Streamer v 6.6.4-8508954355968836270
Poller|1.1.0.0|-62043859|0
Eudora/6.2.3b5 (MacOS)
JNLP/1.0.1 javaws/1.4.2_06 (b03) J2SE/1.4.2_06
AVGINET 70FREE AVI=266.11.1 BUILD=308
  LIC=70FREE-TX-L7Z2U-IB-P1-C01-SIJTY-QEN
  UID={7202675E-49F5-4443-8C8F-6800A3BA21B1}
```

simple splitting strategy can sometimes fail. Alternatives include an iterative search over regex patterns,[a] or context-free grammars (CFG) as in Zhang *et al.* (2015) to allow for better handling of nested structures. These approaches are mostly aimed at *classification*, wherein the objective is to assert which application generated the UAS, out of a list of known applications. They also try to extract detailed information, such as the version of the operating system, which relies on successful parsing of the entire string. There is value in these type of approaches: for example, all traffic from a given host should agree on the version number of the operating system, which renders a mismatch on the operating system version strong evidence of some sort of abnormality.

Unfortunately, the pure syntactic approach does not scale: as we steer clear of browsers, we encounter a fat tail of innumerable, less common applications, which generally fail to adhere to a strict syntax. Some examples are given in Table 2. For example, rules that extract version numbers from browser UASs would have some success with `Datek Streamer` but none with `AVGINET`. Another notable feature is the inclusion of hashes, or very long identifier strings, especially in the case of antivirus updates.

This discussion motivates a hybrid approach that simultaneously takes advantage of the rich structure of browser UASs while still being able to account for the large variability in the non-browser case. We therefore represent each UAS as a structured object with four parts:

(1) "prefix": A single "token-version" tuple, e.g., (`'Mozilla'`, `'4.0'`).
(2) "device": An array of token-version tuples, comprising information about the device. For many applications, this is typically included in the first set of parentheses encountered.

---

[a]The Browserscope project: https://github.com/tobie/ua-parser.

Table 3: Flexibly parsed UASs.

Raw: 'Mozilla/4.0 (Compatible; MSIE 6.0)'
Parsed: {'additional': [],
'device': [('Compatible', ' '), ('MSIE', '6.0')],
'prefix': ('Mozilla', '4.0'),
'unparsable': "}
Raw: 'AIM/5.9.3702
Parsed: {'additional': [],
'device': [],
'prefix': ('AIM', '5.9.3702'),
'unparsable': ' '}
Raw: 'Aquarium/2.1.2 (Windows 2000 Workstation ver 5.1)'
Parsed: {'additional': [],
'device': [('Windows', '2000'), ('Workstation ver', '5.1')],
'prefix': ('Aquarium', '2.1.2'),
'unparsable': ' '}

(3) "additional": Any other token-version tuples besides the above.

(4) "unparsable": Content that cannot be parsed is not thrown away, but rather kept as a raw string.

In Table 3, we show the results of applying this flexible parser on a few example UASs. The process is not infallible, and our distance metric will take this into account. However, it tends to capture the bulk of the structure for most applications including, but not limited to, browsers: the main tokens are stripped of highly variable details such as versioning; the version numbers themselves are stored separately allowing us to operate on them separately, and the device is captured when possible.

2.2. *Distance (or similarity) metrics*

The simplest anomaly detector is based on the identity metric: we could raise an alert every time a UAS is seen for the first time. However, this suffers from a big disadvantage: we have no way of prioritising alerts, as they all appear "equally anomalous". With a data source as volatile as UASs, this is bound to generate too many false alarms that we would then be unable to triage. Instead, we wish to quantify exactly how different two UASs are. We describe several ways to achieve this in what follows, starting from general-purpose techniques to measure distance between strings.

2.2.1. *String distance metrics*

String similarity is a well-researched topic. The simplest example is the *Hamming* distance, which only applies to strings of equal length, and counts the number of places of disagreement: for example, "MSIE" and "MS1E" would have a distance of 1. The assumption that the strings are of equal length makes this an inappropriate metric. An alternative metric is the "Longest Common Subsequence", which counts the length of the longest streak of shared characters. In the example above, this would result in a score of 2. Perhaps the most general-purpose metric is the *Levenshtein* distance, which reports the number of insertions, deletions or substitutions needed to make the two strings match. It is computationally more expensive, but is robust to many real-world contaminations such as typos or shuffling of characters.

All of the above metrics treat the string as a sequence of characters. In many ways, however, we treat strings as sequences of words, or in this case, tokens, rather than sequences of characters. For example, we would treat the strings (compatible; MSIE) and (MSIE; compatible) as almost identical, but they would appear fairly distant under any metric looking at the string character by character. A metric that takes this "order-invariance" into account is the *Jaccard* distance metric, which treats strings as sets of tokens instead, and measures their overlap:

$$J(X, Y) = \frac{|X \cap Y|}{|X \cup Y|} \in [0, 1].$$

Equally, we could apply the LCS or Levenshtein metrics on a tokenised representation of the string, too, so that out-of-order tokens would still be penalised, but independently of the length of each token.

2.2.2. *Shortcomings of string distance metrics*

Generic string distances such as the Levenshtein distance serve as excellent starting points, but must be adapted to the use case to avoid being dominated by irrelevant business-specific issues. We can reveal some of its shortcomings in the case of UASs by way of a simple example. Consider the UASs in Table 4, and the example similarity matrix in Figure 1, where red indicates low similarity and blue large, according to the Levenshtein distance metric

Table 4: Flexibly parsed UASs.

```
Mozilla/4.0 (compatible; MSIE 6 0; Windows NT 5.1)
Mozilla/4.0 (compatible; MSlE 6.0; Windows NT 5.1)
Mozilla/4.0 (compatible; MSIE 6 0; Windows NT 5.2)
Mozilla/4.0 (compatible; MSIE 6.0; AOL 8.0; Windows NT 5.1;
  SV1; .NET CLR 1.1.4322)
Mozilla/4.0 (compatible; MSIE 6.0; Windows NT 5.1;
  {43EE6E71-5B19-424C-9880-28BBBF1360B9})
Mozilla/4.0 (compatible; MSIE 6.0; Windows NT 5.1;
  {FFDC043E-F471-4BC7-99CD-591998C061E3})
```

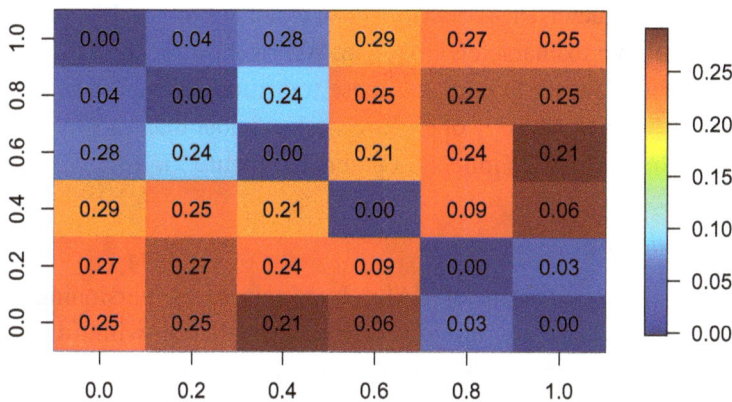

Fig. 1: Distances between the UASs of Table 4 according to the Levenshtein metric.

applied on the raw string. We collected expert feedback on these rankings and two objections were raised: the metric seems to fail to take into account the role of versioning and that of random strings in the UAS. We discuss these in turn.

2.2.3. *Random tokens*

The last two UASs in Table 4 are in fact identical, except in the last token, which is a unique identifier and is expected to differ a lot across an enterprise. Similarly, an Antivirus update will often feature a hash of the update in the UAS: clearly, in any two uploads the hashes will differ. Indeed, hashes and randomly generated identifiers will be viewed as maximally different from the perspective of a distance metric like Levenshtein. Instead, the experts view any two random-looking strings as functionally "identical": the syntax requires that, say, a hash is included at a certain point in the UAS, and that is the only thing we need to know: the actual characters forming it are irrelevant. To capture that insight, we develop a technique to replace all random-looking strings with a keyword, say, @RAND@.

The technique we use is again unsupervised. We model each token as a random sample from a first order Markov chain and compute the transition probabilities between consecutive characters. To reduce the sample space, we focus only on transitions between characters, numbers and non-alphanumeric symbols. For example, MS1E features one transition from character to character, one transition from character to number, one transition from number to character, and so on. We use the entire corpus of tokens in the training data set to compute these transition probabilities, and then compute the relative entropy of each new token under that transition model, which we threshold at its inflection point (see Figure 2).

2.2.4. *Versioning*

Versioning is a key feature of UASs. In certain cases, versioning can be exceptionally verbose and introduce irrelevant variation within UASs that are otherwise identical. However, a top-level version that has never been observed before for a certain application is probably worth attention. Having parsed the UAS in a representation that matches each application with its

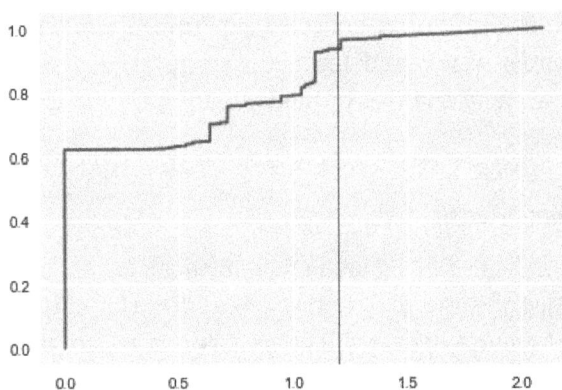

Fig. 2: The cumulative distribution of the relative entropy of the tokens. Thresholding at the inflection point of the chart allows us to separate out effectively random strings such as hashes and unique identifiers, which are replaced with a special keyword.

respective version, we are in a position to introduce the following bespoke distance metric, defined over token–version pairs:

$$d((T_1, v_1), (T_2, v_2)) = \begin{cases} 0 & \text{if } T_1 = T_2 \text{ and } v_1 = v_2 \\ 1 & \text{if } T_1 \neq T_2 \\ \delta(v_1, v_2) & \text{otherwise,} \end{cases}$$

where $\delta(., .)$ is a distance metric defined on version numbers only, which first tokenises the versions (so that, for example, 4.1 becomes [4, 1], and then reports the length of the longest common prefix of the two strings, divided by the *minimum* length. So, for example:

$$\delta(\text{'4.1'}, \text{'4.2'}) = 1/2, \quad \delta(\text{'4.1'}, \text{'4.1.2'}) = 1,$$

$$\delta(\text{'4.10.9'}, \text{'4.10.8.1'}) = 2/3.$$

2.3. *Kernel-based anomaly detectors*

Anomaly detection is an unsupervised machine learning problem where a model is fitted to a population of objects arising from one class, and new objects are scored against it to decide whether they belong to that population or not. Common use cases of this methodology include intrusion detection and fraud detection. Anomaly detection is a well-studied topic (for example, Bhattacharyya and Kalita, 2013; Dunning and Friedman, 2014), albeit poorer in its portfolio of techniques than supervised classification. In this work, we compare two fairly representative techniques: nearest neighbours, and distance-based one-class SVM.

2.3.1. *Nearest-neighbours-based outlier detector*

Outlier detection using a nearest neighbours approach is a straightforward technique. Consider a training data set $D = \{x_i; \ i = 1, \ldots, n\}$, comprising UASs that are deemed to be legitimate in their vast majority, and assume we also have a distance metric $d(., .)$. We may then score a new object, x^* by considering its distance to the training data set, measured by the distance to its nearest neighbour in D:

$$s(x^*, D) = \min_{x \in D} d(x, x^*).$$

2.3.2. *One-class support vector machines*

In the classical Kernel version of the SVM, the Gram matrix K is given:

$$k_{ij} = \langle \Phi(x_i), \Phi(x_j) \rangle,$$

where Φ is typically a projection. Here, the norm between the projections plays the role of a similarity metric: orthogonal pairs of feature vectors (which hopefully represent objects that are fairly different) will produce very small scores, whereas similar pairs will produce larger scores. It is therefore tempting to replace this kernel with a similarity metric. Indeed, the theory of SVMs (Scholkopf, 1997) can support the use of any *Mercer* kernel $K(x_i, x_j)$, a condition needed to ensure that the matrix K remains positive semi-definite. Several authors have proposed ways to convert arbitrary distance metrics, including string distances, into kernels (for example, Li and Jiang, 2005; Neuhaus and Bunke, 2006):

$$K(x_i, x_j) = e^{-\gamma d(x_i, x_j)} \quad \text{or} \quad K(x_i, x_j) = e^{\gamma s(x_i, x_j)}.$$

For γ large enough, the Kernel matrix becomes symmetric diagonally dominant, and hence positive definite (Li and Jiang, 2005).

3. Experiments

In this section, we present experiments that assess performance of different combinations of anomaly detection algorithms and distance metrics. The lack of labelled data introduces challenges not only in the design of methodology, but also in the assessment of its performance. To overcome this challenge, we again look for expert insights that, though they might not be as crystal clear as a labelled data set, might offer clues as to sensible ways of measuring performance. The key insight is that whether they are known or not, it is strongly believed that at any given point only a tiny minority of the UASs observed in the enterprise could represent genuine threats, although a slightly larger minority of "abnormal" strings might still be of interest in the spirit of "knowing-your-network". This ratio is also known to become larger in purposefully high-risk environments such as honeypots, where the defence perimeter is intentionally relaxed to let incoming threats in so that they may be analysed. We capitalise on this insight to create the following assessment framework.

3.1. *Experimental setup*

We train the anomaly detection algorithms on a data set which contains mostly normal traffic in the form of proxy logs with HTTP headers from a Bluecoat proxy installed in an unspecified network (Chuvakin, 2017). We then score data points from a held-out subset of this data, as well as a different data set coming from a honeypot environment (Sconzo, 2017). This data set contains packet headers from network traffic captured by special software installed in isolated and well-monitored parts of the network specifically designed to be attractive to attackers. The latter is guaranteed to differ from the former both in a general, "know-your-network" sense, as well as in the specific sense of containing more genuine threats. Table 5 shows the data sets we used for our experiments. This allows us to use standard classification performance metrics such as area under the curve (AUC), considering any UAS which is included in *bluecoat proxy* data as normal and any user agent included in *honeypot* data as malicious.

We pre-processed the UASs as described in Section 2.2.3 to remove any random strings. We then tested one-class SVMs and k-NN as described in Section 2.3 with the following distance metrics:

- Jaccard distance where every UAS is represented by the set of tokens which constitute the output of the flexible parser described in Section 2.1.
- Jaccard distance where every UAS is represented by the set of overlapping 4-grams of the UAS.
- Levenshtein distance on the UASs.
- The new distance metric we proposed in Section 2.2.4 and is based on version differences.

Table 5: List of data sets used.

Name	UASs	Distinct UASs
Honeypot	994,693	4,048
Bluecoat proxy	7,943,657	2,760

3.2. *Results*

Table 6 shows AUC results of 10-fold cross-validation for the different algorithms and distance metrics and Figure 3 shows the ROC curves for one instance of cross-validation. The cross-validation is performed is such

Table 6: Ten-fold cross-validation AUC statistics for different algorithms and distance metrics.

	Jaccard Tokens	Jaccard *n*-grams	Levenshtein	Version Dist
		1-NN		
Mean	0.69	0.68	0.74	0.71
Std	0.02	0.02	0.01	0.02
		SVM		
Mean	0.65	0.72	0.78	0.68
Std	0.02	0.02	0.01	0.01

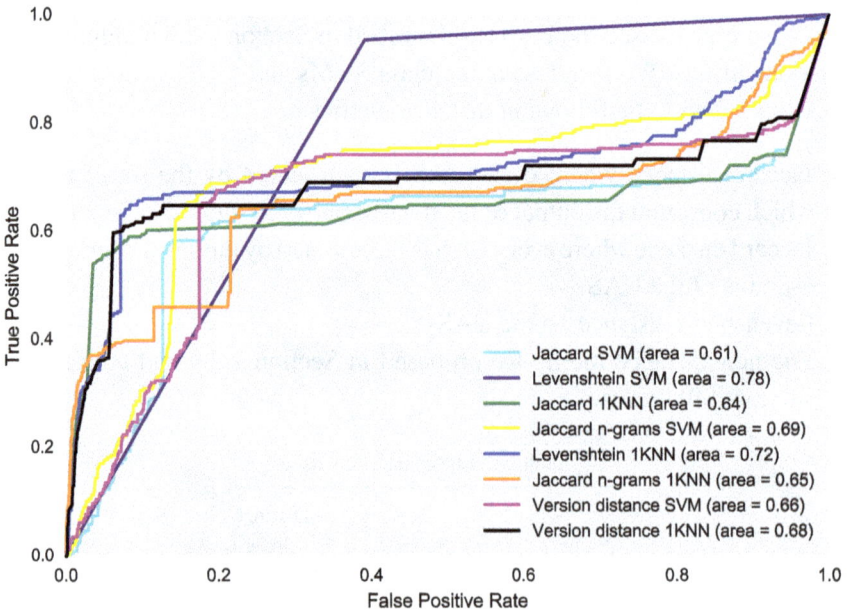

Fig. 3: ROC curves for different algorithms and distance metrics.

a way that in every run the test data comprises one fold of the *bluecoat proxy* data and all of the *honeypot* data.

Interestingly, Levenshtein distance performs best with both algorithms, with SVM being better than k-NN. Our newly proposed version distance performs equally well to Jaccard with n-grams and the simple Jaccard underperforms all of them. These results suggest that structure in the UAS is important for detecting anomalous UASs. Furthermore the distance that only takes versions into account performs equally well to other distances that use all of the string suggesting that versions are highly important for detecting anomalous UASs and should be further investigated.

4. Conclusion

The purpose of this chapter was to address the problem of detecting suspicious UASs using a large set of unlabelled data. Due to the variability of the UAS, we chose the approach where UASs are only characterised by their distances. To this end, our contribution was two-fold. We studied the UAS and presented ways to take into account implicit expert feedback about similarity of UASs either in the choice of similarity metric or in the pre-processing of the strings. We additionally presented an empirical evaluation of the performance of different distance metrics and anomaly detection algorithms namely, k-NN and SVMs. Our results showed that distance metrics that take structure into account perform better than the ones that do not and that differences in versions are highly important and worth further investigation. We believe that the SVM-based approach is worth further exploration as well, as it is more flexible in including partial expert feedback. This can be done either in a semi-supervised setting, or by trying to directly encode expert feedback about classes of similar UASs into the model.

4.1. *Computational considerations*

There are two main aspects of our proposed approach that will need to be considered in order to apply it to larger data sets, namely, the computation of the similarity or kernel matrix and the training of the models. The computation of the similarity matrix is quadratic to the input size. Optimising k-NN is straightforward as there is no training involved and the computation of the similarity matrix between UASs can be improved by using BK-trees (Burkhard and Keller, 1973). A BK-tree is a data structure that stores all strings based on their relative distance according to a distance metric. This data structure can be computed in $O(n \log n)$ time and supports efficient retrieval for any k-NN query. However, SVMs need to either explicitly represent the the kernel matrix or represent a mapping of the original data into a feature space such that the kernel matrix can be computed by means of inner products between points in that space. Although it is hard to think what this mapping could be for the types of kernels that we consider in this chapter, it is an idea worth exploring as in this case stochastic gradient descent can be used for efficiency. When directly computing the kernel matrix, techniques for sampling the original data in a meaningful way could be helpful for approximating it.

4.2. *Future work*

From a methodological perspective, it would be of interest to enhance our analysis to seek out look-alikes, rather than just outliers. A notable example is the comparison between MSIE and MS1E which was used earlier, which was specifically designed to evade detection from visual inspection in the context of Troj/Agent-VUD, a relatively low-sophistication yet fairly successful trojan horse malware. In our current approach, string-level edit distance would consider the strings very similar, whereas token-level edit distance would consider them totally different. Another example is the attempt to masquerade as Internet Explorer albeit using an out-of-date or too-recent version number. A local outlier detection technique would be better suited than the ones we used here to identify UASs that are not altogether foreign to the data set, but are outliers relatively to their nearest cluster. A variant of the k-NN approach used above with k-Means or some form of agglomerative clustering instead would be a first attempt.

An aspect which we did not consider in this work is the role of host-based analysis in anomaly detection for UASs. It is likely that a given host, or perhaps a whole area of the enterprise network, has much greater homogeneity than the entire enterprise network. For example, senior managers might be less likely to use a Linux OS than security experts or developers. At the level of a single host, it is indeed extremely unlikely that there should be two different operating systems for a non-technical user. Consequently, outlier detection might be much more powerful when trained at the host, or business unit level, rather than the enterprise as a whole.

References

Bhattacharyya, D. and Kalita, J. (2013). *Network Anomaly Detection: A Machine Learning Perspective*, CRC Press, Boca Raton, FL, USA.

Burkhard, W. A. and Keller, R. M. (1973). Some approaches to best-match file searching, *Communications of the ACM* **16**, 4, pp. 230–236.

Chuvakin, A. (2017). Public security log sharing site, URL: http://log-sharing.dreamhosters. com/bluecoat_proxy_big.zip.

Dunning, T. and Friedman, E. (2014). *Practical Machine Learning: A New Look at Anomaly Detection*, O'Reilly.

Graham-Cumming, J. (2014). URL: https://blog.cloudflare.com/inside-shellshock/.

Li, H. and Jiang, T. (2005). A class of edit kernels for SVMs to predict translation initiation sites in eukaryotic mRNAs, *Journal of Computational Biology* **12**, 6, pp. 702–718.

Neuhaus, M. and Bunke, H. (2006). Edit distance-based kernel functions for structural pattern classification, *Pattern Recognition* **39**, pp. 1852–1863.

Pfahringer, B. (2000). Winning the KDD99 classification cup: Bagged boosting, *SIGKDD Explorations Newsletter* **1**, 2, pp. 65–66.

Scholkopf, B. (1997). *Support Vector Learning*, R. Oldenbourg Verlag, Munich.

Sconzo, M. (2017). Samples of security related data, URL: http://www.secrepo.com/.

Scott, J. (2017). Signature based malware detection is dead, URL: http://icitech.org/wp-content/uploads/2017/02/ICIT-Analysis-Signature-Based-Malware-Detection-is-Dead.pdf.

Shackleford, D. (2016). Active breach detection: The next generation security technology? URL: https://www.eastwindnetworks.com/wp-content/uploads/2016/03/active-breach-detection-next-generation-security-technology-36812.pdf.

Zhang, Y., Mekky, H., Zhang, Z., Torres, R., Lee, S.-J., Tongaonkar, A. and Mellia, M. (2015). Detecting malicious activities with user-agent-based profiles, *Int. J. Network Mgmt* **25**, 5, pp. 306–319.

Chapter 7

Discovery of the Twitter Bursty Botnet

Juan Echeverria, Christoph Besel and Shi Zhou*

Department of Computer Science,
University College London (UCL), 66–72 Gower St,
London, WCIE 6BT, UK

**s.zhou@ucl.ac.uk*

Many Twitter users are bots. They can be used for spamming, opinion manipulation and online fraud. Recently, we discovered the *Star Wars botnet*, consisting of more than 350,000 bots tweeting random quotations exclusively from Star Wars novels. The bots were exposed because they tweeted uniformly from any location within two rectangle-shaped geographic zones covering Europe and the USA, including sea and desert areas in the zones. In this chapter, we report another unusual behaviour of the Star Wars bots, that the bots were created in bursts or batches, and they only tweeted in their first few minutes since creation. Inspired by this observation, we discovered an even larger Twitter botnet, the *Bursty botnet* with more than 500,000 bots. Our preliminary study showed that the Bursty botnet was directly responsible for a large-scale online spamming attack in 2012. Most bot detection algorithms have been based on assumptions of "common" features that were supposedly shared by all bots. Our discovered botnets, however, do not show many of those features; instead, they were detected by their distinct, unusual tweeting behaviours that were unknown until now.

1. Introduction

Twitter bots are Twitter user accounts created and controlled by hackers, called botmasters, using computer programmes. A Twitter botnet is a group of bots that show the same properties and are controlled by the same botmaster. The Twitter company has identified and removed millions of bots. Researchers[a] claim there are many more bots on Twitter, and they have introduced a number of methods to detect Twitter bots.

---

[a] http://www.public.asu.edu/~fmorstat/bottutorial.

Twitter bots can pose a series of threats to cyberspace security. For example, they can send a large amount of spam tweets to other users; they can create fake trending topics; they can manipulate public opinion; they can launch a so-called astroturfing attack where they orchestrate false "grass roots" campaigns to create a fake sense of agreement among Twitter users (Abokhodair *et al.*, 2015; Ferrara, 2015; Ratkiewicz *et al.*, 2011) and they can contaminate the data from Twitter's streaming API (Morstatter *et al.*, 2016) that so many research works have been based on; they have even been linked to election disruption (Bessi and Ferrara, 2016).

Recently, we discovered the *Star Wars botnet* (Echeverria and Zhou, 2017) with more than 350,000 bots. These bots were discovered because they tweeted uniformly from any location within two rectangle-shaped geographic zones covering Europe and the USA, including sea and desert areas in the zones. Further inspection showed the bots only tweeted random quotations from Star Wars novels. This botnet was discovered and detected in a way completely different from previous bot detection efforts.

In this chapter, we report our discovery of another Twitter botnet, the *Bursty botnet*, which is even larger — with more than 500,000 bots that have not been banned or removed by Twitter at the time of writing. The discovery of the Bursty botnet was inspired by another unusual tweeting behaviour of the Star Wars bots. Our preliminary study showed that the Bursty botnet was directly responsible for a large-scale online spamming attack in 2012.

Our work not only provides valuable ground truth data for research on Twitter bots, but also enabled us to reflect on the limitations of existing methods for detecting Twitter bots. Existing methods are mostly based on "common" features that were supposedly shared by all Twitter bots. Our newly discovered botnets, however, do not show any of those features; instead, they were detected by their distinct, unusual tweeting behaviours that were unknown until now.

2. Background

2.1. *Twitter bots detection*

Twitter, as a company, has been actively identifying and removing suspicious users, many of which are spammers or bots (Thomas *et al.*, 2011).

Researchers have also proposed various methods to classify or detect Twitter bots, many of which are machine learning methods. Many of these works were based on features either measured from ground truth data or assumed by researchers as common properties of all bots. Such features include user properties, including username length (Lee and Kim, 2014), user profile (Zafarani and Liu, 2015), time between tweets (Chu *et al.*, 2010), Levensthein distance between the tweets of a user (Wang, 2010), distribution of tweeting frequency (Chu *et al.*, 2010) and entropy in tweeting frequency (Dickerson *et al.*, 2014); as well as tweet text properties (Chu *et al.*, 2010), including topics (Dickerson *et al.*, 2014) and sentiment analysis (Dickerson *et al.*, 2014). Some researchers claimed that their bot classifiers can achieve high accuracy, as high as 99.99% (Thomas *et al.*, 2013).

The existing efforts on Twitter bots detection, however, suffer a major problem, that despite their ever more sophisticated algorithms, they could only discover small numbers of (mixed types of) bots, mostly hundreds or up to a few thousands — and yet it is well known that there are very large botnets on Twitter.[b]

The performance of bot detection methods is ultimately determined by our knowledge and understanding of Twitter bots. However, there is a well acknowledged lack of ground truth data (Subrahmanian *et al.*, 2016). Twitter's bot data sets are not available to the public. The small number of available data sets are small and contain mixed types of bots.[c] As a result, it is not clear which assumptions on Twitter bots are true, which features are most characteristic or whether Twitter bots should have common features at all.

2.2. *The Star Wars botnet*

Recently we discovered a large botnet, the Star Wars botnet (Echeverria and Zhou, 2017). This discovery stems from the fact that the Star Wars bots create clear rectangular patterns when plotting their location-tagged tweets on a world map. After manual tagging of some of the bots, a Naive Bayes

---

[b]http://www.symantec.com/connect/blogs/green-coffee-and-spam-elaborate-spam-operation-twitter-uses-nearly-750000-account.
[c]http://www.public.asu.edu/~fmorstat/bottutorial.

classifier was trained and some filters were applied. Finally, more than 350,000 Star Wars bots were identified showing the following properties.

- The Star Wars bots exclusively and textually tweet quotations from Star Wars novels, with the only exception of inserting the hash character (#) or special hashtags (such as #followme) at random places.
- The bots were registered with Twitter from June to July 2013, and therefore their user ID numbers are within a narrow range between 1.5×10^9 and 1.6×10^9.
- The tweeting source of the bots is exclusively "Windows Phone", which accounts for only 0.02% of all tweets on Twitter.
- About half of all tweets of the bots are location-tagged. Almost all of the bots have tweeted at least one location-tagged tweet. The tweet location tags are obviously fake because all of them fall in one of the two rectangle zones, uniformly (see Figure 1).
- Because of the fake locations, distance between two consecutive geo-located tweets of a bot is very large, over 2,000 km on average.
- The bots have created no more than 11 tweets in their lifetime, and they have no retweets or mentions.

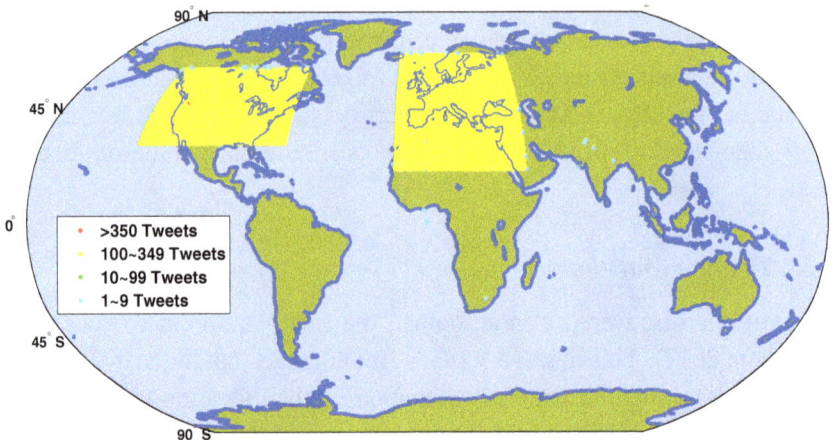

Fig. 1: Distribution of tweet locations of the Star Wars bots. The bots exclusively, uniformly tweet from any location within the two rectangle zones over Europe and North America, including sea and desert areas. This unusual tweeting behaviour was the first clue for discovering the Star Wars bots.

- The Star Wars bots disproportionately follow other Star Wars bots (the botnet follows itself). They have at most 10 followers and at most 31 friends.

The Star Wars botnet provides a valuable data set for studying Twitter bots. It is not only very large, but also contains a single botnet showing the same properties. It provides rich information and clues on how the botnet is designed and created (Echeverria and Zhou, 2017). The Star Wars bots do not show many of the previously assumed "common" features of Twitter bots; instead they exhibit a number of unusual tweeting behaviours that have not been reported. The discovery of the botnet was accidental, but it illustrates the limitations of existing bot detection methods.

3. Discovery of the Bursty Botnet

In this section, we will show how we detect another botnet, with over 500,000 users. This was inspired by an unusual tweeting behaviour that we observed on the Star Wars bots: all the bots only tweeted in the first few minutes after their creation. We call it the bursty tweeting behaviour. We define the *bursty* users as those who tweeted at least 3 times in the first hour following user creation, and then never tweeted again. Figure 2 shows the distribution of bursty users in the Twitter user ID space. When a Twitter user is created, Twitter assigns the user a unique ID number between 0 and 2^{32}. In general, the user IDs are allocated in a sequential manner such that a smaller ID means an earlier creation date.

We can see in Figure 2(a) the bursty users are a tiny fraction of Twitter users. As shown in Figure 2(b), the Star Wars bots can be clearly identified as a cluster of spikes with IDs in the range between 1.5×10^9 and 1.6×10^9, which corresponds to June and July 2013, the period when the Star Wars bots were created. This is as expected, because Star Wars bots are bursty users.

However, in Figure 2(b), there is another much more prominent cluster of spikes. These bursty users were created in February and March 2012 within the ID range between 5.00×10^8 and 5.35×10^8. We manually checked these users and noticed that many of them showed clear characteristics of spamming bots because their tweets contained only a mention and/or

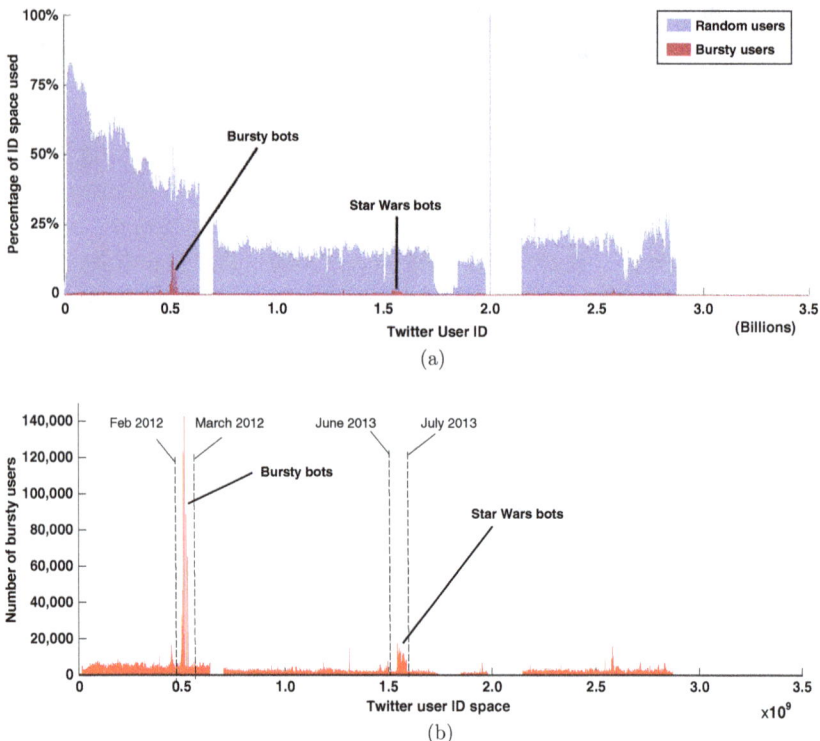

Fig. 2: Distribution of the bursty users in the Twitter user ID space in September 2015. A blue line in (a) near 2.0×10^9 are IDs reserved by Twitter. (a) Percentage of Twitter user IDs allocated to all users and bursty users in each bin of 1 million IDs. (b) Number of user IDs allocated to bursty users.

a URL. Many of the URLs are shortened and pointed to blocked domains. An example of a bursty bot can be seen in Figure 3. Further study showed that these suspicious users were members of an unknown botnet, we call it the *Bursty* botnet.

3.1. *Definition of the Bursty bots*

Here, we define the Bursty bots as Twitter users with all of the following properties.

- They were registered in February and March 2012 with user IDs between 5×10^8 and 5.35×10^8.

Sharron Cashwell @sharronhmsur · 1 Mar 2012
tinyurl.com/7bhvqnf/M8mbbh... @coypeterson

◯　　◻◻　　♡　　✉

Sharron Cashwell @sharronhmsur · 1 Mar 2012
@BeatsByStone tinyurl.com/7rws6s2/6dtt9g...

◯　　◻◻　　♡　　✉

Sharron Cashwell @sharronhmsur · 1 Mar 2012
tinyurl.com/8379tuc/A8bqrl... @MikeCincoSays

◯　　◻◻　　♡　　✉

Fig. 3: Screenshot of a Bursty bot live on Twitter.

- They show bursty tweeting behaviour. That is, they generated at least three tweets and they only tweeted in the first hour after their creation.
- They only tweeted from the source of "Mobile Web".
- They mostly tweet (i) a URL or/and (ii) a mention of another user.

We retrieved about 21 million users in the ID range of 5×10^8 and 5.35×10^8. We collected all of their user account information and all their tweets up to September 2016. According to the above definition, we identified more than 500,000 Bursty bots.

3.2. *Bursty tweeting and bursty creation*

The Bursty botnet shows two bursty properties: they tweeted in a bursty way and they were created in bursts. Figure 4 shows most the Bursty bots and the Star Wars bots only tweeted in the first few minutes since their creation. In particular, the Bursty bots show a strong bursty behaviour that almost all tweets were generated less than 2 minutes after account creation and then stayed silent forever. This is a clear sign of automatised behaviour. This feature also gives us a sharp time frame to look for the possible cyber attacks that the bots were created for.

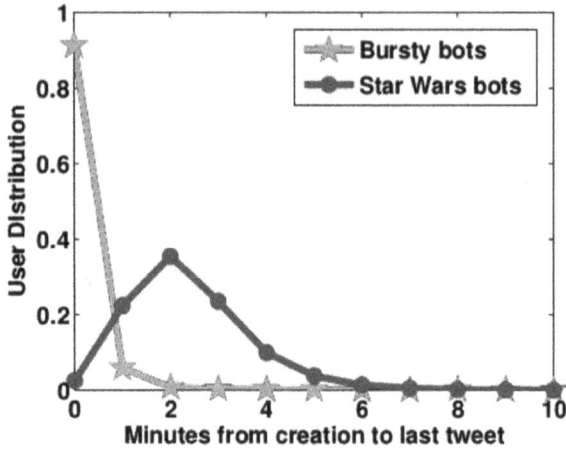

Fig. 4: Distribution of the Bursty bots and Star Wars bots as a function of time (in minutes) from their creation to their last tweet. Most of the bots only generated tweets in their first few minutes.

Figure 5 shows that most of the bursty users created in February and March 2012, with user IDs from 500×10^6 to 535×10^6, are identified as the Bursty bots, showing all the properties defined above. Only a small, stable number of bursty users are not identified as Bursty bots. These are perhaps normal users who accidentally joined Twitter at that time, tried a few tweets and then never return again. Such users appear with a low and almost constant rate throughout the time.

Although we defined the bursty users as those who tweeted only in the first hour, we now know that most of the Bursty bots actually tweeted only in the first two minutes. The fact that almost all bursty users can be identified as the Bursty bots means that bursty tweeting is indeed an unusual, distinct behaviour of this botnet.

3.3. The "disappeared" Bursty bots

We collected the bursty users in September 2015 and again in September 2016. As shown in Figure 5, about 300,000 Bursty bots have disappeared during that period. Notably, there is a whole spike of Bursty bots missing with IDs between 520×10^6 and 525×10^6. It is likely that their accounts were removed by Twitter, we checked many of their accounts, which are indeed suspended. On one hand, this supports our detection of the Bursty

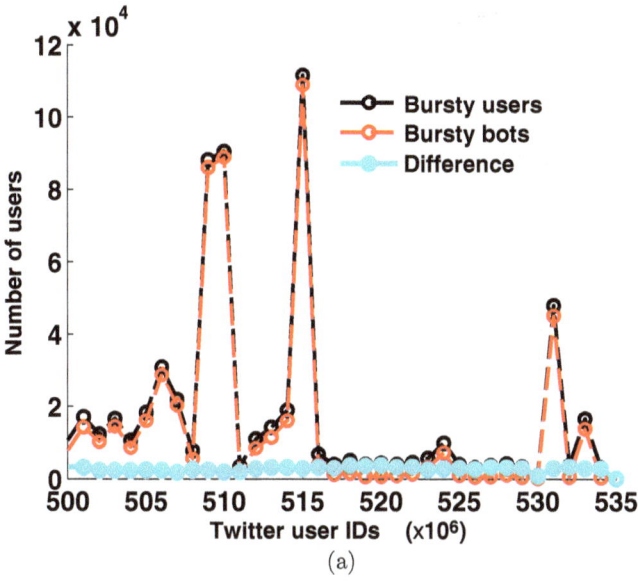

(a)

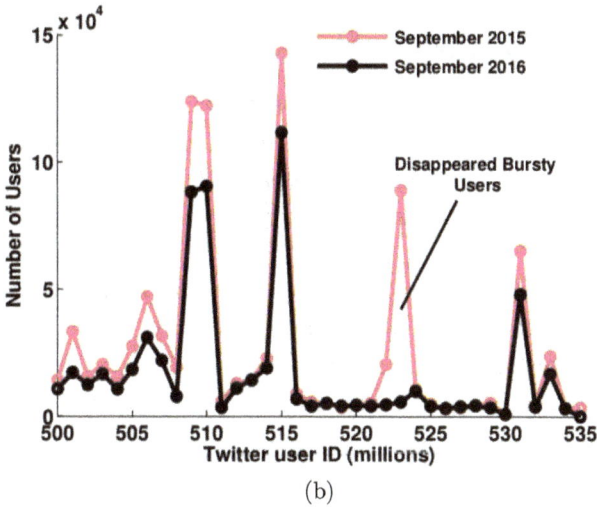

(b)

Fig. 5: Bursty users and the Identified Bursty bots in the Twitter user ID range of 500×10^6 and 535×10^6. (a) Bursty users and the identified Bursty bots as measured in September 2016. Most bursty users are Bursty bots. (b) Bursty bots in September 2015 and 2016. Many bursty bots disappeared during that time.

Table 1:   Properties of the Bursty bots.

Property	Value or Percentage
Bots with no friend	99.0%
Bots with no follower	99.0%
Bots with tweets with URLs	98.0%
Bots with tweets with mentions	97.5%
Bots with tweets with hashtags	0.8%
Average number of tweets	4.74
Total number of tweets	2.8 million
Tweets with URLs	97.6%
Tweets with mentions	64.1%
Tweets with hashtags	2.7%

bots as computer-controlled, malicious users; on the other hand, it shows that Twitter has not identified the Bursty botnet as a whole, leaving the majority of the botnet still alive online.

3.4. *Unusual connectivity*

Table 1 shows the Bursty bots have a number of distinct properties. Most of the bots do not have any followers (outgoing links) or friends (incoming links). It is notable that the definition of the Bursty botnet did not involve user connectivity, yet the detected Bursty bots exhibited such an unusual feature.

This feature is against a popular assumption in previous studies that Twitter bots should tend to have many connections. This feature, however, is expected from the bursty creation of the Bursty bots, as they were designed to be used only once immediately after they were created.

3.5. *The Bursty botnet spamming attack*

It is notable that almost all of the tweets generated by the bots contain a URL, and about 2/3 have a mention. This means that almost all of the tweets that have a mention also have a URL. This indicates that the bots were likely created for spamming attacks; the mentions were used to maximise the reach of the tweet, both by attracting the user being mentioned and his followers to click on the URL.

Table 2: Domains most tweeted by the Bursty bots.

Domain	Count
tinyurl.com	1,179,369
google.com	562,557
bit.ly	328,016
dietagolder670.ru	54,585
goroskopsiris2346.ru	54,414
dietagoliu4758.ru	52,992
dietaseru858.ru	51,894

To find out more details, we examined all the URLs tweeted by the Bursty bots. Of the 2.8 million tweets that the Bursty botnet has created, almost all (over 99.9%) of the URLs were unique, which means most of the URLs were only tweeted once by a single bot. As shown in Table 2, when divided by domain, the most tweeted domain is the URL shortening and redirect service, `tinyurl.com`, with over 42% (or 1.18 million) of the total URLs. We investigated the tinyurl links, and found that 99.9% of them pointed to only two destinations: one was a webpage that had been blocked by tinyurl, which means tinyurl had classified it as malicious or spam; the other is a known phishing webpage www.facebook-goodies. com.[d] By performing a content analysis, we found that the vast majority of all the URLs could be clustered into only two distinct spam campaigns.

It is almost certain that the Bursty botnet was carefully designed and centrally controlled for the purpose of a spamming attack. A number of tricks have been used to hide the attack.

Firstly, the bots were created in large numbers, and each bot was used to generate a small number of tweets in the first few minutes only and then the bots all became silent. Most existing bot detection methods are not able to identify such inactive bots.

Secondly, the bots used a complex network of URL shorteners and redirects to obfuscate the final landing pages, such that the vast number

---

[d]This website has now been deleted, but it is available through Wayback Machine, arguably the most comprehensive digital archive of the World Wide Web.

of URLs were used only once, which could effectively evade most spam filters. Also it was not easy for users to tell on the final destination of the URLs.

Thirdly, the botnet directly targeted over 1.3 million distinct Twitter users by mentioning their usernames, which significantly increased the chance of the URLs being clicked. Our analysis revealed just how successful this technique was: on average over 61% of the posted URLs that lead to a phishing campaign were clicked, which could yield a remarkable revenue by selling stolen personal data.

With the above information and further research, we were even able to track down the alleged botmaster of the Bursty botnet. Our detailed analysis on the spamming attack of the Bursty botnet will be published in another paper.

4. Reflection on Twitter Bot Detection

4.1. *Failure of existing detection methods*

In recent years, there have been many efforts to detect Twitter bots. Some have produced plausible results. Most of them relied on heuristic assumptions on "common" features that should supposedly be shared by all bots.

It is clear that these assumed features are not shared by all bots. For example, the Bursty botnet and the Star Wars botnet show some properties that are diametrically different from those assumptions. As a result, the existing methods have not been successful in detecting large botnets. We have verified that the Bursty bots and the Star Wars bots can fool one of the latest and more advanced bot detection tools (Davis *et al.*, 2016).

One reason was that previous studies were restricted by the lack of ground truth data. Since the available data sets all contained mixed types of bots, researchers had to search for and focus on general features shared by all bots in the data sets.

Another possible reason was that the previously studied features of bots have been "fading", because most of these features could be easily avoided in the design of later botnets as botmasters must have closely followed the development of bot detection.

4.2. *A long-term battle with no silver bullet*

The Bursty botnet and the Star Wars botnet exhibit distinctive properties that have been overlooked so far, namely the tweet location distribution and the bursty tweeting behaviour. But we do not expect that further study on these features will lead to discovery of many other new botnets. There is a strong incentive for botmasters to deliberately create new botnets that do not show any of the features that have already been "exposed" by researchers. Ideally, botmasters would create new botnets that are completely different from existing ones.

Indeed, we expect the battle on bot detection to be a long-term process, where researchers have to keep proposing new detection methods to catch up with new generations of botnets, which are likely to become ever more deceptive. As such, although it has been highly desired for by the research community, we do not believe it will be possible to develop a "generalised" method to detect all types of bots.

5. Conclusion

The discovery of the Bursty botnet and the Star Wars botnet provided valuable ground truth data for the Twitter bot research community. Both botnets are unusually large. Each contains hundreds of thousands of bots. They are different from other data sets because each of the botnets contains a single network of bots that exhibit the same properties and were created and controlled by the same botmaster. It seems Twitter has removed the Star Wars botnet since our publication (Echeverria and Zhou, 2017). As of this writing, most of the 500,000 Bursty bots are still alive on Twitter. Researchers can collect them by following instructions in this chapter. Researchers, however, should hurry to collect them before Twitter deletes these accounts too.

It is interesting to point out that the Bursty botnet and the Star Wars Botnet were discovered by their unusual tweeting behaviours, which is in a rather "unconventional" way that was different from previous bot detection efforts. This also means it does not suffer the biases induced by relying on Twitter's black-box suspension algorithm or URL blacklisting services, which makes it a valuable ground truth for future research.

These new data sets not only enabled us to reflect on the previous assumptions and detection methods, but also provided us a rare and valuable opportunity to investigate how Twitter bots were designed, created and used for a spamming attack in the cyberspace.

References

Abokhodair, N., Yoo, D. and McDonald, D. W. (2015). Dissecting a social botnet: Growth, content and influence in twitter, in *Proceedings of the 18th ACM Conference on Computer Supported Cooperative Work & Social Computing*, CSCW '15, ACM, ISBN 978-1-4503-2922-4, pp. 839–851, doi:10.1145/2675133.2675208, URL: http://doi.acm.org/10.1145/2675133.2675208.

Bessi, A. and Ferrara, E. (2016). Social bots distort the 2016 U.S. presidential election online discussion, **21**, 11, doi:10.5210/fm.v21i11.7090, URL: http://journals.uic.edu/ojs/index.php/fm/article/view/7090.

Chu, Z., Gianvecchio, S., Wang, H. and Jajodia, S. (2010). Who is tweeting on twitter: Human, bot, or cyborg? in *Proceedings of the 26th Annual Computer Security Applications Conference*, ACSAC '10, ACM, ISBN 978-1-4503-0133-6, pp. 21–30, doi:10.1145/1920261.1920265, URL: http://doi.acm.org/10.1145/1920261.1920265.

Davis, C. A., Varol, O., Ferrara, E., Flammini, A. and Menczer, F. (2016). BotOrNot: A system to evaluate social bots, in *Proceedings of the 25th International Conference Companion on World Wide Web*, WWW '16 Companion, International World Wide Web Conferences Steering Committee, ISBN 978-1-4503-4144-8, pp. 273–274, doi:10.1145/2872518.2889302, URL: http://dx.doi.org/10.1145/2872518.2889302.

Dickerson, J. P., Kagan, V. and Subrahmanian, V. S. (2014). Using sentiment to detect bots on twitter: Are humans more opinionated than bots? in *2014 IEEE/ACM International Conference on Advances in Social Networks Analysis and Mining (ASONAM)*, pp. 620–627, doi:10.1109/ASONAM.2014.6921650.

Echeverria, J. and Zhou, S. (2017). Discovery, retrieval, and analysis of the 'star wars' botnet in twitter, in *Proceedings of the 2017 IEEE/ACM International Conference on Advances in Social Networks Analysis and Mining 2017*, ASONAM '17, ACM, ISBN 978-1-4503-4993-2, pp. 1–8, doi:10.1145/3110025.3110074, URL: http://doi.acm.org/10.1145/3110025.3110074.

Ferrara, E. (2015). Manipulation and abuse on social media, pp. 4:1–4:9, doi:10.1145/2749279.2749283, URL: http://doi.acm.org/10.1145/2749279.2749283.

Lee, S. and Kim, J. (2014). Early filtering of ephemeral malicious accounts on twitter, **54**, pp. 48–57, doi:10.1016/j.comcom.2014.08.006, URL: http://dx.doi.org/10.1016/j.comcom.2014.08.006.

Morstatter, F., Dani, H., Sampson, J. and Liu, H. (2016). Can one tamper with the sample API? Toward neutralizing bias from spam and bot content, in *Proceedings of the 25th International Conference Companion on World Wide Web*, WWW '16 Companion, International World Wide Web Conferences Steering Committee, ISBN 978-1-4503-4144-8, pp. 81–82, doi:10.1145/2872518.2889372, URL: http://dx.doi.org/10.1145/2872518.2889372.

Ratkiewicz, J., Conover, M., Meiss, M., Gonccalves, B., Patil, S., Flammini, A. and Menczer, F. (2011). Truthy: Mapping the spread of astroturf in microblog streams, in *Proceedings of the 20th International Conference Companion on World Wide Web*, WWW '11, ACM, ISBN 978-1-4503-0637-9, pp. 249–252, doi:10.1145/1963192. 1963301, URL: http://doi.acm.org/10.1145/1963192.1963301.

Subrahmanian, V. S., Azaria, A., Durst, S., Kagan, V., Galstyan, A., Lerman, K., Zhu, L., Ferrara, E., Flammini, A., Menczer, F., Stevens, A., Dekhtyar, A., Gao, S., Hogg, T., Kooti, F., Liu, Y., Varol, O., Shiralkar, P., Vydiswaran, V., Mei, Q. and Hwang, T. (2016). The DARPA twitter bot challenge, URL: http://arxiv.org/abs/1601.05140.

Thomas, K., Grier, C., Song, D. and Paxson, V. (2011). Suspended accounts in retrospect: An analysis of twitter spam, in *Proceedings of the 2011 ACM SIGCOMM Conference on Internet Measurement Conference*, IMC '11, ACM, ISBN 978-1-4503-1013-0, pp. 243–258, doi:10.1145/2068816.2068840, URL: http://doi.acm.org/10. 1145/2068816.2068840.

Thomas, K., McCoy, D., Grier, C., Kolcz, A. and Paxson, V. (2013). Trafficking fraudulent accounts: The role of the underground market in twitter spam and abuse, ISBN 978-1-931971-03-4, pp. 195–210, URL: https://www.usenix.org/conference/ usenixsecurity13/technical-sessions/paper/thomas.

Wang, A. H. (2010). Detecting spam bots in online social networking sites: A machine learning approach, in S. Foresti and S. Jajodia. eds., *Data and Applications Security and Privacy XXIV*, pp. 335–342, no. 6166 in Lecture Notes in Computer Science, Springer Berlin Heidelberg, ISBN 978-3-642-13738-9 978-3-642-13739-6, URL: http://link.springer.com/chapter/10.1007/978-3-642-13739-6_25, doi: 10.1007/978-3-642-13739-6_25.

Zafarani, R. and Liu, H. (2015). 10 bits of surprise: Detecting malicious users with minimum information, in *Proceedings of the 24th ACM International on Conference on Information and Knowledge Management*, CIKM '15, ACM, ISBN 978-1-4503-3794-6, pp. 423–431, doi:10.1145/2806416.2806535, URL: http://doi.acm.org/10. 1145/2806416.2806535.

Chapter 8

Stochastic Block Models as an Unsupervised Approach to Detect Botnet-Infected Clusters in Networked Data

Mark Patrick Roeling* and Geoff Nicholls

Department of Statistics, University of Oxford,
24-29 St Giles', OX1 3LB, UK
*mark.roeling@stats.ox.ac.uk

Botnets consist of devices connected to the internet, supervised by a botnet owner, performing malicious tasks. The significant impact of botnets on corporate, governmental and civilian operations has resulted in a lot of attention from the machine learning community. However, most studies to date do not respect the linked structure of network data and rely heavily on the availability of a labelled data set. This study applies Stochastic Block Models (SBM) to botnet data with the aim of identifying infected clusters without the need for a labelled data set.

After providing a short review, replication and simulation study, we apply SBMs to a publicly available data set from the University of Victoria, including both neutral background data as well as a capture of the Zeus botnet.

Our findings show that, although SBMs can be of merit in data that includes clusters of infected and uninfected traffic (and users), real-world application is challenging due to the heterogeneity of the data and the way currently available botnet samples have been collected and mapped. We discuss our findings in light of publicly available data sets and put forth suggestions for future research.

1. Introduction

Botnets usually consist of devices connected to the internet, supervised by a botnet owner, performing malicious tasks. Studies focusing on the taxonomy of botnets distinguish Command and Control (C&C) and Peer to Peer (P2P) types (Karim *et al.*, 2014; Vania *et al.*, 2013). C&C botnets

161

consist of infected computers (zombies or bots) that communicate with, and are controlled by, one centralised control centre or server. This follows the classical client–server network model. In contrast, P2P botnets rely on the infected bots to communicate commands to other infected bots. Botnets usually propagate through malware-based infection of computers, and the versatility and scalability (33% of worldwide Internet machines are infected by malware according to Panda Security) has made botnets attractive and useful tools for criminal purposes. Examples of attacks are distributed denial of service (DDoS) and spam as well as fraud and theft of data or computational resources (Chang *et al.*, 2015), illustrating the potential for botnet attacks to have a major impact on infrastructure and users in cyberspace.

Given the threat of botnets, a lot of work has focused on the detection of infected machines. Most of the detection methods rely either on malware analysis of infected machines or on differentiating normal versus malicious traffic with machine learning algorithms (reviewed elsewhere: Elhalabi *et al.* (2014); Hyslip and Pittman (2015); Ismail and Jantan (2016); Karim *et al.* (2016); Stevanovic and Pedersen (2013)). The latter approach relies on the availability of informative features (or covariates) which are generally created by researchers based on expert knowledge and data available in captured network flows. Features can be split into host-based (e.g., number of connections, ratio of source to destination ports) or flow-based (e.g., packet length, number of bytes). Features which are commonly reported to be informative are average payload packet length, average bits per second, the ratio between the number of incoming packets over the number of outgoing packets and duration (Beigi *et al.*, 2014). In the machine learning detection methods presented so far, it is convention to create and compare features from captures of network activity between bots and uninfected users using several techniques. These include *decision trees* (Barthakur *et al.*, 2013; Beigi *et al.*, 2014; Bharathula and Menon, 2016; Bilge *et al.*, 2012; Carl *et al.*, 2006; Feizollah *et al.*, 2013; Haddadi *et al.*, 2014; Haddadi and Zincir-Heywood, 2015; Meng and Spanoudakis, 2015; Singh *et al.*, 2014), *distance-based clustering* (Arshad *et al.*, 2011; Bharathula and Menon, 2016; Davis, 2012; Meng and Spanoudakis, 2015), *support vector machines* (Bilge *et al.*, 2012; Camelo *et al.*, 2014; Davuth and Sung-Ryul, 2013; Feizollah *et al.*, 2013; Meng and Spanoudakis, 2015), *perceptrons* (Bharathula and Menon, 2016; Feizollah *et al.*, 2013), *neural networks* (Karim *et al.*, 2016; Meng and Spanoudakis, 2015; Nogueira *et al.*, 2010), *Bayesian methods* (Barthakur *et al.*, 2013; Carl *et al.*, 2006; Feizollah *et al.*, 2013; Guntuku *et al.*, 2013; Haddadi *et al.*, 2014; Meng and Spanoudakis, 2015) and *clustering* based on local shrinking (Haltaş *et al.*, 2014; Tegeler *et al.*, 2012). Although (P2P) botnets are resilient (Rossow *et al.*, 2013), machine learning approaches have been markedly successful with reported detection rates ≥75% and occasionally ≥90%. However, a technical limitation to the currently used machine learning methods is the need for a labelled training set. Although numerous studies report an excellent performance of detection mechanisms on validation/test data sets, these validation sets often include the same botnets (only split in half randomly to create a training and test set) resulting in the evaluation against a model that is specifically tuned to the connections of the botnet in the training data. Arguably, this provides limited validity to the detection of abnormal network behaviour or other malicious traffic.

Another more relevant and immediate problem with most parametric machine learning methods is that they neglect the linked or networked structure of the data and assume conditional independence of the botnet/non-botnet status given node-based traffic summary statistics. To allow analyses, network data are typically collapsed into summary statistics for every node, indicating the node's position and properties. This assumption is clearly erroneous, as networked data are inherently dependent (Steglich *et al.*, 2010), due to unobserved latent factors acting locally on the network. Neglecting dependence implies throwing away important data and interesting interactions *a priori*, possibly biasing the results of detection methods. For example, if a clustering technique identifies a small distance between two nodes in a network based on their covariates, this could be (partially) explained by the distance of those nodes in the network, especially if calculation of covariate values (e.g., bytes transferred) between nodes directly depends on communication between those nodes. Another reason why neglecting the linked structure of the data may be a bad idea is that botnets are becoming increasingly advanced in mimicking normal traffic, decreasing the effectiveness of machine learning detection.

Some papers have already shown that analyses of the networked structure can be of added value by applying methods from graph theory. One study (Burghouwt *et al.*, 2010) calculated the degree distribution (number of connections in a given time window) to detect visited domains and found that C&C-domains receive an unexpectedly high amount of traffic. Other studies (Bou-Harb *et al.*, 2017; Camelo *et al.*, 2014) present clustering and connectivity techniques to provide more insight in converging patterns of communication, but do not present technical details. Clearly, network properties can influence classification accuracy, which makes the application and development of methods able to model networked data, and its covariates, particularly opportune.

This study aims to extend the application of SBMs to a cybersecurity setting, by fitting SBMs to a capture of network data including botnet infected machines. We think SBMs may assist in the detection of botnets, in a manner that is statistically sensible, without the requirement for a labelled data set. SBMs are extensions of regular latent variable models to networked data, allowing the partitioning of vertices (nodes or addresses on the internet) of a graph into clusters that are more densely connected, and the cluster membership is inferred from the edge pattern (Abbe, 2017). The rationale behind using this approach is to apply an unsupervised method to discover blocks of nodes in the network given the connectivity pattern, with the aim to discover a latent class or multiple classes of malicious traffic as a subset of all classes that also include normal traffic (since some nodes in the network will likely display normal as well as abnormal behaviour).

2. Methods

2.1. *University of Victoria (ISOT) data set*

Data were downloaded from the University of Victoria (https://www.uvic.ca/engineering/ece/isot/datasets/index.php), as made available by Saad and colleagues (Saad *et al.*, 2011), and consisted of a collection of neutral/background data and 4 samples of botnet data.

2.1.1. *Neutral data*

The neutral data were collected from the Traffic Lab at Ericsson Research in Hungary and from the Lawrence Berkeley National Lab (LBNL). The

Ericsson Lab data set contained a large number of general traffic from a variety of applications, including HTTP web browsing behaviour, gaming streams and packets from popular bit-torrent clients such as Vuze (formerly Azureus). The LBNL is a research institute with a medium-sized enterprise network. The neutral data were collected over a 3-month period, from October 2004 to January 2005, include 22 subnets (Saad *et al.*, 2011).

2.1.2. *Botnet data*

A relatively small capture of Zeus botnet traffic was included, with C&C as well as P2P type traffic. Zeus is one of the biggest and most well-known botnets running on Microsoft Windows, spreads through drive-by-downloads and phishing, and is estimated to have infected 3.6 million computers in the United States in 2009. It is able to secretly steal information from the infected machine, allowing the compromise of bank accounts, email and other personal files.

2.2. *Descriptives*

Because the data were collected in separate environments, the addresses of the botnet data have been mapped to match the addresses of the neutral data so that the connections seem to occur within the same network. The neutral data can be split into six blocks based on the time-stamp of the capture (see Table 1). Only one of the six captures (Table 1; Block 1) included IP addresses that overlapped with the Zeus botnet and that capture was

Table 1: Identified blocks of neutral traffic in the ISOT data set.

Block	Start Date	Start Time	End Date	End Time	# Connections	# Unique Addresses
1	08/10/2007	15:21	10/10/2007	2:26	2300385	9274
2	04/10/2004	22:03	05/10/2004	0:19	17694358	12035
3	15/12/2004	09:08	16/12/2004	7:46	65255086	19560
4	16/12/2004	17:15	17/12/2004	4:10	5023778	5122
5	06/01/2005	20:22	07/01/2005	7:28	20511992	10501
6	07/01/2005	11:55	08/01/2005	6:28	26394390	11198
Zeus C&C	17/01/2010	02:02	17/02/2010	02.07	1632	14
Zeus P2P	26/02/2010	04:12	26/02/2010	14.59	1215	3

used in subsequent analyses because, otherwise, the botnet would form an isolated subnetwork, which is trivially identifiable. The used neutral were collected in a capture from 8/10/2007 to 10/10/2007 and included 2300385 connections. The combined Zeus botnet data included 2847 connections. First, we selected all unique pairs of connections (13609 in neutral data and 28 botnet data), and counted the number of unique nodes (9274 and 18 in neutral and botnet data, respectively) after which these matrices were merged (some nodes overlapped, e.g., IP address 172.16.2.12 was involved in both non-malicious and malicious activity). Second, these matrices were transformed into an adjacency matrix using *igraph* in R. The combined data with labels was visualised in Gephi (see Figure 1).

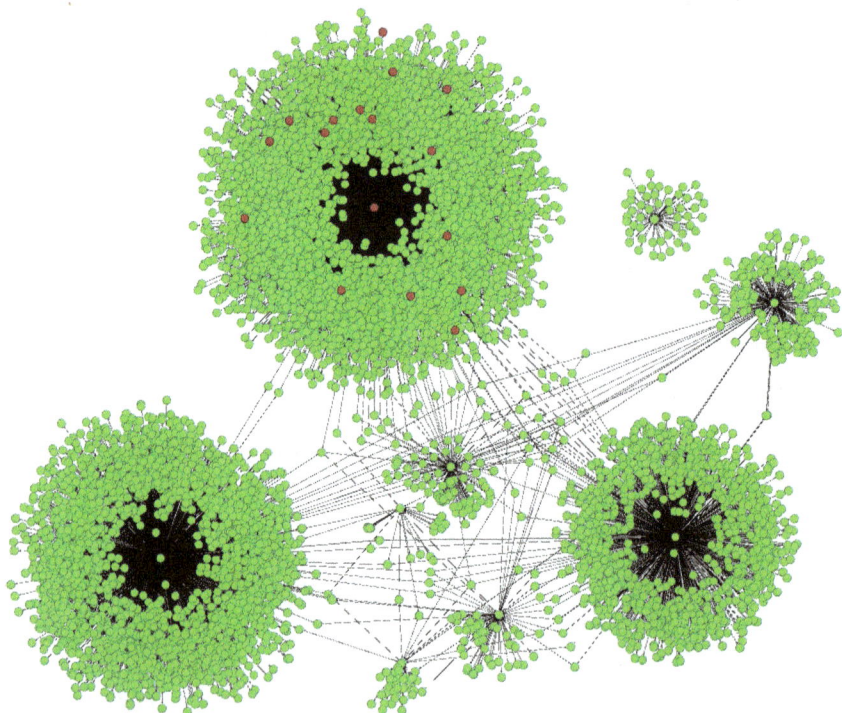

Fig. 1: Network plot of the non-malicious background data and the Zeus botnet data. The colour labels are based on the labels from the original data set with non-malicious data (green) and the Zeus botnet infected nodes (red). Infections are all situated in the highly connected cluster in the top.

2.3. Replication of features from previous studies

Previous studies have mentioned a number of features identified as valid predictors of botnet traffic. In an attempt to replicate previous studies and understand the validity of previously reported features in the current data set, we first present a naive analysis of basic data. We extracted previously reported features and statistically compared these features between non-malicious and malicious data. This is done by collapsing the information available in the network for every node to covariates that are analysed, in replication of previous works, without considering any form of network structure.

2.3.1. Extraction of previously reported features

From the data set, fourteen features could be extracted. These include: number of incoming and outgoing connections, length of the first packet, average packet length, the standard deviation (variability) of packet length, total number of packets exchanged, the ratio of the number of incoming and outgoing connections, the average number of packets per second and the average duration of a connection (see Table 2). In most features, a distinction was made between incoming and outgoing connections. All features were analysed as continuous covariates and, in order to avoid distributional assumptions for non-malicious and malicious data, analyses were based on the non-parametric Wilcoxon rank test. This test was used to detect differences between non-malicious and botnet data.

2.3.2. Replication outcomes

The distributions of fourteen features were compared between the neutral and botnet data. Eleven of the 14 features significantly differed between the two groups (see Table 2). In neutral data, the average number of incoming packets was equal to the number of outgoing packets, whereas in botnet data, these variables are unbalanced. Interestingly, the length of the first packets (incoming and outgoing) was also significantly smaller in botnet data, which is in line with earlier observations that botnets usually start with short connections followed by longer connections after establishing a solid connection (Beigi *et al.*, 2014). Although the average length of the outgoing packets is higher in the botnet data (313.07 bytes) compared

Table 2: Feature comparison between non-malicious and Zeus botnet data.

Feature	Mean (sd) Neutral	Skewness Neutral	Mean (sd) Zeus	Skewness Zeus	p
Number of packets IN	1.47 (25.00)	67.40	0.75 (.44)	−1.19	<0.0001
Number of packets OUT	1.47 (61.05)	74.29	1 (0)	—	<0.0001
First packet length IN	99.27 (32.57)	4.24	62.00 (0)	—	<0.0001
First packet length OUT	119.82 (166.82)	2.83	57.50 (4.09)	0.26	<0.0001
Average length packets IN	104.89 (51.07)	11.58	96.51 (76.29)	2.39	0.0026
Average length packets OUT	241.70 (240.45)	3.19	313.07 (449.61)	1.40	0.0033
Sd length packets IN	25.17 (65.39)	5.61	65.23 (109.98)	1.61	0.4678
Sd length packets OUT	136.39 (166.97)	1.94	150.42 (247.33)	1.38	0.1090
Number packets exchanged	496.40 (18892.76)	65.78	177.94 (433.41)	2.41	<0.0001
IN/OUT packets ratio	1.39 (.99)	4.85	0.69 (.46)	−0.56	<0.0001
Average packets time IN	1.29 (2.29)	18.33	5.23 (6.68)	1.19	0.0027
Average packets time OUT	1.78 (4.61)	13.33	6.58 (12.05)	2.39	0.1943
Average connection duration IN	134.83 (1744.93)	25.25	2.76 (2.73)	2.99	0.0003
Average connection duration OUT	1.98 (10.76)	22.97	2.75 (2.38)	3.30	<0.0001

Note: This table presents the outcomes of the group comparison of features between neutral data and the Zeus botnet data. Degrees of freedom are rounded.
Abbreviations: sd = standard deviation, IN = incoming connection, OUT = outgoing connection.

to non-malicious data (241.70), incoming connections tend to last longer (5.23 seconds in Zeus vs 1.29 seconds in non-malicious data). Standard deviations of incoming (neutral = 25.17, Zeus = 65.23) and outgoing connections (neutral = 136.9, Zeus = 150.42) do not significantly differ, suggesting that there is no increased variability in botnet data. Finally, incoming connections in non-malicious data tend to last significantly longer (134.83 seconds) compared to the botnet data (2.76 seconds), which could be the result of activity such as downloading torrents or gaming.

2.4. Stochastic blockmodels

SBM stems from the merging of blockmodels and stochastic models (Holland *et al.*, 1983). Detailed definitions and derivations have been published elsewhere for directed (Wang and Wong, 1987) and undirected (Snijders and Nowicki, 1997) graphs. Below follows a short outline of the model based on the work presented in Holland *et al.* (1983); Leger (2016).

The botnet data set consists of IP and DNS addresses (vertices) that exist on the internet, which are typically a person manning a computer or a server (hosting a website) connected (edges) in a pairwise manner. These connections can be represented by a directed binary digraph consisting of a set of g nodes. For a single relation between two addresses, the adjacency matrix is given by:

$$X = (x_{ij})$$

with i and j both $\in \{1, \ldots, g\}$, and

$$x_{ij} = \begin{cases} 1 & \text{if } i \text{ connected to } j, \\ 0 & \text{otherwise.} \end{cases}$$

The adjacency matrix was obtained (using *igraph*) after merging the edge-lists of the neutral data and Zeus data. Regardless of how many times identical pairs (e.g., a connection between IP1 and IP2) occurred over time, every ij pair (where $i \neq j$) was 1 if, during the entire capture, at least one connection occurred between address i and address j, and 0 otherwise. The directed nature of the data made X asymmetric as some addresses pairs had a connection in only 1 direction. The lower triangle of X contains outgoing connection $i \rightarrow j$, and the upper triangle contains incoming connection $i \leftarrow j$. Addresses never connected to themselves so, in line with convention, $x_{ij} = 0$, when i equals j. We consider Q classes on nodes, and let the membership matrix Z be

$$Z_{iq} = \begin{cases} 1 & i \text{ is a member of class } q, \\ 0 & \text{otherwise,} \end{cases}$$

for $i \in \{1, \ldots, g\}, q \in \{1, \ldots, Q\}$. The class memberships q of nodes are driven by independently identically distributed multinomial distributions:

$$Z_i \overset{i.i.d.}{\sim} M(1, \alpha),$$

with $i \in \{1, \ldots, g\}$ and where $\alpha \in G$ is a parameter as $\sum_{q=1}^{Q} \alpha_q = 1$.

Next, the model is acquired by obtaining the distribution of each edge (i, j) conditional on the membership of node i in the q-th class and node j in the l-th class:

$$X_{ij}|Z_{iq}Z_{jl} = 1 \overset{ind.}{\sim} \mathbf{B}(\pi_{ql})$$

with $(i, j) \in \{1, \ldots, g\}$ and i never equal to j. $\mathbf{B}$ can be replaced by other distributions giving SBMs their flexibility. There are different models that allow weights on the edge $(i, j) \in \{1, \ldots, g\}$ but in this study edge weights are either 0 or 1, resulting in a Bernoulli model with $[0 \le \pi_{ql} \le 1]$ and $q, l \in \{1, \ldots, Q\}^2$.

Because the diagonals are 0, there are no assortative or disassortative communities (Abbe, 2017). Snijders and Nowicki (1997) argue that models with $Q > 2$ have a complexity that does not allow Maximum Likelihood estimation. Therefore, we used an estimation procedure to determine the optimal number of clusters (Q) based on Mariadassou *et al.* (2010), employing the variational expectation maximisation approach, and the Integrated Classification Likelihood from Biernacki *et al.* (2000). The latter study showed that, in this setting, the ICL can be more robust than the Bayesian Information Criterion and performs well in partitioning mixture models. These algorithms have been recently implemented in the R library *Blockmodels* (Leger, 2016).

2.5. *Simulation study using SBM on simulated network data*

To illustrate the potential of SBMs in identifying clusters of network data in a botnet setting, we first conducted a small simulation study. We simulated a network data set with five users from which four are infected with a P2P botnet (see Figure 2(a). The botnet controller directly connects only to user 1, who connects to user 2, who connects to user 3, who connects to user 4. All users visit between 14 and 30 non-malicious websites including five identical domains (e.g., www.google.com) and 25 unique domains.

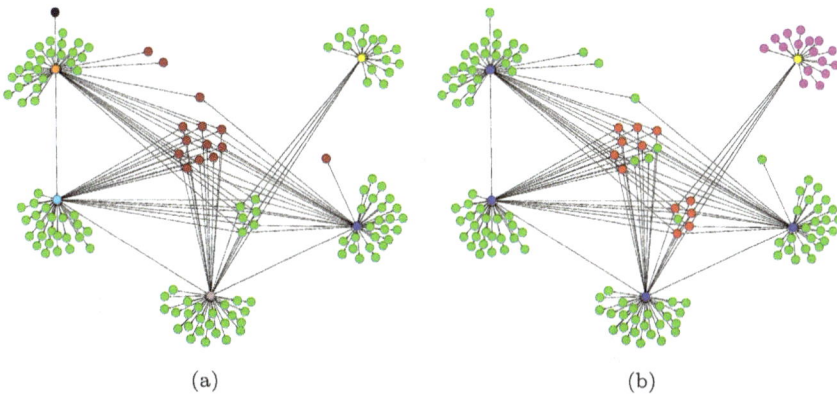

(a)   (b)

Fig. 2: (a) Simulated network with non-malicious activity from four infected users (orange, brown, light- and dark blue nodes) and one uninfected user (yellow) to non-malicious addresses (green nodes), and malicious activity to malicious addresses (red nodes). Nodes in the centre represent addresses visited by multiple users, both non-malicious (green) and malicious (red). The black dot in the left upper corner is the botnet controller communicating to infected user 1 (orange). (b) Simulated network with SBM-generated labels. Five classes capture non-malicious behaviour (green), predominantly malicious behaviour (red), infected users (dark blue) and the uninfected user (yellow) who also connects to unique non-malicious addresses (pink).

The four infected users also visit malicious domains as part of the botnet activity (nine visited by at least two users and three visited by only one user). Ultimately, this data set consisted of 121 non-malicious nodes (120 domains and 1 uninfected user), and 19 malicious nodes (one connector, 14 malicious domains and four infected users).[a]

2.5.1. *Simulation study outcomes*

SBM model fitting on the simulated data revealed that a five class model ($Q = 5$) was optimal with the highest ICL estimate (see Figure 2(b)). This five class model was able to distinguish normal traffic, malicious traffic, and infected users (see Table 3 for the class assignment matrix). The first class captures 99 (81.8%) of the 121 non-malicious nodes and also includes eight malicious nodes (seven domains and the botnet

---

[a] All scripts, data and output from the simulation study can be downloaded from https://github.com/ mproeling/SBM.

Table 3:   Simulation study performance.

Node Type	Class #1	Class #2	Class #3	Class #4	Class #5
Infected users	0	0	4	0	0
Uninfected users	0	1	0	0	0
Non-malicious	99	0	0	16	5
Malicious	7	0	0	0	7
Connector	1	0	0	0	0

Notes: This table presents the frequencies of nodes as distributed over the different classes based on the SBM on the simulation data. Class 1 mostly captures non-malicious nodes and the botnet connector/controller, class 2 includes one uninfected user, class 3 captures all four infected users, class 4 includes non-malicious nodes and class 5 captures a subset of malicious and non-malicious nodes.

manager/connector). The second and third class, respectively, capture the uninfected and infected users and have perfect assignment. The fourth class captures the non-malicious domains only visited by the uninfected user. The fifth class includes the malicious and non-malicious domains visited by multiple users. If we consider classes 1, 2 and 4 as neutral and classes 3 and 5 as malicious, then we have 11 True Positives, eight False Negatives, five False Positives and 116 True Negatives. Hence, the accuracy of the simulation SBM is 90.7%, the sensitivity is 68.8% and the specificity is 93.5%.

3.   Results for ISOT/Zeus Data

3.1.   *SBM outcomes*

The SBM model fitting procedure on the University of Victoria data yielded the highest ICL value in a model with $Q = 9$. From the membership matrix Z, we obtained, for every node g and for every class $q \in \{1, \ldots, 9\}$, a posterior probability, and estimate $\hat{p}_{i,q} = E(Z_{i,q}|X)$, which is an estimate of the posterior probability that node i is in group q. Table 4 shows the distribution of g over q. The infected nodes are distributed over two classes (3 and 5). In class 3, most of the connection $(5150/5166 = 99.7\%)$ is non-malicious. Yet, this class includes 94.1% of all botnet data. Class 5 is a separate class capturing only one node (IP $= 172.16.2.12$) involved in both non-malicious and malicious activity. Classes 1 and 7 both capture clusters

Table 4:   Distribution of malicious and non-malicious nodes across class membership.

Class	# Nodes	# Neutral Nodes	# Zeus Nodes	% Botnet Nodes	Fig. 1 Class Colour
1	1144	1144	0	—	Blue
2	1	1	0	—	Light blue
3	5166	5150	16	94.1%	Purple
4	6	6	0	—	Pink
5	2	1	1	5.9%	Dark green
6	1	1	0	—	Yellow
7	2425	2425	0	—	Green
8	81	81	0	—	Orange
9	465	465	0	—	Black

Note: This table presents the frequencies of nodes as distributed over the different classes of the best fitting model, after assigning class membership to the class with the highest posterior probability.

with neutral data. Class 8 contains nodes that act as a hub and lie between clusters. Class 9 captures several small sub-networks. The other classes contain a small number of central nodes from the neutral data (Figure 3).

4.   Discussion

This chapter presents a first look at the use of the SBM framework for botnet discovery. The simulation study showed that SBMs can be of merit in networks with multiple infected users visiting the same (malicious and non-malicious) addresses. Interestingly, nodes that were wrongly assigned were all visited by multiple users, and botnet nodes that were wrongly identified as non-malicious were all visited by only subgroups of users (e.g., only user 1 and 2). Since botnets usually force a larger number of visitors to the same domains (e.g., DDoS attack), this could strongly increase the detection accuracy. In real-world applications, SBM model performance was significantly lower: if the entire cluster that included botnet data would be treated as infected this would result in a very high false positive rate.

These outcomes should be interpreted in light of some limitations. First, the current model fitting procedure did not include covariates. Given afore-mentioned successes with machine learning features, the performance of our best fitting model could increase if these features (e.g., bytes transferred or packets received) were included in the SBM. Second, modelling the

Data Science for Cyber-Security

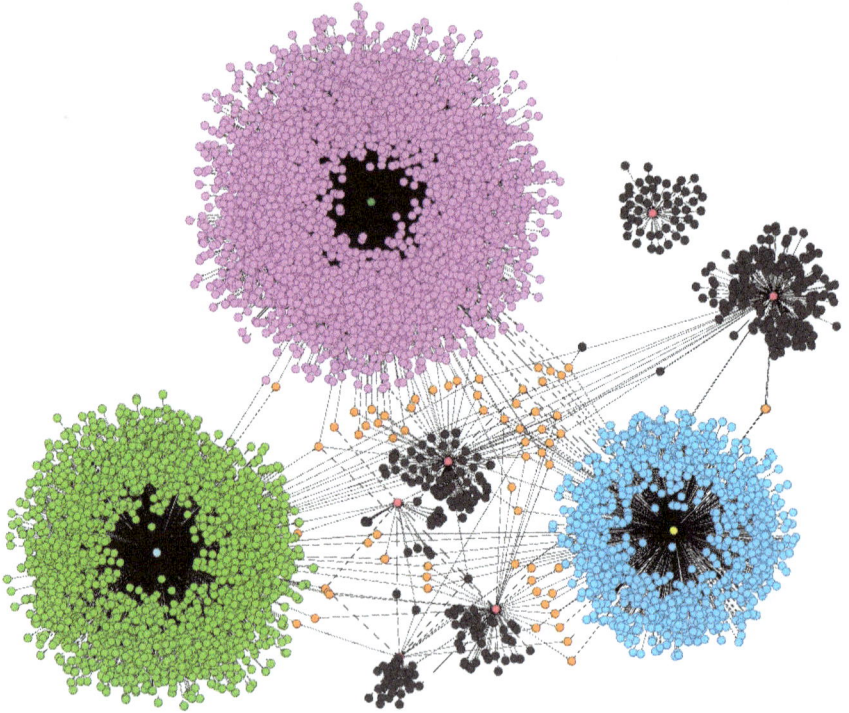

Fig. 3: Network plot of the non-malicious background data and the Zeus botnet data. The colour labels are based on the SBM output with of the best fitting 9 class model, showing three highly connected clusters (purple, green, blue), one class moderately connected sub-networks (black), one class with nodes that connect different clusters (orange) and the remaining four classes capture the nodes that are typically in the centre of the clusters (light blue, yellow, dark green, and pink).

temporal structure of the network data could significantly contribute to an improved detection rate (Holme and Saramäki, 2012), although such analysis would be artificial with current data sets since data are collected in separate environments, at different moments in time. Third, it is possible that the data used here does not provide an adequate capture of real botnet network activity. For example, botnet infections occurred only in one cluster, whereas in P2P botnet activity one would expect multiple clusters (or nodes across clusters) to be infected. Also, connections between clusters were unusually weak and almost always indirect, whereas in P2P traffic one would expect some form of direct link between infected nodes. Unlike the simulation data, where the simultaneous visiting of malicious websites (or the absence of visits) by different users in different clusters was a key marker for botnet detection, those patterns seemed absent in the real-world data analysed here. Finally, these data were collected in separate environments. The botnet data were collected with virtual machines (VM) and IP mapping was used to create one network. Most studies analyse botnet data collected in a VM (Arshad *et al.*, 2011; Beigi *et al.*, 2014; Bharathula and Menon, 2016; Carl *et al.*, 2006; Davis, 2012; Guntuku *et al.*, 2013; Singh *et al.*, 2014), but this can be problematic since there can be many (unobserved) factors that contribute to differences between botnet and background data. The SBM outcomes of this study do not show a strong bias of such difference as there was no immediate distinction between botnet and neutral data. Yet, merging data from different sources can be problematic and ideally one would ask a number of users to work on an infected VM during their normal internet/browsing activity, and then manually classify genuine from malicious traffic afterwards for comparison so that all activity is collected within the same setting. Another benefit of such a design would be that the neutral background data really is uninfected, which improves on current studies that assume that background data, from e.g., a University Campus, is completely free of malicious activity.

References

Abbe, E. (2017). Community detection and stochastic block models: Recent developments, arXiv preprint arXiv:1703.10146.

Arshad, S., Abbaspour, M., Kharrazi, M. and Sanatkar, H. (2011). An anomaly-based botnet detection approach for identifying stealthy botnets, in *2011 IEEE International Conference on Computer Applications and Industrial Electronics (ICCAIE)*, pp. 564–569.

Barthakur, P., Dahal, M. and Ghose, M. K. (2013). An efficient machine learning based classification scheme for detecting distributed command & control traffic of p2p botnets, *International Journal of Modern Education and Computer Science* 5, 10, p. 9.

Beigi, E. B., Jazi, H. H., Stakhanova, N. and Ghorbani, A. A. (2014). Towards effective feature selection in machine learning-based botnet detection approaches, in *2014 IEEE Conference on Communications and Network Security (CNS)*, pp. 247–255.

Bharathula, P. and Menon, N. M. (2016). Equitable machine learning algorithms to probe over p2p botnets, in *Proceedings of the 4th International Conference on Frontiers in Intelligent Computing: Theory and Applications (FICTA) 2015*, pp. 13–21.

Biernacki, C., Celeux, G. and Govaert, G. (2000). Assessing a mixture model for clustering with the integrated completed likelihood, *IEEE Transactions on Pattern Analysis and Machine Intelligence* **22**, 7, pp. 719–725.

Bilge, L., Balzarotti, D., Robertson, W., Kirda, E. and Kruegel, C. (2012). Disclosure: Detecting botnet command and control servers through large-scale netflow analysis, in *Proceedings of the 28th Annual Computer Security Applications Conference*, pp. 129–138.

Bou-Harb, E., Debbabi, M. and Assi, C. (2017). Big data behavioral analytics meet graph theory: On effective botnet takedowns, *IEEE Network* **31**, 1, pp. 18–26.

Burghouwt, P., Spruit, M. and Sips, H. (2010). Detection of botnet collusion by degree distribution of domains, in *2010 International Conference for Internet Technology and Secured Transactions (ICITST)*, pp. 1–8.

Camelo, P., Moura, J. and Krippahl, L. (2014). Condenser: A graph-based approach for detecting botnets, arXiv preprint arXiv:1410.8747.

Carl, L. *et al.* (2006). Using machine learning technliques to identify botnet traffic, in *Proceedings 2006 31st IEEE Conference on Local Computer Networks*, IEEE, FL, USA.

Chang, W., Mohaisen, A., Wang, A. and Chen, S. (2015). Measuring botnets in the wild: Some new trends, in *Proceedings of the 10th ACM Symposium on Information, Computer and Communications Security*, pp. 645–650.

Davis, N. (2012). Botnet detection using correlated anomalies, Masters's thesis, Technical University of Denmark Informatics and Mathematical Modelling, Denmark. Retrieved from: http://www2.imm.dtu.dk/pubdb/views/edoc_download.php/6356/pdf/imm6356.pdf.

Davuth, N. and Sung-Ryul, K. (2013). Classification of malicious domain names using support vector machine and bi-gram method, *International Journal of Security and its Applications* **7**, 1, pp. 51–58.

Elhalabi, M. J., Manickam, S., Melhim, L. B., Anbar, M. and Alhalabi, H. (2014). A review of peer-to-peer botnet detection techniques, *Journal of Computer Science* **10**, 1, p. 169.

Feizollah, A., Anuar, N. B., Salleh, R., Amalina, F., Shamshirband, S. *et al.* (2013). A study of machine learning classifiers for anomaly-based mobile botnet detection, *Malaysian Journal of Computer Science* **26**, 4, pp. 251–265.

Guntuku, S. C., Narang, P. and Hota, C. (2013). Real-time peer-to-peer botnet detection framework based on Bayesian regularized neural network, arXiv preprint arXiv:1307.7464.

Haddadi, F., Morgan, J., Gomes Filho, E. and Zincir-Heywood, A. N. (2014). Botnet behaviour analysis using ip flows: With http filters using classifiers, in *2014 28th International Conference on Advanced Information Networking and Applications Workshops (WAINA)*, pp. 7–12.

Haddadi, F. and Zincir-Heywood, A. N. (2015). Botnet detection system analysis on the effect of botnet evolution and feature representation, in *Proceedings of the Companion Publication of the 2015 Annual Conference on Genetic and Evolutionary Computation*, pp. 893–900.

Haltaş, F., Uzun, E., Şişeci, N., Poşul, A. and Emre, B. (2014). An automated bot detection system through honeypots for large-scale, in *2014 6th International Conference on, Cyber Conflict (CyCon 2014)*, pp. 255–270.

Holland, P. W., Laskey, K. B. and Leinhardt, S. (1983). Stochastic blockmodels: First steps, *Social Networks* **5**, 2, pp. 109–137.

Holme, P. and Saramäki, J. (2012). Temporal networks, *Physics Reports* **519**, 3, pp. 97–125.

Hyslip, T. S. and Pittman, J. M. (2015). A survey of botnet detection techniques by command and control infrastructure, *Journal of Digital Forensics, Security and Law* **10**, 1, p. 2.

Ismail, Z. and Jantan, A. (2016). A review of machine learning application in botnet detection system, *Sindh University Research Journal — SURJ (Science Series)* **48**, 4D, pp. 111–118.

Karim, A., Salleh, R. and Khan, M. K. (2016). Smartbot: A behavioral analysis framework augmented with machine learning to identify mobile botnet applications, *PloS One* **11**, 3, p. e0150077.

Karim, A., Salleh, R. B., Shiraz, M., Shah, S. A. A., Awan, I. and Anuar, N. B. (2014). Botnet detection techniques: Review, future trends, and issues, *Journal of Zhejiang University SCIENCE C* **15**, 11, pp. 943–983.

Leger, J.-B. (2016). Blockmodels: A r-package for estimating in latent block model and stochastic block model, with various probability functions, with or without covariates, arXiv preprint arXiv:1602.07587.

Mariadassou, M., Robin, S. and Vacher, C. (2010). Uncovering latent structure in valued graphs: a variational approach, *The Annals of Applied Statistics* **4**, 2, pp. 715–742.

Meng, X. and Spanoudakis, G. (2015). Mbotcs: A mobile botnet detection system based on machine learning, in *International Conference on Risks and Security of Internet and Systems*, pp. 274–291.

Nogueira, A., Salvador, P. and Blessa, F. (2010). A botnet detection system based on neural networks, in *2010 Fifth International Conference on Digital Telecommunications (ICDT)*, pp. 57–62.

Rossow, C., Andriesse, D., Werner, T., Stone-Gross, B., Plohmann, D., Dietrich, C. J. and Bos, H. (2013). Sok: P2pwned-modeling and evaluating the resilience of peer-to-peer botnets, in *2013 IEEE Symposium on Security and Privacy (SP)*, pp. 97–111.

Saad, S., Traore, I., Ghorbani, A., Sayed, B., Zhao, D., Lu, W., Felix, J. and Hakimian, P. (2011). Detecting p2p botnets through network behavior analysis and machine learning, in *2011 Ninth Annual International Conference on Privacy, Security and Trust (PST)*, pp. 174–180.

Singh, K., Guntuku, S. C., Thakur, A. and Hota, C. (2014). Big data analytics framework for peer-to-peer botnet detection using random forests, *Information Sciences* **278**, pp. 488–497.

Snijders, T. A. and Nowicki, K. (1997). Estimation and prediction for stochastic blockmodels for graphs with latent block structure, *Journal of Classification* **14**, 1, pp. 75–100.

Steglich, C., Snijders, T. A. and Pearson, M. (2010). Dynamic networks and behavior: Separating selection from influence, *Sociological Methodology* **40**, 1, pp. 329–393.

Stevanovic, M. and Pedersen, J. M. (2013). Machine learning for identifying botnet network traffic, Tech. rep., Aalborg University.

Tegeler, F., Fu, X., Vigna, G. and Kruegel, C. (2012). Botfinder: Finding bots in network traffic without deep packet inspection, in *Proceedings of the 8th International Conference on Emerging Networking Experiments and Technologies*, pp. 349–360.

Vania, J., Meniya, A. and Jethva, H. (2013). A review on botnet and detection technique, *International Journal of Computer Trends and Technology* **4**, 1, pp. 23–29.

Wang, Y. J. and Wong, G. Y. (1987). Stochastic blockmodels for directed graphs, *Journal of the American Statistical Association* **82**, 397, pp. 8–19.

Chapter 9

Classification of Red Team Authentication Events in an Enterprise Network

John M. Conroy

IDA/Center for Computing Sciences,
17100 Science Dr, Bowie, MD 20715, USA

conroy@super.org

In this chapter we explore two spectral embeddings, adjacency spectral embedding (ASE) and normalised Laplacian (NL), of the bipartite graph of authentication events from the first release of the Los Alamos Cyber-Security Events data (Kent, 2016). Both ASE and NL require the estimation of the principal singular vectors associated with the largest singular values of a matrix. For comparison, an ensemble of random projections (RP) are also used as a baseline as is the degree sequence of the nodes. The embeddings (spectral, random or degree sequence) are then used as features for a random forest classifier to classify nodes of the graph (computers) into one of two classes: those that have attacked and those that have not. The results indicate that the features produced by ASE are substantially stronger than those of NL, and surprisingly RP outperforms NL — which does outperform the baseline of degree sequence. Finally, the experiments are repeated without the red team events (authentication spoofing attacks) and while the performance degrades, the features still have significant ability to predict which computers will be attacked given a sample of those that would be attacked. Thus, the set of computers that would be attacked are related by their connectivity in the network even when the the edges corresponding to their attack are removed. In this sense, they form a sub-network which may be learned by the connections present in the network when the attacking (red team) events are removed.

1. Introduction

The use of graph theoretic and statistical methods in cyber-defence has recently received much attention. In this chapter, we focus on bipartite authentication graphs. Graphical features such as degree and diameter of these graphs were previously studied by Kent *et al.* (2015) where it was observed that administrators tend to have a higher number of authentication events. Such differences in a user's local graph of authentication events can be used to help classify a user or detect intrusions into the network. Later Heard and Rubin-Delanchy (2016) used a Dirichlet process to model the degree sequence of users to detect malicious authentication events. In this chapter, we study the use of graph embeddings using the singular values of the adjacency matrix corresponding to the bipartite graph. Previously Sussman *et al.* (2012) have used spectral graph embeddings, in particular, the adjacency spectral embedding (ASE) to study statistical classification problems and proved that ASE, in the limit, is consistent for graphs generated by a stochastic block model (SBM). Similarly, Rohe *et al.* (2011) has developed the corresponding machinery and results for embeddings using the normalised Laplacian (NL). Also, Rubin-Delanchy *et al.* (2016) used the NL of graph spectral methods to model the disassortativity of computer networks. In this chapter, we study both ASE and NL for bipartite authentication graphs. We show that the spectra may be computed via a truncated singular value decomposition (SVD), which is quickly computed via fast randomised algorithms such as is found in Python's *sklearn*.[a] These methods will be compared with baselines of random projections (RP) and the degree of the vertices, defined as the number of servers that connect to a client computer.

For all of our experiments, we use the Los Alamos National Laboratory (LANL) "Comprehensive, Multi-Source Cyber-Security Events" data: This data set represents 58 consecutive days of de-identified event data collected from five sources within Los Alamos National Laboratory's corporate, internal computer network. The data sources include Windows-based authentication events from both individual computers and centralised Active Directory domain controller servers, process start and stop events from individual Windows computers, domain name service (DNS) lookups as collected on internal DNS servers, network flow data as collected on at several key router

---

[a]In all of our experiments that required computed a truncated SVD, we called *randomized_svd()* with the default value of five iterations.

locations and a set of well-defined red team events that present bad behaviour within the 58 days. In total, the data set is approximately 12 gigabytes compressed across the five data elements and presents 1,648,275,307 events in total for 12,425 users, 17,684 computers and 62,974 processes.[b] The authentication data, when represented as a bipartite graph consists of 98,513 clients (sources) and 15,876 server (destinations).[c] The resulting graph has a total of 805,201 edges.

2. Graph Embeddings

Given an undirected graph G with n nodes and an adjacency matrix A, we seek to find a low-dimension representation of this graph. Without loss of generality, we assume that the graph is connected as the methods proposed may be applied to each of the components for unconnected graphs.

We first consider the spectral decomposition of a slight adjustment of the adjacency matrix as suggested by Marchette *et al.* (2011) for use in the inner product graph model. We will refer to this decomposition as the ASE. The ASE is a truncated SVD of

$$\tilde{A} = A + \tilde{D} \ (ASE),$$

where $\tilde{D}$ is diagonal matrix whose entries are given by $d_i/(n'-1)$, where d_i is the degree of node i and n' the number of nodes. As $\tilde{A}$ is a symmetric matrix, we may compute the truncated SVD by finding the d principal eigenpairs, the eigenvalues of largest magnitude and their associated eigenvectors. As the largest degree of any node in an authentication graph is much less than n, the number of nodes in the graph, we make the simplification by considering the SVD of the adjacency matrix. In the limit if the degrees of the nodes are bounded above by a constant (or even $O(\log(n'))$), asymptotically the adjusted and non-adjusted adjacency matrices have the same decomposition.

---

[b] See http://csr.lanl.gov/data/cyber1/ for details.
[c] Note that a computer in one authentication event may be a client and in another be a server. Only two computers in the LANL data were seen as both clients and servers in the authentication data.

With this simplification ASE of a bipartite graph may be further simplified as

$$A = \begin{bmatrix} 0 & B^{\mathrm{T}} \\ B & 0 \end{bmatrix},$$

with B an m by n adjacency matrix giving the edges between $n' = m + n$ nodes of the graph with adjacency matrix A. Thus, truncated SVD of A may be derived from the truncated SVD of B, for if $B = U_d \Sigma_d V_d^{\mathrm{T}}$ with Σ_d such that

$$\mathrm{diag}(\Sigma_d) = (\sigma_1, \sigma_2, \ldots, \sigma_d),$$

with

$$\sigma_1 > \sigma_2 > \cdots > \sigma_3 > \sigma_d > 0,$$

then the singular vector of A are given by

$$\begin{bmatrix} V_d & V_d \\ U_d & -U_d \end{bmatrix}$$

and the corresponding singular values are given by

$$\begin{bmatrix} \Sigma_d & 0 \\ 0 & \Sigma_d \end{bmatrix}.$$

Secondly, we consider the NL matrix which is related to the graph Laplacian, L, with

$$L = D - A,$$

where D is the diagonal matrix with $D_{i,i}$ giving the degree of node i. The matrix L is positive semi-definite and the eigenvectors associated with the smallest positive eigenvalues give the ℓ_2 relaxation solution of finding minimal cut sets in the graph G. We represent the k smallest positive eigenvalues of the Laplacian by the matrix $\Lambda^{(L,k)}$ and the corresponding eigenvalues by $Q^{(L,k)}$.

The symmetric NL is a symmetric scaling of the graph Laplacian and this normalisation is given in Equation (2) and is usually preferred over the graph Laplacian as it standardises the matrix based on the degree of the rows and columns as given by

$$\mathcal{L} = D^{-1/2} L D^{-1/2} = I - D^{-1/2} A D^{-1/2} \quad (NL).$$

Note, as with the ASE of a bipartite graph, to compute the spectral decomposition of $\mathcal{L}$ we may compute the rank d truncation of $D_r^{-1/2} B D_c^{-1/2}$ where D_r and D_c are diagonal matrices with the row and column degrees of the bipartite graph whose adjacency matrix is given by B.

As we are restricting our analysis to graphs that are connected, a consequence is that the left and right principal singular vectors, those corresponding to the largest singular values, can be represented as a vector with positive components. This is a result of the Perron–Frobenius theorem (see for example Varga, 2000). We also note that the principal left and right singular vectors of $\mathcal{L}$ are up to scaling, the square roots of row and column sums of the matrix B.

3. Stochastic Block Models

SBM is a random graph model where connections among defined subsets of nodes occur with a fixed probability, that is nodes in subset i will have an edge to nodes in subset j with a given probability p_{ij}. Asymptotically, both ASE (Tang *et al.*, 2017) and NL (Rohe *et al.*, 2011) are known to recover the parameters of the SBM and thus can be used for classification, which will be asymptotically optimal, under the assumption that the graph is generated by the SBM. To illustrate a 2×2 SBM for the LANL data, consider the network flow graph in conjunction with the red team data. We can readily estimate a 2×2 matrix of probabilities and then generate a random graph from this model. Figure 1 is an example of such a graph generated by the red team data and the flow data from LANL. The sizes of the red team subsets were expanded to help illustrate the connection patterns. As we can see in the flow data, there is a degree bias for the red team computers both in those doing the infecting and the infected. While a 2×2 model is not sufficient to give the strongest results possible, it does help illustrate structure within the graph. In the next section, we will illustrate two-dimensional embeddings for ASE and use higher dimensions for classification. But before doing so, we introduce a RP alternative to spectral projections.

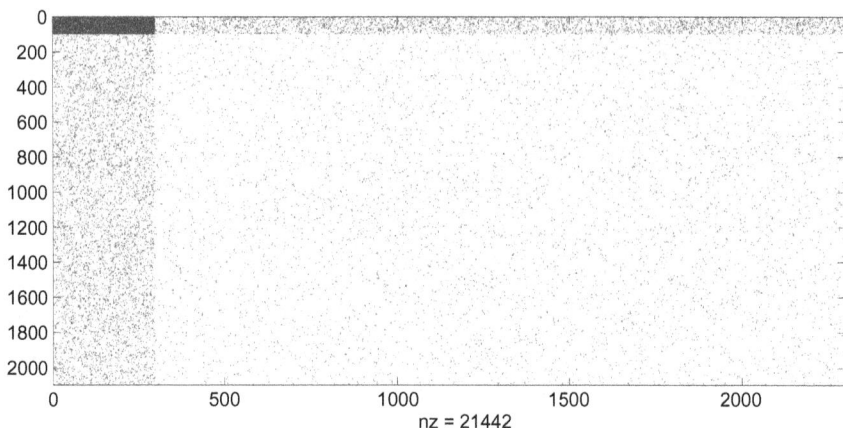

Fig. 1:   SBM of the Graph.

4. Random Projections

RPs are a cheap alternative to spectral embeddings. Specifically, we desire
to embed the nodes corresponding to the rows of B by computing

$$Y_d = BX_d,$$

with the matrix X_d being an n by d matrix whose entries are chosen from
$N(0, 1)$, the standard normal distribution. By the Johnson–Lindenstrauss
Lemma, RP are known to preserve the relative inter-point distances (Johnson
et al., 1986). In the context of graph adjacency matrices, a RP is the expected
value of the squared two-norm, which is preserved, and consequently the
expected value of the squared distance between two nodes is the size of the
symmetric difference of their respective neighbourhoods, which we state
more formally as

Lemma 1. *Let B be an m by n matrix with $b_{ij} = 0$ or 1, r an n long
vector whose entries are chosen from the standardised normal distribution,
$r_i \sim \mathcal{N}(0, 1)$ and $y = Br$. Then the expected value of the sum of squares
of differences in entries of y equals the sum of the corresponding sum of
squares of differences of the rows of B, which is the size of the symmetric*

difference of the neighbourhood of the node i and j in the bipartite graph induced by B.

Proof.

$$E\left[(y_i - y_j)^2\right] = E\left[\left(\sum_{k \in \Delta_{ij}} \text{sgn}(\delta_{ij})r_k\right)^2\right] = E\left[\sum_{k \in \Delta_{ij}} r_k^2\right] = \delta_{ij},$$

with $\delta_{ij} = \sum_{k=1}^{n} |b_{ik} - b_{jk}| = \sum_{k \in \Delta_{ij}} |b_{ik} - b_{jk}|$ and Δ_{ij} the symmetric difference of the neighbourhoods of i and j which is

$$\Delta_{ij} = \{k \text{ such that } |b_{ik} - b_{jk}| \neq 0\}$$

and $\text{sgn}(\delta_{ij})$ is $+1$ or -1 depending on whether k is a neighbour of i or j, respectively. □

5. Results

We now apply the spectral embeddings, RP and degree sequences to the problem of detecting which computers have been attacked via a compromised "red team" authentication event. We consider two experimental designs. In the first, we form the graph using all 59 days of authentication data including the red team events. The authentication attacks were launched from 4 computers and a total of 301 computers were attacked. Table 1 gives the number of nodes and edges in the largest component of the graphs with and without the red team events. When the red team events are included the graph is connected. Without these events the graph is not connected but only a small fraction of vertices are not part of the largest component. None of the attacking or attacked computers are outside this largest component of the graph.

Table 1: Number of clients, servers and events (Edges) in the Los Alamos Authentication Data.

Graph	Clients	Servers	Edges
Without red team events	98509	15876	805201
With red team events	98513	15876	805509

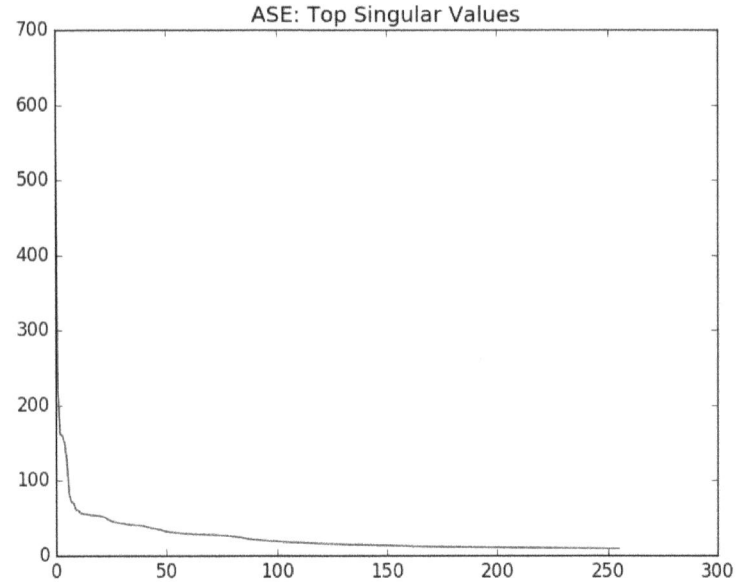

Fig. 2: Adjacency spectral embedding (ASE): Singular values plot (index vs singular value).

The graphs are fairly modest in size and a rank 512 truncated SVD for both ASE and NL are readily computed in Python in about 8 seconds for either decomposition using approximately 6 cores of a Intel(R) Xeon(R) CPU E5-2665 0 @ 2.40 GHz via *scikitlearn*,[d] which employs an implementation of a fast probabilistic truncated SVD developed by Halko *et al.* (2011). By comparison to the spectral methods which took about 8 seconds on 6 cores, 512 RP took about 4 seconds on a single core to compute for the LANL authentication graph. Figures 2 and 3 plot the first 256 singular values for the ASE and NL decompositions for the LANL authentication graph.

Figure 4 illustrates the two-dimensional ASE where the 301 attacked computers are coloured red and the remaining computers are coloured blue. While this two-dimensional scatter plot shows some separation, a higher dimensional embedding can provide a stronger set of features for classification.

---

[d]https://github.com/scikit-learn/scikit-learn.

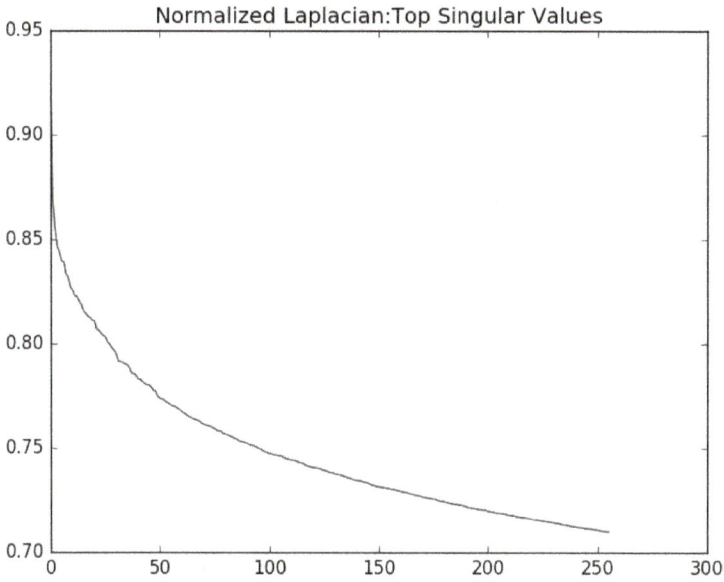

Fig. 3:   Normalised Laplacian (NL): Singular values plot (index vs singular value).

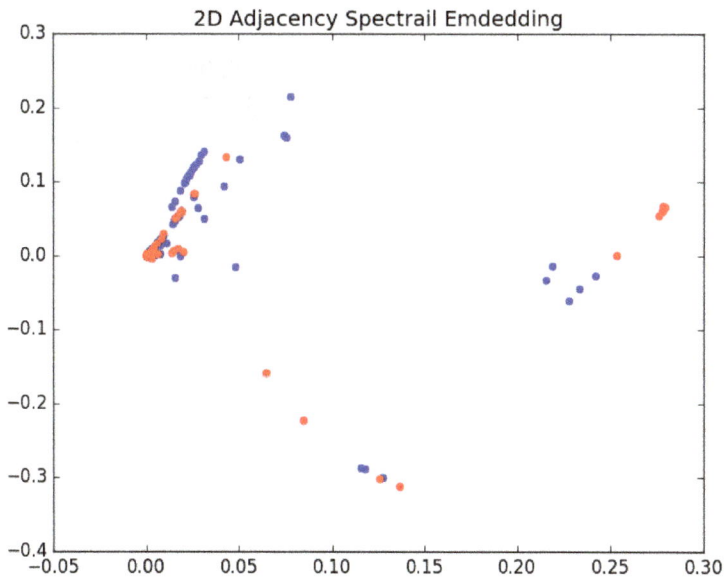

Fig. 4:   ASE: Two-dimensional scatter plot of first two principal right singular vectors.

The classification problem we pose is: given an authentication graph, a subset of the 301 computers which the red team compromised, and a subset of computers that were not compromised, classify each remaining computer as compromised or not compromised. A 2-fold cross-validation experiment for each of these embeddings as well as using the degree sequence (Degree) as a feature was performed. A random forest classifier (Breiman, 2001) as implemented in *scikitlearn*,[e] with 1,000 trees was used to perform the classification, and the true-positive rate (TPR) and the false-positive rate (FPR) as well as the area under the curve (AUC) of FPR vs TPR is given for each approach. The cross-validation splitting of test and train data was done so that approximately an equal number of compromised (and un-compromised) computers were in the test and train data sets. Thus, this ensured that 150 or 151 compromised computers would be in the training (and testing) data and about 7,800 non-compromised computers in each of the test and train data sets. We evaluated dimension 16 and 256 embeddings for ASE, NL and RP. These are denoted ASE16, ASE256, NL16, NL256 RP16 and RP256 in Table 2. We note that ASE256 performs the best and while Degree performs the worst, it is a relatively strong baseline. Finally, we note that RP, while less effective than ASE, far exceeds NL and the baseline of Degree.

To measure to what extent the set of 301 computers that were attacked form a community *without* the red team events, the same set of experiments were repeated with the red team edges removed. Table 3 gives these results.

Table 2: Performance of various embedding with red team events included.

Embedding	AUC	FPR	TPR
Degree	0.71	1.96e−01	0.55
NL16	0.84	8.22e−03	0.07
NL256	0.89	5.97e−03	0.06
RP16	0.87	3.21e−04	0.03
RP256	0.97	0.00e+00	0.01
ASE16	0.97	9.25e−03	0.19
ASE256	0.99	5.78e−04	0.68

---

[e]https://github.com/scikit-learn/scikit-learn.

Table 3: Performance of various embedding with red team events excluded.

Embedding	AUC [AUC w Red]	FPR	TPR
Degree	0.65 [0.71]	1.45e−01	0.39
NL16	0.78 [0.84]	8.93e−03	0.08
NL256	0.79 [0.89]	6.16e−03	0.06
RP16	0.71 [0.87]	7.71e−04	0.02
RP256	0.82 [0.97]	1.93e−04	0.02
ASE16	0.85 [0.97]	8.93e−03	0.06
ASE256	0.91 [0.99]	6.49e−03	0.03

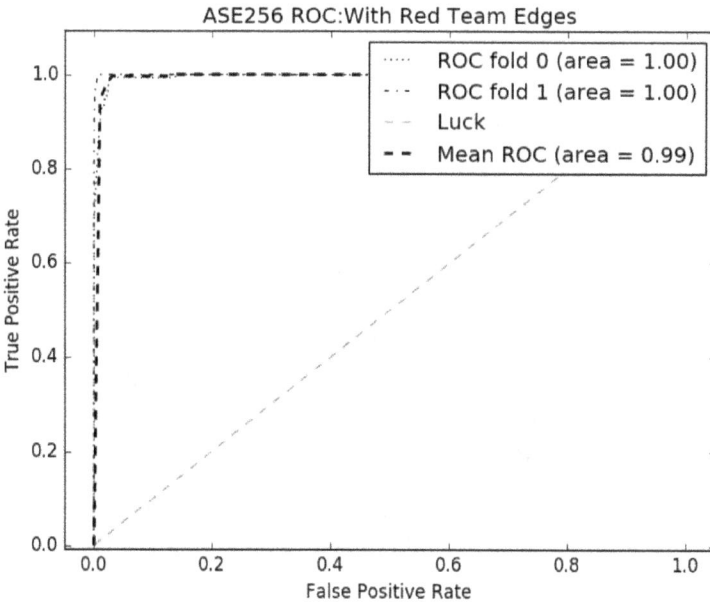

Fig. 5: ASE256: ROC curve with red team edges: 2-fold cross-validation.

For ease of comparison, the AUC for when the red team events were included is displayed in square brackets after the AUC for when these events are excluded. The performance of all features drop, but all perform significantly better than random. Finally, Figures 5 and 6 give the ROC curves for ASE256 both when the red team events are included and excluded, respectively.

ASE256 ROC:No Red Team Edges

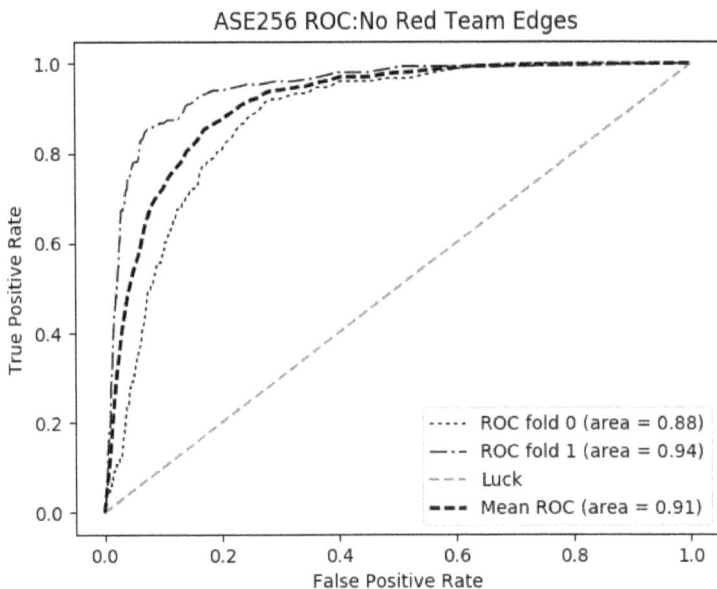

Fig. 6:   ASE256: ROC curve with no red team edges: 2-fold cross-validation.

6. Epilogue

All results presented, so far, used *randomized_svd*(), the default and pre-ferred method called by Python's *TruncatedSVD*() found in sklearn. In a nutshell, the default parameters for the randomised SVD gives rise to the following simple and very fast algorithm:

- Five iterations of block power method with random start with an LU decomposition to normalise after each iteration but the last, where QR decomposition is used.
- One step of Rayleigh–Ritz method.

The Python code is based on the algorithm presented by Halko *et al.* (2011), where a concentration measure theorem is used to show that the method will with high probability compute the matrix decomposition accurately. The Python implementation does not check the accuracy of the solution in any way, presumably to save computation time. The method is the default called by *TruncatedSVD*() as it is generally much faster than the block Lanczos alternatives e.g., *svds*() from the Python *scipy.sparse.linalg* package, and

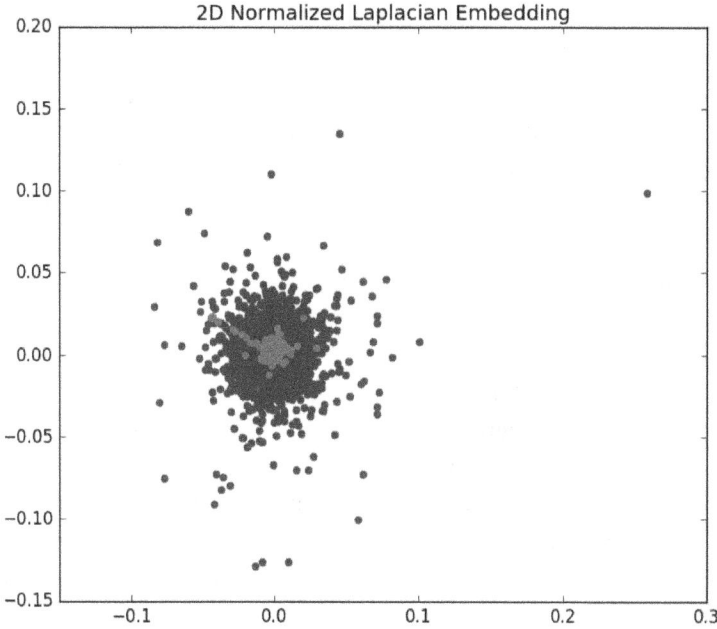

Fig. 7: NL: Two-dimensional scatter plot of first two principal right singular vectors as computed by *randomized_svd()*.

it is thought to give *good enough accuracy* for machine learning tasks. Based on some preliminary testing on the net flow graphs, this seemed to be confirmed. However, scatter plots for the two-dimensional embedding with the NL raised concerns about the accuracy of the *randomized_svd()*. Figure 7 gives a two-dimensional scatter plot when using the principal two right singular vectors of the NL, which embed the server nodes of the graph. Note that the x-axis gives the values which are entries in the first singular vector of the matrix $D_r^{-1/2} B D_c^{-1/2}$, which up to a scale is the vector whose ith entry is $d_i^{1/2}$ where d_i is the number of clients from which server i has had an authentication event. Clearly, this singular vector was computed with low accuracy as its values are both positive and negative. Thus, *randomized_svd()* does not even compute the sign bit correctly for this singular vector! The first singular value corresponding to this vector should be 1; however *randomize_svd()* computed it to be approximately 0.92638.

Note, in contrast, the scatter plot of the two-dimensional embedding for ASE as displayed in Figure 4. This scatter plot is of the first two right singular vectors of B (ASE) and as the plot suggests the first dimension is a positive vector, which is also expected by the Perron–Frobenius Theorem (Varga, 2000). This theorem states that the principal eigenvector of a non-negative irreducible matrix can be represented as a non-negative vector. The right singular vectors of B are the eigenvectors of $B^T B$, which is indeed nonnegative and confirmed computationally to be an irreducible matrix.

As this plot suggests, the numerical inaccuracy of *randomized_svd*() in the computation of the SVD of the adjacency matrix (ASE) was not as severe. Here, the accuracy of the singular values (and the resulting singular vectors) for this matrix line up with those given by the ARPACK (Lehoucq *et al.*, 1998) implementation of block Lanczos computed by *svds*(), in approximately the top half to the computed singular values. Note that ARPACK runs to convergence or reports non-convergence and the singular values were computed to the default tolerance of machine precision and convergence was always observed.

In the end, what is needed is a numerically computed embedding which gives high classification accuracy. To this end, we now compare the effect of the numerical method (*randomized_svd*() vs *svds*()) used in computing the embedding for the red team event classification problem. Table 4 does this

Table 4: Classification performance comparing *randomized_svd*() [RSVD] vs *svds*() [ARPACK].

Method	Embedding	AUC	FPR	TPR
RSVD	ASE16	0.97	9.25e−03	0.19
ARPACK	ASE16	0.97	8.99e−03	0.19
RSVD	ASE256	0.99	5.78e−04	0.68
ARPACK	ASE256	0.99	7.71e−04	0.67
RSVD	NL16	0.84	8.22e−03	0.07
ARPACK	NL16	0.91	1.41e−02	0.12
RSVD	NL256	0.89	5.97e−03	0.06
ARPACK	NL256	0.99	1.14e−02	0.51
	RP256	0.97	0.00e+00	0.01

comparison. As seen, the AUC, FPR and TRP for ASE do not change substantially based on the numerical methods of *randomized_svd*() or *svds*(). In contrast, for the NL using *svds*(), [ARPACK] improves the classification accuracy of NL to the point that is now exceeds that of RP and becomes competitive with ASE.

7. Conclusion and Future Work

In this chapter, we explored the use of spectral and RP embeddings for the classification of malicious authentication events based on just the connection structure of the computers. Our approach was to use a low-dimensional embedding and then to use embedding to train a random forest classifier. We found that using a SVD of the adjacency matrix to generate an embedding ASE gave the best performance and using simply the degree (the number of servers that connected with a client computer) gave the lowest performance. The method of RP outperformed NL when the embedding was computed via the fast approximate method of *randomized_svd*(). When the spectrum were computed using *svds*(), which employs the more accurate block Lanczos method in ARPACK, the performance of NL on classification of red team-attacked computers increased significantly and was competitive with ASE.

The current release from LANL is a modest size data set; once a larger data set is released, these experiments will be be redone to see to what extent they scale to a larger and more diverse data set.

Acknowledgements

I would like to thank Carey Priebe for his discussions on graph classification and the SBM, which greatly inspired this work. In addition, I like to thank Patrick Rubin-Delanchy who suggested using the authentication graph and the experiment of removing the red team events. Patrick also contributed greatly to my understanding of the use of graph embeddings for a bipartite graph. Finally, I like to thank Nick Heard and Niall Adams, both of whom gave good insights and needed feedback for this work.

References

Breiman, L. (2001). Random forests, *Machine Learning* **45**, 1, pp. 5–32.

Halko, N., Martinsson, P. G. and Tropp, J. A. (2011). Finding structure with randomness: Probabilistic algorithms for constructing approximate matrix decompositions, *SIAM Review* **53**, 2, pp. 217–288.

Heard, N. and Rubin-Delanchy, P. (2016). Network-wide anomaly detection via the dirichlet process, in *2016 IEEE Conference on Intelligence and Security Informatics (ISI)*, pp. 220–224.

Johnson, W. B., Lindenstrauss, J. and Schechtman, G. (1986). Extensions of lipschitz maps into banach spaces, *Israel Journal of Mathematics* **54**, 2, pp. 129–138.

Kent, A. D. (2016). Cyber security data sources for dynamic network research, in N. Adams and N. Heard. eds., *Dynamic Networks and Cyber-Security*, Vol. 1, p. 37, World Scientific.

Kent, A. D., Liebrock, L. M. and Neil, J. C. (2015). Authentication graphs: Analyzing user behavior within an enterprise network, *Computers and Security* **48**, pp. 150–166.

Lehoucq, R., Sorensen, D. and Yang, C. (1998). *ARPACK Users' Guide*, Society for Industrial and Applied Mathematics.

Marchette, D., Priebe, C. and Coppersmith, G. (2011). Vertex nomination via attributed random dot product graphs, in *Proceeding of 57th ISI World Statistics Congress*, pp. 5047–5042.

Rohe, K., Chatterjee, S. and Yu, B. (2011). Spectral clustering and the high-dimensional stochastic blockmodel, *The Annals of Statistics* **39**, 4, pp. 1878–1915.

Rubin-Delanchy, P., Adams, N. M. and Heard, N. A. (2016). Disassortativity of computer networks, in *2016 IEEE Conference on Intelligence and Security Informatics (ISI)*, pp. 243–247, doi:10.1109/ISI.2016.7745482.

Sussman, D. L., Tang, M., Fishkind, D. E. and Priebe, C. E. (2012). A consistent adjacency spectral embedding for stochastic blockmodel graphs, *Journal of the American Statistical Association* **107**, 499, pp. 1119–1128.

Tang, M., Athreya, A., Sussman, D. L., Lyzinski, V., Park, Y. and Priebe, C. E. (2017). A semiparametric two-sample hypothesis testing problem for random graphs, *Journal of Computational and Graphical Statistics* **26**, 2, pp. 344–354.

Varga, R. S. (2000). Nonnegative matrices, in *Matrix Iterative Analysis*, pp. 31–62, Springer, Berlin Heidelberg.

Chapter 10

Weakly Supervised Learning: How to Engineer Labels for Machine Learning in Cyber-Security

Christoforos Anagnostopoulos

Mentat Innovations Ltd., Level 39, One Canada Square,
Canary Wharf, London E145AB, UK

canagnos@ment.at

Lack of labelled data is a well-known challenge in cyber-security research. Although confidentiality is often used to explain this scarcity, our experience shows that even within the closed walls of large enterprises with significant in-house expertise, it is not obvious how to turn threat intelligence into a labelled data set suitable for machine learning. This is due to a perfect storm of heavily imbalanced yet massive data sets, scarcity of time for performing manual labelling, and domain-specific idiosyncrasies as to label semantics that drive a wedge between expert know-how and statistical modelling. We hereby try to unpack these incompatibilities, and argue that recent research in *weak supervision*, wherein multiple heuristics are used in place of ground truth, is a more fertile framework for cyber-security research than the classical choices of supervised, semi-supervised and unsupervised learning. We also make a novel methodological contribution in recasting weak supervision as a weighted learning problem, thusly making it straightforward to implement weakly supervised learning using a large number of existing classifiers and software packages. We validate our proposal using a simulation study. An R package has been released in CRAN for weakly supervised learning.

1. Introduction

Supervised classification has seen immense success in recent years, with the advent of a number of techniques such as support vector machines (Cortes and Vapnik, 1995), random forests (Breiman, 2001) and deep learning

195

neural networks (LeCun *et al.*, 2015) that seem to achieve extremely good performance on the majority of use cases where they are applicable, ranging from credit card applications to deep learning architectures driving image classification online. Applicability relies on the ability to cast a learning problem into one of predicting the class y of an object, given a description x of that object and the availability of a corpus of labelled examples to be used for training the classifier, whose job is to algorithmically figure out the relationship between y and x. Unfortunately, in many settings, obtaining a sufficiently large labelled data set is prohibitively expensive or impractical, impairing the ability of scientists in certain domains to take advantage of an otherwise rapidly advancing technology.

One domain where labelled data sets are particularly rare is the field of cyber-security, which, for the purposes of this chapter, can be understood as the defence of a set of information assets that lie within a perimeter (the *firewall*) from malicious agents outside it. A common example is the protection of enterprise data from exfiltration. At first glance, cyber-security is a dreamland for machine learning researchers: most novel defence mechanisms rely almost exclusively on digital data collection using a variety of sensors, producing vast amounts of data in semi-structured forms. For example, *event loggers* record certain aspects of the digital activity taking place in a host computer or across a network link, both within the enterprise and between the enterprise and the broader internet. Moreover, its objective is firmly binary: to detect whether a given piece of behaviour, captured via a sequence of logged digital events, is legitimate or malicious. Nevertheless, obtaining labelled data sets in cyber-security is exceptionally difficult, as it requires manual labelling by security experts, whose time is scarce and invaluable. The problem is aggravated by a dramatic imbalance in the relative frequency of legitimate and illegitimate traffic: although estimates vary depending on the enterprise in question, attacks can be as rare as one a month, or less, pitted against terabytes of legitimate daily traffic.

In the remainder of this section, we review the standard interface of supervised classification, followed by a number of standard ways in which it can be relaxed, including weighted learning, unsupervised, semi-supervised and active learning. In Section 2, we focus on cyber-security from a classification perspective and explain why existing approaches are in many ways lacking. This motivates us to introduce *weak supervision* (Hernández-González *et al.*, 2016) in Section 3, circling back to cyber-security in

Section 4 in an attempt to illustrate how it can address the weaknesses of standard classification. We conclude with a summary and a long list of future work in Section 5, in line with our view that this is an exceptionally promising applied research direction.

1.1. *Supervised classification*

Consider a labelled example (x, y), where $x \in \mathcal{X} \subseteq \mathbb{R}^p$ is a multivariate numeric description of an object, and $y \in \mathcal{Y} = \{l_1, \ldots, l_L\}$. In cases where raw objects are available in non-numeric forms (e.g., a text document), we assume a numeric description x of the raw object ξ can be computed using some mapping $g : \Xi \to \mathbb{R}^p$. A *classifier* is a function $f : \mathcal{X} \to \mathcal{Y}$ that attempts to recover the label given an object description:

$$\tilde{f} = \underset{f \in \Phi}{\operatorname{argmin}} \, \mathbb{E}_{X,Y}[L(f(X), Y)],$$

where $L(\hat{y}, y)$ is a loss function measuring the cost of making a mistake in the label estimate, and the expectation is over some assumed data-generating process, or the empirical process by which we obtain new data.

Typically, the empirical loss over a finite, fixed labelled data set $(x_i, y_i)_{i=1}^n$ is employed as an approximation to the expected loss, yielding:

$$\tilde{f} = \underset{f \in \Phi}{\operatorname{argmin}} \, \sum_{i=1}^{n} L(f(x_i), y_i),$$

subject to the overwhelmingly common assumption of an additive loss. This recasting of an arbitrary learning problem into a relatively straightforward optimisation task, allowed an incredibly rich literature to flourish, proposing exceedingly complex candidates for the function family Φ, as well as the algorithm performing the optimisation implicit in `argmin`, while simultaneously hiding the complexity from the "end user", whose only responsibility remains to provide labelled examples. Indeed, this ability to "learn by example" is the single biggest factor driving the current wave in AI.

Often, the space of possible functions Φ is constrained to a parametric family of functions f_θ, where $\theta \in \mathbb{R}^p$ and θ is a multivariate parameter vector, so that the optimisation target becomes $\sum_{i=1}^n L(f_\theta(x_i), y_i)$ instead, a process known as "parameter fitting". Often, several different candidate parametric families will be considered. Alternative approaches avoid constraining the search space to a finite-dimensional space to begin with and rely on complex algorithms to explore non-parametric function families.

At any rate, in this work we will not concern ourselves at all with techniques for discovering $\tilde{f}$, but rather ways in which the overall abstraction can be generalised so as to better serve reality. This is in tandem to the practical challenges faced in industry today: An abundance of open-source and commercial "classification-as-a-service" offerings has steeply decreased the cost of exploring different choices of classifiers $\tilde{f}$, but has made it no easier to come up with the necessary (x_i, y_i) pairs to begin with.

1.2. *Weighted supervised learning*

A natural extension of the supervised learning framework involves the introduction of weights w_i in the additive loss function of Equation (1.1), which allows the user to place added or reduced importance on certain datapoints:

$$\tilde{f}_w = \underset{f \in \Phi}{\operatorname{argmin}} \sum_{i=1}^{n} w_i L(f(x_i), y_i), \quad \text{where } w_i \in [0, 1].$$

Weighting methods have been employed for a large number of reasons. For example, in the presence of temporal evolution of unknown characteristics (known as "drift"), w_i is often set to an exponential decay factor λ^{n-i} which forces the algorithm to gradually "forget" old datapoints (Anagnostopoulos, 2010). Other uses of weights include ensemble techniques for combining mixtures of experts of varied accuracy (Dietterich, 2000), as well as weighted likelihood techniques where datapoints are assumed to have different, but known, variances (Ruppert and Wand, 1994; Tibshirani and Hastie, 1987). It is important to note that this is a very economical extension of the supervised classification interface, because all classifiers that rely on the optimisation of an additive loss can support it. Indeed, most existing implementations of supervised classification already support the use of weights as an optional parameter.

1.3. *Semi-supervised learning*

The other major assumption is the availability of a labelled training data set. This is often relaxed to what is known as *semi-supervised* learning

(Chapelle *et al.*, 2009), whereby labels are available for some proportion of the training data set. The size of the training data set, and the proportion of examples that are labelled therein, can both vary wildly from one use case to the next. Semi-supervised learning can be modelled as a missing data problem, where some (or most) of the values of y_i in $(x_i, y_i)_{i=1:n}$ are missing. The mechanism by which the labels are missing can and should also be modelled: any non-random mechanism will generate bias in the estimation procedure. A common example of a non-random mechanism for missing labels is one whereby some other filtering process is responsible for selecting which data entries are labelled.

1.4. *Unsupervised learning and anomaly detection*

At the extreme, one can imagine that all labels are missing, resulting in an *unsupervised learning* problem. Unsupervised learning is however qualitatively different to semi-supervised learning, in that the target (1.1) is entirely unavailable. Typically, unsupervised classification takes the form of *clustering*, where we assume that the data examples $(x_i)_{i=1:n}$ neatly separate into (mostly) non-overlapping clusters, the latter hopefully corresponding to the true, but unobserved labels. A related instantiation of unsupervised classification is *anomaly detection*, wherein the assumption instead is that a small number of examples are outliers, lying detectably far from the vast majority of the data (Chandola *et al.*, 2009). Although the optimisation algorithm deployed during the training stage does not feature any labels, it is still meaningful to refer to these problems as *unsupervised classification* (for example Balasubramanian *et al.*, 2011), because the labels do exist, and indeed are eventually observed, which in turn determines the practical success or failure of the respective method.

1.5. *Active learning*

Researchers faced with a scarcity of labelled examples have attempted to experiment with recipes for selecting examples that might have greater "information value", in an attempt to learn faster on the back of fewer, more informative labelled examples (Evans *et al.*, 2013; Settles, 2010). This is a case of an intentionally non-random missingness mechanism, and the resulting bias in the estimation process must be offset against the possibility for faster learning. Although fairly active, this field largely relies on heuristics backed by empirical evidence but with few theoretical guarantees (MacKay, 1992). Nevertheless, it is fairly prominent in practice. Given an intractably large data set available for labelling, very few data scientists will resist the temptation to deploy some heuristic other than plain random sampling to select the precious few that they can afford to have labelled. Another way in which active learning "sneaks into" a classification pipeline is by receiving expert feedback on the few alerts raised per day: this is a form of active learning whereby examples with high (estimated) probability of being malicious are given priority.

1.6. *Summary*

Supervised classification is an area of machine learning that has seen rapid growth in the last decade, and has been the catalyst for a large number of technological breakthroughs. It is applicable to any problem that can be described in terms of the relationship between a numeric description x of an object and a label for that object y, and for which it is possible to acquire a sufficiently large corpus of labelled objects so that the machine learning algorithm can proceed to "learn by example". Conversely, the technology cannot be readily applied in domains where such data sets are unavailable. Variations on the theme of supervised learning have emerged that can handle missing labels, attempt to find patterns in the data without any use of labels, or try to make the best of limited resources by wisely selecting which examples to label. Equipped with these concepts and notations, we proceed to describe the problems faced by cyber-security, and assess the extent to which existing flavours of supervised learning are appropriate.

2.   Cyber-Security as Classification

Classification lies at the core of cyber-security: Distinguishing legitimate behaviour from malicious behaviour is the first and crucial step in mounting defences, mitigating any damage, and apprehending the culprits. In this section, we dig down deeper to establish exactly how we can map this problem to the interface of supervised classification. We begin with a brief survey of available data sets, followed by a description of possible detection technologies and conclude with the realisation that on close scrutiny there is considerable mismatch between the abstraction of a supervised classification problem and the realities of cyber-security monitoring.

2.1. *Data types*

The primary source of information for cyber-security is *computer logs*: These are processes that captured traces of activity on various devices inside a large network for purposes of monitoring, debugging and security. They come in the form of data streams (continually arriving) comprising events with semi-structured descriptions. For example, any interaction between an enterprise employee and the wider internet is typically mediated by a *web proxy*: A server that can inspect the content of the webpages visited by the employee and ban traffic if there is reason for concern. Web proxies generate detailed logs of all user interactions, with information such as the timestamp, the host IP, the destination IP, the user agent, the domain name and other technical information. These logs are fairly structured, and for a given proxy technology can even be considered tabular, but other logs lack such fixed structure. For example, `syslogs` (short for "system logs") record events occurring at the operating system of a single computer, and they comprise events each with a different number of fields, depending on the computer application that is generating it: a text editor might generate an event with three fields, whereas a PDF viewer might log events with five fields. Another rich data source is `NetFlow` (short for "network flow"), which is a data format that captures the number and size of packets flowing between any two connected devices in a large enterprise network. Several more types of logs exist: Authentication logs, DNS records, and more.

A key observation that differentiates cyber from other domains is that attack vectors will usually leave very weak traces in each log type individually, which can strengthen if they are considered jointly. Take the example of an attempt to exfiltrate data from the enterprise. A common first step will be to identify an employee likely to have access to the right internal resources, such as an IT professional, and target them specifically via a *spearphishing* attempt: an email inviting the employee in question to download a file to their local computer, which is masked as coming from a legitimate source.

Unlike most common consumer phishing attempts that can be pretty blatant (consider the infamous Nigerian Prince scam), these can be extremely sophisticated social engineering attempts, that use information extracted from social media to personalise the fake email. If the email recipient is convinced to download the malicious file, then a piece of malware will typically stay dormant on their local computer for a while to avoid immediate detection, then attempt to escalate its privileges in order to traverse the network towards a higher value target, and then finally attempt to send data back to a command and control remote computer. This sequence of events which is known as the *kill chain* leaves small traces on various logs: the email received is recorded in the email headers; downloading the file will be recorded in the web proxy logs; escalation of privileges by the malicious code will be recorded in the system logs; traversing the network will be recorded in network flow; and the final attempt to send data out of the firewall will be recorded again in the web proxy logs of another host (Figure 1). This example emphasises the need for data fusion.

Finally, the size of the data is tremendous. A typical enterprise might generate web proxy logs in the order of a few terabytes a day. Network

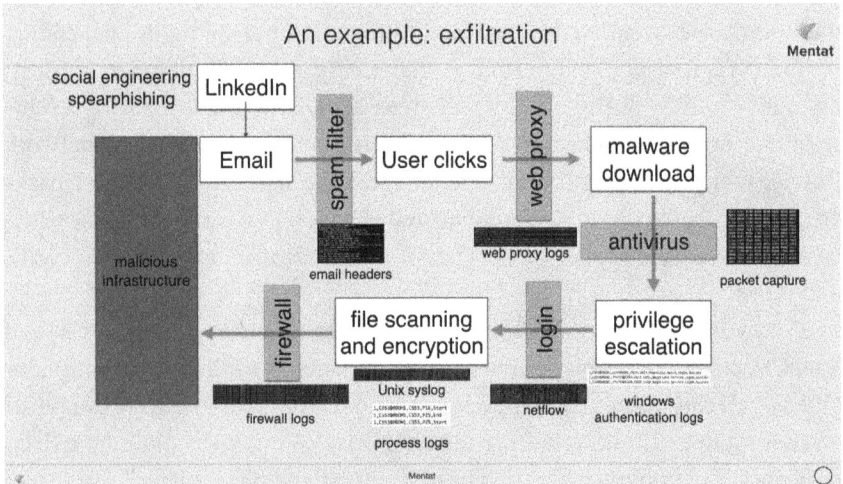

Fig. 1:   Several steps that an attack might involve (also known as the *kill chain* of an attack), in the case of data exfiltration. The attack will appear in all logs, and although its individual trace might appear innocuous, the combined picture is unmistakeable.

flow data can be much larger, as it includes IoT interactions. Querying such data from cold storage is facilitated by the advent of Big Data technology stacks (such as Apache Spark over Hadoop (Meng *et al.*, 2016)), but remains challenging.

2.2. Existing detection technologies

In what follows, we review some common cyber-defence mechanisms. Rather than focusing on the part of the network they are designed to protect, we here attempt a more data-centric categorisation, grouping together technologies according to what type of data operations they rely on.

2.2.1. Rules-based systems

Legacy intrusion detection systems rely on scanning files and logs for specific patterns of attack, often referred to as *signatures*, via the use of fixed rules. Such signature-based detection originated in the antivirus community, and relied on extracting specific snippets of bytecode from known malicious code, and scanning all new files entering the user's filesystem for presence of such code. Although signature-based attacks have exceptionally small false alarm rate, they are by design unable to detect novel threats.

In a similar spirit to file scanning, various types of identifiers that can be found in event logs, such as IP addresses and domain names, can be checked against blacklists of known threats. Via spoofing and larger investments in infrastructure, attackers can relatively easily evade this type of detection, but its presence increases the cost sufficiently that it can act as a deterrent. Identifiers that have previously been associated with malicious activity are known as *indicators of compromise* and are shared across enterprises via threat intelligence crowdsourcing platforms or third-party providers.

2.2.2. Anomaly-based detection and behavioural models

In an attempt to overcome the shortcomings of fixed rules systems, a large number of approaches evolved in the last decade that attempt to construct a model of what "normal behaviour" looks like for a particular user, machine, or for part of the network, and then flag any unusual behaviour as potentially malicious. Simple examples might include the use of a rarely used port, or volumetric analysis that identifies peaks in traffic. More complex approaches take into account subtler behavioural features, temporal dependencies, and user profiling. As a general rule, an anomaly detector will only be as good as the underlying model of normal behaviour. Unfortunately, computer networks exhibit exquisitely complex behaviour, driven by heterogeneity in human and machine behaviour, bursts of activity, erratic temporal patterns influenced by external events, etc. As a result, anomaly detectors tend to offer a large number of false positives which might be genuine statistical abnormalities, but irrelevant to the security analyst.

As threats evolve and become more multifaceted and flexible, simple parametric rules fail to suffice, and models have become accordingly more complex. At the far end of this spectrum lie so-called *black box* techniques, where highly convoluted mathematical models govern the decision of whether to flag an alert or not, so much so that it is impossible for a human to interpret the alert, or fathom why it was raised. Although field trials suggest that this extra flexibility can be useful in capturing a larger percentage of the chaos that constitutes normal behaviour (hence reducing false alerts), there is a cost, namely reduced actionability: the cybersecurity expert finds it harder to decide how to deal with such opaque alerts, and spends more time reviewing the raw data. This increases the cost of each false alert, hence negating some of the benefit of decreasing their number.

Another important distinction which is lost in translation between cybersecurity experts and statisticians/computer scientists is the use of the term "anomaly". In statistical machine learning, as explained earlier, "anomaly detection" has a technical meaning which is linked to unsupervised learning: It presupposes no labels are available. In contrast, the defining characteristic of anomaly detection systems as far as cyber-security experts are concerned is their ability to detect "novel" threats, which, in itself, does not rule out supervised machine learning, given its proven generalisation abilities that allow it to accurately predict the labels of data configurations that it has never precisely observed in the past. It remains true that unsupervised machine learning is in principle even more capable of generalising in that it forms no explicit expectation of the "malicious class" at all. However, using labels where available remains well advised.

2.2.3. *Deception technologies*

In all of the above examples, the logs that are inspected represent genuine events taking place within the enterprise, or at its border (in the case of web proxy logs). This is a high-risk situation: any attack that goes undetected is likely to cause real damage. An alternative is the use of *deception*: the attacker is lured into a fake environment so that more information may be collected about their identity, payload and kill chain. The classical example of deception technologies is a *honeypot* (Provos *et al.*, 2004): a server hosting a web app is duplicated, quarantined away from the real back-end service, and its security measures intentionally downgraded so as to make attackers more likely to choose the honeypot over the real server. Simple honeypots are used by cyber-security companies and communities to attract random attacks by bots that automatically seek out vulnerable servers, but much more sophisticated versions are often used by enterprises to try and lure in targeted attacks and find out more about them so that they can protect the real network. The claimed benefits of deception technologies include a virtually negligible false alarm rate, because by design legitimate users would never have to, or know to access deceptive artefacts. In this sense, they can serve as a highly accurate label generator and intelligence gathering tool.

2.2.4. *Log analysis and threat hunting*

Logs fuel rule-based and anomaly-based detection systems, but also serve as context for human analysts to reach a decision about whether a certain alert represents a genuine threat, and what to do about it if so. A number of technologies are available for running fast queries on such data, both proprietary and open-source (e.g., Elasticsearch (Gormley and Tong, 2015) and Splunk (Carasso, 2012)). The boundary between rule-based decision engines and query engines can sometimes be blurry, since the latter usually support "continual queries" that automatically run in the background on fresh data in regular intervals, and auto-generate an alert whenever a match is found. Alternatively, analysts might use these query engines in interactive mode, iteratively refining a query by inspecting its results, in an attempt to dig up threats that might be too subtle to catch by a simple fixed rule. This process is known as *threat hunting*. Both continually running queries and threat hunting sessions can be a rich source of expert know-how, as we explain in Section 4.1.2.

2.2.5. *Alert correlation and triage*

It has been made clear by the above review that an enterprise security team is required to parse and act upon a potentially large number of alerts, arising from a multitude of distinct sub-systems and technologies. To achieve this, they usually rely on software known as Security Information and Event Management (SIEM) that collects alerts, surfaces them to the security team and records actions taken in response by the analysts for compliance purposes. A busy software industry in its own right, SIEM software mostly dominates the user-facing component of threat detection technologies. From a data analytic perspective, SIEM technologies also offer the ability to "correlate" data (the use of the term being unrelated to its statistical meaning), whereby common attributes across different threats are used to split alerts into groups so that they can be more easily digested. They also offer tools for "triage", or alert prioritisation, which enables analysts to escalate certain alerts to specialised forensic teams within the enterprise. Finally, retention of actions taken in response to each alert (for compliance purposes) can itself serve as an indirect source of labelled data.

2.3. *Challenges surrounding expert labelling*

The exasperation of users over the huge numbers of alerts they need to review per day has come to be known by the term "alert fatigue" (Stanton *et al.*, 2016). Alert fatigue has several adverse consequences, including a reluctance to adopt new threat detection technologies. In addition to the obvious complaint of high false-positive rates, an additional concern is the opaqueness of many alerting systems, which do not offer sufficient context for the user to quickly decide whether the alert is genuine. Requesting labels for machine learning must compete for time and attention in this busy, frustrating routine.

The fundamental challenge is lack of time and size of data: asking users to produce labels for 1,000 events once a week seems like a futile exercise when faced with billions of events per day, especially when it is particularly unlikely that there will be any positive findings in such a small set of events. Helpfully, a distinction must be made between "interesting" and "malicious". Interesting behaviour is anything that would be perceived by an analyst as "worth inspecting". From a statistical standpoint, "interesting" could be simply understood as a noisy label.

Another common complaint is that datapoints are often presented to the analyst for labelling out-of-context, making it impossible or very difficult for them to label. This lack of context also hurts the learning algorithm downstream, as labels might rely on information which is not captured in the labelled data set. For example, a user might geolocate an IP address and label it as suspicious solely on the basis of its geographic origin. If this is the only suspicious behavioural trait, and the geolocation is not available to the classifier, this label is likely to confuse rather than assist the model.

More generally, it is frequently the case that the unit of analysis of the machine learning algorithm is different than that of the analyst. A single event might be viewed as suspicious if it forms part of a suspiciously long session, but innocent otherwise. This multi-view perspective can produce what will be perceived by the algorithm as conflicting labels by different analysts, or even by the same analyst on different occasions. It is hard to overstate the importance of this from a real-world perspective: the constant worry of domain experts involved in training machine learning algorithms is that their heuristics will introduce bias into the algorithm, or plainly erratic behaviour in edge cases that they have not thought of. Expert opinion differs in important ways from "ground truth", and this creates friction.

2.4. *Summary*

Cyber-security is a data-driven exercise, relying on a large number of logs collected via a number of different technologies. Existing detection systems tend to either be rules-based, where fixed patterns or lookups in the data are used to detect known types of attack, or behavioural, wherein a statistical model of normal behaviour is tasked with flagging any behaviour that seems sufficiently abnormal. Although some automation is present, in most cases the expert analyst is the final arbiter who must inspect manually every single alert and reach a decision about the extent of the threat. This results in increased demand for the analyst's time, and a phenomenon known as *alert fatigue*, which speaks against burdening analysts further with the need to manually label large numbers of examples for use in machine learning. Even where possible, producing handcrafted labels is made very difficult by the size of the data and the rarity of attacks. Additional risk factors include lack of context, mismatched units of analysis resulting in labels that are misassociated to the data example and a sense of dread on the part of the expert that they might be misleading the machine learning model with inaccurate labels, and that their time and diligence are the bottleneck standing in the way of an AI promiseland. In Section 4, we will revisit all these issues and try to relieve them by modifying our learning framework.

3. Weak Supervision

We explained earlier how in many expert-driven domains, including cyber-security, labels are mostly not directly observable, but rather proxied by expert opinion, subject to imperfections, incompleteness and disagreement. Rather than dismissing these limitations as data preprocessing issues, we take a different approach and attempt to take them into explicit account, by modelling the relationship between expert heuristics and ground truth, according to the weak supervision framework (Hoffmann *et al.*, 2011; Ratner *et al.*, 2017).

We begin with a brief methodological introduction in Section 3.1, followed by a novel methodological contribution presented in Section 3.2 that offers an approximate but simpler solution for weak supervision using weighted learning. We conclude in Section 3.3.

3.1. *Methodology*

To simplify the exposition, we focus our attention to a parametric classifier $f_\theta(x)$. In the presence of a labelled data set $(x_i, y_i)_{i=1:n}$, we would have sought to minimise the empirical loss as a proxy for the expected loss:

$$\tilde{\theta} = \operatorname*{argmin}_{\theta \in \Theta} \sum_{i=1}^{n} L(f_\theta(x_i), y_i) \approx \operatorname*{argmin}_{\theta \in \Theta} \mathbb{E}_{(X,Y) \sim \pi} L(f_\theta(X), Y).$$

For simplicity, let us assume that our label space is $\{-1, 1\}$, as is common in neural network research. In weak supervision, we assume that ground truth labels are absent, but a set of incomplete, imperfect heuristics is available. We frame each such heuristic as a function that maps each object x to a label $y \in \{-1, 1\}$, or to the value 0 if the heuristic fails to apply for that particular object. For example, a rule that relies on deep packet inspection to classify traffic as legitimate or malicious might fail to provide an answer in the case of encrypted traffic. We can then represent a set of m heuristics in vectorised form as functions of the following form:

$$\lambda_j : \mathcal{X} \to \{-1, 0, 1\}, \quad \text{for } j = 1, \ldots, m.$$

The strength of the weak supervision framework is to rely on a parametric model of the accuracy profile of each labelling rule λ_j, whose parameters can then be estimated from the data. Note that under the data-generating distribution π, the labels produced by the labelling rules are themselves random variables, which we denote by $\Lambda = (\Lambda_j)_{j=1}^m$. Our first attempt at modelling the relationship between Λ and Y is given by assuming rules are *independent* to each other, and that they produce missing labels independently at random, so that each rule Λ_j has a probability β_j of yielding an answer on a random example X, and a probability α_j of getting it right:

$$\mu_{\alpha,\beta}(\Lambda, Y)$$
$$= \frac{1}{2} \prod_{j=1}^m \left(\beta_j \alpha_j \mathbf{1}_{[\Lambda_j = Y]} + \beta_j (1 - \alpha_j) \mathbf{1}_{[\Lambda_j = -Y]} + (1 - \beta_j) \mathbf{1}_{[\Lambda_j = 0]} \right).$$

Knowing the values of α and β would allow us to compute the marginal probability of the observed labels $\Lambda(x_{1:n})$, according to this formula:

$$P_{(\Lambda,Y)\sim\mu_{\alpha,\beta}}(\Lambda = \Lambda(x_{1:n})) = \sum_{i=1}^n \log \left(\sum_{y' \in \{-1,1\}} \mu_{\alpha,\beta}(\lambda(x_i), y') \right).$$

By the same token, the marginal distribution of $\Lambda(x_{1:n})$ yields a likelihood for α, β, which can be maximised to estimate their values:

$$\alpha^*, \beta^* \leftarrow \underset{\alpha,\beta}{\operatorname{argmax}} \sum_{i=1}^n \log P_{(\Lambda,Y)\sim\mu_{\alpha,\beta}}(\Lambda = \Lambda(x_i)).$$

These estimates of α, β allow us to now treat the problem of weak supervision as a noisy label problem, where we use an observed set of imperfect labels with known accuracy to constrain the likely values of the true labels:

$$\tilde{\theta} = \operatorname*{argmin}_{\theta} \sum_{i=1}^{n} \mathbb{E}_{(\Lambda,Y)\sim\mu_{\alpha^*,\beta^*}} \left[L(x_i, y) \mid \Lambda = \lambda(x_i) \right].$$

This problem is solvable for many classifiers [1,2,3,4].

Simulation study. Simple gradient descent on the marginal likelihood with respect to α produces the results of Figure 2(a), where convergence is achieved within a few hundred iterations (for more mathematical detail, please refer to the Appendix). If we decrease the coverage (i.e., the values of β_j) of our labelling rules, we get much poorer convergence (b). Interestingly, the framework can readily support partially observed ground truth: It

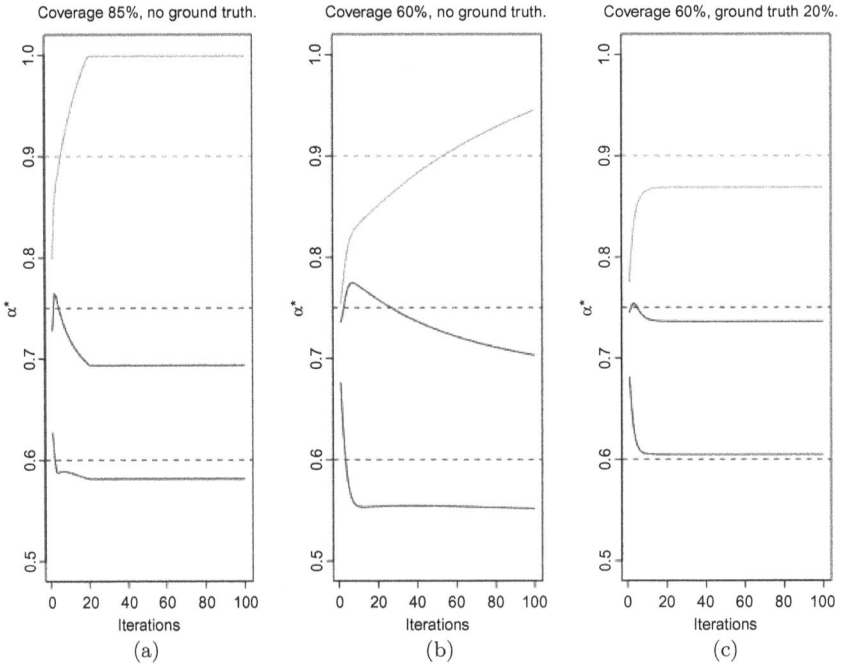

Fig. 2: Gradient descent on the marginal likelihood yields convergent accuracy estimates when the coverage is fixed at 85% for all labelling rules (a). As we decrease the coverage to 60% (b), convergence is compromised, but is restored in the presence of ground truth for 20% of the data (c), albeit with some bias. These results confirm the validity of the approach, but reveal a challenging optimisation problem.

can be represented as another labelling rule with potentially very low coverage, but accuracy *fixed* equal to 1, obtained by fixing the gradient to 0 for this particular rule. Introducing ground truth for 20% of the data recovers our ability of estimating the accuracy of the other three labelling rules (c). Further investigation establishes that the problem of poor convergence in cases of low coverage can perhaps be improved by more sophisticated optimisation techniques, as it is due to the presence of local minima and flat regions in the marginal log likelihood.

3.2. Weak supervision using weighted learning

In the spirit of enabling applied research and maximising the usability of existing software, we illustrate in this section a novel approach for weak supervision that does not require specialised stochastic gradient descent techniques, but can rather employ existing interfaces for *weighted learning*, reviewed in Section 1.2 and naturally supported by most commonly used classifiers. This allows painless and intuitive deployment of weak supervision using existing methodology. In this section, we illustrate the viability of this approach using a simulated study on logistic regression, reserving the pending theoretical analysis of this particular approach for future work.

3.2.1. From weak labels to weighted examples

Consider an estimate α^* and an $n \times m$ matrix of weak labels $\Lambda = \Lambda(\mathbf{x})$, associated with an $n \times p$ feature matrix $\mathbf{x}$. For each labelling function, we consider the index I_j of examples for which it produces labels:

$$I_j = \{i : \Lambda_{ij} \neq 0\}.$$

We then reshape $\mathbf{x}$ by stacking rowwise the blocks of $\mathbf{x}$ corresponding to each I_j. We reshape Λ into a vector using the same partitioning:

$$\mathbf{x}^* = \begin{bmatrix} \mathbf{x}_{i \in I_1, 1:p} \\ \hline \cdots \\ \hline \mathbf{x}_{i \in I_m, 1:p} \end{bmatrix}, \quad y^* = \begin{bmatrix} \Lambda_{i \in I_1, 1} \\ \hline \cdots \\ \hline \Lambda_{i \in I_m, m} \end{bmatrix}.$$

This yields a new regression data set, where $\mathbf{x}^*$ is $N \times p$, y^* is $N \times 1$, and N is equal to the number of non-zero entries in Λ. We then produce a vector of weights w of size N where w_i is the accuracy of the labelling function responsible for producing that particular row of $(\mathbf{x}^*, y^*)$:

$$w = (w[1]|\ldots|w[m]), \quad \text{where } w[j] = (\alpha_j, \ldots, \alpha_j) \text{ a total of } |I_j| \text{ times.}$$

The triplet (X^*, y^*, w) now poses a standard weighted supervised learning problem, with N labelled examples and no missing data.

3.2.2. *Data simulation*

To assess the performance of this method, we draw a data set $(x_i, y_i)_{i=1:n}$ where $x_i \in \mathbb{R}^p$, for $p = 10$, and $y \in \{-1, 1\}$ by letting $x_i \sim N_p(0, 1)$ in an i.i.d. fashion, the regression coefficients $\beta \sim N_p(0, v_\beta)$ and the intercept $\beta_0 \sim N(0, 1)$, and finally the label is generated by letting z_i be a single trial from $\text{Bin}(p_i)$, where $p_i = S(X_i\beta + \beta_0)$ with $S()$ being the sigmoidal function, and $y_i = 2z_i - 1$ so that the sample space of the Binomial with 1 denoting a success and 0 a failure, may map onto our preferred label space $\{-1, 1\}$. We draw training and test data from this generative model. We then posit the following accuracy and coverage for three labelling functions are as follows:

$$a^* = (0.6, 0.9, 0.65), \quad b^* = (0.1, 0.1, 0.1).$$

This means that only one of the three labelling functions is reasonably accurate, and all three have very low coverage, producing missing values for around 90% of the data. We construct an $n \times m$ matrix Λ of weak labels, by utilising $2 \times n \times m$ auxiliary independent binary variables:

$$A_{ij} \sim \text{Bin}(a_j^*), \quad B_{ij} \sim \text{Bin}(b_j^*)$$

and then setting Λ_{ij} accordingly (recalling that $-y_i$ switches the ith label):

$$\Lambda_{ij} = (1 - B_{ij})\left((1 - A_{ij})(-y_i) + A_{ij}y_i\right).$$

3.2.3. *Classification accuracy*

As established in Section 3.1, MLE via simple gradient descent fails to give good estimates for α in the case of very low coverage. To separate out this issue from the ability to use weak labels for accurate classification, we contrast the performance of the following five classifiers:

- *Ground Truth labels* (TL): training on fully observed ground truth, which is available in a simulated setting.

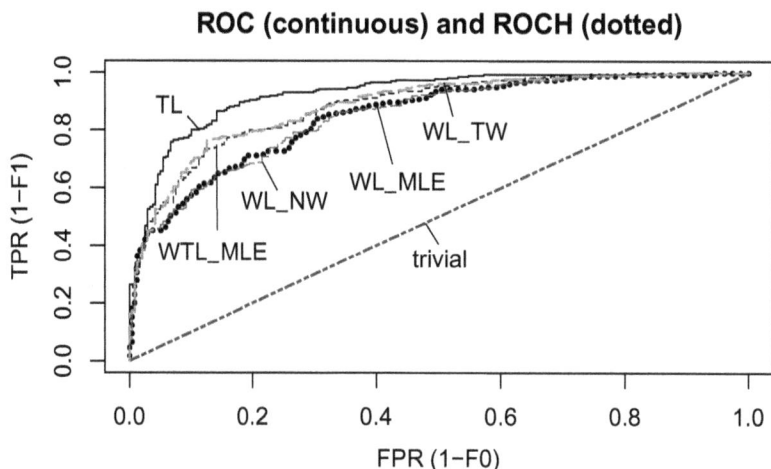

Fig. 3: We contrast the accuracy of five algorithms, establishing the cost of using weak labels rather than ground truth, and the possible improvement afforded by good estimates of the accuracy of each labelling function.

- *Weak and True Labels* (WTL-MLE): training on weak labels as well as ground truth on 5% of the data.
- *Weak Labels only* (WL-MLE): training on weak labels only, using the maximum likelihood estimates for accuracy and coverage.
- *Weak Labels only without weights* (WL-NW): training on weak labels without making use of the weights, in effect forcing the classifier to consider all labelling functions equally accurate.
- *Weak Labels only with True Weights* (WL-TW): training on weak labels but making use of weights obtained from the true accuracy values, rather than the estimated ones.

The results are presented in Figures 3 and 4; in the former, a ROC curve is produced for each classifier using the hmeasure R package, and in the latter, three numeric summaries of performance are displayed for easier comparison. Ground truth (TL) scores highest, followed at some distance by a matching performance for weak supervision using labels (WTL-MLE), and weak supervision using true weights (WL-TW). These two algorithms perform similarly for reasons we have already explained: as seen in Figure 2, even a tiny fraction of ground truth labels allows the MLE procedure to converge to reasonably accurate estimates of the true weights. Interestingly,

	H	Gini	AUC
TL	0.6238149	0.8508147	0.9254073
WTL_MLE	0.4908690	0.7617713	0.8808856
WL_MLE	0.4191900	0.6981368	0.8490684
WL_NW	0.4127802	0.6946763	0.8473382
WL_TW	0.5105231	0.7678271	0.8839136

Fig. 4: Three different performance metrics for the five algorithms under scrutiny. The use of optimal weights and the use of MLE in the presence of some ground truth perform similarly, and outperform the use of MLE in the presence of weak labels only — the latter performs similarly to treating the weak labels as equally accurate.

the presence of ground truth labels for 5% of the data does not seem to offer any additional advantage other than to improve the accuracy estimates.

The two lowest-scoring methods are the classifier using weak labels only and the MLE estimates for the weights, and the classifier using weak labels only and no weights (all weights are set to 1, amounting to the mistaken assumption that all labelling functions are equally accurate). Again, this is a reflection of the characteristics of the MLE procedure for estimating the weights, which with low coverage is unable to produce reasonable estimates of α, rendering these two algorithms effectively identical. This optimisation failure notwithstanding, this result is useful in that it demarcates the "space" of weak supervision: It is the area between the use of weak labels without weights, MLE-NW, and the use of weak labels with optimal weights, MLE-TW. Pushing one's performance from the lower to the higher end of that spectrum is solely reliant on good estimates of α. All code used to produce these experiments has been released as an R software package under the name `wsl`, available at CRAN or at http://www.canagnos.com/software.html.

3.3. *Summary*

In this section, we outlined the weak supervision methodology, which relies on a generative model describing the process through which a labelling function fails to output an accurate label. We demonstrated that maximum likelihood is a viable solution for estimating the parameters of this model without access to ground truth labels, but it suffers when the labelling functions have very low coverage. We took some first steps in the direction of establishing a link between noise-aware empirical loss minimisation and supervised learning with weights, backed by a simulation study. If further work establishes this approximation heuristic to be theoretically valid, it would open the door to straightforward implementation of weak supervision using existing interfaces for weighted learning, with just a few simple matrix transformations. Our simulation study also established that good estimates of the accuracy of each labelling function constitute a performance bottleneck, more so than securing a small percentage of ground truth labels. In practice this means that in spaces where ground truth is exceptionally expensive but labelling rules are cheap, securing fairly inaccurate labelling rules with higher coverage can be a better investment than attempting to obtain a small number of ground truth labels. This stands in contrast with current standard wisdom in applied data science.

Before we move on, it should be noted that both our methodology and simulation study assumed that labelling rules are statistically independent from each other. The formal description of this assumption is:

$$\lambda_i(x) \perp \lambda_j(x) \mid y, \quad y \perp (x \mid \lambda(x)).$$

Violating the independence assumptions can have a fairly dramatic effect on performance. This can be partially mitigated via the use of graphical models for capturing known dependencies between labelling rules, opening up fascinating new directions for research in this area (Bach *et al.*, 2017).

4. Labelling Rules for Cyber-Security

Armed with the framework above, we can now return to cyber-security proper, and consider the implications of switching from ground truth labels to labelling heuristics. First, we need to capitalise on knowledge that is already captured by security teams as part of their daily jobs. This type of frictionless knowledge extraction is cheap and sustainable. Second, we need to ensure that such knowledge is in an appropriate form to map to a programmatic labelling function. We discuss these two issues in turn.

4.1. *Knowledge capture*

Unlike other domains where the expert might perform their decision-making outside the purview of IT systems (e.g., medicine), security analysts are already data-driven, which gives this field a great advantage when it comes to automatic knowledge capture. We can usefully classify such knowledge in four broad groups: (1) whitelists and blacklists; (2) rules and database queries; (3) third-party alerts; (4) soft knowledge. We discuss these types of knowledge in turn, mapping the label of "legitimate" behaviour to -1 (negative, no match) and "malicious" behaviour to 1 (positive, match).

4.1.1. *Whitelists and blacklists*

The primary modern use of blacklists is the automatic flagging of any traffic that includes an IoC, as described in Section 2.2.1 on intelligence-driven security. Conversely, whitelists involve filtering out any traffic originating from high-reputation sites. Blacklists and whitelists are different from other types of knowledge in that they are simple to implement: a mere lookup is involved. Moreover, they can be assumed to have very high accuracy. However, they operate on a limited label space. Blacklists map to $\{0, 1\}$ in that the absence of an IP address on a blacklist says nearly nothing about the probability of it being malicious, so that it is best treated as a missing value, and similarly for whitelists which map to $\{-1, 0\}$. In other words, what is in the blacklist is assumed to be accurate, but the blacklist is not assumed to be complete (and similarly for whitelists). Coverage for blacklists will tend to be extremely low, whereas for whitelists it will tend to be quite high, because high-reputation domains are also frequently popular domains that account for much of the traffic in an enterprise.

Current practice with blacklists typically involves treating hits on blacklists as a ground truth label of 1, but assuming that a non-hit is a ground truth label of -1, which is erroneous. As for whitelisted traffic, data scientists will often remove it in an attempt to reduce their false-positive rate (given that any hit on such data will be a false positive), a crude solution which stands in the way of a fully automated machine learning pipeline.

The challenge with whitelists and blacklists from a learning perspective is that, in many cases, an event might be whitelisted for reasons based on external information that cannot possibly be reflected in the data at hand. Put differently, exactly the same behaviour might be deemed legitimate if originating from google.com, but malicious if originating from evil.com. A way to give the classifier equal footing in such cases is to use whitelists/blacklists as both features and (weak) labels simultaneously: first, a feature is added to the data encoding whether each event is whitelisted or not (resp. for blacklists); second, the whitelist generates a weak labelling heuristic as described above. Although the correlation between the feature and the weak label will be perfect, the presence of other — possibly conflicting — labelling heuristics allows for some degree of nuance and better generalisation performance than crudely enforcing the whitelist by asserting all whitelisted events represent legitimate behaviour.

4.1.2. *Rules and database queries*

A large percentage of the alerts investigated by security analysts result from rules that are either hard-coded in existing software such as IDS, NIDS or firewall security products, or implemented by the analysts themselves in an appropriate query language, such as SQL or the Splunk Query Language. Such rules can have varying intended accuracies, but they generally tend to be much less accurate than blacklists and whitelists, as they attempt to capture weaker signals indicative of an attack. Rules generated as part of threat hunting in particular can be especially valuable complements to fixed rules, as they are intended for data exploration rather than alerting, and therefore they capture different information than alerting rules.

Interpreting a missing value in the case of a database query or complex rule is quite difficult, especially because such rules are often composite decision trees. For example, a rule might state the following: "if a domain that has never been seen before is involved in a higher-than-average upload, produce an alert". Upon further discussion, the analyst might explain that a relatively popular domain that has been seen before producing a higher-than-average upload is probably legitimate (after all, a large proportion of uploads must necessarily be higher-than-average), whereas a rare domain featuring normal-sized uploads is not necessarily malicious. In other words, depending on which branch of the decision tree fails, the rule can either yield a negative label, or a missing label. A discussion with the query author can reveal this, as long as the data scientist asks the right questions.

From an implementation perspective, database queries can be significantly harder to implement, as they often involve baselining. This was the case in the example above: one first has to compute the average upload before they can assess whether a given upload is "higher-than-average". Queries implement these historical operations mostly at run-time, resulting in massive inefficiency when run on a daily basis. In contrast, some more sophisticated databases will cache partial results, refreshing rather than recomputing baseline statistics every time the query runs. Implementation in data science frameworks poses the same engineering dilemmas.

4.1.3. *Third-party alerts*

Most enterprises will additionally face a deluge of alerts produced by third-party software that often operate as black boxes. Given this lack of transparency, it is safer to assume that these systems map onto {0, 1}, and interpret the absence of an alert as a missing label, rather than a negative label. There are exceptions to this rule (for example, as far as firewalls are concerned, any attempted violation of the firewall policy is malicious, and all traffic respecting firewall policy is legitimate). This challenge of deciding whether the absence of an alert is synonymous with a negative or a missing label is a thoughtful exercise that can unlock a lot of insights from the cyber-analysts. Another source of information that can give hints about the correct translation of third-party alerts into labelling functions is alert correlation and triage, as described in Section 2.2.5.

4.1.4. *Soft knowledge*

Soft knowledge is the least processed form of insight that cyber-analysts have, and they often acquire it via experience, or from studying intelligence reports about the tactics, techniques and procedures (TTPs) of threat actors. They will often attempt to encode soft knowledge in queries but might fail to do it accurately or completely, not through lack of skill (cyber-analysts are typically expert users of database query languages) but because of the inherent limitations of database query languages. For example, an analyst might believe that a botnet will tend to produce semi-periodic traffic towards a rare domain. The concept "semi-periodic" can be quite clearly encoded programmatically in a language with strong support for scientific programming such as Python, R or Scala, but it can at best result in a clumsy approximation if an attempt is made to code it in SQL. Capturing such soft knowledge in a modular fashion to be used as components in labelling functions is a key part of building up a knowledge base, and is more broadly referred to in the weak supervision literature as the problem of *encoding domain primitives*, which forms the topic of the next section.

4.2. Domain primitives for cyber-security

A certain amount of translation work like the example of "periodicity" discussed in the last section is in many ways the price of the weak supervision paradigm: although we relieve the user of having to manually produce labels one by one, we do expect them to be able to precisely describe patterns on the basis of which they would reach a labelling decision. A useful notion in this effort is that of a *domain primitive*: this is a concept that an expert would struggle having to decontruct further. It is helpful to categorise domain primitives according to the type of intuition they capture. This allows us to distinguish between three groups of primitives: *cognitive* primitives, *data modelling* primitives and *data grouping* primitives.

4.2.1. Cognitive primitives

Often, a failure to deconstruct further derives from the fact that the pattern in question is recognised using basic brain processes rather than explicit reasoning. For example, a "spike" in traffic would typically be identified visually by an analyst, and they would struggle to define it further. In cyber-security, cognitive primitives are limited to pattern recognition tasks on visualisation of data (e.g., a cluster of activity in a map, or a period in a time series). This is a sub-domain of pattern recognition where it is relatively easy for relatively basic statistical modelling to match or outperform human intuition (in contrast, say, to medical imaging or driving).

4.2.2. Data modelling primitives

The term "data modelling" is unrelated to statistical modelling and refers to a software engineering process used to specify data requirements needed to support a business process via appropriate use of the organisation's information systems (Carlis, 2000; Spyns *et al.*, 2002). A successful data modelling exercise minimises the friction between the user of IT (who owns the *conceptual data model*) and the IT resources themselves (the *logical data model*).

Effective data modelling for data science on cyber-security is a vast exercise that we can only skim here, but perhaps one example will help illustrate the problems. In many enterprises, laptops connected to WiFi will not have static IP addresses. In practice, this means that the traffic from a certain internal IP to the internet over a period of one week might involve more than one human user(s) operating on more than one device(s). Take now the example of a rule describing "stable host behaviour", namely that the probability of a host visiting more than 10 new domains on any given day should be relatively low. A naive attempt to implement this rule on a web proxy data set by utilising the "host IP address" field as the host indicator will fail in the presence of dynamic IPs, because it will mix together traffic from different devices, which might very well differ dramatically from one another without violating the rule above. In general, the onus should not be on the user to have to anticipate every possible mismatch between the fundamental domain concepts that they use daily and the raw data.

4.2.3. *Data grouping primitives*

As illustrated in Figure 1, an attack rarely manifests as a single event: instead, it will appear as a chain of linked events often across several types of logs. The same holds true of any legitimate user action: it will typically leave multiples traces across a number of logs. This has several consequences. First, it means that data must be *linked*: i.e., user identifiers should be consistent across different logs. This is a huge engineering task, as different logging systems identify users in different ways. Second, it often means that data must be grouped over time in subtler ways than hourly or daily aggregation. For example, a key domain primitive here is the notion of a *session*, which in computer networks refers to a temporally concentrated bout of activity by a single user. Sessions are typically computed by looking at the activity of the user in question, and grouping together any events that are preceded and followed by a certain period of inactivity, say 60 seconds. Sessionisation is so fundamental a concept that industry standards such as Netflow perform it on the router itself, in recognition of the fact that individual packets are nearly meaningless in network traffic. Sessionisation is also a domain primitive in the description of human behaviour: many of the characteristics of the behaviour of a human using a computer are in fact session attributes, rather than event attributes: how long did one spend on a certain website; how much time did they spend checking email per day; how much data did they transfer during an average Facebook Messenger chat. Given the fact that network protocols split traffic in small packets, even attributes that at face value seem to be event attributes, such as "the size of a downloaded file", might end up being session attributes. An immediate challenge with event sessions is that the number of events in a session varies, and a data set of sessions cannot therefore be represented in a strictly tabular form. Sessionisation therefore forces us to view the "object" to be classified in an unstructured form, and rely on feature extraction to recast it into a vector form suitable for classification.

Events can also be related in even softer ways. For example, an email by a colleague might drive you to visit the website of a journal and download a paper. This behavioural habit could be leveraged by a spearphisher to trick you to visit a fake website that resembles a journal portal and download a computer virus. Distinguishing between these two behaviours successfully requires a directly observable link between the email, the web browsing and the download. If, as is often the case, we do not have access to the content of the email (for privacy reasons), then there will not be any hard identifier on the basis of which to link these events together with certainty. However, we can use soft indicators of linkage, such as temporal proximity, keyword extraction on the email subject and the website in question, etc. This type of "weak" link poses significant data representation challenges, but is key in mapping human heuristics to programmatic rules.

4.3. *Summary*

In this section, we discussed the design of labelling functions for cyber-security from an applied perspective. The data-driven nature of cyber-threat analysis offers the advantage of pre-captured knowledge in the form of queries, alerts and blacklists or whitelists that can be quickly leveraged to obtain weak labels, with the major challenge being the decision in each case of whether to interpret the absence of an alert as a negative or a missing label. To enable deeper knowledge capture, it is necessary to translate knowledge from the language of the analyst into formal patterns on available data, which involves a solid understanding of domain primitives: These are the fundamental building blocks of the analyst's reasoning. In cyber, domain primitives tend to pose challenges of unique identifiers across disparate logs, as well as different types of event grouping. On balance, any mismatch between the data representation offered to the classifier and that used by the human expert is detrimental, and best bridged.

5. Conclusion

Lack of labelled data is a leading concern of data scientists in cyber-security research, both within industry and academia. The problem in part stems from the lack of time on the part of domain experts, the size of the data and the rarity of attacks, which renders it extremely unlikely that a short manual labelling session will produce any findings. Upon closer scrutiny, multiple more challenges appear, including a mismatch between the notion of a ground truth label in machine learning and that of an example "worth alerting" from the perspective of a cyber-analyst, and several ways in which data examples presented to the analyst for labelling are out-of-context, and often at the wrong level of aggregation or representation. There is, finally, a strong sense that an invitation to handcraft labels for specific examples from scratch is inefficient when considering the fact that cyber-analysts document and capture their knowledge on a daily basis in a variety of systems, such as rule-based alerts, blacklists and whitelists created using threat intelligence, and database queries that they use for drill-down.

This has led the community to abandon the use of supervised learning in favour of semi-supervised or unsupervised learning. Although valid, this approach is wasteful in that it fails to capture the knowledge already present in the enterprise. In contrast, the relatively novel framework of *weak supervision* which we present here attempts to explicitly model the noise and challenges inherent in employing expert opinion as a proxy for ground truth. In weak supervision, the expert is not asked to label individual examples, but rather to produce labelling rules, capable of producing potentially inaccurate labels on a subset of examples. The three main main benefits of weak supervision are: First, relaxing the requirement for labels to be perfectly accurate is both a relief to the expert and a more realistic an assumption. Second, asking for a rule rather than a label is extremely efficient as a rule can be used to mass-label future points. Third, allowing for that rule to often produce missing labels allows a lot of flexibility to the expert to describe rules that apply in a limited setting without having to worry about how they generalise outside this setting. In effect, weak supervision models the label generating process, in other words the expert's reasoning itself, by suggesting that their decision-making process is an ensemble of imperfect heuristic rules, that get it right on average.

To facilitate the quick adoption of weak supervision in industry, we illustrated how the interface of weighted learning which is already supported by most supervised classifiers can be used to handle weak labels, as long as an estimate of the accuracy of each labelling heuristic is produced using the generative model mentioned above. We identified some challenges in using simple gradient descent for maximum likelihood estimation of accuracy (to be addressed in future work), but otherwise confirmed that weak supervision is a valid proposition for handling imperfect, often missing labels.

We also discussed how to smoothen the translation of heuristics into programmatic labelling rules by recognising the existence of domain primitives, namely fundamental concepts that experts use as building blocks to express their knowledge. We broke down domain primitives into three groups: cognitive primitives relate mostly to visual pattern recognition; data modelling primitives abstract away tedious IT details in favour of respecting simple concepts like that of a user, a device and a programme; and data grouping primitives concern aggregation or grouping of events into examples more closely resembling a "behavioural unit", like that of a user session, removing the irrelevant complexity introduced by network routing and logging.

Viewed from this perspective, the task of preparing data in a way that is consistent with expert domain primitives should not be downplayed as a preprocessing task, but is instead a critical part of the modelling exercise.

5.1. *Future research*

This new approach for learning in environments where we have a multitude of heuristics in place of ground truth opens up a large number of potential future research directions. An obvious one is the improvement of the MLE framework for estimating the accuracy of each labelling function, and its robustness under violation of the independence assumption (Bach *et al.*, 2017).

Another direction for fundamental methodology is to make room for scoring functions, rather than labelling functions, where the output is a continuous score rather than a label. This reflects the fact that many heuristics are in fact natively represented as scoring rules that the expert expects are monotonically related to the probability of the example being malicious, and that are then (somewhat arbitrarily) thresholded to produce a label. To

avoid the arbitrariness of the choice of threshold and the resulting information loss, a different generative model must be posited, as well as a different
encoding of missing labels.

Finally, a concern pertinent to all streaming contexts is the evolving
nature of the data generating process, which might cause the relationship between the features and the response to gradually shift over time
or abruptly change on occasion, a phenomenon referred to as *concept drift*.
In the standard streaming framework, some form of windowing or exponentially decay is applied so that old pairs (X_t, y_t) are gradually forgotten
to make room for a shifting relationship between X_t and y_t. In the presence
of a labelling rule which continues to provide labels for novel examples, it
is interesting to ask ourselves whether exponential decay might best take
place at the level of the rule, rather than the label. This reflects existing
practice of security analysts in "retiring" old alerting rules. In this case, as
well as more generally, the harmonisation of supervised learning with rule-
based alerting is one of the most appealing characteristics of the proposed
framework.

Finally, exploring the potential for weak supervision beyond cyber-
security is an exciting applied research direction. In principle, the framework applies in all domains that satisfy the following characteristics: the
data are big; positive events are rare; ground truth is not readily available;
and rule-based systems are already in place. Examples include anti-money
laundering, fraud detection and fault detection in industrial manufacturing.
This hybrid between rule-based and machine learning classification offers
a different sort of interaction between human and machine.

Appendix: Gradient Computations

There is clearly a closed-source solution for β, given by

$$\beta_k^* = \frac{\sum_{i=1}^n \mathbf{1}_{\Lambda_{ik}=0}}{n}.$$

We plug in β^* and take the derivative with respect to α:

$$\nabla_\alpha \mathcal{L}(\alpha, \beta^*; \Lambda) = \sum_{i=1}^n \frac{\sum_{y' \in \{-1,1\}} \nabla_\alpha \partial \mu_{\alpha,\beta^*}(\lambda(x_i), y)}{\sum_{y' \in \{-1,1\}} \mu_{\alpha,\beta^*}(\lambda(x_i), y')},$$

where the partial derivative of $\mu()$ with respect to α_k is

$$\frac{\partial \mu_{\alpha,\beta}(\lambda(x_i), y)}{\partial \alpha_k} = \frac{(\beta_k \mathbf{1}_{[\Lambda_k = Y]} - \beta_k \mathbf{1}_{[\Lambda_k = -Y]}) \mu_{\alpha,\beta}(\lambda(x_i), y)}{\beta_k \alpha_k \mathbf{1}_{[\Lambda_k = Y]} + \beta_k (1 - \alpha_k) \mathbf{1}_{[\Lambda_k = -Y]} + (1 - \beta_k) \mathbf{1}_{[\Lambda_k = 0]}}.$$

References

Anagnostopoulos, C. (2010). *A Statistical Framework for Streaming Data Analysis*, Ph.D. thesis, Imperial College London.

Bach, S. H., He, B., Ratner, A. and Ré, C. (2017). Learning the structure of generative models without labeled data, arXiv preprint arXiv:1703.00854.

Balasubramanian, K., Donmez, P. and Lebanon, G. (2011). Unsupervised supervised learning II: Margin-based classification without labels, *Journal of Machine Learning Research* **12**, pp. 3119–3145.

Breiman, L. (2001). Random forests, *Machine Learning* **45**, 1, pp. 5–32.

Carasso, D. (2012). *Exploring Splunk*, published by CITO Research, New York, USA, pp. 978–0.

Carlis, J. (2000). *Mastering Data Modeling: A User Driven Approach*, Addison-Wesley Professional.

Chandola, V., Banerjee, A. and Kumar, V. (2009). Anomaly detection: A survey, *ACM Computing Surveys (CSUR)* **41**, 3, p. 15.

Chapelle, O., Scholkopf, B. and Zien, A. (2009). Semi-supervised learning (Chapelle, O. et al., eds.; 2006)[book reviews], *IEEE Transactions on Neural Networks* **20**, 3, pp. 542–542.

Cortes, C. and Vapnik, V. (1995). Support vector machine, *Machine Learning* **20**, 3, pp. 273–297.

Dietterich, T. G. (2000). Ensemble methods in machine learning, *Multiple Classifier Systems* **1857**, pp. 1–15.

Evans, L. P., Adams, N. M. and Anagnostopoulos, C. (2013). When does active learning work? in *International Symposium on Intelligent Data Analysis*, pp. 174–185.

Gormley, C. and Tong, Z. (2015). *Elasticsearch: The Definitive Guide: A Distributed Real-Time Search and Analytics Engine*, "O'Reilly Media, Inc.".

Hernández-González, J., Inza, I. and Lozano, J. A. (2016). Weak supervision and other non-standard classification problems: A taxonomy, *Pattern Recognition Letters* **69**, pp. 49–55.

Hoffmann, R., Zhang, C., Ling, X., Zettlemoyer, L. and Weld, D. S. (2011). Knowledge-based weak supervision for information extraction of overlapping relations, in *Proceedings of the 49th Annual Meeting of the Association for Computational Linguistics: Human Language Technologies — Volume 1*, pp. 541–550.

LeCun, Y., Bengio, Y. and Hinton, G. (2015). Deep learning, *Nature* **521**, 7553, pp. 436–444.

MacKay, D. J. (1992). Information-based objective functions for active data selection, *Neural Computation* **4**, 4, pp. 590–604.

Meng, X., Bradley, J., Yavuz, B., Sparks, E., Venkataraman, S., Liu, D., Freeman, J., Tsai, D., Amde, M., Owen, S. *et al.* (2016). Mllib: Machine learning in apache spark, *The Journal of Machine Learning Research* **17**, 1, pp. 1235–1241.

Provos, N. *et al.* (2004). A virtual honeypot framework. in *USENIX Security Symposium*, Vol. 173, pp. 1–14.

Ratner, A., Bach, S. H., Ehrenberg, H., Fries, J., Wu, S. and Ré, C. (2017). Snorkel: Rapid training data creation with weak supervision, arXiv preprint arXiv:1711.10160.

Ruppert, D. and Wand, M. P. (1994). Multivariate locally weighted least squares regression, *The Annals of Statistics* **22**, 3, pp. 1346–1370.

Settles, B. (2010). Active learning literature survey, *University of Wisconsin, Madison* **52**, 55–66, p. 11.

Spyns, P., Meersman, R. and Jarrar, M. (2002). Data modelling versus ontology engineering, *ACM SIGMod Record* **31**, 4, pp. 12–17.

Stanton, B., Theofanos, M. F., Prettyman, S. S. and Furman, S. (2016). Security fatigue, *IT Professional* **18**, 5, pp. 26–32.

Tibshirani, R. and Hastie, T. (1987). Local likelihood estimation, *Journal of the American Statistical Association* **82**, 398, pp. 559–567.

Chapter 11

Large-scale Analogue Measurements and Analysis for Cyber-Security

George Cybenko[*,‡] and Gil M. Raz[†,§]

*Thayer School of Engineering,
Dartmouth College, Hanover, NH 03753, USA
†Systems & Technology Research,
600 W. Cummings Park, Woburn, MA 01801, USA

‡gvc@dartmouth.edu
§Gil.Raz@STResearch.com

All digital logic and data in a computing system are subject to compromise by an attacker. As a result, any security monitoring or analysis done within the same communications and computational fabric is also subject to compromise. Moreover, many embedded processors do not have the additional memory or computational resources to coexist with security solutions. As a result, there is interest in using out-of-band analogue side-channel measurements and their analyses to monitor expected programme execution. This chapter describes an approach to this problem that involves measuring external electromagnetic emanations from a commodity processor and analysing those measurements to estimate various aspects of application software execution. It is of particular importance to alert the user to deviations from the logically constrained execution paths determined by the programme structure. Our approach uses analogue RF measurements made in multiple bands at GHz rates which generate enormous amounts of data at high sampling rates. These measurements are used initially for developing the appropriate classification and analytics, and subsequently for implementing those classifiers and trackers operationally in real time. We describe our implementation of machine learning and information theory-based algorithms for identifying the most useful features for tracking an application's control flow graph. Moreover, we describe a hierarchy of control flow graph models in which different models have different execution tracking performance properties.

227

1. Introduction

Data modelling and analysis have played a central role in intrusion detection since the earliest days of the cyber-security field (Denning, 1987). Despite this long history, the basic problems and solution frameworks have remained largely the same. Computer systems, networks and/or application programmes (the "systems") are instrumented to produce observations related to the security state of the instrumented systems. Those observation are analysed, preferably in real time, with the ultimate goal of classifying the operation of the system as being benign, abnormal or outright malicious.

The volume and diversity of security-related system observations have become staggering since the inception of intrusion detection. Networks, operating systems and applications programmes can be instrumented in multiple places and at multiple levels of granularity, resulting in significant observation-type heterogeneity (Granadillo *et al.*, 2016). Moreover, network speeds and processor clocks have continued to increase according to Moore's Law, resulting in observation data rates in the gigabytes per second rates (Jose and Gireeshkumar, 2016; Mahmood and Afzal, 2013).

Concurrently, it has also recognised that the data analysis required for effective and robust solutions could not be based solely on classical statistical tests and techniques, resulting in efforts to apply different types of data analytics to the observations (Forrest *et al.*, 1996; Lee *et al.*, 1998). Today, a wide variety of data mining, machine learning and, more generally, data science approaches have been brought to bear on the intrusion detection problem in cyber-security (Dua and Du, 2016).

As a result, the "perfect storm" of high data rates and high data diversity in cyber-security is today challenging data science across many fronts.

In this chapter, we describe a novel cyber-security problem that involves a new type of observational data and a new approach to temporal analysis of that data. Specifically, we are using involuntary electromagnetic (EM) emanations from a microprocessor as the observation source and control flow graphs (CFGs) as baseline models for correct execution. As we will demonstrate, both the observation sequence and the execution model pose big data science problems.

The chapter is organised as follows. Section 2 contains a more detailed description of the underlying problem and its intended use cases. Section 3 describes the underlying classification problem, while Section 4 goes into details of our current solution approaches. Section 5 is a summary together with a discussion of current results and future work.

2. Cyber-Defence Using Analogue Side Channels and Control Flow Graphs

Detecting malware and its effects on a system using intrusion detection systems (IDS) running on the same system is inherently risky. In such situations, malware could have full access to machine and/or network state and may therefore circumvent common detection techniques. Moreover, malware can actually compromise security monitoring and analysis systems if those systems are "in-band" with respect to the processor and memory architecture which is ostensibly being protected. In particular, subversions of virtual machines and hardware-based isolation mechanisms have been demonstrated in various ways (Horn, 2018; Rutkowska and Tereshkin, 2008).

Not only are such "in-band" solutions subject to compromise themselves, but low-powered embedded devices that are prevalent in the Internet-of-Things (IoT) and industrial control systems (ICS) lack the computational horsepower and/or memory to implement IDS approaches. Such embedded devices are the initial systems of interest for this line of research. The ultimate goal is to develop an IDS capability for platforms that cannot themselves host security add-ons due to power, memory or throughput constraints.

As a result, the authors and their respective organisations have been conducting research into cyber-defence methods based on principled analyses of involuntary, "out-of-band," analogue emissions. Our methods provide a principled approach to analysing and exploiting such analogue side-channel information as security information sources as well as providing insights into achievable performance bounds.

Our approach involves four areas of innovations that we describe in more detail later in this chapter:

- modelling of the target application programme for accurate associations between observations and programme state;

- selection of the best subset of EM frequencies/features to identify programme state;
- algorithms for tracking programme execution accurately and efficiently; and
- techniques for improving such tracking performance.

By focusing primarily on EM emissions, our approach isolates the security functionality by an air gap from the target host. A major challenge is obtaining sufficient programme state via such unintended emissions to accurately characterise the execution. We have considered some other analogue signals such as power fluctuations, infrared, thermal, vibrational, and acoustic signals to determine the full range of available side channel information using multi-modality sensing extensions to other types of systems but those results are preliminary and will not be reported here.

To summarise, the basic technical challenge we are addressing here is the question of whether "out-of-band" analogue emissions can be used to characterise whether a known executing programme is operating "as expected" or not. Weaker variants of this question ask which of N known programmes are currently executing, some of which might be malware.

3. Review of the Measurement to Control Flow Graph Problem

We formulate the Measurement to Control Flow Graph Problem (M2CFG) as a classification problem in which analogue measurements are features and the classes are basic blocks in the target programme executing. Representing basic blocks as nodes and the allowed transitions, according to the programme semantics, between basic blocks as directed edges, the CFG is a directed graph as depicted on the right side of Figure 1. M2CFG is thus a mapping of analogue measurements to nodes in the CFG as depicted in that figure.

It should be noted that the overall problem discussed here involves two levels of classification. The one described in this section deals with the classification of measurements using basic blocks as classes while, at a higher level, we are ultimately interested in labels such as "normal," "abnormal" and "malicious" being applied to sequences of measurements.

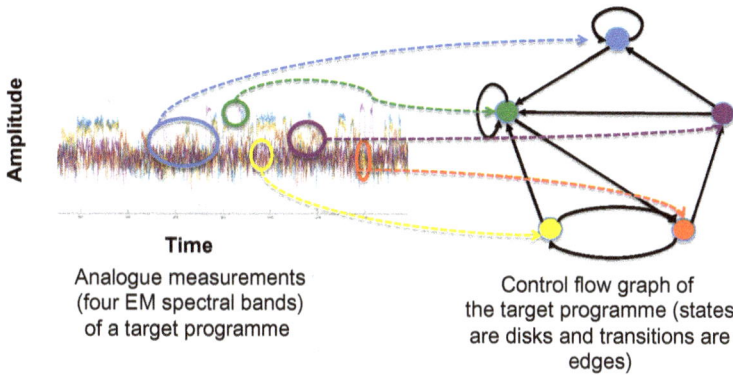

Analogue measurements
(four EM spectral bands)
of a target programme

Control flow graph of
the target programme (states
are disks and transitions are
edges)

Fig. 1: The measurement to control flow graph (M2CFG) problem is to classify analogue measurements (on the left) as belonging to basic blocks in the executing programme (on the right). This example is ideal in a sense described below.

Readers not familiar with the "basic block" concept of programme analysis are encouraged to review a seminal work in the area (Allen, 1970). Briefly, a basic block of instructions in an executable representation of a programme is a maximal sequence of instructions to which control can only be passed at the start of the block and from which control is passed to another block only at the end. All instructions within a basic block are executed sequentially and unconditionally. One can think of basic blocks as atomic elements from the point of view of control flow within a programme.

It has been observed by many authors that the average size of basic blocks across a variety of real-world applications programmes is relatively small, namely smaller than 10 instructions per basic block (Patel *et al.*, 2000). This suggests that a programme with 100,000 instructions would have about 10,000 basic blocks. This observation has implications for some analyses of control flow graphs that we describe below because some analyses and constructs require determining properties of a graph with n^2 nodes constructed from a programme that has n basic blocks.

Our present approach to M2CFG involves four steps:

(1) Performing experiments in which the analogue measurements are taken using a clock that is synchronised at start time with the programme execution so that we know both the measurement and basic block at

start time, although we have relaxed this synchronisation in our most recent experiments.

(2) Using a statistical machine learning technique to construct a classifier using the data from Step 1 as the training data.

(3) Combining the classifier from Step 2 and CFG structure in a tracking algorithm that uses the constraints of the CFG in addition to the class labels produced by the classifier to more accurately estimate which basic block corresponds to a measurement.

(4) If the use case requires more accuracy, modifying the programme in a way to improve tracking without changing its functionality.

Several observations about the M2CFG problem and our approach are important to make:

- Steps 1 and 2 are typically iterated because our raw measurements (namely, power in multiple frequency bands) are high dimensional and the classifier developed in Step 2 can be used to select a smaller number of frequencies/features that are most important to the classifier. We describe some examples of such feature selection below.
- The measurements are inherently noisy and there is possible clock drift between the measurement instruments and the processor clock. As a result, the training data is noisy, and the resulting measurement-to-node mapping of the classifier is imperfect and probabilistic. This is in contrast to the CFG dynamics, which can be regarded as nondeterministic and so not treated as stochastic in our present approach. That is, transitions between basic blocks are either possible or not according to the programme semantics and, although they may occur normally at different rates, we do not model the different transition rates as probabilities nor the nodes in the CFG as "states" of the programme in the classical sense.
- The structure of the CFG has bearing on the performance of the tracking algorithm implemented in Step 3 in a manner that can be rigorously described and quantified. Our initial investigations into that are described below.
- Just as Step 1 and Step 2 can be iterated to identify a smaller set of measurements or features without sacrificing intrusion detection performance, all of Steps 1–4 can be iterated to find programme

modifications that improve tracking performance as required for a specific use case.

It should be pointed out that monitoring aspects of a programmes control flow with the goal of intrusion detection and, more generally, security and correctness has been proposed and implemented by several authors in various ways (Abadi *et al.*, 2005; Erlingsson and Schneider, 1999; Hofmeyr *et al.*, 1998; Keromytis and Stolfo, 2016; Oh *et al.*, 2002; Song *et al.*, 2009). Those efforts however were based on measurements made within the memory and processor boundaries of the system. The work described here is among the first efforts to use "out-of-band" sensors and measurements to estimate the security properties of an executing programme. Other related efforts are currently underway in a multi-year research programme funded by the US Department of Defense (Keromytis, 2015).

The next section describes in detail this approach as well as several experiments we have performed to gauge the performance of the above four steps and provide insights from lessons learned.

4. Implementations Details and Results

4.1. *Observation of EM emissions (Step 1)*

Our approach to data collection consists of two steps. The first is collecting a considerable amount of instantaneously wide-bandwidth, high-fidelity, RF emissions from the devices under test, to perform offline analysis and system training. These analyses provide the foundation for understanding bands of interest and calculating the achievable performance bounds. This is followed by online operation using narrower band software defined radios (SDRs), which provide a cost-effective and mobile solution for operationally relevant use. Here, broadband measurements consist of sample rates up to 4 Giga samples per second and lower sample rates are up to 200 Mega samples per second with a selectable centre band between DC and 6 GHz.

The measurements used to generate the examples described here were measured using Beehive Electronics near field probes and amplifier at a 10 mm distance. Measurements at 35 cm distance were conducted using monopole antennas such as the VERT2450 antenna from Ettus Research. The broadband measurements were sampled using a TI

4GSps ADC12J4000 board and the SDR used for narrowband operations is the Ettus ×310 board. The combination of these sensing modalities provides comprehensive depth and breadth of data collected under multiple conditions, yielding accurate waveforms and distributions of both signals-of-interest and interference sources. Signal quality as measured by signal-to-noise-ratio (SNR) and signal-to-interference-and-noise ratio (SINR) is compared against the theoretic bounds provided by an analogue link analysis parametrised by emission source, distance, modality and channel conditions. The measurements were conducted in shielded and unshielded environments with distances ranging from 10 mm to 35 cm.

The main device under test (DUT) described here is the Arduino Uno. This device has two independent clocks. One at around 8 MHz and a second at around 16 MHz. The target programme-related artefacts are related to the current instruction length or block length and are therefore primarily at typical bandwidths well under 8 MHz. These artefacts are then modulated by the relatively strong clock signal and harmonics. Therefore, we concentrate on the DC-500 MHz range for extracting features for use in downstream processing. This frequency range covers the first few tens of clock harmonics and the upmodulated programme-related artefacts.

Within this 500 MHz spectrum band, one can observe several thousand separate signal artefacts emitted from the DUT during operation of any programme. Figure 2 depicts a typical signal collected at a distance of 10 mm. These artefacts include multiple clock harmonics and intermodulation artefacts, artefacts that are due to programme loops whose frequency components are related to loop length, many broadband modulations of stronger tones due to transients, artefacts generated by clock dividers, etc. Many of these artefacts are useful as features for programme analysis while others are nuisance factors.

For the Arduino Uno, instruction clock (~16 MHz) movements related to the current instruction being processed are of particular usefulness since the clock stability is limited and therefore its frequency is informative. Figure 3 depicts a single spectral clock shift artefact when the DUT is running simple loop programmes where only the innermost instruction in the loop is varied. Hence both the complex amplitude of the various artefacts and their (limited duration) frequency shifts are useful as features. This requires collection and processing of both short-duration measurements for capturing transitions in

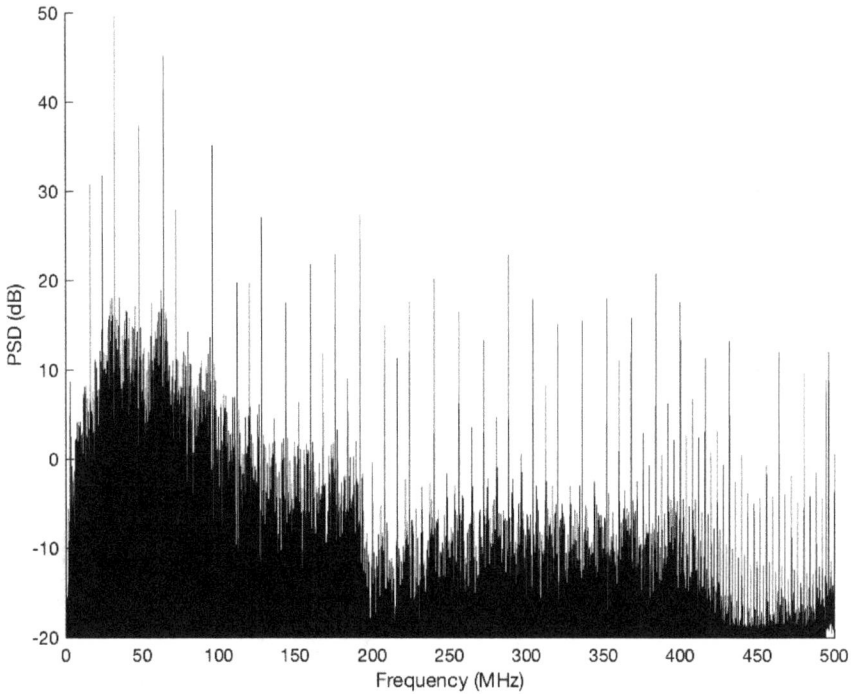

Fig. 2: Example of measured RF power spectrum density (PSD) emitted by an Arduino Uno.

the programmes as well as longer sample rages which provide more accurate frequency estimation.

In addition to the signals emitted from the DUT, many interfering RF signal sources are present in this band. These include RF emissions from nearby devices as well as a wide variety of communications signals, in particular FM radio station signals are observed throughout the band. Such interference signals are handled at all stages of the sensor system starting from the measurement setup, through signal processing to mitigate known interferences without impacting the signals of interest, through training the learning steps to account for the residual interference related artefacts. Figure 4 shows the measurement setup inside a shielded anechoic chamber. Figure 5 shows the typical difference of the spectrum when measured inside the shielded environment vs outside. Multiple very strong interference artefacts are clearly present.

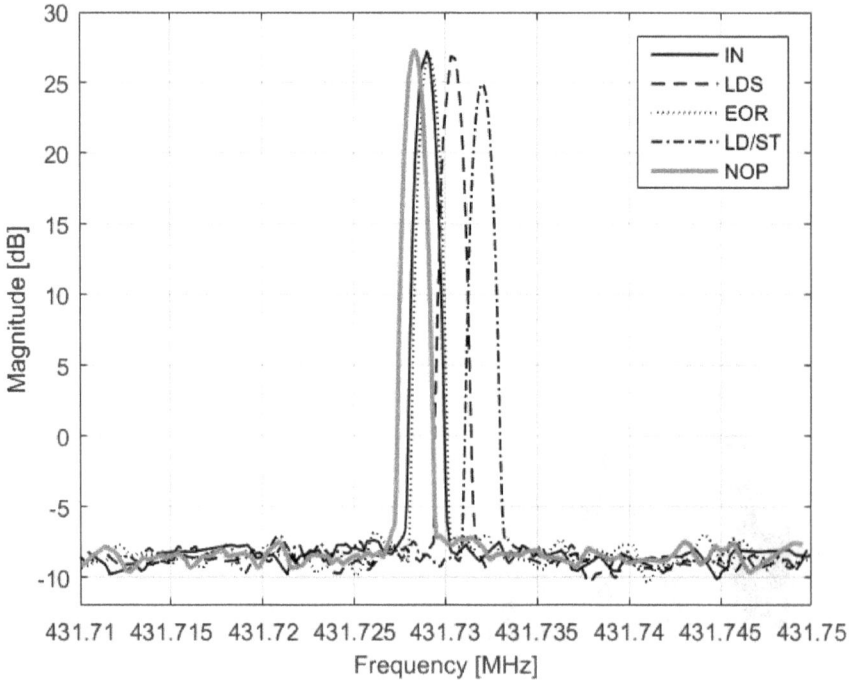

Fig. 3: Example of a target processor clock shift spectral artefact emitted by an Arduino Uno.

4.2. *Machine learning and the measurement to basic block mapping* (*Step 2*)

We have conducted a variety of experiments in which a simple programme is executed and the corresponding EM emissions are measured. Because the execution timing of the programme on the Arduino processor is known, we can correlate it, modulo clock drift, with the measurements. Figure 6 depicts the results of one such experiment where only four of the measured frequency bands are shown to make the plot readable.

While some correlation between the analogue features and the discrete states is evident to the eye, specifics are hard to pick out. Figure 7 zooms in on this graph and the correlation becomes more apparent. We experimented with various techniques for learning a classifier based on this data.

The training data used had 135 features (frequency bands) per sample together with the correctly labelled basic blocks for each sample. The

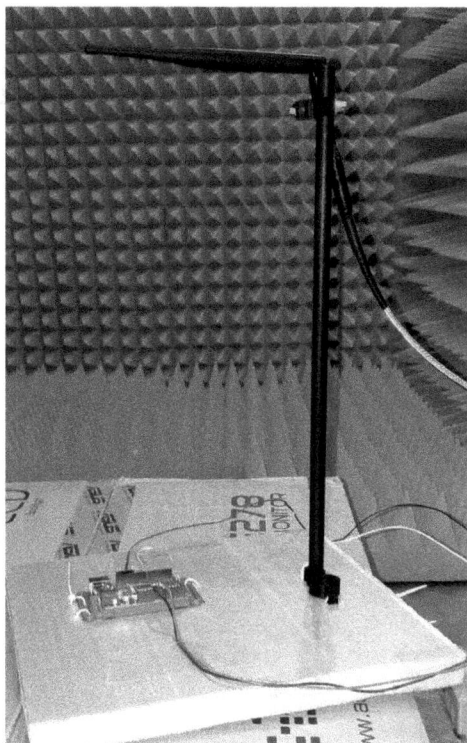

Fig. 4: Measurement setup inside our anechoic chamber.

results described here were based on about 32,000 samples drawn from the programme with 14 basic blocks depicted in Figure 8.

The machine learning technique we selected is based on the Matlab implementation of random forests of classification trees. The specific Matlab functions used were:

```
mdl1 = ClassificationTree.template('NVarToSample','all');
 RF1 = fitensemble(Xtrain,Ytrain,'Bag',150,mdl1,'type',
'classification');
```

with a holdout of 10% of the training data used for validation testing. A total of 150 trees were randomly constructed for the ensemble and the performance as a function of the number of trees is depicted in Figure 9.

Figure 9 shows that no more than 50 trees are sufficient to achieve the minimally achieved error and that trees with surrogate splits (typically used

Data Science for Cyber-Security

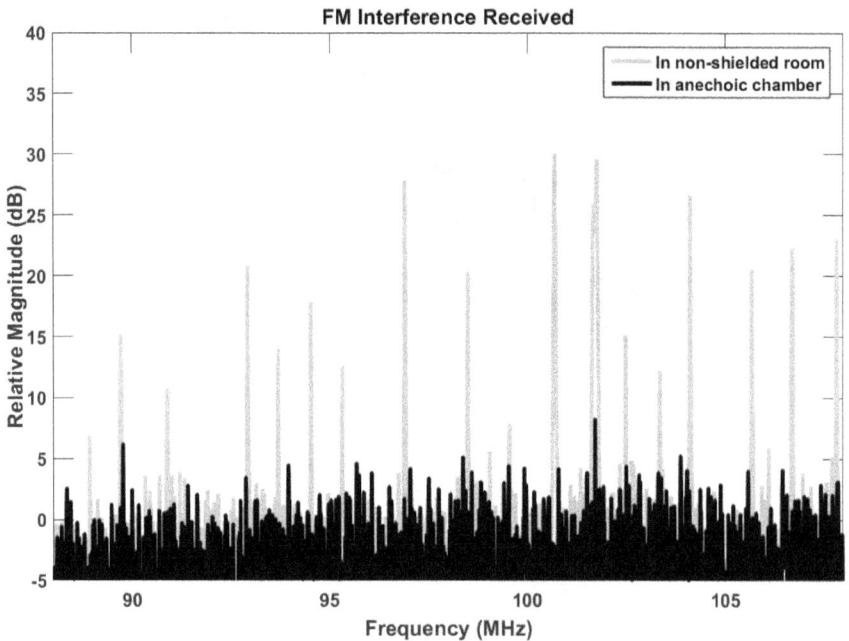

Fig. 5: Comparison of measurements performed inside anechoic chamber vs outside.

for problems with missing features in the data) made no significant difference. While we did not have any missing features in the experiments we
ran, it is possible that some future deployment or use case might require
handling missing features in measurements. (Readers unfamiliar with decisions trees, surrogate splits and the associated mechanisms for handling
missing data can find tutorial expositions in the decision tree literature such
as Rokach and Maimon (2005)).

Figure 10 shows the importance of the 135 features ordered by both their
indices as features (on the left) and sorted by decreasing importance (on the
right). The importance computed is based on the increase in mean-squared-
error when a single feature is removed from the decision tree ensemble, and
so does not take into account the importance of tuples of features. With that
caveat, there seem to be between 40 and 60 features of the 135 that play
any significant role in the classification, about 25 of which are dominant in
that respect.

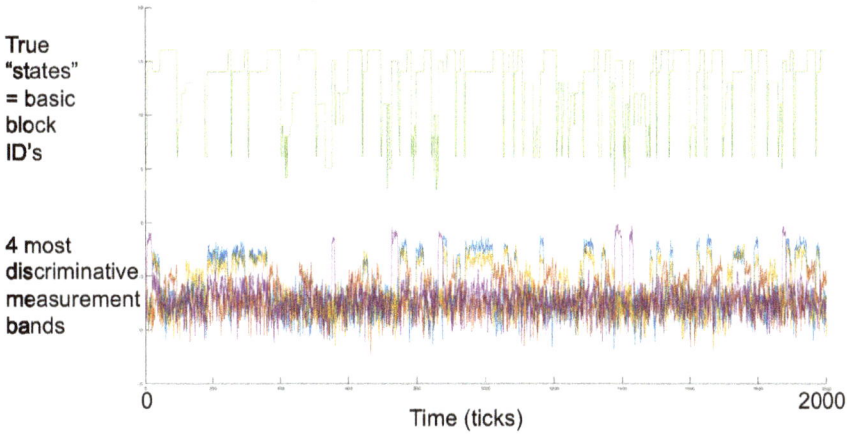

Fig. 6: Amplitudes of four measured frequencies (the bottom four coloured graphs) with the states of the executing programme (the top green graph). The horizontal axis is time.

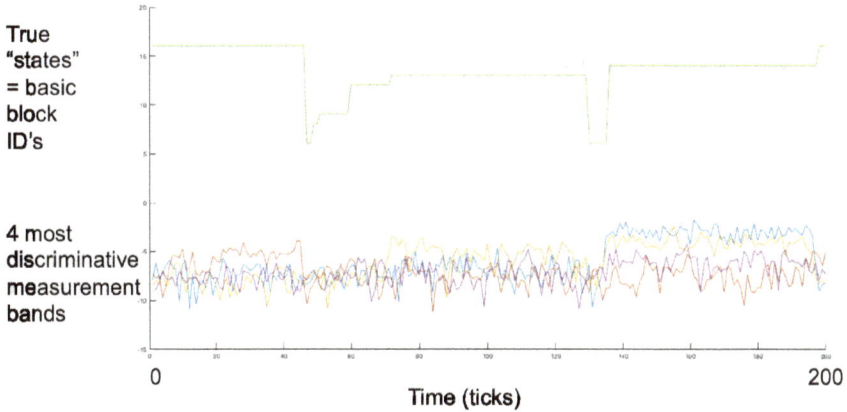

Fig. 7: This is a zoomed in portion of Figure 6, showing the correlation between four frequency measurements and the basic blocks (nodes or states) of the CFG.

The resulting confusion matrix for this classifier is shown in Figure 11. By the standards of many machine learning and classification problems, the misclassification rate should be considered very low, in fact quite remarkably so. It might be unlikely that this error rate can be improved much more although we will continue to explore other techniques as outlined below. In particular, when we consider that the sample rates for a LADS deployment

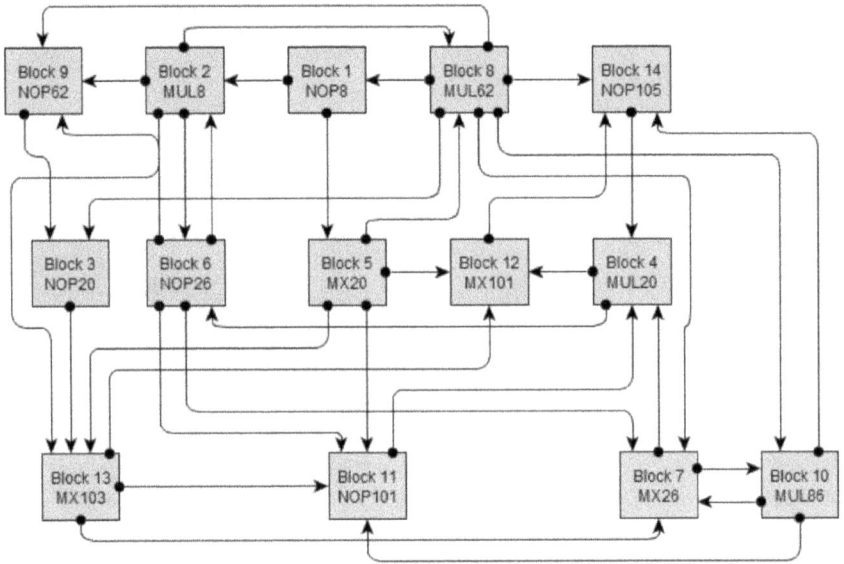

Fig. 8:   The control flow graph of the programme used in the described experiments. Each node represents a basic block and each directed edge is a legal control transition.

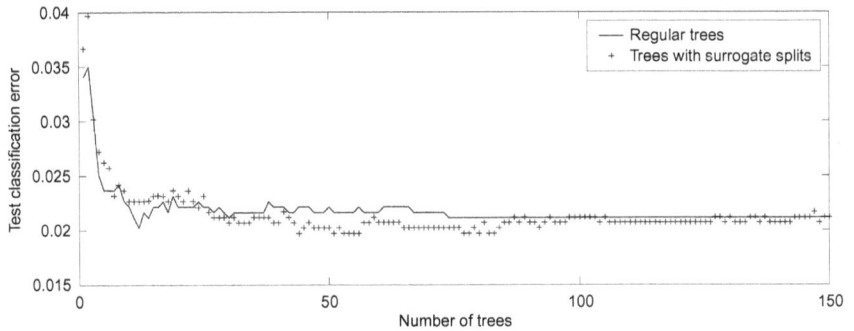

Fig. 9:   The performance of the random forest levels off after 50 trees in the ensemble.

may be at multiple megahertz to gigahertz, a one in a thousand error rate will result in thousands or millions of misclassification errors per second. It is evident that some form of mitigation in the form of extra processing will be required to reduce such error rates. In particular, for typical LADS use cases, misclassification of measurements cannot be determined solely by

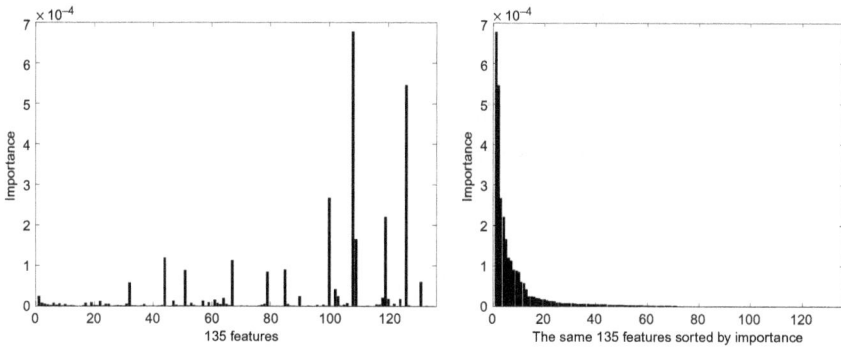

Fig. 10: The bar chart on the left shows the importance of the 135 original features. The bar chart on the right is a sorted version of the left chart, suggesting that only about 25 features are highly relevant to classification accuracy. This is important for selecting a reasonable number of features for performance requirements of an operational version of this technology.

Classification

44	0	0	0	0	0	0	0	0	0	0	0	0	0
0	83	0	0	0	1	0	0	0	0	0	0	0	0
0	0	1500	0	0	0	1	0	0	0	0	0	0	0
0	0	0	1179	0	2	0	0	0	0	0	5	0	3
0	0	0	0	40	0	0	0	0	0	0	0	0	0
0	0	0	1	0	705	1	0	0	0	0	0	0	0
0	0	0	0	0	0	1932	0	0	2	0	0	0	0
0	0	0	0	0	0	0	2327	0	1	0	0	0	0
0	1	4	0	0	2	0	2	5530	0	0	0	0	0
0	0	0	0	0	0	0	2	0	294	1	0	0	0
0	0	0	1	0	0	0	0	1	0	2007	0	0	0
0	0	0	2	0	0	0	0	0	0	0	5260	0	4
0	0	1	0	0	0	0	0	0	0	0	3	1603	0
0	0	0	3	0	0	0	0	0	1	0	0	0	9502

True state (BB)

Fig. 11: The confusion matrix indicates that the computed classifier is relatively good by most machine learning standards.

the measurements themselves since ground truth of the executing program may not be known and instead will be inferred.

4.3. *Evaluating the classifier in the context of the confusion matrix and the control flow graph (Steps 3 and 4)*

Ideally, the confusion matrix for a classifier would have all off diagonal elements equal to zero, namely there is no ambiguity about which basic block is responsible for the observed measurement. Figure 1 depicts such a situation whereby the colours of the nodes are meant to convey the unambiguous classification of such an ideal classifier.

We have explored a hierarchy of control flow graph structures from the point of view of measurement to basic block classification performance. A directed graph together with a specific node colouring is called *observable* if there exists a finite number, k, with the property that any k consecutive observations of node colours results in unique identification of the node in the CFG responsible for the last colour (that is, measurement).

Because the graph depicted on the right of Figure 1 has each node coloured uniquely, the observation of any single node colour uniquely identifies the node, or basic block in the context of the LADS problem. Jungers and Blondel (2011) have discovered an effective algorithm for determining whether a given directed graph and colouring is observable in this sense.

Without going into details, the algorithm first constructs an auxiliary graph with n^2 nodes where the original graph has n nodes. The edges in this auxiliary graph are determined by the colours and edges in the original graph. This auxiliary graph is then checked for cycles. If it has a cycle, the original graph together with its colouring is not observable. If it has no cycles, then the longest path in the auxiliary graph determines the number, k, of observations required to uniquely identify the basic block executing in the programme (that is, the length of the longest path equals the minimal number of required observations). Details can be found in Jungers and Blondel (2011).

Figure 12 shows a simple example of the construct to check observability of a coloured graph.

As previously noted, it has been empirically observed that the average basic block size across a wide variety of applications programmes in an

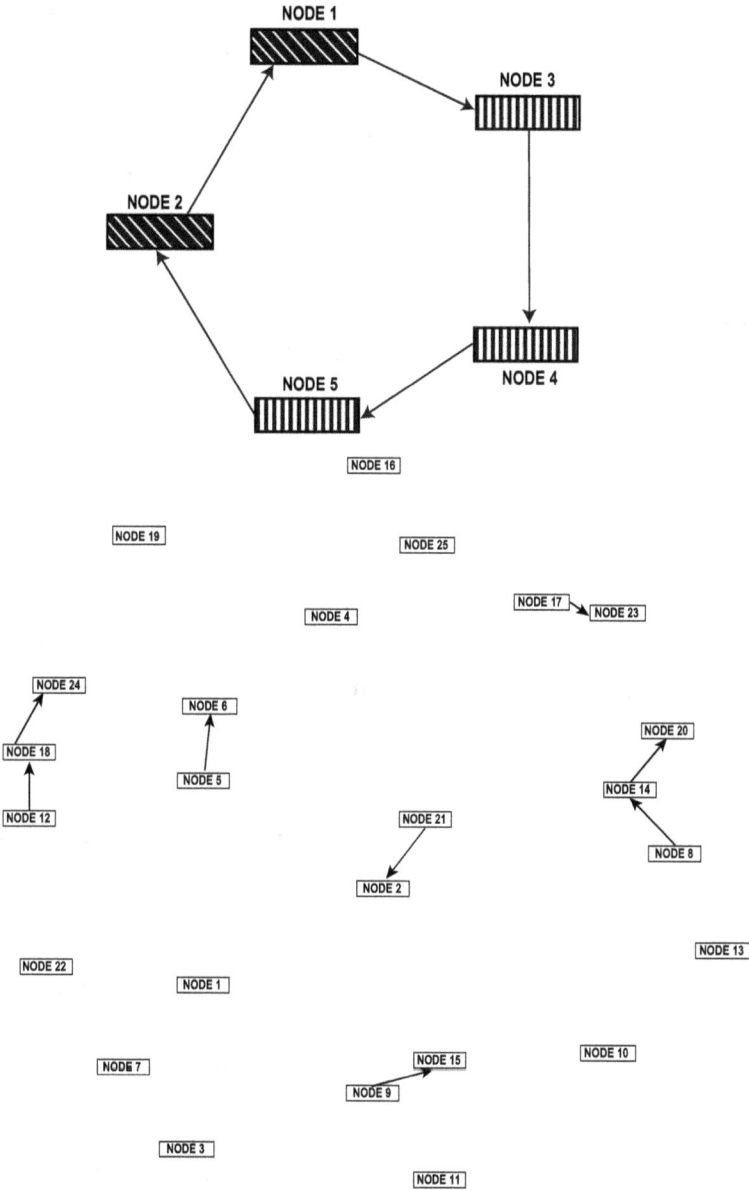

Fig. 12: The two-colour directed graph on the top results in an auxiliary graph on the bottom which has no cycles and a longest path with two edges so that three observations are necessary and sufficient in the original graph to determine any node uniquely.

industry-wide benchmark suite is less than 10 and based on this we noted that, for example, a 100,000 instruction programme might therefore have as many as 10,000 basic blocks. The auxiliary graph construct would have about $10,000^2 = 10^8$ nodes which would have to be tested for the existence of cycles. Fortunately, this analysis is done "off-line" before the detection system is implemented. Nonetheless, analyses of graphs of this size gets into the big data realm.

As the confusion matrix in Figure 11 shows, the association between measurements and basic blocks is not exact in that some measurements are misclassified. In terms of colouring, this means that nodes in the confusion matrix can have multiple colours and so we need to extend the observability construction described above to that case.

We have developed a method for this extension by creating clone nodes for nodes that are multicoloured. Specifically, if a node can be assigned one of c colours according to the empirical confusion matrix, we create c copies of that node that have the same incoming and outgoing edges as the original together with incoming and outgoing edges to and from each of its sibling clones. Each of the c clones is assigned one of the c colours; if node i can be confused with n_i other nodes, the final graph in this clone construction will have $n + \Sigma_i n_i$ nodes in total where n is the number of nodes in the original CFG.

It should be clear that even with a nontrivial confusion matrix, this construction leads to a simply coloured graph whose observability properties are identical to the observability properties of the original multicoloured graph. An example of that construct is shown in Figure 13.

Another important issue that can be dealt with similarly has to do with the asynchronicity of the measurements with respect to transitions between nodes. That is, the dwell time in a basic block can vary or drift depending on various runtime factors. If basic block dwell times are unbounded, this creates self-loops in the coloured CFG so that the coloured CFG is observable if an only if all nodes are assigned unique colours (measurements). However, if dwell times are bounded then a construct similar to the one described above can be made resulting in observability even for programmes that have some bounded variation in basic block dwell time.

Using this construct, we expanded the control flow graph in Figure 8 using the confusion matrix in Figure 11 to get the graph shown in Figure 14

Node Adjacency Matrix

$$\begin{bmatrix} 0 & 1 & 0 \\ 0 & 0 & 1 \\ 1 & 0 & 0 \end{bmatrix}$$

New Node Adjacency Matrix

$$\begin{bmatrix} 0 & 1 & 0 & 1 \\ 0 & 0 & 1 & 0 \\ 1 & 0 & 0 & 1 \\ 1 & 1 & 0 & 0 \end{bmatrix}$$

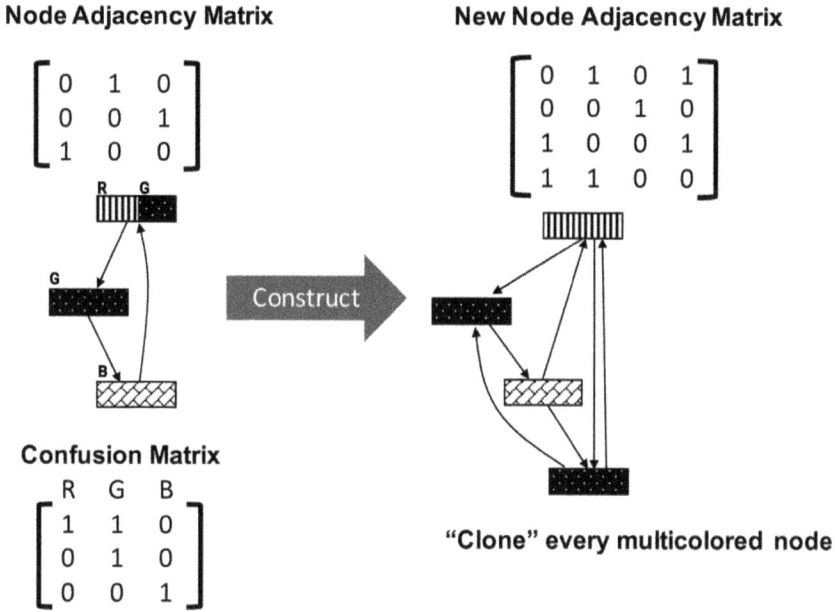

Construct

Confusion Matrix

$$\begin{array}{ccc} R & G & B \end{array}$$
$$\begin{bmatrix} 1 & 1 & 0 \\ 0 & 1 & 0 \\ 0 & 0 & 1 \end{bmatrix}$$

"Clone" every multicolored node

Fig. 13:   This shows the construction for expanding a graph which has multicoloured nodes into an equivalent graph with single coloured nodes. This figure shows how a two-coloured node is cloned into two new nodes singly coloured nodes.

that has 37 nodes and an auxiliary graph with $1369 = 37^2$ nodes that has to be checked for cycles. It turns out that graph does have cycles so that even though the classifier has remarkably high accuracy, the small amount of error creates enough possible confusion that even with arbitrarily long observation sequences, we cannot ever guarantee uniquely identifying the current node. This indicates that perhaps a different measurement strategy will lead to a confusion matrix that results in an observable colouring of the control flow graph, which is the iteration of Steps 1 and 2 outlined above.

4.4.   *Tracking algorithms and their performance*

We have performed a number of experiments with different tracking algorithms to see if the actual observed sequences of real basic block transitions

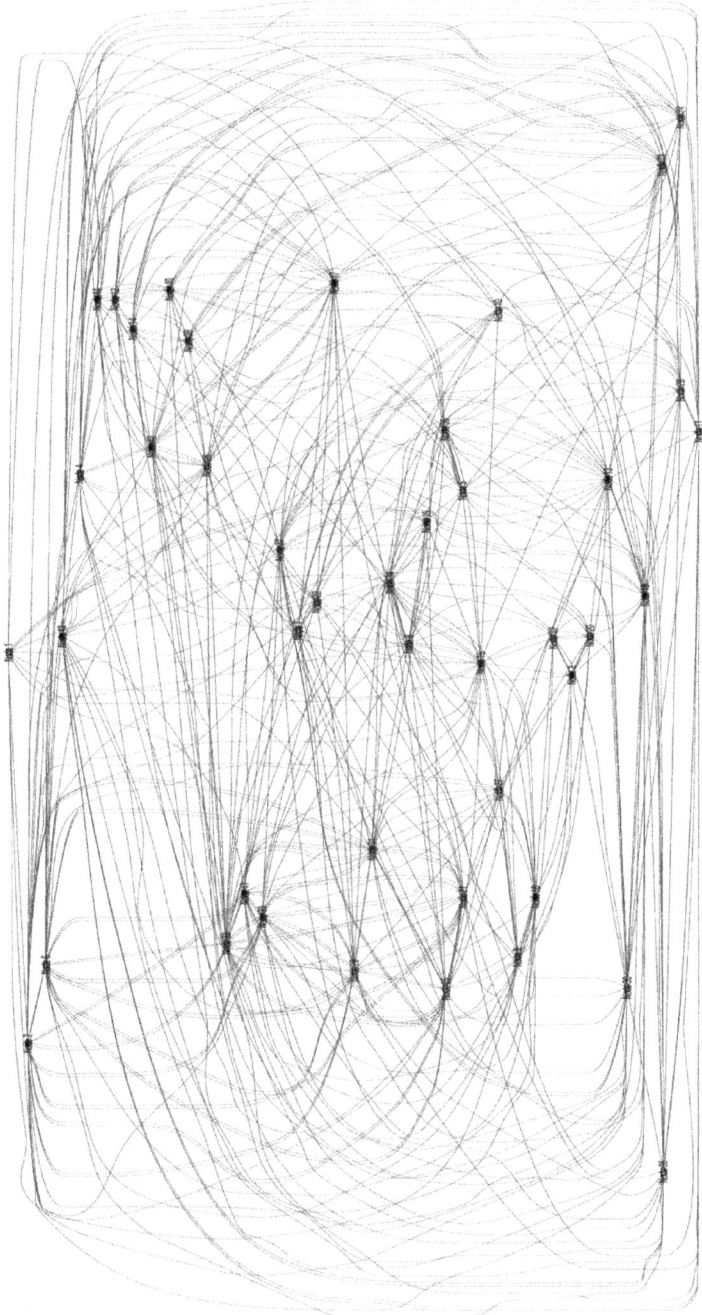

Fig. 14: The graph constructed from the original CFG in Figure 8 and confusion matrix in Figure 11. It has 37 nodes.

typically lead to observable sequences of measurements — in the sense that only one actual basic block is possible, given the observed data, confusion matrix and control flow graph. That is, it is possible that even though the control flow graph is not observable, all observed execution paths lead to measurement sequences that disambiguate the basic blocks nonetheless. Those efforts indicate that a wide variety of tracking algorithms are possible and that the selection of specific algorithms might depend on the use cases and threat models.

There is an extensive literature on tracking algorithms that make a variety of assumptions about the underlying processes being tracked, the measurement to process node mapping and associated statistics (Blackman and Popoli, 1999; Blackman, 2004; Crespi *et al.*, 2008). Moreover, while we have introduced the concept of an observable CFG, other properties that are weaker than observable graphs are possible. In particular, we mention the notion of a "trackable" process in which the rate of growth of possible node sequences as a function of the length of the observation sequence is polynomial (Crespi *et al.*, 2008). Another class of models are so-called "unifilar" models which are information theory analogues of deterministic finite state machines (Ash, 1990).

With respect to modelling an application programme as a CFG, it should be noted that nodes in the CFG are not "states" of the executing programme and should not be conflated with them. In particular, one should be cautious about treating nodes in a CFG as states in a Hidden Markov Model (Rabiner, 1989) and measurements as observations on those states because basic blocks do not represent the state of an executing programme except in some trivial examples. Moreover, transitions between basic blocks are, in general, not Markovian. That said, it might be possible to gain some insights and approximations through such modelling.

5. Discussion and Future Work

The approach to programme identification via tracking of involuntary RF emission from devices has shown the ability to correctly identify the embedded programme running on IoT devices with over 90% accuracy at distances of over 30 cm using commercial SDRs and low-cost antennae. This was shown for a number of device types and performs consistently across multiple devices of the same type without retraining.

In the near future, our team is focused on extending these results to more complex devices including FPGAs, thin-client compute platforms and laptops. In addition, the work aims to extend the sensing distance to over 3 meters and enhance the identification granularity from programme-level identification to block-level identification and eventually to single instruction differences. Moreover, we are extending the ability of the implementation to handle multiple similar devices in the same vicinity, as well as ability to adapt to other external interference signals.

To achieve these aggressive goals, we are enhancing all aspects of the current sensor implementation. These enhancements include augmenting the antenna and analogue front-end to provide higher gain and the ability to beamform and mitigate interference signals. Our embedded signal processing code is being adapted to faster real-time operation with augmented capabilities for noise rejection and signal separation. Of particular focus are enhancements to the control flow graph tracking approaches described above to handle significantly larger scale programmes on devices that are capable of running in a multi-threaded operation and interrupt driven processes with an operating system running in the background. Some of the approaches we are pursuing include feedback mechanisms from the tracker and classifier operations for informing the signal processing and filtering operations, feature selection and analogue sensor controls. These help select configurations and features that are optimal for the back-end processing (for example, the classification and tracking computations) while limiting the data rates required at earlier stages of the sensor data flow.

Acknowledgements

The authors wish to thank the Defense Advanced Research Projects Agency (DARPA) for funding this work as part of the LADS programme. In particular, we thank Dr. Angelos Keromytis, the DARPA programme manager of LADS, for his encouragement and support throughout the programme. In addition, the authors thank the following individuals for many useful discussions and for their work on various part of the project: Isaac Dekine, Nils

Sandell, Michael Tran, Robert Argo and Yi-San Lai. Moreover we thank our collaborators at the University of Pennsylvania who are investigating other forms of analogue side channels in conjunction with our work on RF missions: Jonathan Smith and Matt Blaze.

This research was developed with funding from DARPA.

The views, opinions and/or findings expressed are those of the author and should not be interpreted as representing the official views or policies of the Department of Defense or the US Government.

Approved for Public Release, Distribution Unlimited.

References

Abadi, M., Budiu, M., Erlingsson, U. and Ligatti, J. (2005). Control-flow integrity, in *Proceedings of the 12th ACM Conference on Computer and Communications Security*, pp. 340–353.

Allen, F. E. (1970). Control flow analysis, in *ACM Sigplan Notices*, Vol. 5, pp. 1–19.

Ash, R. (1990). *Information Theory*, Dover Publications Inc., New York.

Blackman, S. and Popoli, R. (1999). Design and analysis of modern tracking systems, *Norwood, MA: Artech House*.

Blackman, S. S. (2004). Multiple hypothesis tracking for multiple target tracking, *IEEE Aerospace and Electronic Systems Magazine* **19**, 1, pp. 5–18.

Crespi, V., Cybenko, G. and Jiang, G. (2008). The theory of trackability with applications to sensor networks, *ACM Transactions on Sensor Networks (TOSN)* **4**, 3, p. 16.

Denning, D. E. (1987). An intrusion-detection model, *IEEE Transactions on Software Engineering* **SE-13**, 2, pp. 222–232.

Dua, S. and Du, X. (2016). *Data Mining and Machine Learning in Cybersecurity*, CRC press, Boca Raton.

Erlingsson, U. and Schneider, F. B. (1999). SASI enforcement of security policies: A retrospective, in *Proceedings of the 1999 Workshop on New Security Paradigms*, pp. 87–95.

Forrest, S., Hofmeyr, S. A., Somayaji, A. and Longstaff, T. A. (1996). A sense of self for unix processes, in *Proceedings of the 1996 IEEE Symposium on Security and Privacy*, pp. 120–128.

Granadillo, G. G., El-Barbori, M. and Debar, H. (2016). New types of alert correlation for security information and event management systems, in *2016 8th IFIP International Conference on New Technologies, Mobility and Security (NTMS)*, pp. 1–7.

Hofmeyr, S. A., Forrest, S. and Somayaji, A. (1998). Intrusion detection using sequences of system calls, *Journal of Computer Security* **6**, 3, pp. 151–180.

Horn, J. (2018). Reading privileged memory with a side-channel, Google Project Zero, https://googleprojectzero.blogspot.com/2018/01/reading-privileged-memory-with-side.html.

Jose, A. E. and Gireeshkumar, T. (2016). Gigabit network intrusion detection system using extended bloom filter in reconfigurable hardware, in *Proceedings of the Second International Conference on Computer and Communication Technologies*, pp. 11–19.

Jungers, R. M. and Blondel, V. D. (2011). Observable graphs, *Discrete Applied Mathematics* **159**, 10, pp. 981–989.

Keromytis, A. D. (2015). Leveraging the analog domain for security (LADS), https://www. darpa.mil/program/leveraging-the-analog-domain-for-security.

Keromytis, A. D. and Stolfo, S. J. (2016). Methods, media, and systems for detecting an anomalous sequence of function calls, US Patent 9,450,979.

Lee, W., Stolfo, S. J. *et al.* (1998). Data mining approaches for intrusion detection. in *USENIX Security Symposium*, pp. 79–93.

Mahmood, T. and Afzal, U. (2013). Security analytics: Big data analytics for cybersecurity: A review of trends, techniques and tools, in *2013 2nd National Conference on Information Assurance (NCIA)*, pp. 129–134.

Oh, N., Shirvani, P. P. and McCluskey, E. J. (2002). Control-flow checking by software signatures, *IEEE Transactions on Reliability* **51**, 1, pp. 111–122.

Patel, S. J., Tung, T., Bose, S. and Crum, M. M. (2000). Increasing the size of atomic instruction blocks using control flow assertions, in *Proceedings 33rd Annual IEEE/ACM International Symp Microarchitecture (MICRO-33)*, pp. 303–313.

Rabiner, L. R. (1989). A tutorial on hidden Markov models and selected applications in speech recognition, *Proceedings of the IEEE* **77**, 2, pp. 257–286.

Rokach, L. and Maimon, O. (2005). Decision trees, in *Data Mining and Knowledge Discovery Handbook*, pp. 165–192, Springer.

Rutkowska, J. and Tereshkin, A. (2008). Bluepilling the Xen hypervisor, *Black Hat USA*, pp. 1–27.

Song Y., Keromytis A. D., and Stolfo, S. J. (2009). Spectrogram: A mixture-of-Markov-chains model for anomaly detection in web traffic, in *Sixteenth Annual Network and Distributed Security Symposium (NDSS)*, Vol. 9, pp. 1–15.

Chapter 12

Fraud Detection by Stacking Cost-Sensitive Decision Trees

Alejandro Correa Bahnsen[*,‡], Sergio Villegas[*,§], Djamila Aouada[†,¶]
and Björn Ottersten[†,||]

*Cyxtera Technologies,
8550 NW 33 Street, Doral, FL 33122, USA

†Interdisciplinary Centre for Security,
Reliability and Trust University of Luxembourg,
2, avenue de l'Université,
4365 Esch-sur-Alzette, Luxembourg

‡alejandro.correa@cyxtera.com
§sergio.villegas@cyxtera.com
¶djamila.aouada@uni.lu
||bjorn.ottersten@uni.lu

Worldwide, billions of euros are lost every year due to credit card fraud. Increasingly, fraud has diversified to different digital channels, including mobile and online payments, creating new challenges as innovative new fraud patterns emerge. Hence, it remains challenging to find effective methods of mitigating fraud. Existing solutions include simple if-then rules and classical machine learning algorithms. Credit card fraud is by definition an example-dependent and cost-sensitive classification problem, in which the costs due to misclassification vary between examples and not only within classes, i.e., misclassifying a fraudulent transaction may have a financial impact ranging from a few to thousands of euros. In this chapter, we propose an extension to the cost-sensitive decision trees (CSDT) algorithm, by creating an ensemble of such trees, and combining them using a stacking approach with a cost-sensitive logistic regression (CSLR). We compare our method with standard machine learning algorithms and state-of-the-art cost-sensitive classification methods using a real credit card fraud data set provided by a large European card processing company. The results show that our method achieves savings of up to 73.3%, more than 2% points more than a single CSDT.

1. Introduction

Classification, in the context of machine learning, deals with the problem of predicting the class of a set of examples given their features. Traditionally, classification methods aim to minimise the misclassification of examples, in which an example is misclassified if the class it predicts is different from the true class. Such a traditional framework assumes that all misclassification errors carry the same cost. This is not the case in many real-world applications. Methods that use different misclassification costs are known as cost-sensitive classifiers (Elkan, 2001).

Fraud detection has been shown to be a classification problem in which this traditional cost-insensitive approach is not suitable (Correa Bahnsen *et al.*, 2013). This is because incorrectly predicting a legitimate transaction to be fraud makes the financial institution incur several different kinds of administrative costs. On the other hand, failing to detect a fraudulent transaction may have a financial impact of a few to thousands of euros, depending on the particular transaction and card holder (Ngai *et al.*, 2011).

Some methods have been proposed to deal with these example-dependent costs. Standard solutions consist of re-weighting the training examples based on their costs, either by cost-proportionate rejection-sampling (Zadrozny *et al.*, 2003), or by cost-proportionate sampling (Elkan, 2001). Recently, we have proposed different methods that take into account the different example-dependent costs, in particular: Bayes minimum risk (BMR) (Correa Bahnsen *et al.*, 2013, 2014b), cost-sensitive logistic regression (CSLR) (Correa Bahnsen *et al.*, 2014a), and cost-sensitive decision tree (CSDT) (Correa Bahnsen *et al.*, 2015b).

A comparison of the above-mentioned methods was performed in Correa Bahnsen *et al.* (2015b); the results showed that the most successful algorithm for detecting credit card fraud is the *CSDT* algorithm. This method is based on a new splitting criteria, which is cost-sensitive, used during the tree construction. Then, after the tree is fully grown, it is pruned by using a cost-based pruning criteria. The CSDT algorithm only creates one tree in order to make a classification; however, individual decision trees typically suffer from high variance (Louppe and Geurts, 2012). A very efficient and simple way to address this flaw is to use them in the context of ensemble methods.

Ensemble learning is a widely studied topic in the machine learning community. The main idea behind the ensemble methodology is to combine several individual base classifiers in order to have a classifier that outperforms each of them (Rokach, 2009). Nowadays, ensemble methods are one of the most popular and well-studied machine learning techniques (Zhou, 2012). The core principle in ensemble learning is to induce random permutations into the learning procedure in order to produce several different base classifiers from a single training set, then combining the base classifiers in order to make the final prediction. Typically, these base classifiers are combined using majority voting (Zhou, 2012).

In this chapter, we propose a new method to create an ensemble of example-dependent cost-sensitive decision trees (ECSDT) by combining them using a cost-sensitive stacking algorithm. The stacking algorithm consists of combining the different base classifiers by learning a second-level algorithm on top of them (Wolpert, 1992). Following the logic used in Nesbitt (2010), our proposed cost-sensitive stacking consists of learning the second level classifier using a CSLR (Correa Bahnsen *et al.*, 2014a). Furthermore, our source code, as used for the experiments, is publicly available as part of the *CostSensitiveClassification*[a] library.

The remainder of the paper is organised as follows. In Section 2, we expose the downsides of the traditional classification methods on credit card fraud and present an evaluation method based on savings. In Section 3, we present the proposed stacking of CSDT algorithm. In Section 4, we describe our experimental setup and present the results of the experiments. Finally, conclusions are given in Section 5.

2. Credit Card Fraud Detection

Online fraud costs the global economy more than \$400 billion, with more than 800 million personal records stolen in 2013 alone (Center for Strategic and International Studies and McAfee, 2014). Increasingly, fraud has diversified to different digital channels, including mobile and online payments, creating new challenges as innovative fraud patterns emerge. One of the tools used to identify fraudulent transactions is machine learning.

---

[a] https://github.com/albahnsen/CostSensitiveClassification.

At its essence, machine learning is the study and creation of algorithms that learn and make relevant predictions from data. Within machine learning, a sub-family of algorithms called classification methods are being used to distinguish between fraudulent and non fraudulent transactions. The following are examples of models that have been used in the past in fraud detection: neural networks (Maes *et al.*, 2002), Bayesian learning (Maes *et al.*, 2002), artificial immune systems (Bachmayer, 2008), association rules (Sánchez *et al.*, 2009), hybrid models (Krivko, 2010), support vector machines (Bhattacharyya *et al.*, 2011), peer group analysis (Weston *et al.*, 2008), online learning (Dal Pozzolo *et al.*, 2014), discriminant analysis (Mahmoudi and Duman, 2015) and social network analysis (Van Vlasselaer *et al.*, 2015). In this section, we will talk about how the traditional evaluation methods for classification methods on credit card detection fail to take into account monetary costs associated with fraud and fraud detection. Afterwards, we will present an evaluation method that corrects for this downfall by optimising for savings rather than raw predictive power. This correction will serve as a definition for the following machine learning models in subsequent sections.

2.1. *Fraud detection evaluation: Traditional vs cost-sensitive approach*

A credit card fraud detection model is based on a classification algorithm that attempts to predict class y_i of a set S of transactions, given their k features $\mathbf{x}_i \in \mathbb{R}^k$. The objective is to construct a function $f(\cdot)$ that makes a prediction c_i of the class of each example using its variables $\mathbf{x}_i$. Traditionally, such systems are evaluated using a standard binary classification measure, such as misclassification error, receiver operating characteristic (ROC), Kolmogorov–Smirnov (KS) or $F_1 Score$ statistics (Bolton *et al.*, 2002; Dal Pozzolo *et al.*, 2014; Hand *et al.*, 2007). However, these measures may be not the most appropriate evaluation criteria when evaluating fraud detection models because they seek to minimise the misclassification rate assuming all hits and misses carry the same value. This assumption does not hold in fraud prevention, since wrongly predicting a fraudulent transaction as legitimate carries a significantly different financial cost than in the case of a false positive. Furthermore, the accuracy measure also assumes that the class distribution among transactions is constant and

Table 1: Credit card fraud detection cost matrix.

	Actual Positive $y_i = 1$	Actual Negative $y_i = 0$
Predicted positive $c_i = 1$	$C_{TP_i} = C_a$	$C_{FP_i} = C_a$
Predicted negative $c_i = 0$	$C_{FN_i} = Amt_i$	$C_{TN_i} = 0$

balanced (Provost *et al.*, 1998), and typically the distributions of a fraud detection data set are skewed, with a percentage of fraud ranging from 0.005% to 0.5% (Bachmayer, 2008; Bhattacharyya *et al.*, 2011).

To take into account the costs of fraud detection operation during evaluation, different costs are assigned to the different misclassification errors. Table 1 is an example matrix representation of the different classification outcomes with the associated costs. Hand *et al.* (2007) proposed a cost matrix, where in the case of a false positive the associated cost is the administrative cost $C_{FP_i} = C_a$ related to analysing the transaction and contacting the card holder. This cost is the same assigned to a true positive $C_{TP_i} = C_a$, because in this case, the card holder will have to be contacted. However, in the case of a false negative, in which fraud is not detected, the cost is defined to be one hundred times larger, i.e., $C_{FN_i} = 100C_a$. This same approach was also used in (Bachmayer, 2008).

Nevertheless, in practice, losses due to a particular fraudulent transaction can vary from a couple to thousands of euros, meaning that assuming constant cost for false negatives is unrealistic. In order to address this limitation, we propose a cost matrix that takes into account the actual example-dependent financial costs. Our cost matrix defines the cost of a false negative to be the amount $C_{FN_i} = Amt_i$ of the transaction i. We argue that this cost matrix is a better representation of the actual cost, since when a fraud is not detected, the losses of that particular fraud correspond to the stolen amount. The costs are summarised in Table 1.

2.2. *Credit card fraud detection model evaluation*

Once the different costs have been defined, we must incorporate them into the classification model so it can maximise savings. We first define the cost given a model f. After, we define a way to measure the savings of the model f compared to using no model at all. Both of these definitions are going to be used in further sections.

Let S be a set of N transactions, $\mathbf{x}_i$, where each transaction is represented by the augmented feature vector $\mathbf{x}_i^* = [\mathbf{x}_i, C_{TP_i}, C_{FP_i}, C_{FN_i}, C_{TN_i}]$ and labelled using the class label y_i. A classifier f which generates the predicted label c_i for each transaction i is trained using the set S. Using the cost matrix, an example-dependent cost statistic (Correa Bahnsen *et al.*, 2013), is defined as:

$$\mathrm{Cost}(f(\mathbf{x}_i^*)) = y_i(c_i C_{TP_i} + (1 - c_i)C_{FN_i})$$
$$+ (1 - y_i)(c_i C_{FP_i} + (1 - c_i)C_{TN_i}),$$

leading to a total cost of:

$$\mathrm{Cost}(f(S)) = \sum_{i=1}^{N} \mathrm{Cost}(f(\mathbf{x}_i^*)).$$

However, the total cost may not be easy to interpret. A better way to analyse the performance of an algorithm is by using the savings (Correa Bahnsen *et al.*, 2014a). The savings corresponding to using an algorithm are defined as the cost of the algorithm vs the cost of using no algorithm at all. To do that, the cost of the costless class is defined as

$$\mathrm{Cost}_l(S) = \min\{\mathrm{Cost}(f_0(S)), \mathrm{Cost}(f_1(S))\},$$

where $f_0(S)$ and $f_1(S)$ are trivial classifiers that predict all examples of S to be either negatives or positives, respectively. Then, the cost improvement can be expressed as the cost of savings as compared with $\mathrm{Cost}_l(S)$

$$\mathit{Savings}(f(S)) = \frac{\mathrm{Cost}_l(S) - \mathrm{Cost}(f(S))}{\mathrm{Cost}_l(S)}.$$

3. Stacking Cost-Sensitive Decision-Trees

In this section, we present our proposed framework for stacking of ECSDT. The framework is based on expanding our previous contribution on CSDT (Correa Bahnsen *et al.*, 2015b). In particular, we create many different CSDT on random subsamples of the training set, and then we stack them using a CSLR (Correa Bahnsen *et al.*, 2014a).

The remainder of the section is organised as follows: First, we introduce the ECSDT. Then we show how to ensemble different ECSDT. Finally, we present our proposed cost-sensitive stacking algorithm.

3.1. *Cost-sensitive decision tree*

Introducing the cost into the training of a decision tree has been a widely studied way of making classifiers cost-sensitive (Lomax and Vadera, 2013). However, in most cases, approaches that have been proposed only deal with the problem when the cost difference between false positives and false negatives is constant (Draper *et al.*, 1994; Kretowski and Grześ, 2006; Li *et al.*, 2005; Ling *et al.*, 2004; Ting, 2002; Vadera, 2010). In order to take into account the varying costs for the different misclassification errors, in Correa Bahnsen *et al.* (2015b), we proposed an ECSDT algorithm that takes into account the example-dependent costs during the training and pruning of a tree.

The CSDT method uses a new splitting criteria during the decision tree's construction. In particular, instead of using a traditional splitting criteria such as Gini, entropy or misclassification, the example-dependent cost, as defined in (2.2), is calculated for each tree node. Then, the gain of using each different split is evaluated as the decrease in total cost.

The cost-based impurity measure compares the costs when all the transactions in a leaf are classified as legitimate and as fraudulent,

$$
I_c(\mathcal{S}) = \min\left\{ \text{Cost}(f_0(\mathcal{S})), \text{Cost}(f_1(\mathcal{S})) \right\}.
$$

Afterwards, using the cost-based impurity, the gain of using the splitting rule $(\mathbf{x}^j, l^j)$, that is the rule of splitting the set $\mathcal{S}$ on feature $\mathbf{x}^j$ on value l^j, is calculated as:

$$
\text{Gain}(\mathbf{x}^j, l^j) = I_c(\mathcal{S}) - \frac{|\mathcal{S}^l|}{|\mathcal{S}|} I_c(\mathcal{S}^l) - \frac{|\mathcal{S}^r|}{|\mathcal{S}|} I_c(\mathcal{S}^r),
$$

where $\mathcal{S}^l = \{\mathbf{x}_i^* | \mathbf{x}_i^* \in \mathcal{S} \wedge x_i^j \le l^j\}$, $\mathcal{S}^r = \{\mathbf{x}_i^* | \mathbf{x}_i^* \in \mathcal{S} \wedge x_i^j > l^j\}$, and $| \cdot |$ denotes the cardinality. Afterwards, using the cost-based gain measure, a decision tree is grown until no further splits can be made.

Lastly, after the tree is constructed, it is pruned by using a cost-based pruning criteria

$$PC_c = \text{Cost}(f(S)) - \text{Cost}(f^*(S)),$$

where f^* is the classifier of the tree without the pruned node.

3.2. *Ensembles of cost-sensitive decision trees*

The main idea behind the ensemble methodology is to combine several individual classifiers, referred to as base classifiers, in order to have a classifier that outperforms every one of them (Rokach, 2009). The most typical form of an ensemble is made by combining T different base classifiers. Each base classifier $M(S_j)$ is trained by applying algorithm M to a random subset S_j of the training set S. For simplicity, we define $M_j \equiv M(S_j)$ for $j = 1, \ldots, T$, and $\mathcal{M} = \{M_j\}_{j=1}^{T}$ a set of base classifiers. Then, these models are combined using majority voting to create the ensemble H as follows

$$f_{mv}(S, \mathcal{M}) = \arg \max_{c \in \{0,1\}} \sum_{j=1}^{T} \mathbf{1}_c(M_j(S)).$$

Importantly, the base classifiers are typically created by selecting random subsamples S_j for $j = 1, \ldots, T$, of the training set S. Then, a *CSDT* algorithm is evaluated on each one of the partitions. To create the different random subsamples, we used three different methods: bagging (Breiman, 1996), pasting (Breiman, 1999) and random patches (Louppe and Geurts, 2012).

The bagging method consists in randomly drawn bootstrap subsets of the original data. Pasting is a similar method in which the random samples are extracted without replacement. Lastly, the random patches algorithm consists of creating base classifiers by randomly drawn bootstrap subsets of both examples and features.

3.3. *Cost-sensitive stacking*

Once different base classifiers are learned, the next step involves combining them. Typically, this is done by majority voting as described in (3.2). However, majority voting gives the same weight to all the base classifiers, but our hypothesis is that individual classifiers should have different weights according to their performance measured by financial savings. To get there, we use so-called stacking learning.

The stacking algorithm consists in combining the different base classifiers by learning a second-level algorithm on top of them (Wolpert, 1992). In this framework, once the base classifiers are constructed using the training set S, a new set is constructed where the output of the base classifiers is now considered as the feature, while keeping the class labels.

Even though there is no restriction on which algorithm can be used as a second-level learner, it is common to use a linear model (Zhou, 2012), such as

$$f_s(S, \mathcal{M}, \beta) = g \left(\sum_{j=1}^{T} \beta_j M_j(S) \right),$$

where $\beta = \{\beta_j\}_{j=1}^{T}$, and $g(\cdot)$ is the sign function $g(z) = \text{sign}(z)$ in the case of a linear regression or the sigmoid function, defined as $g(z) = 1/(1 + e^{-z})$, in the case of a logistic regression.

Following the logic used in Nesbitt (2010), we propose learning the set of parameters β using a CSLR (Correa Bahnsen *et al.*, 2014a). The CSLR algorithm consists of introducing example-dependent costs into a logistic regression, by changing the objective function of the model to one that is cost-sensitive. For the specific case of cost-sensitive stacking, we define the cost function as:

$$J(S, \mathcal{M}, \beta) = \sum_{i=1}^{N} [y_i(f_s(\mathbf{x}_i, \mathcal{M}, \beta) \cdot (C_{TP_i} - C_{FN_i}) + C_{FN_i})$$

$$+ (1 - y_i)(f_s(\mathbf{x}_i, \mathcal{M}, \beta) \cdot (C_{FP_i} - C_{TN_i}) + C_{TN_i})].$$

Then, the parameters β that minimise the logistic cost function are used in order to combine the different base classifiers. However, as discussed in Correa Bahnsen *et al.* (2014a), this cost function is not convex for all possible cost matrices, and therefore we use genetic algorithms to minimise it.

This method guarantees that the base classifiers that contribute to a higher increase in savings have more importance in the ensemble. Furthermore, by learning an additional second-level cost-sensitive method, the combination is made such that the overall savings measure is maximised.

4. Experiments

In this section, the data set used for the evaluation of the algorithms is described. Then the partitioning of the data set and the algorithms used for fraud detection are given. Lastly, we present the experimental results.

4.1. *Database*

For this chapter, we use a data set provided by a large European card processing company. The data set consists of fraudulent and legitimate transactions made with credit and debit cards between January 2012 and June 2013. The total data set contains 750,000 individual transactions, each one with 27 attributes as summarised in Table 2. The database also includes a fraud label indicating whenever a transaction is identified as fraud. This label was created internally in the card processing company, and can be regarded as highly accurate. In the data set 0.467% of the transactions correspond to fraud. Moreover, the total financial losses due to fraud are 866,410 euros.

Using the initial attributes we derived 260 additional attributes using the transaction aggregation methodology (Bhattacharyya *et al.*, 2011; Correa Bahnsen *et al.*, 2015a; Correa Bahnsen *et al.*, 2016; Whitrow *et al.*, 2008). The idea behind the derived attributes consists of using a transaction

Table 2: Database attributes.

Attribute Name	Description
Date	Date and hour of the transaction
Account number	Identification number of the account
Card number	Identification number of the card
Transaction type	Type of transaction (Internet, Card present, ATM)
Amount	Amount of transaction in euros
Merchant ID	Identification of the merchant
Merchant group	Merchant group identification provided by the card processing company
Country	Country where the transaction took place
Country 2	Country of residence of the card holder
Type of card	Card brand (Visa debit, Visa Classic, Mastercard ...)
Gender	Gender of the card holder
Age	Card holder age
Bank	Issuer bank of the card
Fraud	Whenever the transaction was or not fraud

aggregation strategy in order to capture consumer spending behaviour in the recent past. The derivation of the attributes consists of grouping the transactions made during the last given number of hours, first by card or account number, then by transaction type, merchant group, country or other, followed by calculating the number of transactions or the total amount made in those transactions. An example of a derived attribute is: number of transactions made during the past 6 hours on the internet by the same individual in the same country.

4.2. *Database partitioning*

First, the database is partitioned in 3 different sets: training (t), validation and testing, each one containing 50%, 25% and 25% of the transactions, respectively. Afterwards, we perform the cost-proportionate rejection-sampling (r) (Zadrozny et al., 2003) and cost-proportionate over-sampling(o) (Elkan, 2001) procedures. The rejection-sampling approach consists of selecting a random subset S_r by randomly selecting examples from S, and accepting each example i with probability $w_i / \max_{1,...,N}\{w_i\}$, where w_i is defined as the expected misclassification error of example i:

$$w_i = y_i \cdot C_{FN_i} + (1 - y_i) \cdot C_{FP_i}.$$

Lastly, the over-sampling method consists of creating a new set S_o, by making w_i copies of each example i. However, cost-proportionate over-sampling increases the training since $|S_o| >> |S|$, and it also may result in over-fitting (Drummond and Holte, 2003). Furthermore, none of these methods uses the full cost matrix, only the misclassification costs.

Table 3, summarizes the different sets. It is important to note that the sampling procedures were only applied to the training data set since the validation and test data sets must reflect the real distribution.

4.3. *Results*

For the experiments we first used three classification algorithms, decision tree (DT), logistic regression (LR) and random forest (RF). Using the implementation of Scikit-learn (Pedregosa et al., 2011), each algorithm is trained using the different training sets: training (t), under-sampling (u), cost-proportionate rejection-sampling (r) (Zadrozny et al., 2003) and cost-proportionate over-sampling (o) (Elkan, 2001). Afterwards, we evaluated

Table 3:   Summary of the data sets.

Set	# Examples	% of Positives	Cost
Total	236,735	1.50	895,154
Training (t)	94,599	1.51	358,078
Under-Sampling (u)	2,828	50.42	358,078
Cost-Sensitive Rejection-Sampling (r)	94,522	1.43	357,927
Cost-Sensitive Over-Sampling (o)	189,115	1.46	716,006
Validation	70,910	1.53	274,910
Testing	71,226	1.45	262,167

the CSDT (Correa Bahnsen *et al.*, 2015b) and CSLR (Correa Bahnsen *et al.*, 2014a). Lastly, we calculated the ensemble of cost-sensitive decision trees algorithms using majority voting (mv) and cost-sensitive stacking (s), and the following random inducer methods: bagging (CSB), pasting (CSP), random forests (CSRF) and random patches (CSRP). Unless otherwise stated, the random selection of the training set was repeated 50 times, and each time the models were trained and results collected; this allows us to measure the stability of the results.

The results are shown in Table 4. Observing the results on the t data sets are not as good as the ones on the u, this is highly related to the unbalanced distribution of the legitimate and fraudulent transactions.

In the case of cost-proportionate sampling methods (CPS), specifically the cost-proportionate rejection-sampling (r) and cost-proportionate over-sampling (o), it is observed that these methods do not outperform the algorithms trained on the under-sampled set. This may be related to the fact that in this database the initial percentage of positives is 1.5%, which is similar to the percentage in the r and o sets. However, it is 50.42% in the u set, which may help explain why this method performs much better as measured by savings. Moreover, if we see the results of the family of algorithms in the cost-sensitive training, which includes the CSLR and CSDT techniques, we can observe a significant increase in the performance of the algorithms. The CSDT significantly outperforms the previous algorithms.

Lastly, we evaluate the proposed ECSDT algorithms. Initial results show that the bagging algorithm does not improve the results of the CSDT regardless of the method used for combining the base classifiers. This is already

Table 4:   Results of the algorithms measured by savings and F1Score.

Family	Algorithm	Savings	F1Score
CI	DT-t	0.3176 ± 0.0357	0.4458 ± 0.0133
	LR-t	0.0092 ± 0.0002	0.1531 ± 0.0045
	RF-t	0.3342 ± 0.0156	0.2061 ± 0.0041
	DT-u	0.5239 ± 0.0118	0.1502 ± 0.0066
	LR-u	0.1243 ± 0.0387	0.0241 ± 0.0163
	RF-u	0.5684 ± 0.0097	0.0359 ± 0.0065
CPS	DT-r	0.3439 ± 0.0453	0.4321 ± 0.0086
	LR-r	0.3077 ± 0.0301	0.1531 ± 0.0045
	RF-r	0.3812 ± 0.0264	0.2171 ± 0.0100
	DT-o	0.3172 ± 0.0274	$\mathbf{0.4495 \pm 0.0063}$
	LR-o	0.2793 ± 0.0185	0.1776 ± 0.0117
	RF-o	0.3612 ± 0.0295	0.2129 ± 0.0080
CST	CSLR-t	0.6113 ± 0.0262	0.2031 ± 0.0065
	CSDT-t	0.7116 ± 0.2557	0.2522 ± 0.0980
ECSDT	CSB-mv-t	0.7124 ± 0.0162	0.2112 ± 0.0125
Majority	CSP-mv-t	0.7106 ± 0.0113	0.2098 ± 0.0126
Voting	CSRP-mv-t	0.7220 ± 0.0082	0.2691 ± 0.0054
ECSDT	CSB-s-t	0.7181 ± 0.0109	0.2072 ± 0.0103
Stacking	CSP-s-t	0.7212 ± 0.0067	0.2064 ± 0.0069
	CSRP-s-t	$\mathbf{0.7336 \pm 0.0108}$	0.2735 ± 0.0148

Note: The model with the highest savings and F1Score are marked as bold.

an indicator of the good overall performance of the CSDT algorithm. It is in the case of the random patches that we see an increase in performance measured by savings. In particular, we see that by using CSRP with majority voting, there is an increase to 72.2% of savings, and by using the proposed cost-sensitive stacking, we achieve financial savings of 73.3%.

5.   Conclusion and Future Work

In this chapter, we proposed a new method for stacking ECSDT. The proposed method was applied to credit card fraud detection using a real-world database. We have shown experimentally that our method outperforms state-of-the-art classification algorithms and example-dependent cost-sensitive methodologies, when measured by financial savings.

The best results are found when creating and stacking CSDT created by sub-sampling the training data using the random patches algorithm. Furthermore, the random patches algorithm is the one with the lowest complexity, as each base classifier is learned on a smaller subset than with bagging or pasting. We also found that the proposed stacking method provides an additional percentage point in savings compared to using only majority voting to combine the base classifiers.

Moreover, our results show the importance of using the real example-dependent financial costs associated with credit card fraud detection. In particular, we found significant differences in the results when evaluating a model using a traditional cost-insensitive measure such as F1Score, than when using financial savings.

To improve the results, future research should be focused on developing an example-dependent cost-sensitive boosting approach. For some applications, boosting methods have proven to outperform the bagging algorithms. Furthermore, the methods covered in this work are all batch, in the sense that the batch algorithms keeps the system weights constant while calculating the evaluation measures. However, in fraud detection, the evolving patterns in fraudster behaviour are not captured by using batch methods. Therefore, there is a need to investigate this problem from an online-learning perspective.

References

Bachmayer, S. (2008). Artificial immune systems, *Artificial Immune Systems* **5132**, pp. 119–131.

Bhattacharyya, S., Jha, S., Tharakunnel, K. and Westland, J. C. (2011). Data mining for credit card fraud: A comparative study, *Decision Support Systems* **50**, 3, pp. 602–613.

Bolton, R. J., Hand, D. J., Provost, F. and Breiman, L. (2002). Statistical fraud detection: A review, *Statistical Science* **17**, 3, pp. 235–255.

Breiman, L. (1996). Bagging predictors, *Machine Learning* **24**, 2, pp. 123–140.

Breiman, L. (1999). Pasting small votes for classification in large databases and on-line, *Machine Learning* **103**, pp. 85–103.

Center for Strategic and International Studies and McAfee (2014). Net losses: Estimating the global cost of cybercrime, URL: https://csis-prod.s3.amazonaws.com/s3fs-public/legacy_files/files/attachments/140609_rp_economic_impact_cybercrime_report.pdf.

Correa Bahnsen, A., Aouada, D. and Ottersten, B. (2014a). Example-dependent cost-sensitive logistic regression for credit scoring, in *2014 13th International Conference on Machine Learning and Applications*, IEEE, Detroit, USA, pp. 263–269.

Correa Bahnsen, A., Aouada, D. and Ottersten, B. (2015a). Detecting credit card fraud using periodic features, in *2015 14th International Conference on Machine Learning and Applications*, IEEE, Detroit, USA.

Correa Bahnsen, A., Aouada, D. and Ottersten, B. (2015b). Example-dependent cost-sensitive decision trees, *Expert Systems with Applications* **49**, 19, pp. 6609–6619.

Correa Bahnsen, A., Aouada, D. and Ottersten, B. (2016). Feature engineering strategies for credit card fraud detection, *Expert Systems with Applications* **51**, 1, pp. 134–142.

Correa Bahnsen, A., Stojanovic, A., Aouada, D. and Ottersten, B. (2013). Cost sensitive credit card fraud detection using Bayes minimum risk, in *2013 12th International Conference on Machine Learning and Applications*, IEEE, Miami, USA, pp. 333–338.

Correa Bahnsen, A., Stojanovic, A., Aouada, D. and Ottersten, B. (2014b). Improving credit card fraud detection with calibrated probabilities, in *Proceedings of the fourteenth SIAM International Conference on Data Mining*, Philadelphia, USA, pp. 677–685.

Dal Pozzolo, A., Caelen, O., Le Borgne, Y.-A., Waterschoot, S. and Bontempi, G. (2014). Learned lessons in credit card fraud detection from a practitioner perspective, *Expert Systems with Applications* **41**, 10, pp. 4915–4928.

Draper, B., Brodley, C. and Utgoff, P. (1994). Goal-directed classification using linear machine decision trees, *IEEE Transactions on Pattern Analysis and Machine Intelligence* **16**, 9, pp. 888–893.

Drummond, C. and Holte, R. (2003). C4.5, class imbalance, and cost sensitivity: Why under-sampling beats over-sampling, in *Workshop on Learning from Imbalanced Datasets II, ICML*, Washington, DC, USA.

Elkan, C. (2001). The foundations of cost-sensitive learning, in *Seventeenth International Joint Conference on Artificial Intelligence*, pp. 973–978.

Hand, D. J., Whitrow, C., Adams, N. M., Juszczak, P. and Weston, D. J. (2007). Performance criteria for plastic card fraud detection tools, *Journal of the Operational Research Society* **59**, 7, pp. 956–962.

Kretowski, M. and Grześ, M. (2006). Evolutionary induction of cost-sensitive decision trees, in *Foundations of Intelligent Systems*, pp. 121–126, Springer, Berlin Heidelberg.

Krivko, M. (2010). A hybrid model for plastic card fraud detection systems, *Expert Systems with Applications* **37**, 8, pp. 6070–6076.

Li, J., Li, X. and Yao, X. (2005). Cost-sensitive classification with genetic programming, in *2005 IEEE Congress on Evolutionary Computation*, Vol. 3, IEEE, pp. 2114–2121.

Ling, C. X., Yang, Q., Wang, J. and Zhang, S. (2004). Decision trees with minimal costs, in *Twenty-first International Conference on Machine Learning — ICML '04*, ACM Press, New York, USA, p. 69.

Lomax, S. and Vadera, S. (2013). A survey of cost-sensitive decision tree induction algorithms, *ACM Computing Surveys* **45**, 2, pp. 1–35.

Louppe, G. and Geurts, P. (2012). Ensembles on random patches, in *Proceedings of the 2012 European conference on Machine Learning and Knowledge Discovery in Databases (ECML PKDD'12)*, Springer Berlin Heidelberg, pp. 346–361.

Maes, S., Tuyls, K., Vanschoenwinkel, B. and Manderick, B. (2002). Credit card fraud detection using Bayesian and neural networks, in *Proceedings of the 1st International Congress on Neuro Fuzzy Technologies*, pp. 261–270.

Mahmoudi, N. and Duman, E. (2015). Detecting credit card fraud by modified Fisher discriminant analysis, *Expert Systems with Applications* **42**, 5, pp. 2510–2516.

Nesbitt, T. A. (2010). *Cost-Sensitive Tree-Stacking: Learning with Variable Prediction Error Costs*, Ph.D. thesis, University of California, Los Angeles.

Ngai, E., Hu, Y., Wong, Y., Chen, Y. and Sun, X. (2011). The application of data mining techniques in financial fraud detection: A classification framework and an academic review of literature, *Decision Support Systems* **50**, 3, pp. 559–569.

Pedregosa, F., Varoquaux, G., Gramfort, A., Michel, V., Thirion, B., Grisel, O., Blondel, M., Prettenhofer, P., Weiss, R., Dubourg, V., Vanderplas, J., Passos, A., Cournapeau, D., Brucher, M., Perrot, M. and Duchesnay, E. (2011). Scikit-learn: Machine learning in Python, *Journal of Machine Learning Research* **12**, pp. 2825–2830.

Provost, F., Fawcett, T. and Kohavi, R. (1998). The case against accuracy estimation for comparing induction algorithms. in *Proceedings of the Fifteenth International Conference on Machine Learning*, Morgan Kaufmann, pp. 445–453.

Rokach, L. (2009). Ensemble-based classifiers, *Artificial Intelligence Review* **33**, 1–2, pp. 1–39.

Sánchez, D., Vila, M., Cerda, L. and Serrano, J. (2009). Association rules applied to credit card fraud detection, *Expert Systems with Applications* **36**, 2, pp. 3630–3640.

Ting, K. (2002). An instance-weighting method to induce cost-sensitive trees, *IEEE Transactions on Knowledge and Data Engineering* **14**, 3, pp. 659–665.

Vadera, S. (2010). CSNL: A cost-sensitive non-linear decision tree algorithm, *ACM Transactions on Knowledge Discovery from Data* **4**, 2, pp. 1–25.

Van Vlasselaer, V., Bravo, C., Caelen, O., Eliassi-Rad, T., Akoglu, L., Snoeck, M. and Baesens, B. (2015). APATE: A novel approach for automated credit card transaction fraud detection using network-based extensions, *Decision Support Systems* **75**, pp. 38–48.

Weston, D. J., Hand, D. J., Adams, N. M., Whitrow, C. and Juszczak, P. (2008). Plastic card fraud detection using peer group analysis, *Advances in Data Analysis and Classification* **2**, 1, pp. 45–62.

Whitrow, C., Hand, D. J., Juszczak, P., Weston, D. J. and Adams, N. M. (2008). Transaction aggregation as a strategy for credit card fraud detection, *Data Mining and Knowledge Discovery* **18**, 1, pp. 30–55.

Wolpert, D. H. (1992). Stacked generalization, *Neural Networks* **5**, pp. 241–259.

Zadrozny, B., Langford, J. and Abe, N. (2003). Cost-sensitive learning by cost-proportionate example weighting, in *Third IEEE International Conference on Data Mining*, IEEE Comput. Soc, pp. 435–442.

Zhou, Z.-H. (2012). *Ensemble Methods Foundations and Algorithms*, CRC Press, Boca Raton, FL, US.

Chapter 13

Data-Driven Decision Making for Cyber-Security

Mike Fisk

Los Alamos National Laboratory,
Los Alamos, New Mexico, 87545, USA
mike.fisk@lanl.gov

Businesses and government face a daunting option space of cyber-security improvements that could be made. However, resources are limited and improvements have direct costs and opportunity costs, and can impede other business objectives. Thus, deciding how much to invest and in which improvements is a key challenge for decision makers. The paucity of data-driven decision tools today results in decisions that are often based solely on regulatory requirements, product marketing claims and peer benchmarking. Given the role of adversary decision-making and adaptation in cyber-security, we pose new ways to quantitatively evaluate options based on factors like reachability, adversary delay time and adversary productivity. In the absence of sound decision-making, defenders can bankrupt themselves enacting "enhanced security" without actually thwarting an intruder. We demonstrate through quantitative analysis that well-intentioned actual policy decisions may be ineffective at thwarting the adversary.

1. Introduction

Cyber-security is a field of seemingly endless measures and countermeasures between offence and defence. Organisations have a seemingly endless number of security tools, appliances and policies and can bankrupt themselves trying, and failing, to prevent attacks and intrusions. In this chapter, we present a data-driven methodology for more optimal use of resources. This quantitative risk management methodology is based on measuring the effectiveness of candidate security improvements, in terms of impact to impede intruders. We show examples of how to quantify this effectiveness using data, and models informed by empirical data and policies and standards.

Cyber-defence is difficult because of the large, and growing, number of pathways an intruder can use to obtain their objective and the general lack of provable or even high-assurance defences against any of those pathways. Cyber-security is inherently asymmetric in that the offence need only find one pathway to success while the defence must concern itself with all possible offensive pathways. For example, firewalls have matured to the point that they generally protect enterprise internal networks from being exploited through direct, unsolicited network protocol attacks. However, adversaries have continued to be successful at reliably penetrating networks by using phishing and tricking an internal user into initiating the exploitation.

So how does one manage this asymmetry and tilt the balance in favour of the defence? We propose a simple, yet elusive, goal for all cyber-security policies and investments: The marginal cost to the defence of making a cyber-security improvement should be less than the marginal cost incurred to the offence. If the cost to the defence exceeds the cost to the offence, then that course of action is counterproductive for the defence. The defence can bankrupt itself if it continually chooses actions that cost itself more than the attacker. In fact, bankruptcy could even be the attacker's desired outcome. The defender should instead invest in alternative security improvements that penalise the attacker more than the defender.

That conclusion is relatively obvious, but the challenge is in quantifying the costs and effectiveness of security improvements. We start with measuring effectiveness, since an improvement with zero effectiveness is unwise at any cost. Zero intrusions is a goal, but not fully achievable and not a strategy. Intrusion tolerance, in the sense of fault tolerance, is an underutilised engineering principle that leads to systems that are better at containing, constraining and slowing an intruder. Our choice of quantitative measure is based not on a Boolean outcome of intrusion or non-intrusion, but instead on the impact that system and policy have on an intruder's freedom of motion. In this chapter, we will show that this data-driven measure of effectiveness can improve on existing decision-making regardless of the ability to accurately and precisely estimate cost.

In Section 2, we examine cost–benefit and cost-effectiveness strategies as applied to cyber-security and identify new measures of effectiveness. In

Section 3, we discuss security measures for complex system security problems in which adversaries have multiple avenues of attack and introduce some analytical approaches. We perform a detailed case study of objective cost-effectiveness for authentication technology and policy against different adversarial capabilities in Section 4. We offer conclusions in Section 5.

2. Measuring Cost–Benefit and Cost-Effectiveness

It is common practice in business to steer resources to opportunities that offer the highest expected return on investment. Classic cost–benefit and cost-effectiveness starts with the cost term. For this discussion, that is the cost of making a security improvement. That cost is captured as an Information Technology (IT) project cost, combined with any resulting loss in user productivity. While estimating such costs is far from trivial, we yield to the body of knowledge on IT projects. In this analysis, we instead focus our attention on the challenge of measuring the effectiveness or financial benefit achieved by that improvement.

In security, it is common to measure *return* as avoidance of costs incurred by security breaches. For example, Wei *et al.* (2001) compute annualised cost savings of a security improvement based on the fraction of the annualised cost due to incidents that a new security improvement will prevent. A classic *return on investment* analysis as applied to security compares the increased cost to the defence to the expected reduction in costs.

The return on investment construct is sound, but organisations are challenged to estimate the financial value of losses, particularly when including impact on reputation, trust and brand. Even if historical data is used a predictor of future loss, there is little objective basis for estimating the reduction in loss *likelihood* that will be caused by a security improvement. Effectiveness of security controls against adversaries is not well understood. Worse, even when a security control hinders an intruder, the intruder may quickly adapt and there may be no realised change in the amount or impact of breaches. Attackers are not really limited to single attempts. At best, a security improvement might eliminate the lowest cost pathway for an intruder. A well-resourced and persistent attacker may still succeed with equally high probability, albeit with more effort (cost) required to do so. In this sense, most security improvements do not objectively have a favourable return on investment because they do not necessarily prevent a successful attack or result in any cost avoidance.

To address this failing, Cremonini's *Return on Attack* metric (Cremonini and Martini, 2005) ignores the cost incurred by the defence and instead measures the increased amount of effort required by the attacker to obtain its objective. Specifically, Cremonini measures the impact on attacker costs in terms of the probability of a security improvement being defeated in a single attempt. But again, a persistent attacker may be willing to perform multiple attempts in order to penetrate a system. For example, the probability of correctly guessing a secret with a single guess is low, but the rate at which guesses can be made is an equally important factor that is ignored with this metric.

We address this concern by instead measuring *intruder delay*, the amount of time required by an intruder to successfully gain access. This measure allows us to include both probability and rate, as well as other dynamics such as dependencies on user behaviour.

An even more nuanced measure is the *intruder productivity*, which also includes the effectiveness of a successful intrusion in terms of the length of time that the intruder will retain that access. We define intruder productivity as follows:

$$\text{Intruder Productivity} = \frac{\text{Duration of access}}{\text{Delay to obtain access}}.$$

Intruder productivity approaches zero when a large amount of time is required to obtain a small amount of access. For values greater than 1, the intruder can be assumed to always have access.

This dimensionless productivity ratio allows us to compare options that have the same delay time, but grant different durations of access after that delay. However, in some scenarios, instantaneous access is all that is required for the intruder to achieve their objective or to establish persistence independent of the initial access (by installing malware on a host, for example). In those cases, delay may be the more apropos measure. Thus we argue that changes in intruder delay and productivity can be useful measures of effectiveness.

2.1. *No universal relationship with cost*

In order to perform a true cost–benefit analysis, we would need to convert effectiveness to monetary units. We argue that there is no universally appropriate conversion between those units. In a ransomware scenario, an attacker might generate revenue proportionate to how quickly he or she can compromise additional hosts before their infrastructure is disabled. In this case, increased delay may linearly reduce revenue. In a different scenario, an intruder may not have a fixed period in which to succeed and may have enough potential victims being attacked simultaneously that he or she can remain productive regardless of the delay against an individual target. Finally, if a would-be intruder has a single objective and needs sustained access time on a target, increased productivity may linearly reduce costs.

To a defender, there is financial value of reducing the number of successful intrusions per unit time. This value may be difficult to predict when incorporating impacts such as brand value, reputation, and impact to stock value. CGI commissioned an Oxford Economics study that measured an average loss of £120 million when a FTSE 100 company suffers a major data breach.[a] The resources and strategies of would-be intruders determines the relationship between delay and intrusion rate. In the following scenarios, the impact ranges from none to complete protection from intrusion:

- If each adversary could work all of its desired targets in parallel, then a change in delay time only adds that amount of latency to the beginning of their work, but does not affect the throughput of the adversary or the number of successful intrusions for each defender.
- If each adversary picks targets in a random order, can only work on a finite number of targets in parallel, and each target increases the delay time by a factor k, then the throughput of each adversary is reduced by k. If the defender has a fixed number of adversaries, then its frequency of successful intrusion will be slowed by factor k.
- If it is the only defender to increase delay for the intruder, then there is no expected change in intrusion frequency.

---

[a]CGI IT UK Ltd, The Cyber-Value Connection: https://www.cgi-group.co.uk/system/files/cyber valueconnection_full_report_final_lr.pdf.

- If an intruder initiates intrusions against a batch of targets simultaneously but stops as soon as it succeeds with one, then the defender that always causes the most intruder delay will never be intruded.

Each of these scenarios is plausible, and thus we do not offer a universal mapping from change in delay time to defender cost savings.

3. Complex Systems with Multiple Pathways

In this section, we turn our attention to the fact that intruders usually have multiple pathways that lead to an objective. Our professional experience is that in an absence of data, the defence is psychologically prone to focusing too narrowly on the offence's most recent modality for exploitation. There is a desire to completely remove that avenue of attack at all costs. However, the rational objective for the defence is only to make that avenue of exploitation at least as expensive to the offence as the other options at the offence's disposal. Adversaries will choose the least-cost alternative at their disposal, and so there is no return on investment for eliminating one avenue of intrusion when other equal-cost alternatives remain. However, in the absence of quantified costs of other avenues of attack, the defence is prone to over-securing the most salient failure mode. This problem of "fighting the last war" is not unique to cyber-security.

Attack Trees and Attack Graphs (Sheyner *et al.*, 2002) describe the options that an intruder has in reaching their objective. A rational and informed, well-equipped intruder will choose the most effective method to reach that objective. However, many automated and self-propagating attacks have a very small number of intrusion vectors and simply try them all. Another method may be equally or more effective, but simply not implemented in the automation and therefore not attempted. Less-equipped intruders may behave similarly. There is therefore some reason to pay attention to both the most frequently used or predictable vectors as well as the most effective vector. But importantly, there is little expected return from shoring-up an already stronger and unpopular pathway. For the remainder of this discussion, we give the would-be intruder credit for being persistent and well-equipped. While not precisely describing the behaviour of less-capable intruders, this approach is more robust against rapid sharing of information and tools in the offensive community.

When the defence is selecting from multiple security improvements, it must determine if the improvement would change the weakest link in security. If it eliminates or complicates the intruder's most-effective option, then it has an effect. If it only changes an option that is not one of the weakest links, then it is not effective.

3.1. *Measuring effectiveness in multiple pathway graphs*

The weakest link may be a different kind of vulnerability, or it may be the same vulnerability instantiated in a different pathway through a complex system. Given multiple pathways for an intruder, and multiple steps required to achieve objectives, there are many ways that one can potentially improve security and where effectiveness needs to be measured. Our research group at Los Alamos National Laboratory has studied several of these circumstances both theoretically and empirically. The general form of this analysis is a graph of nodes in a computer network where directed edges are constructed between pairs of nodes i, j if and only if there is a trust relationship that allows j to be controlled by i.

In our models, we define classes of nodes and quantify the size of those classes. A simple example of this counted class graph is shown in Figure 1. A traditional directed graph is constructed from a counted class graph by first creating the specified number of nodes for each class (represented by a colour in the figure). An edge is constructed between two nodes if and only if there is a corresponding edge between the classes of those two nodes. The counted class graphs provide a simpler representation and are naturally elicited from computer policy and expert elicitation. Finally, graph statistics can be computed on them directly, thus simplifying otherwise large combinatoric calculations.

This author first pursued discrete modelling of these connectivity relationships from expert knowledge of engineered trust relationships. For example, central authentication and configuration management servers explicitly have control over the systems that use those services. They can grant access to, or install targeted software on, all of those systems. Protecting or eliminating these single points of compromise is crucial to intrusion tolerance within a distributed system. These trust digraphs (directed graphs)

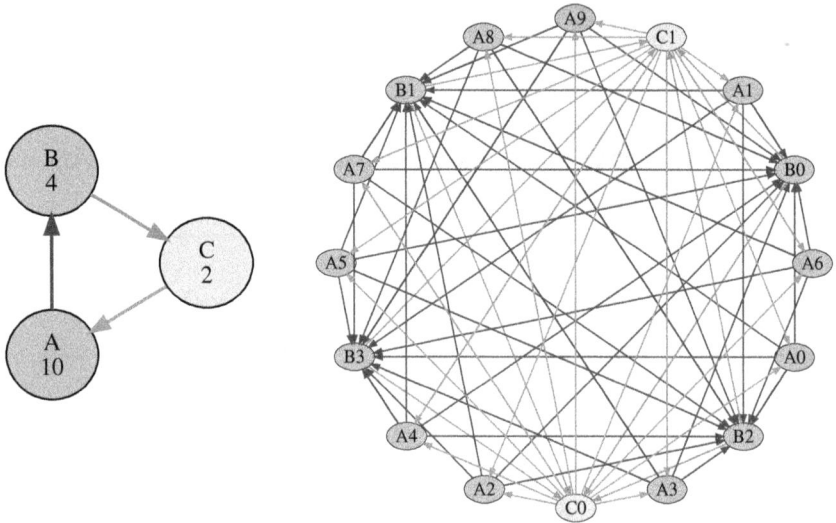

Fig. 1: An example of a counted class graph (left) and the induced supergraph when each class node is substituted by a given number of instance nodes that each share the same edge structure as the class graph.

are the basis for much of our work and are inspired by previous work in network interdiction (Corley and Sha, 1982; Morton *et al.*, 2007).

The most basic statistic is how much of the graph can be reached, on average, from a random point of compromise. A strongly connected digraph contains a path from every node to every other node and therefore has a reachability of 100%. A less connected digraph has a lower reachability and, on average, greater intrusion tolerance.

Figure 2 shows an example of every combination of two policy decisions: The first factor (the columns) is whether or not clients trust other clients. The second factor (the rows) is whether or not administrator credentials are allowed to be used on general-purpose systems that normal clients can access. Microsoft strongly recommends not allowing this in order to prevent a compromised general user from leading to the compromise of an administrator credential (Jungles *et al.*, 2012). The 2 × 2 chart shows that reachability is 100% without either protection and reduces to 1% only when both mitigations are applied.

Subsequent work at Los Alamos constructed bipartite graphs of users and computers based on empirical authentication data (Hagberg *et al.*, 2014).

	Clients trust clients	Clients do *not* trust clients
Admin Credentials	Reachability: 100%	Reachability: 100%
Protect Admin	Reachability: 98%	Reachability: 1%

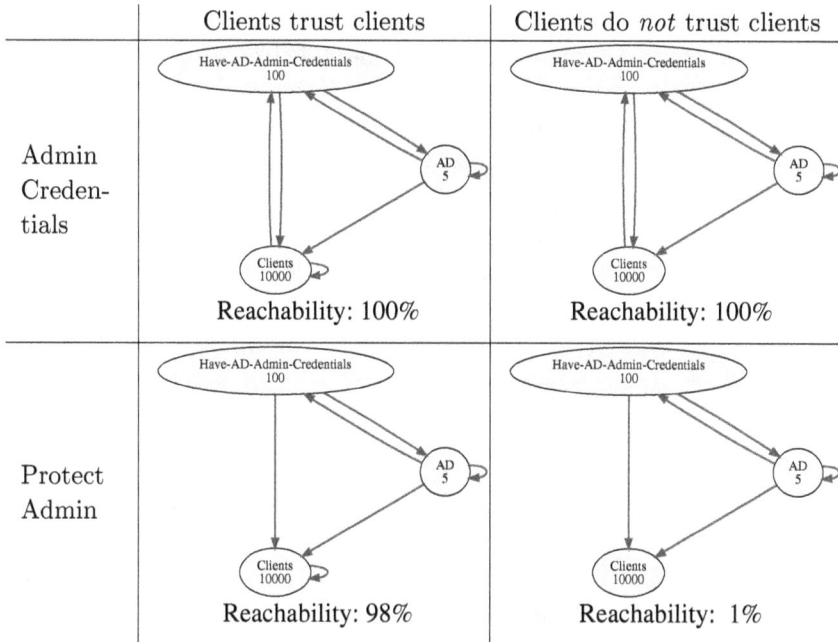

Fig. 2: Trust relationship model graphs for combinations of two policies. Trust relationship model graphs.

In that work, the efficacy of different credential caching policies was studied in terms of impact on the size of the largest connected component. More recently, reachability has become a time-valued metric through analysis of reachability in temporal graphs where a traversal may be delayed waiting for an edge to be present in the graph (Hagberg *et al.*, 2016). This work, which continues, allows us to move from average reachability statistics on static graphs to intruder delay time metrics in temporal graphs.

4. Case Study: Multi-Factor Authentication

In this section, we examine a more detailed case study in cost-effectiveness. The White House Cyber Sprint[b] (Donovan and Scott, 2015) made it a

---

[b]US Department of Homeland Security and Executive Office of the President of the United States, FY 2016 CIO FISMA Metrics: https://www.dhs.gov/publication/fy17-fisma-documents.

priority across the US Government to require the use of multi-factor authentication and specifically to use a NIST 800-63-2 (Burr *et al.*, 2013) "Level of Assurance (LOA) 4 credential" to "log onto the network." This requirement can only be met by storing a cryptographic key (the credential) on a hardware token such as a smart card (Fancher, 1997). Was this policy an effective improvement in security? Does it improve security by itself or is it even a necessary component of a larger strategy? In this section, we present a quantitative analysis to answer those questions.

Credentials and tokens are only part of the authentication process. The accompanying network protocols that allow a credential to access network resources are also important to security. Many protocols use a "secondary authenticator" (Burr *et al.*, 2013) or "session secret" (Grassi *et al.*, 2017). As a prominent example, Microsoft Windows uses the NTLMv2 protocol, introduced in 1998, which relies on a long-lived session secret for a user that is, by itself, sufficient to access any service from any client as that user (Jungles *et al.*, 2012). This session secret is only invalidated by changing the user's password (National Security Agency, 2016). This session secret does not meet even Level of Assurance 1 requirements in NIST 800-63-2. This weakness was reported in 1997 (Ashton, 1997a,b) for NTLMv1 and is regularly exploited to this day by intruders (Hummel, 2009). Since 2008, there have been publicly available software tools such as the Pass-The-Hash Toolkit (Ochoa, 2008), and Mimikatz (Delpy, 2014) to exploit this design weakness.

As a result of this mismatch in assurance levels, many organisations now require the use of high-assurance hardware tokens rather than passwords, and yet intruders still easily impersonate those users without having access to the token. The Cyber Sprint mandate occurred as a result of the well-publicised breach of personnel and security information for nearly all US Government employees that reportedly occurred when an intruder was able to obtain the credential of an authorised user (US Government, 2015). Does this mandate actually address that problem?

To objectively answer that question, we calculate the effectiveness of several different authentication mechanisms across several credential misuse scenarios. Those scenarios are as follows:

(1) *Guess*: The intruder wants to remotely access a network portal without any access to user credentials. Brute force guessing is required.

(2) *Phish*: The intruder tricks a user into providing credentials that can be used by the intruder.
(3) *Pivot*: A user's client computer has been compromised and the intruder is leveraging that access to move laterally across the network as that user.

The objective of each scenario is to gain authenticated access as a user to other network services of the intruder's choosing. In Verizon's most recent annual data breach analysis report,[c] it is reported that 34% of breaches involve phishing and 33% involve use of stolen credentials. Less than 4% involved brute force guessing methods. 51% involve malware — the typical enabler for pivot actions. This analysis is based on the VERIS Community Database,[d] an evolving open data set of breach data using the vocabulary for event recording and incident sharing (VERIS).

For each scenario, we analyse two measures of effectiveness. Both of these quantities are measured from the perspective of the would-be intruder. The *delay* is the amount of time the adversary has to wait before obtaining the desired access. The *duration* is the length of time that access persists once it is obtained. We calculate *productivity* as the ratio between the duration and the delay. We use $\epsilon = 1$ minute as the minimum value for the delay time.

Duration is measured in terms of the authentication mechanism itself and the duration of the adversary's ability to authenticate one or more times. It does not count the duration of access granted by a single authentication. A single authentication might be used to authorise a single discrete action. In many cases, a single authentication event creates a longer-lived session such as a remote login or remote access connection. It is a standard security control (National Institute of Standards and Technology, 2014) to define a maximum session duration, but there is no standard value for that duration. That security risk posed by that duration is independent of the authentication mechanism and we do not include it in our productivity calculations.

Our analysis is based on several parameters specific to the target environment. For policy values, we use published standard recommendations. For user behaviour, we use only rough models. A more targeted analysis

---

[c]http://www.verizonenterprise.com/verizon-insights-lab/dbir.
[d]http://veriscommunity.net.

Table 1: Expected intruder productivity ($\lambda = 90\,\text{d}$, $u_1 = 15.4\,\text{h}$, $\epsilon = 1\,\text{m}$, y = year, d = day, h = hour, m = minute).

Mechanism	Scenario		
	Adversary Productivity (duration/delay)		
	Guess	Phish	Pivot
Password	10^5 (λ/1m)	10^2 (λ/1 d)	10^2 (λ/u_1)
One-Time Password	10^{-3} (45 s/28 h)	10^{-3} (45 s/1 d)	10^{-3} (74 s/u_1)
Smartcard (worst)	0	0	10^6 (1.5 y/ϵ)
Smartcard (best)	0	0	10^{-3} (ϵ/u_1)
NTLMv2	0	N/A	10^5 (λ/ϵ)
Workday SSO	0	N/A	10^0 (8 h/u_2)

for a given environment would measure distributions of activity observed in that environment. However, our results show differences in policies and are measured in orders of magnitude.

Table 1 summarises the results described in the following analysis.

4.1. *Scenario 1: Guess*

Our first scenario is that of a remote intruder with no prior access or knowledge. For example, consider an intruder wants to remotely access a network portal (a remote desktop server, virtual private network (VPN) service, etc.) without any access to user credentials. In this scenario, delay time is based on the strength of the authentication mechanism against brute force attacks.

4.1.1. *Password*

The time to guess an individual's password varies significantly based on what sort of password the individual uses. For example, in one empirical study, 26% of passwords come from a small dictionary of 10,143 common passwords (Dell'Amico *et al.*, 2010). When an adversary has a multiple accounts to probe, the odds are good that at least one of those accounts will use a password that is easy to guess, and Bonneau estimates that they are equivalent to only about 10-bits of random values (Bonneau, 2012). Thus, the expected number of attempts required before success is only 512.

It is a best practice to limit the number of incorrect guesses that can be made per account per unit time. The recommended value for high-security

US government systems is three failures every 15 minutes (Committee on National Security Systems, 2014). However, we are giving the adversary credit for performing round-robin attempts against a large number of accounts. Thus, the allowed rate increases linearly with the number of accounts. We assume an enterprise with at least 342 user accounts which allows for 1024 guesses (3 per account) to occur without rate limiting. In this case, we use the minimum allowed delay time of 1 minute. Enterprise-class systems are capable of accepting 512 guesses per minute, so we do not consider that a technical limitation.

The maximum allowed password lifetime is part of security control IA-5 in the NIST cyber-security framework (National Institute of Standards and Technology, 2014). We use 180-days as the maximum allowed password lifetime,[e] as recommended for high-security environments (Committee on National Security Systems, 2014). The expected duration of access is half of that, or $\lambda = 90$ days. The resulting productivity is 129,600.

4.1.2. *One-time password (OTP)*

One-time passwords are intended to be uniformly distributed across a large number of character combinations. For this analysis, we use 7-digit numeric passwords for which there are 10^7 possible values. The TOTP (M'Raihi *et al.*, 2011) standard recommends that new passwords be generated every 30 seconds and that the server accept passwords from a 90 second window to allow for clock skew. Thus, three passwords are valid at any point in time. Again, we assume attempts against multiple accounts in which the adversary can pick a single password value and try it for all accounts. Each attempt will have an independent $p = 3/10^7$ chance of success. We assume that at least 90 seconds go by before beginning the next guess on each account, an assumption that is easily met with the policy limit of three attempts per account per 15 minutes. In that case, by the time a second round of guesses is made all three valid passwords per account will have changed and the next guess (which could in fact reasonably use the same value as the first guess) will have the same $p = 3/10^7$ chance of success per account. Thus, the expected number of guesses required is $1/p = 10^7/3$.

---

[e]Although there is newer prevailing wisdom that user passwords should have much longer lifetimes (Grassi *et al.*, 2017).

With the same policy limit of three attempts per account per 15 minutes, the intruder will be rate limited before the expected number of guesses occurs unless there are at least $10^7/9 = 1,111,111$ accounts. While this would be possible for very large enterprises, we assume a more common enterprise with at most 10,000 accounts. At 30,000 attempts every 15 minutes, we expect to need more than 1,666 minutes before success.

Because the server accepts passwords for 90 seconds, the expected remaining lifetime of the password is 45 seconds. The resulting intruder productivity is 0.00045. If we consider increasing the length of one-time passwords to 8-digits and including alphanumeric characters, productivity decreases to 10^{-5} and 10^{-9}, respectively.

4.1.3. *Smart card*

The basic mechanisms for computer authentication using smart cards remains relatively unchanged since the first Personal Computer/Smart Card standard in 1997 (Bull CP8 *et al.*, 1997). For this analysis, we examine the use of RSA with 2048-bit keys, as that is considered a contemporary minimum standard for security (Polk *et al.*, 2015). The recommended validity period for the key — for example, 3 years (National Institute of Standards and Technology, 2013) — is significantly less than the time required to perform the 2^{111} offline guesses NIST estimates that would be expected to defeat that algorithm (Barker, 2016). We therefore assign a duration of access, and hence productivity, of 0. We assume the smart card is used as part of an online authentication protocol such as TLS 1.2 (Rescorla and Dierks, 2008) with all known protocol deficiencies mitigated.

4.1.4. *NTLMv2*

In addition to the above authentication mechanisms that the user uses to initially authenticate, we also look at the security of session authenticators such as those used in NTLMv2. NTLMv2 is the predominant authentication protocol used in Windows environments. Regardless of the initial authentication mechanism and protocol, a session credential is created for the user, stored on the user's computers, and sufficient by itself to access network services. For example, even for users who only have a smart card, Microsoft authentication servers still maintain a randomised password that is unknown to the user (National Security Agency, 2016). This practice allows various legacy authentication mechanisms that rely on a hash of a password.

Contemporary NTLMv2 authentication uses a challenge–response protocol that includes cryptographic hashes of random values combined with a 128-bit MD4 hash of a password. Guessing against a 2^{128} search space using the same limitations of 3 attempts per account per 15 minutes and 10,000 accounts would require 2^{97} years. The odds of guessing correctly within the lifetime of the user's credential (and in fact the user) are essentially 0.

When users have passwords, the hash is derived from the password and the overall security is the same as analysed above for passwords.

4.1.5. *Workday single sign-on (SSO)*

Single sign-on protocols such as Kerberos (Zhu *et al.*, 2005) and SAML (Cantor *et al.*, 2005) are often used to increase user productivity by enabling access to multiple services over some fixed period of time without the user participating in additional authentication events. These protocols use one of the previously analysed authentication mechanisms combined with an additional cryptographic protocol to establish a session credential used for subsequent accesses. Those sessions have a maximum lifetime, often set to not require re-authentication during a work day.

A good single sign-on protocol uses cryptography effectively and provides a standard 128 bits worth of security. As discussed above, the odd of successfully forging a session credential are essentially 0.

4.2. *Scenario 2: Phish*

As brute force attacks are become better protected against, intruders moved to man-in-the-middle attacks where they can interfere with the communications between an authorised user and a network service. Cryptographic protocols such as TLS (Rescorla and Dierks, 2008) prevent many classic network-based man-in-the-middle attacks. A second variety of these attacks, sometimes called pharming, redirects traffic to a different service that the user requested using techniques such as ARP spoofing, or DNS cache poisoning. Infrastructure protections such as DNSSEC and ethernet switch port security (Abad and Bonilla, 2007) address these attacks, but are less thoroughly implemented. However, we focus on a third variety of attacks which is much more prevalent and in which a phishing e-mail tricks a user into visiting a malicious site that looks to the user like a trusted site. In this scenario, the delay time is the same for each authentication mechanism since it is entirely dependent on the user clicking on the phish. We assume that at least one user will click on a well-formed phish an average of 1 day after receiving it, so our delay time is 1 day. Verizon reported that in their data, 7.3% of phish recipients take the bait.

Password: As before, we have a $\lambda = 90$-day expected duration and productivity is 90.

One-time password: We expect that on average the one-time password is obtained halfway through its 90-second valid period which leaves a 45-second duration for the intruder. Therefore, the productivity is 0.75.

Smart card: Smart card authentication over the network uses end-to-end cryptographic operations that prevent a man-in-the-middle attack. Productivity is zero since the intruder cannot obtain access to a legitimate site this way.

Active directory: As before, the expected duration is $\lambda = 90$ days. Productivity is 90.

4.3. *Scenario 3: Pivot*

A user's client computer has just been compromised and the intruder is leveraging that access to move laterally across the network as that user or to access a remote access server (Jungles *et al.*, 2012; Kent *et al.*, 2015). The intruder has escalated to privileged access on the client computer and can eavesdrop and perform man-in-the-middle attacks between the user and a network service.

For this analysis, it is necessary to understand when the user initiates authentication events. For this chapter, we use the model shown in Figure 3. Each week consists of five work days that each begin with an authentication event. Each hour of the work day begins with an authentication usage event (to login, unlock the screen, access a service, etc). The user is present for two 4-hour periods with a 1-hour break in between. No activity occurs during the remainder of the day or on weekends.

A week is comprised of Four types of intervals: For 23.8% of the week, the user is active immediately. On lunch hours (3.0%) of the week, the user

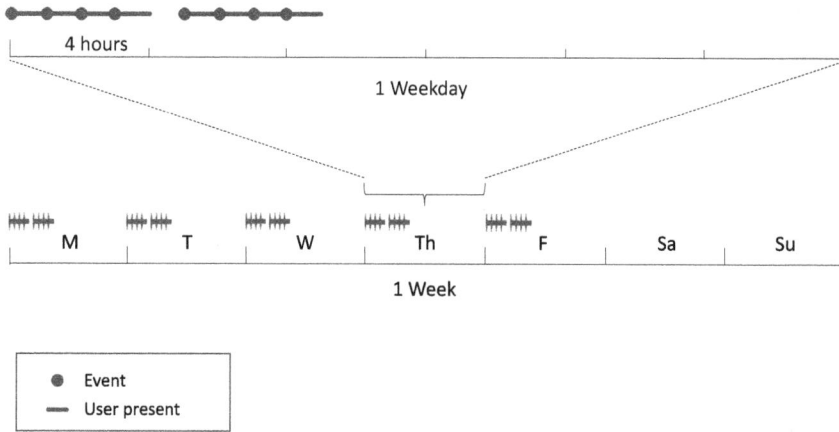

Fig. 3: User authentication event timeline.

will be active within an hour. 35.7% of the week is weekday evenings when the user will be active within 15 hours. 37.5% of the week is weekends when the user will be active within 63 hours. Given a uniform distribution of the time of week that the intruder begins activity, the expected delay time until the user is active is $u_2 = 14.5$ hours.

The time until the user performs an authentication event is slightly different. 17.9% of the week is 6 hours per week day in which the next authentication will occur within the hour. 6.0% of the week is the 2-hour workday period including lunch in which authentication will occur within 2 hours. 38.0% of the week is Monday–Thursday evenings which are 16 hours long in which authentication will occur within 16 hours. Finally, 38.1% of the week is a 64-hour period over the weekend with a 32-hour average delay time until the start of the next work week. Overall, the expected time until the next authentication event is $u_1 = 15.4$ hours. We will use this time repeatedly throughout this section.

Clearly, these times are dependent on user behaviour in a network and could be measured empirically to achieve a more tailored result.

4.3.1. *Password*

An intruder must wait until an authentication event, an expected delay time of $u_1 = 15.4$ hours, before a key logger can record the password. The expected duration of that access is $\lambda = 90$ days, as before for passwords. Intruder productivity is 140.

4.3.2. *One-time password*

Recall from before that the server provides a window of up to 90 seconds to use a one-time password. We expect that the password is discovered halfway through its valid period and that the intruder has a duration of 45 seconds to use it. The clocks are in sync, the victim will provide a password that is, on average, 15 seconds old. That gives the intruder a duration of 74 seconds to use it. The expected time between one-time passwords being presented is the same as the expected delay time for a reusable password ($u_1 = 15.4$ hours). The intruder productivity is 0.0013. This is the method frequently-used for bastion hosts and remote access into a network.

4.3.3. *Smart card*

We will show that the operational security of smart cards is not robust to the behaviour of users or operating systems. Intuitively, one-time password tokens are not connected to the client computer and therefore have some robustness against actions taken on the computer. However, smart cards are physically inserted into the computer and the computer is typically used to authenticate the user to the card with a PIN. This mode of operation has several vulnerabilities (Dasgupta *et al.*, 2007) and has been actively exploited in the wild (Blasco, 2012). While the smart card is inserted into a computer, an attacker can use the smart card to access resources as the card holder. The intruder may need the PIN, but the PIN can be obtained from memory (Delpy, 2014) or a keystroke logger.

In the best case (for the defender) the user only puts their card in when using it and the intruder has the same $u_1 = 15.4$-hour expected delay time as the password case. The intruder can capture and reuse the user's PIN to access the card for additional transactions while it is inserted. The user must typically leave the password in for many seconds in order for the operating system to finish using it. We use the minimum, $\epsilon = 1$ minute, duration for that access. Attacker productivity is 0.001 for this best-case scenario.

However, it is not uncommon for users to leave the card in the reader for extended periods of time. Some environments even require this by setting the screen to lock automatically when the card is removed. In that case, the intruder must wait until the user is logged in, an expected delay of $u_2 = 14.5$ hours. Microsoft Windows keeps the user's PIN in memory, so we do not require any additional delay time to obtain the PIN. The duration of access is governed by the lifetime of the PIN and the smart card. PINs are seldom required to change. Three years is a standard certificate lifespan (National Institute of Standards and Technology, 2013). With an expected 18-month life left, intruder productivity is 906 for this case.

If a credential is left in the client computer at all times (rather than just during working hours), security is even worse. Many modern computers have secure key storage hardware such as a Trusted Platform Module that can be used like an embedded smart card. For example, Microsoft Windows now has "Virtual Smart Cards" that use that hardware as a smart card. In that case, the credential is always present and the delay time is $\epsilon = 1$ minute. With an 18-month expected remaining credential lifespan, the productivity is 788,400. This startlingly high intruder productivity is the highest of all cases examined in this chapter. Worse, the credential will almost certainly be refreshed before it expires so that the user can maintain access. Thus, the duration of access may have no practical limitations imposed by the authentication system.

4.3.4. *NTLMv2*

NTLMv2 credentials do not expire and stay present as long as the user is logged in. Practices vary, and the delay time varies between 0 (if the user is always logged in) and 499.7 (if the user is only logged in during the 9-hour work day). The former scenario is common and the latter scenario is disruptive to users and difficult to enforce, so we use the minimum value of $\epsilon = 1$ minute. We use the same $\lambda = 90$-day expected duration for passwords. Note that the initial authentication mechanism used (password, smart card, etc.) does not change Windows networks' internal use of passwords, even if the user is not aware of the password (National Security Agency, 2016). The intruder productivity is 129,600.

4.3.5. *Workday SSO*

The single sign-on system explicitly determines the lifetime of a session. It can even change that lifetime circumstantially or choose to invalidate it for subsequent use if usage is suspicious. However, for our analysis we use a typical 9-hour session lifetime designed to allow a user to not have to re-authenticate during a work day. Thus, a valid session credential will be present throughout the workday and the intruder delay is $u_2 = 14.5$ hours. The expected remaining duration is 4.5 hours for intrusion during a work day and 9 hours if the intruder has had to wait for the beginning of the work day. The overall duration is therefore 8 hours.

4.4. *Policy evaluation and recommendations*

For the first two scenarios, Guess and Phish, smart cards are clearly the most preferred technology. Table 2 summarises this result. Intruders generally go after the weakest link they can find. We therefore show the *maximum productivity* across the included scenarios and the *min delay* is the amount of time that an attacker must wait to obtain any amount of access. We also report *feasibility* is a binary measure of whether a patient would-be intruder can obtain any amount of access. Feasibility is true if and only if intruder productivity is non-zero.

This analysis shows the strengths of cryptography against these threats and why smart cards are categorised by NIST in its highest level of assurance for authentication (Burr *et al.*, 2013). For protecting against authentication attacks as the *initial vector* into a system, smart cards are the most effective option and the only form of authentication that makes phishing for authentication credentials unfeasible. Both forms of single sign-on are also robust in this scenario.

Table 2: Initial vector security: The maximum intruder productivity (smaller is better for the defender) afforded by mechanisms. *min delay* is the smallest amount of time (in minutes) that an intruder would expect to wait before being able to access a user's credentials (larger is better for the defender).

Rank	Mechanism	*max productivity*	*min delay*	*feasibility*
Worst	Password	10^5	10^3 (1d)	Feasible
	One-Time Password	10^{-3}	10^3 (1d)	Feasible
	NTLMv2 SSO	0	0	Unfeasible
	Workday SSO	0	0	Unfeasible
Best	Smart card (any)	0	0	Unfeasible

For authenticating from the Internet, the most effective authentication method is a smart card, or more generally a non-duplicatable hardware token used in an end-to-end cryptographic protocol. The federal government is wise to require that any remote access and Internet-accessible services be upgraded to a smart card. This step prevents authentication from being a feasible initial vector into a system.

4.5. *Post-exploitation security*

However, the analysis is incomplete unless one lives in an idealised world where no computer has been compromised. In reality, computers are routinely compromised and intruders leverage those initial compromises to spread throughout networks to achieve their objectives. For example, an intruder may begin with a phishing attack that installs malware on a computer rather than eliciting a password from the user. Once that step has already occurred, the *pivot* scenario comes into play and a system's ability to defend itself against authentication-based exploitation is more limited. This phase is sometimes referred to as "post-exploitation."

Smart cards are particularly and notably vulnerable in this circumstance. The smart card is connected to a compromised computer and all human input to the card (specifically, the PIN) traverses the compromised computer. When used in with worse-case behaviour (always in the computer and with Windows caching the PIN in memory), the smart card is nine orders of magnitude less secure than a one-time password. However, smart card security ranges wildly from being the worst option to tied for best. Smart card cryptography can be used effectively here only when it is tied to a physical action by a user. Most smart cards cannot enforce this user interaction. A card could, in theory, be configured to require a removal and reinsertion for each transaction. A non-standard form factor could include some form of physical user interaction such as a biometric or at least a simple touch by a person. The Yubikey product (Jacobs, 2016) can be used as a smart card and can be configured to require the user to use its touch sensor for each transaction. Secure PIN Entry, in which a dedicated and trusted hardware reader (a "terminal" in smart card standards) is used to enter the PIN and unlock the card is the norm for financial transactions using smart cards. These trusted readers even display information about the transaction for the user to accept. Unfortunately, Secure PIN Entry is not well supported in commodity operating systems as there are no standard ways to technically require it.

However, many enterprises actually utilise multiple authentication technologies concurrently. For example, within most Windows-based enterprises, one is unable to not use NTLMv2 authentication. When multiple technologies are used together, the intruder can choose which to attack and the overall intruder productivity is the maximum of that of the allowed technologies. For example, when password authentication is used with NTLMv2, the Guess scenario has an intruder productivity of 10^5 because password guessing is allowed and the Pivot scenario has productivity 10^5 because of the pass-the-hash vulnerability of NTLMv2. Similarly, when combined with even best-case smart cards, Pivot productivity is still 10^5 because the intruder will pivot using pass-the-hash rather than the smart card. Hence *max productivity* for an environment that uses NTLMv2 is 10^5 regardless of what mechanism users use. As long as NTLMv2 is used, there is no return on investment for changing the user authentication mechanism on Windows computers from reusable passwords to something else. Or, put another way, one should decouple services from Windows authentication (NTLMv2) wherever possible, if security is a consideration.

Some enterprises require users to use smart cards for logins at the console of a computer, but still allow the user to have a domain password to be used for other purposes. In fact, we believe this is more common than not since many client and server applications function poorly if the user does not have a password. This configuration only impacts users or intruders that already have physical access to a computer. It does nothing to thwart over-the-network attacks — the mainstay for intruders — including our three scenarios. Again, there is no return on investment against our three scenarios from requiring the use of smart cards only on console and not over the network. If anything, the effectiveness is negative because introducing smart cards, when used in their worse case, actually reduces security because the Pivot intruder productivity actually increases from 10^5 to 10^6 and raises *max productivity* accordingly.

Table 3 summarises the security when all three scenarios are available to an intruder. In this analysis, we see that requiring smart cards may be completely ineffective. To improve the security of a typical Windows environment that has NTLMv2 enabled, one would need to implement the following

Table 3: Secondary vector security: The maximum intruder productivity (smaller is better for the defender) afforded by mechanisms. *min delay* is the smallest amount of time (in minutes) than an intruder would expect to wait before being able to access a user's credentials (larger is better for the defender).

Rank	Mechanism	*max productivity*	*min delay*	*feasibility*
Worst	Smart card (worst)	10^6	$10^0(\epsilon)$	Feasible
	NTLMv2	10^5	$10^0(\epsilon)$	Feasible
	Password	10^5	$10^0(1m)$	Feasible
	Workday SSO	10^0	$10^3(u_2)$	Feasible
Best	One-Time Password	10^{-3}	$10^3(u_1)$	Feasible
Best	Smart card (best)	10^{-3}	$10^3(u_1)$	Feasible

4-element policy: disable NTLMv2, eliminate domain passwords, prohibit Virtual Smart Cards, and either train users to keep their smart cards disconnected most of the time or use a smart card technology that enforces physical user interaction. A policy that allows one or more of those items to remain is ineffective because it leaves a weaker pathway for the adversary. The US Cyber Sprint policy does not address any of these other factors, and so it is ineffective in adding security to commodity, likely exploitable computers that are used for legitimate authentications. In a typical enterprise network, all users' computers fall into that category.

However, enterprises can make policy decisions that are distinct for different services. For example, remote access and bastion hosts typically require the highest available levels of authentication and have a higher security posture than other applications (including those that use NTLMv2 authentication). In these limited and important cases, it is cost-effective to implement the entire 4-element policy above and require a one-time password or a smart card that can only be used with physical input from the user.

5. Conclusion

We have demonstrated a methodology for quantitatively measuring cost-effectiveness of security improvements, in the context of multiple other concurrent avenues for an intruder. We have shown several quantitative effectiveness measures including average reachability, intruder delay time and intruder productivity. We have shown how to model distributed system security as a graph and a shorthand graph construction that allows for more straightforward elicitation and analysis. For the important problem of authentication, we demonstrated how an objective, quantitative cost-effective analysis using these approaches can enable more cost-effective policy decisions than policymakers otherwise make. In doing so, we showed that some "security improvement" can be ineffective at any cost, or may only improve security when implemented in concert with other improvements that may be too costly to implement widely. In addition, we quantified the impact and necessity of establishing physical participation by a user in smart card transactions.

References

Abad, C. L. and Bonilla, R. I. (2007). An analysis on the schemes for detecting and pre-venting arp cache poisoning attacks, in *27th International Conference on Distributed Computing Systems Workshops (ICDCSW)*, IEEE, pp. 60–60, doi:10.1109/ICDCSW. 2007.19.

Ashton, P. (1997a). LSA secrets, ntbugtraq e-mail list, URL: https://marc.info/? l=ntbugtraq&m=87602837719664&w=2.

Ashton, P. (1997b). Vulnerabilties of service passwords, ntsecurity e-mail list, URL: https:// marc.info/?l=ntsecurity&m=87602727619593&w=2.

Barker, E. (2016). Recommendation for key management, part 1: General, SP 800-57 part 1 rev 4, doi:10.6028/NIST.SP.800-57pt1r4.

Blasco, J. (2012). Sykipot variant hijacks DOD and Windows smart cards, Tech. rep., AlientVault Blogs, URL: https://www.alienvault.com/blogs/labs-research/ sykipot-variant-hijacks-dod-and-windows-smart-cards.

Bonneau, J. (2012). The science of guessing: Analyzing an anonymized corpus of 70 million passwords, in *Proceedings of the 2012 IEEE Symposium on Security and Privacy*, SP '12, IEEE Computer Society, Washington, DC, USA, ISBN 978-0-7695-4681-0, pp. 538–552, doi:10.1109/SP.2012.49.

Bull CP8, Gemplus SA, Hewlett-Packard Company, IBM Corporation, Microsoft Corporation, Schlumberger SA, Siemens Nixdorf Informationssysteme AG, Sun Microsystems, Inc., Toshiba Corporation and VeriFone, Inc. (1997). Interoperability specification for iccs and personal computer systems, Tech. rep., PC/SC Workgroup, URL: ftp://ftp.iks-jena.de/pub/mitarb/lutz/chipcard/standards/pc-sc/p1v10.ps.

Burr, W. E., Dodson, D. F., Newton, E. M., Perlner, R. A., Polk, W. T., Gupta, S. and Nabbus, E. A. (2013). Electronic authentication guideline, SP 800-63 rev 2, doi: 10.6028/NIST.SP.800-63-2.

Cantor, S., Kemp, J., Philpott, R. and Maler, E. (2005). Assertions and protocols for the OASIS 3 security assertion markup language 4 (SAML) v2.0, Tech. Rep. saml-core-2.0-os, OASIS, URL: http://docs.oasis-open.org/security/saml/v2.0.

Committee on National Security Systems (2014). Security categorization and control selection for national security systems, Tech. Rep. CNSSI 1253 v3, URL: https://www.cnss.gov/CNSS/issuances/Instructions.cfm.

Corley, H. and Sha, D. Y. (1982). Most vital links and nodes in weighted networks, *Operations Research Letters* **1**, 4, pp. 157–160, doi:10.1016/0167-6377(82)90020-7.

Cremonini, M. and Martini, P. (2005). Evaluating information security investments from attackers perspective: the Return-On-Attack (ROA), in *4th Workshop on the Economics on Information Security*.

Dasgupta, P., Chatha, K. and Gupta, S. K. S. (2007). Vulnerabilities of PKI based smartcards, in *MILCOM 2007 — IEEE Military Communications Conference*, IEEE, doi:10.1109/MILCOM.2007.4455333.

Dell'Amico, M., Michiardi, P. and Roudier, Y. (2010). Password strength: An empirical analysis, in *Proceedings of the 29th Conference on Information Communications*, INFOCOM '10, IEEE, Piscataway, NJ, USA, ISBN 978-1-4244-5836-3, pp. 983–991, doi: 10.1109/INFCOM.2010.5461951.

Delpy, B. (2014). mimikatz, Version 2.0, Software, URL: https://github.com/gentilkiwi/mimikatz.

Donovan, S. and Scott, T. (2015). Cybersecurity strategy and implementation plan (CSIP) for the federal civilian government, URL: https://obamawhitehouse.archives.gov/sites/default/files/omb/memoranda/2016/m-16-04.pdf.

Fancher, C. H. (1997). In your pocket: Smartcards, *Spectrum* **34**, 2, pp. 47–53, doi:10.1109/6.570830.

Grassi, P. A., Fenton, J. L., Newton, E. M., Perlner, R. A., Regenscheid, A. R., Burr, W. E. and Richer, J. P. (2017). Digital identity guidelines: Authentication and lifecycle management, SP 800-63B, doi:10.6028/NIST.SP.800-63b.

Hagberg, A., Lemons, N., Kent, A. and Neil, J. (2014). Connected components and credential hopping in authentication graphs, in *Proceedings 2002 IEEE Symposium on Security and Privacy*, IEEE, pp. 416–423.

Hagberg, A., Lemons, N. and Misra, S. (2016). *Temporal Reachability in Dynamic Networks*, pp. 181–208, Security Science and Technology, World Scientific (Europe).

Hummel, C. (2009). Why crack when you can pass the hash, SANS Institute InfoSec Reading Room, URL: https://www.sans.org/reading-room/whitepapers/testing/crack-pass-hash-33219.

Jacobs, T. A. (2016). Secure token-based authentication with yubikey 4, *Linux Journal*, 265, URL: http://dl.acm.org/citation.cfm?id=2953926.2953927.

Jungles, P., Simos, M., Margosis, A., Robinson, L. and Grimes, R. (2012). Mitigating pass-the-hash (PtH) attacks and other credential theft techniques, Tech. rep., Microsoft, URL: https://download.microsoft.com/download/7/7/A/77ABC5BD-8320-41AF-863C-6ECFB10CB4B9/Mitigating%20Pass-the-Hash%20(PtH)%20Attacks%20and%20Other%20Credential%20Theft%20Techniques_English.pdf.

Kent, A. D., Liebrock, L. M. and Neil, J. C. (2015). Authentication graphs: Analyzing user behavior within an enterprise network, *Computers & Security* **48**, Supplement C, pp. 150–166, doi:10.1016/j.cose.2014.09.001.

Morton, D. P., Pan, F. and Saeger, K. J. (2007). Models for nuclear smuggling interdiction, *IIE Transactions* **39**, 1, pp. 3–14, doi:10.1080/07408170500488956.

M'Raihi, D., Machani, S., Pei, M. and Rydell, J. (2011). TOTP: Time-based one-time password algorithm, RFC 6238, doi:10.17487/RFC6238.

National Institute of Standards and Technology (2013). Personal identity verification (PIV) of federal employees and contractors, FIPS 201-2, doi:10.6028/NIST.FIPS.201-2.

National Institute of Standards and Technology (2014). Security and privacy controls for federal information systems and organizations, SP 800-53 rev 4, doi:10.6028/NIST. SP.800-53r4.

National Security Agency (2016). Long-lived hashes associated with smartcard-required accounts in windows active directory domains are being used in pass-the-hash attacks, Tech. Rep. ORN U/OO/803300-16, U.S. National Security Agency, URL: https://www.iad.gov/iad/library/ia-advisories-alerts/long-lived-hashes-for-ad-smartcard-required-accounts.cfm.

Ochoa, H. (2008). Pass-the-hash toolkit for windows implementation & use, in *HITB 2008*, URL: https://www.coresecurity.com/system/files/publications/2016/05/Ochoa_2008-Pass-The-Hash.pdf.

Polk, W. T., Dodson, D. F., Burr, W. E., Ferraiolo, H. and Cooper, D. (2015). Cryptographic algorithms and key sizes for personal identity verification, SP 800-74 rev 4, doi: 10.6028/NIST.SP.800-78-4.

Rescorla, E. and Dierks, T. (2008). The transport layer security (TLS) protocol, Version 1.2, RFC 5246, doi:10.17487/RFC5246.

Sheyner, O., Haines, J., Jha, S., Lippmann, R. and Wing, J. M. (2002). Automated generation and analysis of attack graphs, in *Proceedings of the 2002 IEEE Symposium on Security and privacy*, pp. 273–284, doi:10.1109/SECPRI.2002.1004377.

US Government (2015). Cybersecurity: The Department of the Interior, Tech. Rep. 114-52, U.S. House of Representatives, URL: https://oversight.house.gov/wp-content/uploads/2016/04/7-15-15-Cybersecurity-The-Department-of-the-Interior.pdf.

Wei, H., Frinke, D., Carter, O. and Ritter, C. (2001). Cost-benefit analysis for network intrusion detection systems, in *28th Annual Computer Security Conference*, Computer Security Institute, URL: http://citeseerx.ist.psu.edu/viewdoc/download?doi=10.1.1.20.5607&rep=rep1&type=pdf.

Zhu, L., Wasserman, M. and Astrand, L. (2005). The Kerberos network authentication service (v5), RFC 4120, doi:10.17487/RFC4120.

Index